Draft Horses
an Owner's Manual

Draft Horses

an Owner's Manual

Beth A. Valentine, DVM, PhD
Michael J. Wildenstein, CJF

A **RURAL HERITAGE** Book
PO Box 2067
Cedar Rapdis IA 52406
(319) 362-3027

Published by RURAL HERITAGE
PO Box 2067
Cedar Rapids IA 52406
319-362-3027
www.ruralheritage.com

RURAL HERITAGE magazine has served its readers since 1976 in support of farming and logging with horses, mules and oxen.

Edited by Gail Damerow & Marion Hudson
Cover design and layout by Allan Damerow
Cover photo by Dusty L. Perin
Back cover photos by Barry Cooper (top) and courtesy of Mike Wildenstein
Line drawings by Bethany Caskey
Indexed by Gail Damerow

Printed in the USA
First Printing, December 2000
09 10 11 12 13   10 9 8 7 6 5

        Library of Congress Cataloging-in-Publication Data

Valentine, Beth A., 1954-
    Draft Horses: an owner's manual / Beth A. Valentine, Michael J. Wildenstein
        p. cm.
    Includes bibliographical references (p.).
    ISBN: 1-893707-12-1 (pbk.)
    1. Draft horses. I. Wildenstein, Michael J., 1958- II. Title.

SF311. V36 2000
636.1'5--dc21

                                        00-046003

Contents

"Everything in this book was learned from me."

Acknowledgements

We hope this book proves useful and enlightening and helps make the lives of draft and draft cross horses and ponies healthier and happier. Sincere thanks to the following people for their contributions: Dr. Barry Cooper, Dr. Peter Daels, Dr. Tom Divers, Dr. Robin Gleed, Dr. William Rebhun (sadly, deceased), Dr. David Murphy, Dr. Sarah Ralston, Dr. Harold (Skip) Hintz, Dr. Kent Thompson, Dr. David Kronfeld, Dr. Al Volpini, Dr. Katharine Houpt, Dr. Normand Ducharme, Dr. Mary Smith, Dr. Sarah Fryer, Dr. Ron Riis, Dr. Jim Brendemuehl, Dale Wagner, Clint Dern, Norman Foley, Bill Lowe, Chris Gregory and especially the draft horse owners whose experiences, both happy and sad, have been incorporated into this book.

Photo by Phil Krahn

Introduction

Are Draft Horses Different from Other Horses?

For generations draft horses have been selectively bred for size, strength and temperament, and certain things set them apart from their light horse cousins.

A 2,000-pound Belgian, for example, does not necessarily require twice the feed of a 1,000-pound Arabian. A draft definitely does not need twice the amount of medication to achieve a good state of sedation. The draft horse's hooves are big and carry a lot of weight, and are more susceptible to certain problems than are the hooves of other horses. The easy-going, workaholic temperament of draft horses makes detecting problems in the early stages more difficult.

> **Draft horses**
>
> The word draft is an American term for the English word *draught,* which relates to pulling power or traction power. Any horse in harness is a draught or draft horse. This book focuses on the horses more appropriately known as heavy horses, although the terms draft breeds, draft horses and drafts are also commonly accepted.

Our horses are always talking to us. As horse owners we need to learn to listen and understand. A light horse may shout when it has a problem, where the draft horse may only whisper. Of the draft breeds, the Clydesdale may be the most sensitive and often speaks the loudest.

Although many light horses will do everything they can to avoid working, many drafts seem to enjoy their work. Semi-retirement for a previously hard-working draft may be healthier, physically and mentally, than full retirement. Drafts were bred to work, and working may perk up a dejected draft horse.

Many folks ask "Can I ride my draft?" The answer is, "Of course." Just ask all those folks who are doing it. A draft trained to drive should adjust easily to being ridden. The gait of most drafts is exceedingly smooth, making them comfortable for both the Western and the English rider. Don't let anyone tell you that drafts can't canter properly, because a healthy draft is ready and willing to give you a lovely rocking horse canter.

The biggest problem with riding drafts is finding tack to fit. A harness maker may be able to make appropriate tack. Some tack designed for extra-large Warmbloods can be adjusted to fit a draft. You'll need a saddle with a wide or extra wide tree; long billets will make it easier to find a girth to fit. Even though a street-wise bomb-proof draft may be the ideal horse to ride on roads and trails, we still advise you to wear a helmet when riding. If nothing else it will help protect your head from the branches you are likely to hit riding up there.

Not everything owners say about their draft horses is true. Just because the horses are big and heavy doesn't mean they can't stand on three legs for hoof care. Many folks believe the working life and the total life span of drafts are shorter than for other horses, which may be part of the reason drafts are sometimes trained and put to work at a young age. Some drafts, however, have lived 40 years. With proper care and attention, there's no reason a draft horse shouldn't live to a ripe old age.

The easy-going reputation of the draft breeds leads many horse owners to believe that a draft horse normally has a low energy level in harness or under saddle and rarely kicks up its heels in the pasture. They may fail to realize that a sluggish draft horse may have something wrong.

Since the poor times of the Great Depression draft horses have been making an incredible comeback. Draft breeds are no longer working only on farms or pulling carriages. Drafts and draft crosses have been slowly and steadily making their way into every aspect of the horse world. They are fox hunting. They are performing in dressage, hunter/jumper competitions, competitive trail and eventing. Drafts are used in team penning; can you imagine the powerful effect on the steers seeing a full-sized draft horse coming at them? Some of the problems said to be uncommon in drafts, such as bowed tendons and splints, may now become more common. Given the sturdy cannon bones of a draft, however, we suspect their legs will hold up better than those of many light breeds.

Folks often ask, "Which draft breed is best?" The answer is easy—all of them. A better question is, "Which draft breed is best for me?" The answer depends on many things. If you like a flashy horse and are willing to spend the extra time keeping feathers clean you may want a Clydesdale or Shire. If you want a sturdy working horse, the smaller drafts such as the Suffolk and American Cream, and the draft ponies such as the Haflinger and Norwegian Fjord, may outwork the larger breeds pound for pound. Don't overlook the crossbred or grade drafts. Like mixed breed dogs, crossbred horses are often healthier and smarter than their purebred parents.

Today the world probably has more draft horses than at any time since the turn of the century. It is an exciting time to write this book because of the resurgence of the popularity of draft breeds and because recent findings have begun to shed light on some of the problems that have plagued draft horses for as long as anyone can remember. Examples of these problems include Monday morning disease, shivers and the low tolerance some draft horses have for general anesthesia.

Recent studies have shown that these and many other problems are likely to be related to the fact that most draft horses are metabolically different from other horses and do not derive enough energy from the traditional horse feeds. This newly recognized problem, called equine polysaccharide storage myopathy (EPSM), is referred to many times in this book under many different headings. We have seen so many different possible problems in EPSM drafts that you may begin to wonder if we believe draft horse disorders can have any other cause. Of course they can, and we have tried to describe all possibilities.

The information on EPSM in drafts is so new, though, that you will have a hard time finding out about it elsewhere. This problem is so common in draft horses that it is vital for you to be aware of it—you may find yourself educating your veterinarian about it. Even more exciting than the recognition of this disorder is the development of new ways to feed draft horses that show remarkable results and seem to prevent many different problems.

This book is geared toward all draft breeds, including the heavy or draft pony breeds such as Haflinger and Norwegian Fjord. Much of the information it contains is common sense and pertains to light horses as well. We hope this book will help you, the draft horse owner, hear what your horses are saying so you will know how to feed and care for them to enable your horses to live the longest, fullest and healthiest possible lives.

After a day logging in the woods this Clydesdale-Percheron cross demonstrates the versatility of draft horses by giving his owner a lift home.

Courtesy of Coffey family

Keeping Draft Horses Safe

Maintaining a safe environment should be your primary concern as a horse owner. Whether you are creating a new facility or modifying an existing one, careful design of stabling and turnout areas will minimize the risk of injury and other health problems. Attention to detail and a little common sense goes a long way towards protecting draft horses at the farm, while in harness and during shipping. Many excellent references are available on designing and building barns and fences, managing pasture, and safely harnessing, hitching and driving draft horses. Some issues that are important to good draft horse health are outlined below.

The Barn

Heavy-duty barn, stall and fence construction is important for all horses, but especially for drafts. Some folks say draft horses have no respect for barns. The power of a draft seems to increase exponentially; a 2,000-pound draft horse has more than twice the power of a 1,000-pound horse. A draft horse leaning on a door or fence may result in some amazing architectural alterations, and rubbing that itchy butt may be enough to knock a wall down.

The barn must have excellent ventilation or the horse is likely to suffer from respiratory allergies and infections. Good ventilation means the air in the barn is not stagnant but rather has a continuous inflow of fresh air. If, even after regular cleaning of stalls, you walk into your barn and the air smells musty or of ammonia, or your barn develops heavy water condensation on the walls from moisture in the horse's breath, you probably need more ventilation. Many barns are equipped with windows that can be closed. Unless severe winds or

rains are blowing directly on the horse leave the windows open. A light breeze in the barn is fine, but of course a gale-force wind in the horse's face is undesirable.

High ceilings provide ventilation and ensure that a tall horse will not injure its head by hitting the ceiling. Determining the proper ceiling height for a draft horse can literally be a tall order. The horse should have enough head room, at least two feet, to allow for the occasional head toss. Most ceilings are not high enough for a horse that rears, but let's hope our drafts are sensible enough not to rear where doing so might be dangerous. Just in

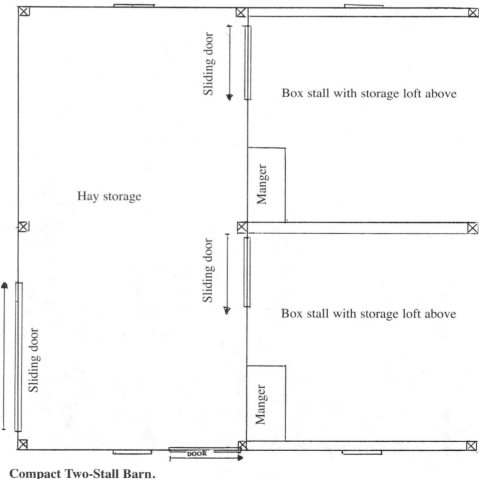

Compact Two-Stall Barn.

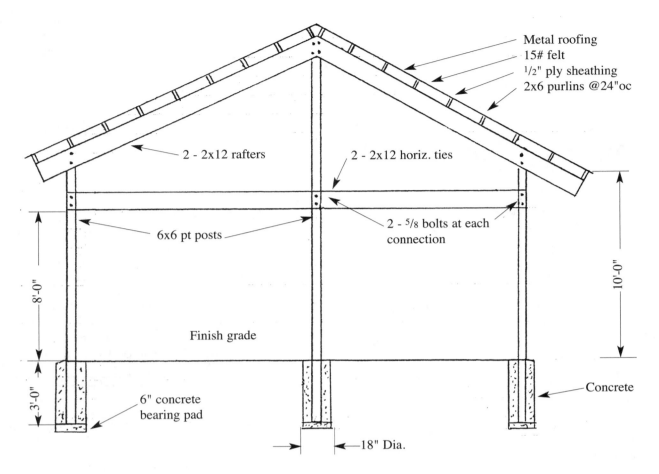

Metal roofing
15# felt
1/2" ply sheathing
2x6 purlins @24"oc

2 - 2x12 rafters

2 - 2x12 horiz. ties

6x6 pt posts

2 - 5/8 bolts at each connection

10'-0"

8'-0"

Finish grade

3'-0"

6" concrete bearing pad

Concrete

18" Dia.

Frame Cross Section.

Artwork by Pete Cecil

Two-stall barn showing hay-loading door at one end.

Photos by Pete Cecil

case, use metal cages to protect light fixtures in stall ceilings.

Make the barn a pleasant environment by ensuring plenty of artificial light combined with natural sunlight. Too much sunlight in stalls encourages flies to congregate.

Include a clean, dry, level and well-lit area for farrier work. Rubber stall mats laid together provide an excellent surface that is easily swept clean. Good airflow helps the farrier and the horse in hot weather and during hot shoeing.

If you live in a climate with heavy snow, design your building to avoid having barn door or stall door openings blocked by drifting snow or snow falling from the roof.

If you feed grain, you *must* store it in such a way that a horse getting loose in the barn cannot get into the grain and gorge itself. Grain overload is the number one cause of colic and founder, both of which can be deadly. Keep grain in a separate room, in a latched bin, or in a trash can closed with tight bungee cords.

Stalls

A stall is important to protect your horse from the worst weather and to provide a safe environment for a horse recovering from an injury or illness. A stall allows you to know exactly what and how much the horse is eating, and therefore lets you worry less about injuries or inadequate feed intake because of competition for food and water.

Many owners prefer tie stalls because more horses will fit into the barn, and the harnesses may be hung conveniently so the horses may easily and quickly be harnessed for work. For the horses' health and well being, however, box stalls are better because they allow the horses to move around. Stiff joints and muscles just get stiffer when a horse is forced to stand in one place for long periods of time.

How big a box stall should be depends on the size of your horse and the amount of time it will spend in the stall. A small draft kept in the stall only for feeding, for really bad weather, and for layups may do fine in a 10- by 10-foot stall. For a larger horse, and for a horse spending more time in the stall, a 12- by 12-foot stall would be more comfortable. For foaling, or for layups in which some exercise is important, an ideal stall is 12-feet by 15-feet or even larger.

Horses are happiest when they can see other horses. Dutch doors, half gates or stall gates with U-shaped cut-outs allow the horses to see and play with the horses next door. Some folks, however, prefer to limit contact among horses to decrease the chance of injury or spread of disease. Be careful not to place any valuable tack within reach of a curious draft horse.

The stall floor must first of all be solid. Concrete, however, is hard on a

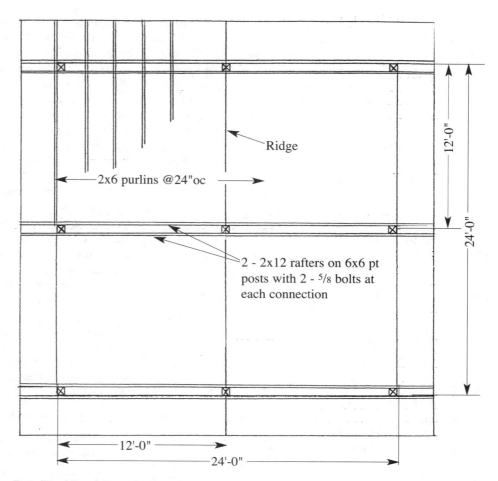

Details of Roof Framing.

Two-stall barn showing two open box stalls at the other end.

horse's feet and joints unless stall pads and heavy bedding are used. The stall floor should ideally allow for drainage of urine, although regular (at least once daily) stall cleaning will remove urine. Packed dirt or fine gravel works fine as a stall floor.

Bedding should be clean, soft and as free of dust and pollen as possible. Wood shavings are easiest to clean, but often contain more dust than straw does. If you use straw, you may find that your horses use it as an additional source of fiber in their diet. Munching on the bedding is not a problem from a nutritional standpoint, but might mean that your horses have less bedding to lie down on and to soak up urine. Shredded newspaper is a good stall bedding for horses.

Bedding to avoid

Black walnut shavings cause founder.

Wheat straw should not be used for a horse with respiratory allergies, as it contains more fungal spores than do shavings.

Newsprint may stain the haircoat of a light-colored horse.

Stall Vices

Too much time spent in a stall may result in the development of stall vices such as cribbing, weaving or stall walking.

Cribbing is an action in which the horse grasps the edge of a board in its teeth, sharply bends its neck, sucks in air and makes a grunting noise. Cribbing supposedly gives the horse a high due to the release of endorphins in the brain, but we have no proof that this is true. Cribbing is hard on a horse's teeth and even harder on the barn. A collar designed to keep the horse from bending its neck sharply may help control cribbing.

The stall weaving horse stands and sways from side to side for minutes or hours. The stall walking horse continuously walks in circles, which can wear the stall floor, not to mention the horse's shoes and hooves.

Stall vices probably begin out of boredom. Fortunately, most draft horses are too sensible to develop these bad habits. A bored draft horse is much more likely to occupy itself by eating the barn.

Chewing, too, is often a sign of boredom. All horses like to constantly do something with their mouths and draft horses seem to be the worst. Numerous bad-tasting products, applied like paint, are available to try to prevent horses from chewing wood. You can also protect top boards with metal sheeting.

Once any of these habits is established it may be difficult to break. Prevent these habits from getting started by allowing your horses plenty of exercise and toys to keep them occupied. Horse toys including rubber or plastic balls, as well as ordinary tires, plastic jugs containing a few rocks, feed tubs, inexpensive bath towels, hay or other horses to chew on all help prevent boredom. Preventing boredom helps prevent not only the development of stall vices, but also damage to the barn and fence.

The best way to prevent stall vices is to minimize the time your horse is confined to a stall.

Avoid placing tack within reach of a curious draft horse.

Photo by Bonnie Nance

The Cast Horse

A horse is cast by getting itself into a situation where it is down and cannot get its feet into the right position to allow it to stand. Providing plenty of stall room for the horse to maneuver to stand helps avoid a cast situation, but in any size stall a young horse or one that just doesn't know any better can roll up against a wall and need help getting up. Some stalls are built with walls that are reasonably easy to dismantle to give the horse and the handlers room to maneuver. A horse in a tie stall with a manger should have enough room in its tie rope to lie down, but not enough to allow it to climb into the manger.

If you find your horse cast and you can safely place ropes on its head, tail or legs to pull or roll the horse away from the wall, you may be able to solve the problem yourself. If the horse is panicked, or you are not able to resolve the problem soon, call a veterinarian to help. The horse may require mild sedation and possibly treatment for injuries that may occur during its struggles.

Getting cast against a pasture fence is less common than getting cast in a stall, but it can happen. Avoid it by making the bottom fence wire or board one and one-half to two feet above ground.

Do not wait for the cast horse to find its own solution. If it could, it would have already done so.

Fences

Although electric fence seems to work well for many horses, a board, pipe, or mesh wire fence is safer. If you build a fence with boards make sure the posts and the boards are strong, and fasten the boards securely on the *inside* of the posts. Otherwise you may find your horses popping off boards as they lean over to get at grass on the other side. If leaning is a problem, a hot wire on the inside should eliminate the habit. Check the fence frequently for broken or loose boards that could cause an injury or breakout.

No matter what kind of fence you have, horses can still get themselves into trouble. A heavy-duty mesh fence with mesh holes small enough that a horse or foal can't get a foot through is expensive, but is the safest kind of fence. The turnout paddocks at the Cornell Veterinary College are surrounded by six-foot chain link fences. Chain link is relatively safe, but costs more than the average horse owner can afford.

Avoid a situation in which two horses can get on opposite sides of the same fence. They may delight in positioning themselves across the fence and spending hours play fighting or really fighting, rearing, biting and kicking through and over the fence.

If your fence is difficult to see, such as one composed of wire strands, tie plastic-tape flags onto the wire before letting your

Fasten boards to the insides of the posts to keep them from popping off when your horses lean on the fence.

Photo by Vickie Darnell

horses out for the first time to help to avoid collisions with the fence. The color of the flags does not matter. You can remove the flags after the horses are aware of the fence boundaries. Although most horses become fully familiar with the fence within the first few hours of turnout into a new area, give them a couple of weeks to explore before removing the flags.

Pasture or Turnout Area

The ideal situation gives a horse 24-hour turnout with plenty of trees or a three-sided shed where it can escape flies and bad weather. The shed should be large enough to accommodate all your horses, although you may be amazed at how much draft horseflesh can squeeze into a 10- by 10-foot space. Doorways to sheds should be wide enough to allow at least two horses to pass. The barn may be constructed in such a way that stalls are open to the pasture or paddock as well as to the barn interior, thus providing both stalls and a turnout shelter.

The ideal situation is 24-hour turnout with trees or an open shed where the horses can escape flies or bad weather.

Photo by Debby Peterson

The amount and quality of your turnout area will depend on your geographic area, number of horses, budget and whether you want to feed the horses on pasture or just provide a place for exercise. The larger the pasture the better, but any space where your horse can stretch its legs for a good run is the bare minimum. The rule-of-thumb for feeding light horses on ideal pasture is to allow at least one acre per horse, which equates to about one and one-half acres per draft horse. You can easily see why most draft horse owners supplement pasture with additional hay. Dividing the pasture to allow for pasture rotation is a good idea. Pasture improvement may include soil analysis and regular addition of needed fertilizer. Periodic raking of accumulated manure will help spread this natural fertilizer as well as helping kill parasites by drying them out.

Well-drained soil free of rocks is great, but how many of us have that luxury? Rocks can cause bent and lost shoes, sole bruises and broken hooves. Try to keep the turnout area as free of rocks as possible. A rock-free pasture is more of a dream than a reality in many places. You can only do your best. Upstate New York grows a great crop of rocks. We sometimes wonder whether rocks fall from the sky, as we often find grass growing under them.

If the pasture has boggy areas, and you get tired of searching for lost shoes or wondering if you'll ever see your horse's feet again, you may want to look into improving drainage. Improved drainage might involve careful placement of agricultural pipes, thick layers of crushed rock or both. Constant exposure to moisture may predispose horses to the development of skin infections such as scratches and hoof infections such as thrush and canker.

Horses on sandy soil should have their feed placed off the ground to minimize sand intake that could cause impaction or sand colic. If your area is sandy, ask your veterinarian for advice. Products are available to help deal with this problem.

Regular examination of pastures and paddocks for broken fences, rocks, sticks and holes is part of good horse management. Walk your turnout areas regularly. Sometimes you may find a missing shoe or fly mask.

Exercise

Exercise is important to equine health, especially for young growing horses. Pasture exercise helps build strong bones. For horses with muscle stiffness or pain, turnout after exercise may bring some relief.

Horses need turnout for exercise as well as for grazing.
Photo by Vickie Darnell

Although regular exercise, including daily turnout, is best, Dr. Katharine Houpt at Cornell University did a study showing that adult horses kept in confinement for long periods of time—to simulate conditions at PMU farms, where mares are kept in tie stalls for weeks at a time for the collection of pregnant mare urine for medical use—do not suffer serious adverse effects.

Unless you have a good reason to keep your horses inside, though, the more exercise they get the better. Even after hard work, a draft horse should be turned out or at least allowed the freedom of a box stall, rather than being confined to a tie stall. Turnout is usually best because it lets horses exercise at will. Some horses are naturally more active on pasture than others; a low activity level is not necessarily a sign that something is wrong.

Ponds and Streams

Having a pond or stream in your horse pasture is always a convenient way to provide your horses with water. In areas with Potomac horse fever, however, horses that drink from ponds and streams may be at a higher risk of exposure to the causative agent. Areas of highest risk include parts of Maryland, northern California, southern Oregon, Ohio, Kentucky, the northeastern states and the mid-Atlantic states. This disorder is highly regional, so if you are in doubt about whether it occurs in your area ask your veterinarian or county Extension agent.

During the summer in the Plains states ponds may contain blue-green algal blooms that can, although rarely do, cause severe liver damage and sudden death.

To be safe, offer horses on pasture a stock tank of clean water from the tap to discourage them from drinking from ponds and streams. We'd prefer our drafts to use the pond only to play in during hot weather.

Poisonous Plants

Many pastures contain a variety of plants that are potentially poisonous to horses. An inventory of your pasture plants may

Educate neighboring children about plants that are, and are not, safe to feed a horse.
Photo by Bonnie Nance

generate a list of many of them. Most plants listed as poisonous to horses cause problems only when the horse has nothing else to eat or when the plants are baled into hay.

Landscape plants can cause problems to neighborhood horses when families bring lawn clippings to feed the horses. If this activity is popular in your neighborhood, try to educate your neighbors as to what is and is not safe to feed a horse.

The plants described here are only those we consider to be particularly dangerous. If you have doubts about any of your local plants, ask your veterinarian, local agricultural cooperative extension or local college.

Japanese Yew

Japanese yew (ground hemlock) is a popular ornamental evergreen that is often used in residential landscaping. It must *never* be planted in an area where horses are turned out or tied, and cuttings must *never* be fed to horses. This plant is deadly. Only a small amount will kill a horse quickly. The toxic compound interferes with heart function, causing sudden and rapid death.

One teamster who was having construction work done around his house transplanted an uprooted yew into the horse pasture. The family didn't know what to think when the first horse died. Within a day or so, the second one died and they began to wonder. A postmortem examination of the second horse found the deadly plant needles in the horse's mouth and stomach. Whether or not damage to the heart would be permanent is unknown because few horses survive eating Japanese yew.

compounds in oleander and foxglove are known as cardiac glycosides. Milkweed also contains these compounds, but we have never heard of a horse being poisoned by milkweed, even though it commonly grows wild in many pastures. Oleander is a popular ornamental plant, especially on the West Coast and Deep South. Horses browsing on oleander plants or fed garden clippings containing oleander may die so rapidly they exhibit few symptoms, and the plant leaves may still be found in the stomach and mouth.

Oleander
(Nerium oleander)

Japanese yew or ground hemlock (Taxus cuspidata)

Oleander and Foxglove

Oleander and foxglove are similar to the Japanese yew in containing compounds that affect heart function. The

Foxglove
(Digitalis purpurea)

Foxglove is cultivated in gardens and grows wild in pastures and on roadsides in western North America. Since it is particularly bad tasting to horses, poisoning by foxglove is rare. Poisoning occurs only when other plants are not available to graze or when portions of these plants are included in lawn clippings or hay.

One group of drafts was poisoned by foxglove after woodchips containing this plant were spread on their paddock. Signs of staggering and weakness may precede death. Although horses may occasionally survive mild cases of poisoning, permanent damage to the heart may later result in signs of heart failure or sudden death from severe cardiac failure.

Black Walnut

Ingestion of wood, leaves, or bark from the black walnut tree will not cause problems, but wood shavings containing black walnut will quickly result in severe laminitis and founder. Horses often browse on bedding after their feed is gone. Prompt removal of the horse from the offending bedding and aggressive treatment for laminitis and founder generally results in recovery. Prevention is the best cure, and careful questioning of the content of shavings purchased for bedding will prevent this serious problem.

Yellow Star Thistle

Yellow star thistle and the related plant Russian knapweed grow wild in the western part of the United States. Both plants cause degeneration of parts of the brain. Paralysis of the swallowing muscles is the most obvious sign of poisoning.

Yellow star thistle
(Centaurea spp.)

Potentially Toxic Plants

Many plants that are present in pasture and turnout areas only rarely cause problems. As with the severely toxic plants, making sure your horses have plenty of safe food available should keep them from getting into trouble.

Red Maple

Red maple is a common wild tree found in the northeastern, north central, and southeastern United States. In other areas it is planted as an ornamental tree. Many pastures in the Northeast contain numerous red maples, as do the woods and hedgerows. Horses often browse on leaves in passing and browse on the leaves and bark of trees in their pasture. The bark seems to be particularly tasty and may provide hours of entertainment for horses stripping it off.

Red maple or swamp maple
(Acer rubrum)

The leaves are the potentially toxic portion, but are toxic to horses only when wilted. Problems occur most often in the autumn when the leaves fall and wilt. Red maple leaves may cover other available forage. Horses occasionally get into trouble when a tree or branch falls and the leaves are eaten after they wilt.

The toxins in these leaves cause a breakdown of red blood cells. The symptoms are pale gums and mucous membranes of the eyes (conjunctiva), both characteristic of anemia. You may notice red urine, a condition called hemoglobinuria, caused by

hemoglobinuria	
hemo	= blood
globin	= protein
hemoglobin	= the oxygen-carrying protein of red blood cells
uria	= urine

pigments released from damaged red blood cells. If this should happen, get your horse away from the areas with fallen leaves and call your veterinarian immediately. Recovery is possible provided the kidneys have not been severely damaged by the red blood cell pigments in the urine. Horses with access to adequate hay or other forage rarely consume enough wilted red maple leaves to cause problems.

Wild Cherry

The leaves, seeds, saplings and bark of the wild cherry tree contain cyanide, a poison that can cause death because cyanide blocks the transfer of oxygen from the blood to the cells that need it. As with many potentially poisonous plants, a horse must have little or nothing else to eat to be poisoned by wild cherry.

**Hoary alyssum
(*Berteroa incana*)**

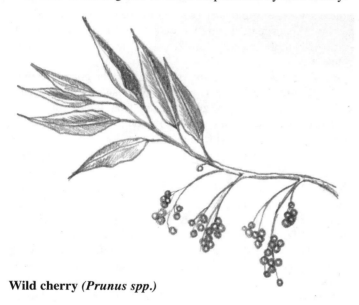

Wild cherry (*Prunus spp.*)

Hoary alyssum

Hoary alyssum, found in the North, may be eaten by horses if other forage is not available. Of particular importance is its presence in hay, where it may resemble alfalfa. This plant causes stocking up (swelling of the lower legs), fever and diarrhea in horses consuming sufficient quantities. Horses usually recover within two to three days after being removed from the plant source.

Sorghum

Sorghum, or sudan grass, is common in the central states and Southern Great Plains. Sometimes horses on sorghum pasture develop damage of the nerves to the bladder and hind legs. They develop hind leg incoordination or paralysis, and may dribble urine and develop urine scalding of affected skin. Recovery is not possible. This syndrome may resemble clinical signs of rabies or neuritis of the cauda equina (end of the spinal cord). Sorghum may also contain cyanide that can cause acute death similar to wild cherry toxicity.

Sorghum or sudan grass (*Sorghum vulgare var. sudanense*)

Kleingrass and Fall Panicum

Kleingrass is a common pasture grass of the Southwest, similar to fall panicum in the East. As pasture or hay each is toxic to horses when it is the only source of roughage. Affected horses may be depressed and perform poorly. With heavy exposure they may develop jaundice and nervous signs from liver failure.

Kleingrass and fall panicum *(Panicum spp.)*

Locoweed
(Astragalus spp. and Oxytropis spp.)

Locoweed

Locoweeds are found in the West, where they may be present on range pastures. Horses raised on western ranges are less likely to be poisoned than are horses newly introduced to range. A horse must consume about 30 percent of its body weight over a period of weeks before it begins to show nervous signs such as hyperexcitability, trembling, incoordination and paralysis. Horses removed from these ranges apparently recover, but are still considered dangerous to drive or ride.

Plants Containing Pyrrolizidine Alkaloids

A number of plant families contain toxins called pyrrolizidine (pronounced peer-row-LIZ-a-dean) alkaloids that cause damage to the liver when grazed by horses. Some of these plants include hound's tongue, groundsel (with numerous modifiers such as wooly, thread-leaf, Riddell's and broom), tansy ragwort, rattlebox, heliotropum, stinking willie, bitterweed and fiddleneck.

Horses grazing these plants may show poor condition with low exposure. Higher levels of exposure result in jaundice and nervous signs that may progress to death from liver failure. Less severe liver damage may result in a build up in the skin of substances that react with sunlight to cause a form of skin irritation known as photosensitization (sensitivity to sunlight).

Plants Causing Photosensitization

Photosensitization, in addition to being caused by pyrrolizidine alkaloid-containing plants, may also be caused by St. John's wort and buckwheat, both of which contain compounds that accumulate in the skin and react with sunlight. St. John's wort grows on roadsides, abandoned fields and open woodlands throughout the United States. Buckwheat, however, is a cultivated plant, and exposure in horses is rare. Keep horses away from areas or feeds containing either plant, fresh or dried.

Feed-Associated Toxicities

Feed associated toxicities are caused, not by toxic compounds contained within the plant itself, but by toxic substances that contaminate grasses, grains or hays. Such toxins include those produced by certain endophytic fungi (molds that grow within the plant and are not visible to the naked eye), other fungi, and toxic insects, as well as bacterial and chemical toxins.

Red Clover

Red clover is a common plant in pastures and hay fields and is not toxic. Problems occur when plants are infected with a fungus (*Rhizoctonia leguminicola*) that causes the production of too much saliva, resulting in slobbering. Affected clover has brown or black spots on the leaves. Although affected horses are not in danger of losing their lives, they should be kept off infected pasture or hay and provided with adequate water and salt to replace the fluids and sodium they lose in the excessive

Some Plants Poisonous to Horses

Common name(s)	Scientific name	Where found	Toxic parts	Sign(s)	How Serious	Outcome
black walnut	*Juglans nigra*	widespread	shavings	laminitis/founder	variable	variable
fall panicum	*Panicum dichotomiflorum*	eastern pastures	all parts	depression, jaundice, nervous signs	serious	variable
foxglove	*Digitalis purpurea*	widespread in gardens, grows wild in the West	all parts	weakness, staggering	serious, but rare	permanent heart damage or death
hoary alyssum	*Berteroa incana*	Northeast and Midwest	all parts	stocking up, fever, diarrhea	moderate	curable
Japanese yew; ground hemlock	*Taxus cuspidata*	widespread in landscaping	all parts	sudden death	serious	death
kleingrass	*Panicum coloratum*	Texas and Southwest pastures	all parts	depression, jaundice, nervous signs	serious	variable
locoweed	*Astragalus spp.* and *Oxytropis spp.*	Western range and pasture	all parts	hyperexcitability, trembling, incoordination, paralysis	serious	possible recovery in mild cases
oleander	*Nerium oleander*	landscaping: West Coast and Deep South	all parts	colic, tremors, diarrhea, sudden death	serious	permanent heart damage or death
red maple; swamp maple	*Acer rubrum*	northeastern, north central, southeastern states	wilted leaves	pale gums, red urine	serious	variable
sorghum; sudan grass	*Sorghum vulgare var. sudanense*	central and southern Great Plains	all parts	incoordination or paralysis of hind legs, urine dribbling, sudden death	serious	recovery is rare
yellow star thistle; Russian knapweed	*Centaurea spp.*	western states range and pasture	all parts	inability to eat	serious	no recovery: starvation leads to death
wild cherry	*Prunus spp.*	widespread	leaves, seeds, saplings, bark	sudden death	serious, but rare	death

saliva. On rare occasions this same fungus will infect alfalfa or white clover.

Blister Beetle

Blister beetles contain a powerful irritant, cantharidin, known in certain circles as Spanish fly. Horses become exposed to the toxins only when they eat hay containing dead adult insects that had been feeding on alfalfa in mid- to late summer and were baled into the hay. Cases of blister beetle poisoning have also been associated with feeding alfalfa cubes or pellets containing beetles.

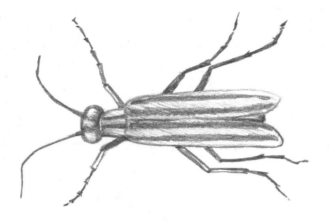

Affected horses develop serious gastrointestinal and urinary tract irritation resulting in colic and increased urination. Blister beetle toxicity is often fatal. Just two to five beetles fed to a horse may cause signs of colic. Blister beetle contamination is mostly a problem in the South and Midwest, where horse owners may be reluctant to feed alfalfa products. Careful examination and use of insecticides on infested fields will control the beetles, and responsible hay producers in these areas will produce a safe and nutritious product.

> *endophyte*
> endo = inside or internal
> phyte = plant
> endophyte = fungi that grow within plants that may produce harmful toxins

Fescue

Fescue grass is a popular feed in the Southeast, and the grass itself is not a problem. Fescue toxicity—which may result in reproductive problems such as lack of milk, premature placental separation, retained placentas, stillbirths and prolonged pregnancy—is due to toxins produced by endophytic fungi (endophytes) that grow in the grass as a parasite. Fescue hay or grass may be tested for levels of specific endophytes. Although some fungal-resistant strains of fescue have been developed, they are not as hardy as the parent plants.

Fescue Foot

On rare occasions a foal grazing on infected fescue pasture may lose the blood supply to a hoof, causing loss of the hoof. This serious condition may be treated with nitroglycerin patches placed over the digital arteries to cause them to open and reestablish the blood supply. This treatment is similar to that for acute laminitis and founder.

The best prevention is to avoid feeding fescue pasture or hay to pregnant mares, especially during the last one to two months of pregnancy. Providing supplemental alfalfa or clover hay to pregnant mares grazing fescue is not effective. Mares are much more sensitive than cows are to fescue endophyte toxicity. The drug domperidone may be used to help counteract some of the effects of endophytes, such as lack of milk in mares. Prevention, however, is much more effective than treatment.

Ryegrass Staggers

Ryegrass is a common pasture plant in the Southeast and the West Coast of the United States. The plants may become parasitized by an endophytic fungus that produces a toxin causing incoordination and staggering in horses and other livestock. Removing the horses from the affected pasture or hay will result in their recovery.

Botulism

Botulism may be caused either by production of the powerful paralyzing toxin of the causative organism *Clostridium botulinum* in the intestinal tract or by ingestion of toxin present in the feed. Most cases of equine botulism occur due to ingestion of the toxin, but intestinal toxin production occasionally occurs in foals.

This bacterial organism is present in the soil, but does not produce its toxin unless conditions are just right. The bacteria are particularly fond of moist environments in which oxygen availability is low and the pH is not too acidic. Contamination of feeds by animal carcasses is one way adult horses get botulism.

Dairy farmers sometimes use silage or haylage as horse feed. Silage and haylage are moist feeds that are not always sufficiently acidic to keep out the toxin. Some horse owners have gotten away with feeding these products, but it takes only one outbreak of botulism to make them aware of the danger. Horses are much more sensitive to botulism than are cattle, sheep, goats, cats or dogs.

The toxin causes a profound weakness and paralysis of muscles, especially of the muscles involved in chewing and swallowing. Horses often go down and die. If diagnosed in early stages, administration of botulinum antitoxin and good nursing care may enable a horse to pull through. Like so many equine diseases, botulism is a problem that is much better prevented than cured. Should your horses begin to show signs of weakness—especially after having eaten from a new batch of silage, haylage, moist hay, or hay cubes or pellets—immediately change the feed and call a veterinarian.

Silage and haylage are not safe feeds for horses.

Moldy Corn Toxicity

Moldy corn toxicity occurs within one to several weeks of feeding corn, especially corn screenings, contaminated by a fungus known as *Fusarium moniliforme*. The toxins produced by this fungus cause massive liver and brain damage, leading to death or lifelong neurologic problems. The best way to avoid this problem is to not feed corn to horses.

Ionophore Toxicity

Ionophores are compounds that are often added to cattle and poultry feeds to improve feed efficiency. The most commonly fed ionophores are monensin (trade name Rumensin or Coban), lasalocid (trade name Bovatec or Avatec), narasin and salinomycin. Although feeding ionophores may be beneficial to cattle and poultry, horses are exquisitely sensitive to poisoning by these compounds. Death may occur following ingestion of only small amounts.

Affected horses show a variety of signs including loss of appetite, colic, diarrhea, sweating, rapid breathing, recumbency and sudden death. Although no specific treatment is known, some horses survive with supportive care. Cardiac scarring in horses surviving ionophore exposure may result in sudden death at a later date.

If you keep horses and cattle or poultry on the same farm, do not allow your horses access to ionophore-containing feeds or to buckets that once contained these feeds.

Safe Driving

If you are new to drafts and driving find someone in your area who can help you learn, or travel to one of the draft driving schools. Harnesses and hitches come in numerous configurations, and excellent reference books are available to help you determine what you need and how to use it. Hands-on learning with an experienced teamster, however, has no substitute. Work with an experienced horse or team, under the guidance of an experienced driver.

If you are new to draft horses, make sure your first horse or team is well-trained and steady. A horse trained to work in a team may not have a clue about driving single, and a horse that drives single may not work well in a team. Developing a team takes time, patience, training and experience.

Once you are on your own, carefully check everything about your harness and hitch before setting out. Don't rely on your horse's good temperament and training to allow you to drive safely if you have forgotten to attach the lines to the bridle.

When you unhitch *never* remove the bridle before you have completely unhitched the horse. Lots of unexpected things happen that can spook even the quietest horse. A mature draft or team running amok is dangerous enough, but an out-of-control draft or team pulling a vehicle or machinery is just plain deadly.

Shipping Safety

Shipping can be a stressful for your horse, although most short hauls are not a problem. Light horses are often shipped covered in bulky shipping boots, blankets and head bumpers. Many drafts travel in stock trailers, and many folks load them already harnessed.

For most horses, especially for heavily muscled draft horses, excessive heat production rather than loss of heat in the trailer is a problem. If you want to blanket your draft horses during shipping, use a light sheet instead of a heavy blanket. Open a few or all the windows to allow adequate air circulation, or use an open-sided stock trailer.

The stress of long-distance shipping will decrease a horse's natural immunity to bacterial and viral infections. The enclosed space will increase exposure to any microbes ("bugs") in the air. Allow your horses as much room as is safely possible so they can move their heads, as well as drop their heads to allow gravity to help clear microbes out of their breathing passages. Letting your draft horse travel loose in the trailer may be safer than tying its head.

Protecting a horse's lower legs and head from injury during shipping sounds like a good idea, but where can you get shipping boots and head bumpers to fit a draft? Shipping boots may be dangerous because a loose wrap can get a horse tangled, upset and possibly injured. Not bothering with leg wraps simplifies loading preparations and the horses don't

Before setting out carefully check your harness and hitch. *Photo by Vickie Darnell*

have to deal with the strange sensation of having heavy wraps on their legs. Have you ever seen a horse walk after having leg wraps put on? Horses with hind leg wraps often appear to have suddenly developed the condition of shivers or stringhalt. They lift their hind legs abnormally high, which we can explain only as a response to something about their legs that feels funny. Unless you know your horse is likely to bash its head on the ceiling or step on itself don't feel guilty about shipping it without extra paraphernalia.

Make sure your trailer has enough headroom and side to side room for your horses to stand naturally and brace themselves for turns, accelerations and decelerations. Padding and the elimination of sharp surfaces decrease the chance of injury. *Drive carefully and maintain a safe rig.*

Photo by Vickie Darnell

Feeding the Draft Horse

Teamsters and racehorse trainers have at least one thing in common—they all know exactly what their horses need to eat, and it is entirely different for each teamster or trainer. Few other horse-related subjects provoke more differences of emotionally charged opinion. With such controversy, and all the different horse feeds available, no wonder some horse owners are just plain confused, yet nothing else under your control as the horse's owner has as much impact on your horse's health.

A horse requires water, fiber, protein, vitamins, electrolytes, minerals and a source of energy. Fiber in the diet keeps the intestinal tract healthy and is broken down by fermentation in the large intestine for energy, primarily in the form of fatty acids. Sufficient protein builds growing organs, rebuilds damaged tissues and maintains body tissues.

A horse needs adequate vitamins, including vitamin A and E, that are not made by intestinal bacteria (as are vitamin C and the B vitamins) or made in the skin following sun exposure (as is vitamin D). Essential electrolytes and minerals, such as salts, calcium, phosphorus, selenium, iron, copper and zinc, are needed—along with a source of additional energy—for growth and to allow the horse to perform work over and above carrying its own weight around the pasture. Energy helps horses stay warm during cold weather and helps ensure successful pregnancy and lactation.

Water

The one thing a horse needs lots of, that costs little or nothing, is plain old water. A big horse may drink 10 to 15 gallons or more per day, and that's just standing around. If the horse is working, especially on a hot, humid day, its daily water requirement may increase to 30 to 45 gallons or more. Since the capacity of even a large horse's stomach (about four to five gallons) is nowhere close to the amount of water it needs to drink, you can see why frequent drinking is necessary to maintain the horse's proper hydration.

Draft horses may be more inclined than other horses to play with their water, causing a wet soggy mess in the stall. Barns with tie stalls are often not designed for water buckets to be readily refilled. Some draft owners feel that monitoring how much a horse drinks is more important than providing free choice drinking water. For most horses, however, there is no good reason for measuring how much each horse is drinking, and every reason to ensure that your horses have as much water to drink as they want, whenever they want it.

Few circumstances occur in which a horse does not voluntarily drink enough water. If your horse doesn't want to drink, what would you be able to do about it? Healthy horses know exactly how much water they need to drink. Only a sick horse might need extra water, which may need to be provided by fluids dripped directly into the jugular vein. Far more problems are associated with limiting a horse's access to water than with allowing free access to water. Horses need water especially during or after mealtime, when food should be mixed with liquid in order to keep moving through the gastrointestinal tract.

Draft horses need lots of water, which they should be able to get from a stock tank full of clean tap water.

Photo by Vickie Darnell

If you are in the habit of bringing your horse to the water trough after or during work, you may need to do so several times to ensure that the horse is well hydrated. After hard work a horse should always be provided with plenty of drinking water before it is given grain or hay. Supplying a ready source of water all day long is much easier and safer than occasionally visiting the trough. The pasture or paddock is a good place to provide a large water trough or natural source of water such as a pond or creek.

Winter Watering

In many parts of the world, winter brings frozen streams, ponds, water buckets and troughs, resulting in an increased incidence of horses needing intensive care because of bad impaction colics. Where freezing is a problem, many ingenious ways may be found for keeping water available. Bubbling devices in ponds or troughs, floating tank de-icers, insulation of water troughs by man-made or horse-made (manure) materials, and gadgets with floating balls in a top opening are just a few of the ways to make water available all winter.

Devices that warm the water slightly are more expensive to run, but have the advantage of enticing a horse to drink more during the winter and may pay off in decreased veterinary bills for impaction colics. Horses will get a small amount of water from green grass and from licking snow. Neither of these water sources comes close to providing a sufficient amount of water.

Ganting

Owners of pulling horses that compete in lightweight or middleweight divisions often limit a horse's access to water to make the weight requirements, a practice known as ganting. Although the tradition is well established, the danger to the horse of competing while slightly dehydrated and with an altered electrolyte balance is enormous, and we cannot recommend this practice.

Surveys of draft horse owners have found that tying up and colic are the two most common health problems reported by owners of pulling horses. Ganting must certainly contribute to this finding. Feeding a slightly less bulky feed—such as a low carbohydrate, high fat feed—is a better way to decrease the gut-ballast weight of the horse and help ensure that the horse's weight is in well-hydrated muscle for maximum performance.

Fiber

The horse is a grazing animal with the ability, and the need, to process large amounts of fiber that is indigestible to humans, cats or dogs. Forage—either pasture or hay—supplies fiber and is the mainstay of the equine diet. Fiber is critical to a horse's health.

A draft horse must be fed the best possible quality hay or pasture. If good forage is not available as pasture or baled hay, supplement the horse's diet with one of the pelleted or cubed hay products available as alfalfa, grass hay or a combination of both.

When feeding hay to more than one horse in a pasture or paddock, spread the hay into one or two more piles than the number of horses you are feeding. Competition for food among horses can be fierce, and those at the low end of the pecking order could lose out.

To qualify for the midweight or lightweight pulling class, the best way to reduce gut-ballast weight is with low carbohydrate high fat feed. *Photo by Phil Krahn*

If you are feeding only one or two horses, or you live in an area where the soil is extremely sandy, you may want to put the hay in a trough or haybox, which should be low to the ground. A horse that can lower its head while eating is unlikely to inhale various dusts and pollens, and the mucus in its nose that catches many of these dusts and pollens can readily drain out of the horse. Avoid spreading the hay on ground or bedding that is heavily soiled by manure. Although horses will not graze on grass contaminated by manure, they do not seem to mind hay being placed on manure-contaminated ground or bedding. Pellets and cubes are best fed in buckets or troughs.

Never compensate for poor quality forage by feeding extra grain.

Whether you feed alfalfa hay, pellets or cubes, grass hay, or a mixture of alfalfa and grass hay products depends on local cost, availability and individual preferences. Under many

To ensure that all horses get their share, spread hay into one or two piles more than the number of horses you are feeding.
Photo by Vickie Darnell

circumstances—such as feeding debilitated horses, hard working horses and nursing or growing horses—we like the added calcium, vitamins and calories available in alfalfa products, but good quality grass hay is better than poor quality alfalfa or other clover hay. Good quality pasture provides most, if not all, essential vitamins and minerals. Good quality hay of any kind provides excellent levels of calcium, vitamin A and essential trace minerals.

Beet Pulp

Beet pulp is a popular added feed with draft horse owners. It provides roughage and calories similar to alfalfa hay. Arguments have been made for and against the need for soaking beet pulp pellets prior to feeding them, since they expand greatly in water. We don't feed beet pulp ourselves and therefore can't speak from experience, but presoaking, especially when feeding more .than a few pounds, seems prudent.

Forage is the mainstay of the equine diet.
Photo by Bonnie Nance

Beet pulp is not particularly tasty to many horses, and contains a bit more soluble carbohydrates than does hay. Although we cannot recommend beet pulp as a substitute for good hay or pasture, a small amount may help soak up the vegetable oil many draft horses need in their diets (as described in the next chapter).

Bran Mash

For some reason word has gotten around that feeding your horse a warm wheat bran mash is beneficial. We understand that in some stables in Canada bran mashes are a regular part of the evening meal during cold weather. Bran provides fiber, but so does forage. Bran does not provide a laxative effect in the amounts that can be easily fed to a horse. Bran has a high phosphorus and low calcium content and can therefore lead to an imbalanced diet. Wheat bran also contains soluble carbohydrates that we prefer not to feed our horses. The only possible benefit to feeding a warm wheat bran mash in cold weather is to increase a horse's water intake. A bucket of slightly warmed water would do the same thing, only better.

Horses should be able to lower their heads to eat, reducing the chance they will inhale dusts and pollens.

Photo by Bonnie Nance

Protein

Most horses are overfed protein. A diet that is about 10 percent protein is adequate for most adult horses. Feeding excess protein, however, has no adverse effects. Too much protein does not lead to kidney or liver damage. It does not cause a horse to get hot or develop so-called protein bumps, and does not cause tying up.

All the nutritional studies performed to date that we know of have involved healthy light horses. Given the draft horse's heavy musculature and its incidence of muscle problems, erring on the side of more protein than the horse needs may be a more reasonable approach than to risk feeding too little. But feeding the same amount of a higher protein feed could result in feeding additional calories. The horse must either use these extra calories to make fat or burn them through extra activity. If your horse appears to get hot (unmanageably energetic) when switched to a higher protein feed or hay, try feeding a bit less of it before you condemn that feed as inappropriate for your horse.

The only suggested down side to feeding too much protein (besides the unnecessary extra cost) is an increased urine volume because of the extra protein breakdown products passing through the kidneys. Unless something is drastically wrong with the horse, its kidneys are capable of handling the extra load. The potential for a loss of electrolytes in the increased urine volume is a problem only in hard working heavily sweating horses. These lost electrolytes are easily replaced with commercially available electrolytes designed for horses.

Burning protein for energy results in a slightly increased production of body heat during exercise, which can be effectively counteracted by substituting fat for carbohydrates in the feed. Whether certain protein sources are better than others for maximal performance and health in horses remains to be determined through research.

Vitamins

The bacteria in a horse's intestine produce many of the vitamins essential to equine health. These vitamins are known as the water-soluble vitamins and include the many forms of B vitamin—such as thiamin, riboflavin, pantothenic acid, choline, niacin—as well as vitamin C. Any extra water-soluble vitamins in the horse's diet are passed in the urine, so these vitamins are considered non-toxic.

The fat soluble vitamins A, D and E are stored in the body's fatty tissues and other cells, and can build up to high levels. These vitamins are therefore often referred to as potentially toxic vitamins. A high level of vitamin E in a horse is, however, not known to be toxic but may be quite beneficial. Although synthetic vitamin A is potentially toxic, vitamin A toxicity is rare. No toxicity is associated with even extremely high levels of the natural vitamin A, beta-carotene, abundantly present in carrots, alfalfa and other clover hays. You cannot, therefore, poison your horse with too much vitamin A by feeding too many carrots.

Vitamin D is produced by the action of sunlight on skin, and is contained within green plants. A horse fed only marginal or poor quality hay and kept indoors for long periods of time may become vitamin D deficient. Vitamin D deficiency could affect the strength of bones and teeth and the horse may require supplementation. Under these circumstances, consult with your veterinarian or an equine nutritionist to determine whether supplementation is required to prevent problems. Over supplementation of vitamin D is most often associated with errors of mixing at the feed manufacturer. Be sure you buy from reputable feed companies. Horses in Texas and Florida that graze on wild jasmine (*Cestrum diurnum*), which contains vitamin D-like compounds, can develop vitamin D toxicity resulting in weight loss and lameness due to calcification (hardening) of tendons and ligaments. As with most plant toxicities, provide adequate good quality pasture or hay to reduce the likelihood that your horse will eat potentially poisonous plants.

Many horses without access to good quality pasture, alfalfa or other clover hay or hay products are slightly to severely vitamin E deficient. These horses require supplementation. Vitamin E deficiency in young growing horses may cause spinal cord disease (equine degenerative myelopathy). In older horses deficiency may result in performance problems due to muscle dysfunction or may predispose the horse to developing a disease called equine motor neuron disease, which is similar to amyotrophic lateral sclerosis (ALS, or Lou Gehrig's Disease) in people. Alternatively, a vitamin E deficient horse may simply age faster and not have the lifespan of a horse with plenty of vitamin E.

Each horse needs 1 to 2 IU (international units) of vitamin E per pound of horse per day.

Minerals

Good quality pasture or hay may contain all the vital minerals your horse needs. Equally important to providing the right minerals is ensuring a proper ratio of minerals, particularly of calcium to phosphorus. In some areas, soils may be lacking in essential minerals such as selenium.

Calcium and Phosphorus

The two major minerals horses require are calcium and phosphorus, which are particularly important for building and maintaining strong bones and teeth. A ratio in the diet of two parts calcium to one part phosphorus is ideal. A ratio of one-to-one is considered the bare minimum. Anything lower than one-to-one is dangerous to the horse's health.

Calcium is present in high levels in alfalfa and other clover grass and hay, and is added to commercial feeds. No evidence suggests that a higher calcium level, up to four parts calcium to one part phosphorus, is dangerous. Some people believe that high calcium levels may predispose a horse to tying up or to "thumps," a condition akin to hiccups in which the diaphragm spasms at regular intervals, but this theory is by no means proven.

In certain parts of the United States, including California, the high levels of magnesium present in the soil (and therefore in the forage grown in the soil) added to the usual calcium in alfalfa may predispose a horse to the formation of intestinal stones, or enteroliths. In these areas feeding a grass or mixed grass and alfalfa product may be prudent. Addition of vinegar to the feed may also help prevent stones from forming by decreasing the pH of the intestinal content.

Serious problems occur when the level of calcium in the diet is lower than the phosphorus level. This situation causes calcium to be taken out of the bones in large amounts to maintain the proper amount of calcium in the blood. The bones then become thickened and soft. These changes are most obvious in the bones of the head, resulting in a condition called big head. If the imbalance is not rapidly corrected, the horse may lose teeth and/or its demineralized bones may fracture.

Poor quality grass hay, grains such as corn and oats, and wheat and rice brans are high in phosphorus and low in calcium. If your horse's diet contains large amounts of grains or brans and no alfalfa or other clover hay, remedy the imbalance by changing to a commercial feed in which the calcium-to-phosphorus ratio has been corrected.

> *enterolith*
> entero = intestine
> lith   = stone

Selenium

One of the most important trace minerals needed by horses of all ages is selenium. This mineral is taken up from the soil by the growing plants that horses graze. In areas of the American West where horses can survive in the wild, the soil contains more than enough selenium. In many other parts of the world, the selenium content of the soil is low or nonexistent. In such areas good forage alone will not provide sufficient nutrition for horses. Selenium is essential for proper function of many cells of the body, particularly muscle cells. Along with vitamins E, A, and C, selenium is also a powerful antioxidant. Antioxidants are compounds that counteract the potentially damaging effects of both the cells' use of oxygen and exposure to ultraviolet radiation from the sun.

If selenium levels are low in your area, your horse may still be getting sufficient selenium from other sources, such as a commercial grain mix, pellets or extruded feed to which selenium has been added. If your feed is grown and mixed locally, and you are in a selenium-deficient area, check that your

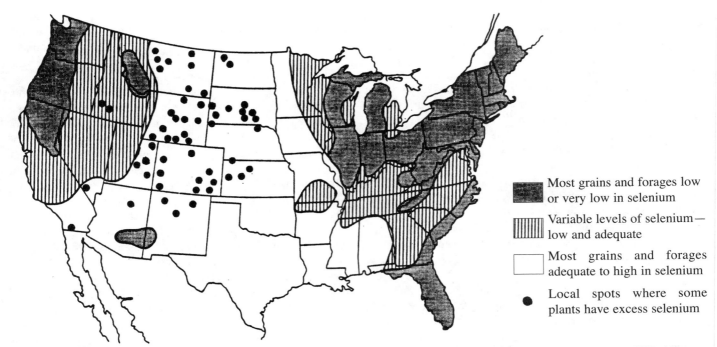

Most grains and forages low or very low in selenium

Variable levels of selenium— low and adequate

Most grains and forages adequate to high in selenium

● Local spots where some plants have excess selenium

Relative selenium contents of crops in relation to animal requirements. Adapted from map prepared by Dr. W.H. Allaway and co-workers, USDA.

local mill is adding selenium. If you feed whole grains such as oats and corn, find out if the selenium content has been analyzed and selenium added if needed. Selenium-containing salt blocks often do not provide adequate daily intake for horses in selenium-deficient areas.

Deficiency

If your horse is fed only selenium deficient pasture or hay, with little or no added grain, or if no selenium is added to the whole grains you feed, you would be wise to invest in one of the many inexpensive selenium supplements on the market. Although your selenium-deficient horse may appear to be perfectly healthy, adequate selenium intake will offer the following benefits:

● aid in more rapid muscle conditioning
● improve maintenance of condition
● improve reproductive capacity
● perhaps delay the natural aging process.

Many selenium products contain added vitamin E, which is not a problem even if vitamin E is being supplied by good pasture, alfalfa or other clover hay sources, but in such cases buying a straight selenium supplement may be more economical. Some hard working horses, and those on a high fat diet, may benefit from additional selenium and vitamin E.

Each horse needs 1 to 2 mg of selenium per 1,000 pounds of horse per day

---

How Much Is Too Much?

Although selenium may be toxic at high levels, in most parts of the world you would have to work hard to poison a horse with this mineral. Selenium has about a 10-times safety factor, meaning that a draft horse would need to eat 10 to 20 mg or more of selenium per day to be in the danger zone. Remember to factor in *all* possible sources of selenium in your horses' diet to determine their intake. When in doubt, have your veterinarian submit a blood sample for selenium analysis. Signs of selenium toxicity include transverse (side-to-side) cracks in hooves that may progress to loss of the hoof wall, and loss of mane and tail hairs.

Iron and Copper

Iron is a necessary component of the oxygen-carrying protein of red blood cells (hemoglobin). An iron deficiency may cause anemia. Significant anemia in horses is, however, an uncommon condition except in horses that have had serious blood loss or red blood cell damage. Unfortunately anemia is frequently diagnosed when a horse with unexplained performance problems comes up with a slightly lower-than-normal total red blood cell count or a mild iron deficiency. Adding iron-containing supplements to "build the blood" is unlikely to result in improved performance because the real problem may be less obvious than anemia. Mild anemia may accompany any longstanding infection or disease. Poor performance in a draft horse is more likely to be due to muscle disease than to anemia.

Iron may be a more important issue when it is fed in excessive in doubt, have your water tested. Excessive iron interferes with the absorption of other minerals such as copper and zinc. Too much iron may result in accelerated aging because iron is involved in cell damage due to oxygen-derived free radicals. These free radicals, produced when cells utilize oxygen to produce energy, are potentially damaging to the cells. The body's antioxidants, including vitamin E and selenium, are present to help control free radicals.

An adequate copper level in the diet of a pregnant mare or growing foal is important for the prevention of developmental bone diseases such as osteochondrosis dissecans (OCD). Ever since the importance of copper was recognized in the 1980s, horse feed manufacturers have increased the copper levels in their feeds. Horses are tolerant of even high levels of copper and do not develop copper toxicity.

Electrolytes

Electrolytes include the salts and minerals that are needed for the proper functioning of cells, especially those of the nervous system, heart and other muscles. Supplying salt in the form of a salt block allows a horse to replace salts lost in sweat and urine.

Trace mineralized salt blocks may be preferable to plain salt, because they contain iron and other trace minerals. Probably the most important trace mineral they contain is iodine, which is essential to equine health. All other trace minerals added to salt blocks do not clearly do anything other than make us horse owners feel better about providing what we believe to be the best for our horses.

The iodine added to salt blocks, however, is necessary for the proper functioning of the thyroid, a gland in the neck just below the larynx. The thyroid gland is composed of two portions called lobes, one on each side of the neck. Foals born with iodine deficiency may have goiter, a condition in which the thyroid glands become markedly enlarged and function poorly. Too much iodine in the diet, especially of adult horses, may also result in thyroid enlargement, but does not appear to seriously affect the thyroid's function.

Occasionally a horse develops an apparent craving for salt and will devour a large salt block in a matter of days. Such a horse needs to drink a lot of extra water and will urinate great volumes. For a salt monster such as this, take the salt block away and add a couple of tablespoons of regular iodized table salt and of lite salt (containing potassium) to provide the horse with the electrolytes it needs.

Supplements

Pound for pound the draft horse does not require the same amount of feed as a light horse. Vitamins and minerals, however, should be fed according to the horse's weight. Depending on the nature of your feed, vitamin and mineral supplementation may be in order. Many supplements are on the market, some designed especially for draft horses. Most, however, do not supply the

minimum daily requirement of vitamin E.

Electrolyte supplementation is generally not necessary unless your horses are working and sweating hard for long periods of time. Electrolytes may be especially important for hard working horses fed a slightly higher than needed protein level.

Supplements designed for improving hoof quality may be important for a draft or draft cross with problems such as hoof cracking or splitting, sole bruises or abscesses and for horses that do not seem to be able to keep their shoes on. Supplements with high levels of methionine as well as biotin are often beneficial, resulting in faster growth of more hoof and sole.

You will undoubtedly read about many other vitamins, minerals and electrolytes you may, under certain circumstances, need to consider for your horse's diet. Some come with more believable credentials than others. We have quite likely left out something you may feel is a critical element of your horse's diet. We acknowledge that our view of the basics of equine nutrition is just that—the basics. We look forward to future studies that help define and refine what makes the best diet for our horses.

Treats

Some teamsters never treat their horses to a carrot, apple or sugar cube and the horse wouldn't know what to do if offered one. The health of these horses is not jeopardized by the lack of treats. Horses not hand-fed treats are not likely to be constantly looking in your pockets or nuzzling, nibbling or biting your hands and shoulders for food.

Other horse owners like to see their horses enjoy treats and use them as positive reinforcement for a job well done. Although we do not advocate sugar cubes for horses, we cannot deny them carrots and apples in moderate amounts and have not seen any adverse effects. Some horses may relish other delicacies such as watermelon rind and blackberries. Provided these treats don't become a major part of the horse's diet, we cannot consider them potentially unhealthy. We do, however, try to avoid heavily sugared products such as donuts, pies, cookies and Twinkies. We no longer feed our horses corn on the cob, as we are concerned about the high levels of soluble carbohydrates (starches and sugars) in corn.

A small handful of Kellogg's Cracklin Oat Bran is another treat we like to feed occasionally. We can keep this cereal in the barn even during hot or cold weather because it does not go limp or freeze. We can't remember why we started offering this treat, but our horses (and our dogs) enjoy it and we're happy because it supplies about 20 percent of calories from fat.

Photo by Kay Fellows

Fat Is Good

Nothing is natural about feeding grain to a horse. Wild horses do not eat grain. Wild horses, of course, are not required to be high performance animals, and no member of the wild equid family resembles a draft horse. Our modern horses often require extra energy to support growth and performance.

Energy is produced in living cells through the breakdown of nutrient compounds to result in the production of a molecule known as ATP (adenosine triphosphate), which is essential for the proper functioning of body cells. The main reason animals and people need to breath is to provide oxygen to the mitochondria, the cells' microscopic powerhouses that use oxygen to produce much of the ATP. The two main energy sources for body cells are carbohydrates and fats. Protein is also a source of energy, although it is much less efficient than are carbohydrates and fats.

Energy Requirements

Most horses in temperate climates stay fat and healthy solely by grazing good pasture or eating good quality hay. Sufficient energy may not be present in forage, however, to meet the dramatically higher requirements of a hard working horse, a broodmare, a young growing horse, or a horse that must deal with a cold climate. Extremely old horses and those with metabolic problems may not be able to derive enough energy from an all forage diet. Hard working horses and those that do not enjoy an unlimited supply of pasture or good quality hay may need to be fed concentrated feeds to supply needed calories.

Estimating Intake

Although the feed requirements of light horses are known, the requirements for draft horses have yet to be accurately determined. What is known is that the requirements for a 2,000-pound draft horse are not twice those for a 1,000-pound light horse.

The total energy requirement for a draft horse may be *estimated* by calculating the amount needed for a comparably sized light horse (if such a thing existed), then multiplying by 0.75. For example, the maintenance diet of a 1,000-pound light horse calls for about 15,000 calories per day. The maintenance diet for an adult 2,000-pound draft horse would be be 2 x 15,000 x 0.75, or about 22,500 calories per day. Increased activity increases a horse's caloric needs.

Measuring Feeds

The calories a horse requires may be adequately supplied by feeding plenty of good quality grass or hay. Horses need to eat about two to three percent of their body weight per day when forage is their only feed. Even allowing for the improved feed efficiency of a draft, that comes out to 30 or 40 pounds of forage per day.

To better know how much your horses are being fed, use a scale to determine what your hay weighs and what your full scoop of feed weighs. Some rice brans and other feeds come with a one-pound measuring cup.

Hard working horses and those in cold climates may not derive all the energy they need from forage alone.

Photo by Susan Greenall

Estimating Calorie Needs			
		Calorie Needs	
Activity	Factor	1,000 lb. light horse	2,000 lb. heavy horse
Maintenance		15,000	22,500
Pleasure and equitation riding, pleasure driving	1.25	18,750	28,125
Roping, cutting, jumping farming, light logging	1.50	22,500	33,750
Distance training, polo, competition pulling, heavy logging, plowing, combined driving	2.00	30,000	45,000
Broodmare (last 3 months of gestation)	1.1-1.2	16,500-18,000	24,750-27,000
Lactating mare	1.75	26,250	39,375

The calorie needs of a 1,000-pound light horse, with multiplication factors for activities of various intensity, have been established. To estimate the calorie needs of a draft horse, multiply the needs of a comparably sized light horse doing work of similar intensity by 0.75. The calorie needs for any given horse must be adjusted to that horse's own weight.

Energy from Carbohydrates

Horse feeds contain two kinds of carbohydrates:

1. soluble carbohydrates, also known as nonstructural carbohydrates, which include the starches and sugars that are abundant in grains and molasses. Enzymes present in the horse's mouth and small intestine break down these carbohydrates into glucose and other simple sugars.

2. insoluble carbohydrate, or structural carbohydrates, which constitute most of the calories in forage such as hay and pasture, and come from plant wall materials such as cellulose. These carbohydrates are broken down by microorganisms in the horse's large intestine and are absorbed, in large part, as fatty acids.

Grains and grain-based concentrates contain nothing that a horse on good balanced forage needs, except extra energy. The energy in grains is primarily in the form of soluble carbohydrates. The energy of carbohydrates has been the traditional choice of horse owners probably because grains are readily available at an affordable price. When draft horses put in a full day of work six days a week, feeding three meals a day was the norm and probably allowed for a sufficient amount of feed without overloading a horse's system. Working hard almost every day probably also helped protect the horse's muscles.

For some horses a soluble carbohydrate based energy source works fine, but comes with the risk of causing colic or laminitis and founder. Grain is not a good diet for horses that have had problems with stomach ulcers, colic, laminitis or tying up. Grain gives some horses a sugar high that does little to add to their productivity or ease of handling.

The metabolism of some horses is not geared for the adequate use of soluble carbohydrates as energy. The highly concentrated soluble carbohydrates present in grain and sweet feeds may be a problem. The energy a horse gets from grass and hay is mostly derived from protein and from insoluble carbohydrates from the cellulose in the plant wall. To our knowledge these insoluble carbohydrates are not a problem for any horse.

Horses with problems involving soluble carbohydrate metabolism may temporarily be able to compensate but will eventually become energy deficient. This condition particularly affects muscles and is the basis for the disease known as equine

polysaccharide storage myopathy	
poly	= many
saccharide	= sugar
storage	= refers to the carbohydrates stored in the muscle
myo	= muscle
pathy	= disease

Counting Calories	
Feed	Approximate Calories Per Pound
Timothy or other grass hay	800-900
Alfalfa pellets or hay	900-1,000
Beet Pulp	1,000
Sweet feeds	1,200-1,400
Oats	1,450
Purina Strategy	1,500
Rice bran	1,550
Soybean meal	1,600
Barley	1,620
Corn, wheat	1,750
Buckeye Ultimate Finish	1,980
Vegetable-based oil	4,000
Animal fat designed for horses or pigs	4,000

polysaccharide storage myopathy (EPSM, also sometimes called PSSM or EPSSM).

Before the onset of an obvious problem, muscle samples from affected drafts and other breeds show an increase in stored glycogen and other even more complex polysaccharides. Blood testing may reveal that these horses are undergoing some degree of muscle damage caused by a lack of adequate muscle energy production, even if their only exercise is turnout. Normal blood tests do not, however, rule out this problem.

Energy from Fat

Horse owners, and especially draft horse owners, may avoid the problem of muscle damage by feeding a low soluble carbohydrate and high fat diet. What we call a high fat diet for horses (20 to 25 percent of total daily calories from fat) would be considered a low fat diet for humans. Horses do not metabolize dietary fats into the nasty low-density lipoproteins (LDLs) that lead to the clogging of human arteries. A low soluble carbohydrate and high fat diet is therefore safe to feed horses from weaning to old age.

Severely affected EPSM horses may or may not respond well to the high fat, low soluble carbohydrate diet recommended for draft horses. The first three to four months after a diet change determine whether the horse is quickly adapting to the high fat diet and regaining sufficient strength to survive. About half of such severely affected horses have pulled through, but the other half continued to worsen until they died or required euthanasia.

Lessons from the Drafts

I (Dr. Beth) came to my conclusions about the importance of a high fat diet as a result of focusing on some previously unexplained problems in draft horses that might relate to the recently recognized and apparently common muscle disease known as equine polysaccharide storage myopathy (EPSM). I

quickly began to realize that EPSM could explain a wide range of draft horse problems. The problems I reviewed range from Monday morning disease to an inability to get up after anesthesia, to poor performance, to shivers. Since I began focusing on draft horse problems, draft horse owners have often asked me about shivers: What is it? What causes it? What can be done for it?

I did not learn about this disease in veterinary college, probably because most veterinarians don't have a good idea of what shivers looks like. Many savvy draft horse folks can explain what it looks like, even if they don't have all the answers.

Shivers is usually described as a gait problem and is often confused with stringhalt (sometimes called springhalt). The name indicates that the hind end has quite a bit of a hitch. Normal body shivering or trembling in horses may be related to excitement, at which time the horse's whole body shows quivering associated with head tossing and pawing. Cold horses will shiver to increase body heat. What about a horse whose muscles or body trembles during or after exercise? This trembling is recognized as a sign of weakness. It may be associated with excessive sweating and may be the earliest indication that your horse is going to develop full blown shivers.

Shivers

Dr. A.J. Neumann has written the best description of shivers in draft horses that I have ever seen. In addition to the characteristic hiking of the hind limbs while backing or turning in a tight circle, Dr. Neumann describes the lifting and fine trembling of the tail that sometimes helps distinguish shivers from stringhalt. He also recognizes shivers as both an inherited and a progressive problem, eventually resulting in a severely disabled horse. This progression is not a feature of stringhalt, but with the first signs of a hitch in the hind, who's to know whether that horse is developing stringhalt or shivers?

Dr. Neumann suggests shivers may be a disease of the nerves, which have a limited capacity for repair. No one has any treatment for nerve disease. It would be better if shivers were a muscle disease, because muscle cells can repair following injury. No one has been able to explain exactly how either a nerve or a muscle problem results in the exaggerated lifting of the legs, which may also occur while the horse is standing still.

This leg lifting is not seen when the horse starts trotting out or while it is cantering. The lifting may be due to muscle cramping. It may be similar to a horse that hikes its hind leg because it has a foot abscess or because you have put a wrap on the leg— something in the leg may feel funny to the horse.

Jerry's Story

Because of my interest in draft horse diseases, Dr. Bob Orcutt in Massachusetts who was dealing with a Belgian with shivers

Jerry (right wheel) was a willing hitch horse for many years, until at the age of 14 his muscles began wasting away.

Courtesy of Beth A. Valentine

Early one morning Jerry arrived from Massachusetts on a trailer. The clinic admitted him, filled out all the necessary paperwork, and put him in a stall. I went to examine him and was shocked. Nothing I had seen before in affected draft horses had prepared me. Jerry was remarkably muscle wasted, although he had a good fat layer and was obviously well cared for. He was covered in sweat—the trailer ride had been rough on him. He stood with his front legs well under him to take weight off the hind. The hind legs were planted widely apart for support. He would first lift one hind leg, hold it tightly up and then stomp it down in order to lift the other hind leg, followed by a front leg, and then the other front leg. During these episodes he was clearly in discomfort. If allowed to do so, he would walk out of the episodes by circling in his stall.

While I worked with him I found Jerry to be one of the nicest, gentlest, best trained horses I have ever worked with. He wanted to do whatever I asked of him, but he wasn't always capable. Backing was particularly difficult, although after a brief hesitation he always tried. His head went up, and then his tail went up and showed the characteristic fine trembling. He often scuffed his hind feet on the ground when not hitching them high. After backing he looked particularly uncomfortable with whole body tremors, and he would place his front feet so far under that he actually leaned forward. He would then lift a front leg, hold it close to the other front leg, and place it down abruptly, often in a crossed position so he stepped on his other front hoof. His whole body would start to tremble and lean, and he looked as if he would fall over.

Although he would stand if that was what he thought you wanted, it was obvious that what he really wanted was to walk,

contacted me. Dr. Bob told me that the owner of the horse felt the problem had gotten so severe it was time to put the horse down, and he wondered if I was interested in accepting the horse as a donation to the Equine Hospital at Cornell so we could learn from him. I said "yes" and made plans to admit the horse to the Equine Hospital.

From my studies of previous cases of draft horses with shivers, I thought the diet change we had been testing could at least halt the progression of the problem and alleviate some of the weakness and abnormal gait. I began to think of folks I knew who might want to adopt him because I already had two affected horses—a Belgian-Percheron cross and a Belgian-Thoroughbred cross.

Jerry, a 14-year-old Belgian gelding, had for many years been a hitch horse—single, double, and unicorn lead horse. As his owner described it, Jerry had a slight hitch in his hind end since he bought him as a four-year-old, but for years had never shown the problem while in harness.

Eventually Jerry's disease caught up with him. His hitch grew steadily worse until it involved both front legs, as well as both hind legs. He steadily lost weight no matter how much hay and grain he was fed. He developed an abnormal stance in which he stood under himself in the front. He had become difficult to shoe during the last year and a half, especially in the hind, and even the stocks and other apparatus didn't work anymore. This horse was clearly special because his owner had kept him for more than a year after he had become so severely affected that he could no longer be hitched.

As Jerry's muscles wasted away, his gait became markedly affected by his shivers and his hitch-horse days were over.

Courtesy of Beth A. Valentine

and walk, and walk, because by walking he seemed to become more comfortable. A distinct circle developed in the shavings in his stall, and he often interrupted eating to circle.

I knew immediately that I could do nothing for this horse—the disease had gone too far. We gave him the best alfalfa hay we could find, plenty of water and exercise. I knew that most veterinarians, especially at a referral center like Cornell, would never see a case like Jerry. Such horses are usually either sent for slaughter or die and are buried on the farm. Only because Jerry's owner thought so much of him and wanted us to learn from him was he there at all.

For the several days he was at the clinic I made sure that everyone—faculty, residents, technicians and students—got to see real draft horse shivers. Jerry came to the neurology rounds held for students and faculty once a week. Our neurologist, Dr. Alexander (Sandy) de Lahunta, who is undoubtedly the world's foremost veterinary neurologist, had thoroughly examined him for any evidence of nervous system problems and found none.

We talked about shivers, about the little that was known about it and what we thought Jerry was telling us. Since our patients can't talk to us about what's bothering them, we veterinarians have to learn to interpret the horse's actions, attitude and signs. It seemed apparent to us that Jerry's abnormal lifting of the legs was caused by muscle cramping. Sometimes it appeared that his whole body was cramping. Despite his obvious discomfort, his attitude was remarkable. Jerry was a great horse. The students brought him apples, and everyone brought their cameras and video cameras.

Although we wanted to keep him and help him, his discomfort and profound weakness prompted us to make a hard decision. He loved being outside. We took him out to a grassy spot under a pine tree. As my colleague put the needle into his vein, Jerry leaned down to me and breathed softly into my face. His breath fogged my glasses, which was good because it hid my tears. Then something in the distance caught Jerry's attention. He held his head high, fascinated by something, and stood quietly. The intravenous barbiturates hit quickly and painlessly. At last Jerry got the peace he had lacked for so many years as he lay down gently on the grass.

EPSM

Despite no clinical evidence of a neurological problem, Dr. de Lahunta agreed to examine Jerry's nervous system. I examined many of his muscles. Nothing was wrong with Jerry's nervous system, and his internal organs were all healthy. In his muscles I found the characteristic changes of EPSM, the muscle disease I have been studying. I had seen the same changes in several other draft horses and Warmbloods with shivers, but I had never before been able to examine the nervous system of affected horses to show that nerves were not the problem.

EPSM appears to cause affected horses to be unable to derive sufficient energy from the grains and other soluble carbohydrates in their diet for proper muscle function. Severely affected horses may begin to break down their own muscle to use the protein for energy. Some EPSM draft horses are well muscled and may appear normal for many years. The disease slowly saps their strength until some crisis occurs, which may cause the horse to become a poor performer or to suddenly lose weight despite a good appetite. The horse may appear stiff in the rear, may seem to be colicking or may be found down and unable to rise. Painful muscle cramps are common in people with similar problems, and also may be caused by insufficient muscle energy.

Jerry's condition was caused by a muscle disease that I believe we could have halted or even reversed with a diet change that replaces soluble carbohydrates with fat. In Jerry's case it was too late. Do all draft horses with shivers have a muscle disease that is treatable with a low carbohydrate, high fat diet? Only time and continued studies will tell. Meanwhile feeding a high fat diet to a horse exhibiting the signs of shivers can't hurt the horse, and just may save its life.

Myths about feeding fat

Horses cannot digest fat. It is true that horses do not have gall bladders, but it is *not* true that horses cannot digest fat. Horses digest fat just fine.

Feeding fat blocks the absorption of fat soluble vitamins such as vitamin E and vitamin A. This is just plain nonsense. If fat has any effect on these vitamins, it aids in their absorption.

Fat Advantages

Feeding your draft horses a high fat, low soluble carbohydrate diet has the following advantages:

1. Decreases body heat production with exercise. The heavy muscling of a draft horse makes it more likely to overheat than, for example, a lean Arabian. Compared to its body mass, a draft has a proportionately lower skin surface area and a more difficult time cooling itself by sweating. Although a slightly higher than maintenance protein diet (higher than about 10-percent protein) is preferred for draft horses to maintain and repair muscle fibers, a higher protein diet may result in increased heat production with exercise. Replacing the concentrated carbohydrates with fats should result in overall lower exercise-related heat production.

2. Decreases risk of colic, founder and gastric (stomach) ulcers. Well-documented by numerous studies, carbohydrate overload is the number one cause of founder, colic and gastric ulcers in horses. High fat, low soluble carbohydrate feeds should be given to horses with a previous history of founder, colic or gastric ulcers or to horses believed to be at risk for these conditions.

3. Provides a ready source of energy that does not have to be chewed. Less chewing is an advantage for mature horses whose teeth may be worn with age and whose ability to adequately grind up grains for digestion and absorption may be impaired. A low soluble carbohydrate, high fat diet is also excellent for a horse with intestinal absorption problems from parasite damage or from surgical removal of portions of the intestine.

4. Provides a high energy feed in a low volume. Given the small total volume of the horse's stomach, it is not safe or even possible to feed enough grain and hay in two meals to provide needed calories for an 8- to 12-hour work day. In days gone by, working drafts were fed three meals a day. Most horses are now fed twice a day. A low bulk, high energy feed is advantageous for hard working horses with high caloric requirements and should appeal especially to owners of pulling horses. The decreased weight in the gut reduces gut ballast for horses needing to make weight. For the owner of a hard keeper, this diet offers a safe way to add meat to an otherwise unthrifty horse.

5. Improves respiratory function in horses with chronic respiratory disease. Although they are still hypothetical, studies by Dr. David Kronfeld of the Virginia-Maryland Regional School of Veterinary Medicine suggest that horses with chronic respiratory problems such as heaves may benefit from using fat instead of soluble carbohydrates for energy. Dowsing the pellets with vegetable oil is probably even better than soaking them in water for decreasing the inhaled dusts that may contain molds or other allergens. Dust and allergens cause the lungs' small airways (bronchioles) to close down in a horse with heaves or allergic bronchitis, causing difficult breathing and coughing.

For long periods of strong steady work, fat is better than carbohydrates as a fuel for muscle cells. *Photo by Bonnie Nance*

6. Enhances oxidative metabolism. Draft horses are rarely asked to run the quarter mile. Instead they perform strong, steady work for long periods — also known as aerobic exercise. Relying on fat, which is burned aerobically and which is the preferred fuel for muscle cells, makes more sense than feeding soluble carbohydrates, which are often metabolized anaerobically.

7. Controls or prevents EPSM. Because of the high incidence of this metabolic problem in draft horses, feeding fat instead of soluble carbohydrates could be life saving. EPSM can result in decreased performance, a reduced life span, or catastrophic events such as severe tying up, going down or sudden death.

8. Avoids OCD. Studies by Dr. Sarah Ralston, an equine nutritionist at Rutgers University, suggest that high soluble carbohydrate feeds are a major factor in the development of osteochondrosis dissecans (OCD), a joint disease in young growing horses. Our EPSM diets, which minimize soluble carbohydrate intake and maximize fat, provide more than adequate protein and safe energy to support growth in foals.

9. Improves haircoat and skin. Adding fat to a horse's diet has for many years been known to enhance haircoat and skin quality. The addition of a pound of linseed meal per day to a horse's feed was advised as early as 1917. At that time linseed meal had a five-percent fat content. Modern linseed meal processing techniques result in meal with only 1.5 percent fat. Linseed or flax oil is 100-percent fat, and the use of these products remains a mainstay of many teamsters and other horse owners. Linseed and flax oil contain high levels of certain fatty acids, such as omega 3, which may be beneficial for horses with conditions involving inflammation of tissue or organs. Linseed and flax oil fed at high levels (such as 4 cups per day), however, may cause colic.

Any vegetable oil can add fat, yet some folks feel strongly that they should continue giving their horses linseed or flax oil. A small amount, up to 1/2 cup per day, is fine if additional fat is added in the form of soy, canola, corn or other vegetable-based oil.

The shiny haircoat of a horse on a high fat diet is one of the reasons why this diet is excellent for horses being shown or offered for sale. Many horse owners comment on this change in the coat, even in horses that had great coats to begin with.

10. Possibly protects from post-anesthetic muscle problems. EPSM has a possible role in post-anesthetic problems in which draft horses can have difficulty standing up and staying up. Studies of this problem are still in their infancy. Preliminary research strongly suggests that underlying muscle weakness from EPSM is common in drafts that develop life-threatening post-anesthesia problems. If your horse cannot stand up and stay up, you and your horse have a serious problem.

Changing to a high fat, low soluble carbohydrate diet shows some promise in protecting horses from post-anesthetic problems. For horses undergoing elective surgery (any surgery that is not an emergency) such as for OCD or partial laryngeal paralysis (roaring), starting this diet well before surgery may be prudent. One prominent veterinary surgeon we know now advises owners of draft horses to change their horse's diet prior

A shiny haircoat is one good reason to put your horses on a high fat diet.

Photo by Sue Greenall

to surgery. As research reveals more about EPSM and post-anesthetic problems in drafts, preventive measures and treatments will continue to evolve.

Potential Problems

Feeding your draft horses a high fat, low soluble carbohydrate diet presents the following potential problems:

1. Finding the right low soluble carbohydrate feed. Sweet feed or textured feed, oats, corn, barley or any combination of these is high in carbohydrates. It is impossible to recognize a low soluble carbohydrate horse feed from the label, because no manufacturer includes carbohydrate content. Manufacturers of horse feeds are not even required by law to list their ingredients in the order of decreasing volume. The total amount of carbohydrates in the feed is important. The most important information is knowing the percentage of calories from soluble

carbohydrates (starches and sugars) per pound of feed. Unfortunately, at this time only the nutritionists who designed the feed can determine this information. Maybe someday the horse feed manufacturers will get wise and start providing us with more useful information.

Forage-based products such as alfalfa or other hay-based pellets are ideal, if your horse will eat them with added fat. Alfalfa cubes also work, but need to be soaked in water so they will break down and mix well with added oil. Although beet pulp is not our favorite feed, a few pounds soaked in water will help soak up added oil. Adding fat directly to hay or water works well for some draft horse owners.

2. Finding a palatable, inexpensive fat source. Feeding a full-sized draft horse with our recommended diet requires up to 4 cups (1 quart or 2 pounds) of fat per day. Multiply that by more than one draft horse, and you will find yourself going through a lot of fat.

The most economical way to supply fat for a draft horse is with bulk vegetable oil in 35-pound (about five-gallon) jugs. Canola and soy oil are usually the least expensive. Cocosoya, coconut, wheat germ, corn, cottonseed and safflower oils may be purchased in bulk but are often pricier. Even olive oil is apparently effective, although expensive. Sources of bulk oil include restaurant suppliers, discount warehouses and your local feed mill. Some people feel that unrefined soy oil is more beneficial to the horse's health, as it may contain higher levels of vitamin E and beneficial fatty acids that may be altered by processing. Although this hypothesis has yet to be rigorously tested, if you live near a soy processing plant you may find that you can get bulk unrefined soy oil at an even lower price than processed soy oil.

Another effective and inexpensive source of fat is powdered animal fat products designed for simple-stomached animals such as horses and pigs. The products marketed for pigs are similar to those marketed for horses, but cost a lot less. Animal fat products designed for cattle and other ruminants cannot be completely digested by horses, so you would need to feed more of them. The expert nutritionists we have consulted feel that feeding extra of these ruminant products to horses will not cause any problems.

3. Dispensing oil from a large volume container. Five-gallon buckets are difficult to pour from, but many ways may be used to get around this problem. You may divide the oil into one-gallon jugs, or find a top with a plastic pump that fits a five-gallon jug, such as those on bulk liquid laundry detergent. Or you might invest in an apparatus for pumping automobile fluids, such as lubricant and transmission fluid. Available at any auto

---

Reading horse feed labels

Reading feed labels is easy, but interpreting them is almost impossible. Most labels give information only on percentages of protein, fat and fiber. Any feed containing primarily forage products such as grass or alfalfa hay is low in soluble carbohydrates. Any feed with whole, cracked, or crushed grains of any kind is high in soluble carbohydrates. Fat has a caloric density of more than twice that of carbohydrates and protein provides about the same amount of calories as carbohydrates. A pelleted or extruded feed that is high in fat and high in protein is likely to be lower per pound in soluble carbohydrate calories than a low fat and low protein feed.

A dandy device for storing and dispensing vegetable oil is a five-gallon bucket fitted with a pump designed for dispensing automotive fluids.

Photo by Beth A. Valentine

parts supply store, this gadget consists of a five-gallon bucket with a lid containing a pump and a flexible hose with a curved metal end.

4. Keeping vegetable oil from gelling in cold climates. The change of consistency caused by cold temperatures makes pouring the correct volume difficult. One of the ways to avoid gelling is to keep the oil in a warm place. You might build an insulated box with a 40-watt bulb in a false bottom. You could buy corn oil instead of soy or canola oil during cold weather; corn oil stays liquid at lower temperatures than many other oils.

5. Keeping vegetable oil from going rancid in warm weather. Oil usually does not go rancid until after the container is opened and the oil is exposed to air. Rancidity is unlikely to be a problem when feeding drafts because of the volume used.

6. Keeping jackets, feed buckets and horses' noses clean. Vegetable oil is admittedly a messy feed and can result in oilskin jackets, an oil-based slime in the feed bucket or manger, and the oily slime mixed with dirt on a horse's nose. Try relegating one jacket for barn chores only. The feed bucket

problem may necessitate more frequent scrubbing of the bucket. Powdered laundry or other detergent, a stiff brush, a metal pot-scrubbing pad and plenty of elbow grease work well. Power cleaning hoses, such as those available at car washes, may also do the trick. If the buckets stay oily, horses may develop mild skin irritation from the build up of oil residue and dirt on their faces. An obviously dirty nose is usually a problem only on a horse with a white blaze. Although the problem may be at its worst in late winter, clean new hair will appear after the spring shed.

7. Introducing the diet to your horse. Draft horses can be fussy eaters, perhaps from their strong sense of habit. If a draft horse has been fed grain or sweet feed, some persuasion may be needed to get it to accept the new diet. To avoid colic any change to a horse's feed should be made gradually, but in this case a gradual change to the high fat diet is more to allow the horse's taste buds to adjust than to prevent colic.

If fat is added too quickly to the horse's diet, the worst problem you may see is soft manure for a few days. Horses adjusted to high fat diets have manure that is well formed, but not dry, possibly giving them less chance of impaction. If a horse has been on grain or a grain-based concentrate, gradual replacement with a lower carbohydrate feed and gradual increase of fat by about 1/4 cup per feeding every few days should do the trick. Sometimes you have to get tough and leave the feed until the horse decides to eat it.

Given the high caloric density of fat, aim for a lower volume of feed in the bucket than you had before. Exactly how much you end up feeding depends on whether the horse needs to regain lost weight or lose excessive fat. Both are possible with the low soluble carbohydrate, high fat feeds. Be conscious of total daily calories and total daily exercise.

Oils to avoid

Do not feed your horse recycled vegetable oil that has been superheated for deep frying. Such oils may be available from fast food franchises. Recycled cooking oils contain potentially harmful products produced by degradation during the high heat phase.

Do not feed your horse products marketed as frying oil. Although such oils may be quite inexpensive, they contain many chemical additives.

Do not feed your horse large volumes of any oil you would not put in your salad.

Recipe for a healthy draft horse

Based on current knowledge of draft horse metabolism and nutritional needs, the following recipe represents ideal nutrition for a draft horse. The ingredients are listed as daily requirements to be divided into two or three equal meals. For some horses with severe problems such as shivers, feeding even more fat than we recommend here may help. Provided the fat level is increased gradually we have never seen any problems develop in horses on even an extremely high fat diet.

6 to 9 pounds (2 to 6 good-sized scoops) alfalfa or alfalfa/grass hay pellets
3 to 4 cups soy, canola, corn or other vegetable-based oil
1 to 2 ounces vitamin E and selenium supplement
15 to 20 pounds grass or alfalfa hay (or good pasture)
Free choice water
Trace mineralized salt block

Alternative Strategies

For the fussy draft horse or the horse with a poor appetite, try the following alternative feeding strategies:

1. Substitute a low soluble carbohydrate commercial feed. Some suitable substitutes for all or part of the hay pellets are listed under Resources at the back of this book.

2. Substitute a high fat feed. Suitable substitutes for some or all of the hay pellets are listed under Resources. Reduce added vegetable oil to one to 1½ cups per day.

3. Use five pounds of rice bran per day in place of two cups of vegetable oil. If you are wealthy you may replace all the oil with rice bran and feed 10 pounds of rice bran per day to your 2,000 pound draft horse. You will need to either feed a rice bran product with added calcium or feed alfalfa products to balance the calcium to phosphorus ratio. By the way, mixing rice bran and vegetable-based oil is not a problem, no matter what you might read or hear elsewhere.

4. Use a powdered animal fat product designed for simple-stomached animals (horses or pigs) in place of vegetable oil. A source is listed under Resources at the back of this book.

5. Try using Cocosoya oil. This product, although more expensive than other vegetable-based oils, seems to be readily accepted by many horses. A source is listed under Resources. A fussy horse that begins to feel better on an expensive diet may have an improved appetite, allowing you to gradually switch to a more economical diet.

6. For the fussiest horses you might carefully force-feed the vegetable oil with a large syringe or turkey baster.

Try It

Based on what we know about the muscle metabolism of draft horses, and from observing results of diet change in our own and other drafts and draft crosses, we believe that a low soluble carbohydrate, high fat diet is the best way to feed a draft-related horse and many other horses as well.

You may read or hear about many other ways to feed a draft horse, that others may claim is the "only way to feed a draft." Many horses seem to do just fine on those diets. Remember, though, that some people can eat all the wrong things and live forever, but for most people the wrong diet will eventually catch up with them. Some horse owners have found that adding one to two cups of vegetable oil to regular grain helps make their horses' coats shine and allows them to feed less grain. This diet, however, is too low in fat to prevent muscle problems from developing in a predisposed horse.

If your horse has any performance, gait or weight problems or has foundered, at least *try* the high fat diet. The cashier where you buy the oil and the folks who pick up your recycling may wonder what you're up to. You can either explain why you are feeding your horses fat or you can just let them wonder. Whatever you feed your draft, keep the grain to an absolute minimum, invest in good quality forage and provide plenty of water.

"Since we put her on the low carbohydrate, high fat diet she hasn't been the old gray mare anymore."

With thanks to Joe E. Buresch

Routine Health Care

No "right" way exists when it comes to routine health care for your draft horses. All we can offer are guidelines, to be modified depending on where you live and the circumstances of how your horses live. Advice from your veterinarian and the experienced horse owners you might know, along with reading a few good reference books, are valuable ways to learn to care for your horses. Knowledge of the parasites and diseases most commonly found in your local region will help you and your veterinarian determine the best maintenance programs for parasite control and vaccinations.

Internal Parasites

A variety of parasites attack horses. The most important of these are the intestinal worms that can cause damage to both the intestinal wall and the blood vessels supplying the intestine, resulting in severe colic. Intestinal parasites are more dangerous in horses than in any other domestic species. A large number of horses on a relatively small pasture or turnout area, and a temperate climate in which developing stages of these parasites are not killed by cold or drying out, can result in a high exposure rate and high parasite loads if management practices are not employed to help to keep the parasites under control.

Large strongyles are small intestinal worms that pass their eggs in the manure. The immature forms (larvae) hatch, are swallowed, and burrow into the intestinal wall to migrate through various tissues before returning to the intestine as adults. Of the several species of large strongyles, *Strongylus vulgaris* is the most damaging because the larval forms migrate through and can severely damage intestinal blood vessels, resulting in decreased blood flow or blockage of blood flow to the intestines. Rarely, strongyle larvae migrate into the brain or spinal cord, with serious consequences.

Small strongyles are tiny intestinal worms. They are less damaging than the large strongyles, but occasionally a heavy load in the intestinal wall results in intestinal damage and severe colic.

Bots are fly larvae that attach to the inside of the stomach and the first part of the small intestine. They are not a particularly dangerous parasite, but heavy bot loads may interfere somewhat with digestion.

Tapeworms most commonly found in horses do not achieve the great lengths of some of the tapeworms of other species. They cluster only in one area, the ileocecal junction between the end of the small intestine (the ileum) and the beginning of the large intestine (the cecum). They are about one to three inches long, wide and flat, and in large numbers may resemble cooked pasta.

Tapeworms are not generally considered a serious threat to a horse's digestion or absorption. They may, however, cause enough irritation at their sites of attachment to predispose the

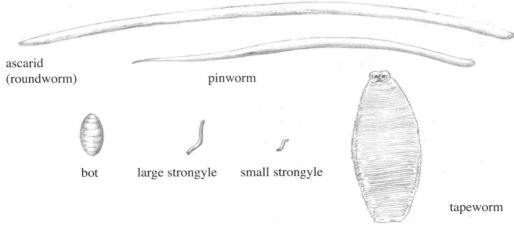

ascarid
(roundworm)

pinworm

bot   large strongyle   small strongyle

tapeworm

Internal Parasites

horse to intussusception (telescoping) of the end of the small intestine into the cecum, which can result in a surgical colic and possibly death. They have also been implicated as the cause of bouts of gas, or spasmotic colic, and of ileocecal impaction (blockage by feed).

Pinworms are thread-like worms that lay their eggs around the anus and can cause rectal irritation and tailhead rubbing. Pinworms of horses are much larger than most other pinworms, sometimes several inches long. With the safe, effective wormers available today, pinworms are much less likely than allergic skin disease to be the cause of tail rubbing. These worms are not infectious to humans or other species.

Ascarids, or roundworms, do not damage the tissues of the intestine or the blood vessels, but large numbers could result in altered intestinal activity or in an intestinal blockage. They are primarily a problem in horses less than one year of age. A mature horse's immune system seems to effectively eliminate them.

Non-intestinal parasites. The most important of the non-intestinal parasites are the larvae of the worms onchocerca and habronema. They can be carried by biting flies and transferred to the skin, where they migrate and cause skin irritation. The larval forms of these worms may create non-healing skin sores called summer sores, or the horse may develop an allergic hypersensitivity to the worms, resulting in itchy, irritated skin. Occasionally the larva migrate into other places, such as the eye, where they may cause inflammation. These microscopic larvae cannot be seen by the naked eye. Regular use of ivermectin has much reduced the incidence of these skin parasites.

Horse parasites and human health

None of the common internal parasites of horses is infectious to people. The risk of infection by any horse parasite is quite low. Even the occasional horse that passes in its manure the protozoal organism giardia—certain strains of which cause human illness and diarrhea, such as Montezuma's revenge and beaver fever—pose a relatively low risk to humans.

An exception is another protozoal organism called cryptosporidia. A severely affected young draft horse with uncontrollable diarrhea due to cryptosporidia resulted in several exposed people also getting sick. Fortunately such a situation is quite uncommon.

Worming

Worming a horse in bygone days could be performed only by a veterinarian passing a tube through the horse's nose and into its stomach. Through the tube were pumped the various solutions that killed intestinal parasites. This potentially dangerous procedure was often performed only once or twice a year.

Since the early 1980s the advent of new compounds and the development of paste wormers have made worming our horses safe, easy and effective. Several formulations are now available, and some discussion goes on about which ones are best. Another much-discussed topic is whether to rotate wormers or to use one single compound.

Wormers

Two of the best wormers are ivermectin and pyrantel pamoate. Ivermectin, a powerful compound sold under many brand names, is effective against bots and migrating larval strongyles, as well as adult large and small strongyles. It effectively kills the parasites that affect the skin, such as onchocerca, habronema, pinworms, mange mites and many lice.

Injectable ivermectin is available for use in cattle, sheep and goats. Horses often develop severe reactions to injectable ivermectin, so this product should not be used in horses. Some folks have given injectable ivermectin orally to horses because it is less expensive than ivermectin pastes. We cannot recommend this worming treatment, as its efficacy has not been proven. Treating for internal parasites is one place where cutting costs should not be allowed to compromise our horse's health.

Pyrantel pamoate (Strongid is the original brand name) is effective against adult large and small strongyles, ascarids and pinworms. It is safe to administer, even in high doses. The only effective treatment for tapeworms is to give a double dose of pyrantel pamoate at least once a year, which for an adult draft horse can mean getting close to four tubes of wormer at one time. This amount might appear excessive to some teamsters and may be the reason why so many draft horses have tapeworms. The only danger is to your bank account. This compound may be purchased as a liquid; a product designed to treat children with pinworms may prove to be economical. The liquid formulation may be either added to a horse's feed (the banana flavor is apparently not a problem for most horses) or given by oral dose syringe.

A related compound, pyrantel tartrate (Strongid C is the original brand name), may be fed daily, which is particularly useful on farms with high parasite loads or for individual problem horses. Although daily Strongid C is somewhat effective at controlling tapeworms, we advise using a yearly double dose of pyrantel pamoate.

Worming Schedule

Some horse owners worm religiously every six weeks, but a better plan is to consult your veterinarian about developing the best program for your region and your horses. The appropriate interval between wormings depends on your locality, the season and the density and type of your horse population. We generally worm our horses about four times a year, but we have only a few horses and are not breeding and raising youngsters.

Heavy parasite loads can be really damaging to youngsters. Foals may be given wormers at two months of age, but use only medications proven to be safe for young horses. Read the package instructions carefully. Do not worm pregnant mares within one month prior to delivery.

Fecal Examination

To get a handle on your parasite loads, have periodic fecal examinations performed to evaluate for strongyle egg counts. The procedure is inexpensive and may save you money in the long run as you determine the ideal worming program. Collecting a handful or so of relatively fresh manure and storing it in a sealed container (jar or zipper-sealed bag) in the refrigerator will keep it in good shape prior to analysis.

Some worms, such as pinworms and tapeworms, do not show up on standard fecal examinations. Although clear adhesive tape may be used to try to pick up pinworm eggs around a horse's anus, and blood tests are available to look for evidence of tapeworm infection, neither of these parasites is likely to be a problem if your worming program is appropriate.

Wormer Rotation

Despite the claims of some manufacturers that parasites demonstrate no resistance to compounds such as ivermectin and pyrantel pamoate, history tells us parasites are remarkably adaptable creatures and, with time, may develop resistance to many drugs. This development of resistance has been well documented with the use of benzimidazole compounds such as fenbendazole, mebendazole, oxifendazole, oxibendazole and thiabendazole. Common sense suggests that rotation of anthelmintic compounds (wormers) helps decrease the likelihood of the development of parasitic resistance.

We advocate alternating ivermectin and pyrantel pamoate, with ivermectin administered in the spring before horses are put on pasture and in the fall after the bot flies have hatched. We also recommend double dosing once a year with pyrantel pamoate for tapeworm control.

Although today's wormers for horses are safe, they still contain powerful toxins that act on the nervous system of the parasites to cause their death. Horses should not be stressed at the time of worming. Give the horse a day off or engage in only light work on the day after worming.

> *anthelmintic*
> ant = against
> helminth = worms

Flies

Where you find horses, you'll find flies. Where you find cattle near horses, you'll find more flies. The kind of pests you'll see, especially during warm seasons, varies from one geographic area to the next.

Non-Biting Flies

Certain flies may not give painful bites, but they sure can be annoying. Who likes to be covered by crawling flies sucking up secretions from your skin, eyes and nose?

Face flies and house flies are closely related. They both feed through a vacuum device, rather than through a bite. These flies breed in almost any decaying organic material. They congregate in great numbers on horses and cattle kept on pasture. House flies vacuum up debris from the skin. Face flies cause increased secretions of fluid from the eyes and nose on which they feed. Face flies are quite annoying and irritating to most horses. In California a plant known as tarweed (*Hemizonia multicaulis*, ssp. *vernalis*) exudes a black, sticky tar-like substance that horses bothered by flies may deliberately cover their faces with. Although we have never seen this, we are told that when horses get into tarweed they resemble our horses on vegetable oil when we haven't cleaned the feed buckets regularly.

Bot flies as adults lack mouthparts and live for a short time, during which they do not feed. These flies resemble honey bees in size and appearance. They mate and deposit their eggs on a horse's hair, usually on the legs and around the mouth. The eggs hatch in the warmth and moisture of the horse's breath, and burrow into the skin to migrate to the stomach and first part of the small intestine. They attach, feed and mature to pass out in the manure. They then develop into adults and repeat the cycle. Although finding large numbers of larvae attached to a horse's stomach and the first part of its small intestine is a revolting sight, the damage to the horse is usually minimal. Removal of bot eggs from the horse's haircoat by clipping or scraping with a bot knife will decrease the number of bots making it to the horse's stomach and intestine.

Non-Biters

house fly/face fly   bot fly

The non-biting house fly/face fly look similar to the biting stable fly/horn fly, the main difference being the biting mouthpart of the latter in contrast to the former's vacuuming mouthpart.

Maggots are the larvae of a number of different fly species that lay eggs in unattended wounds. The eggs hatch and the larvae feed on dead tissue. These maggots do not cause infection or tissue damage, but rather may aid in the removal of dead material. Their presence is clearly not desirable, though, as it indicates the wound has been left untreated for too long. Treatment is easily performed by flushing and cleaning the wound and applying an appropriate insecticide.

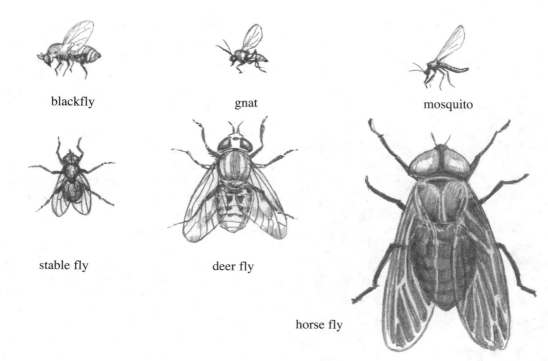

blackfly

gnat

mosquito

stable fly

deer fly

horse fly

Biters

Biting Flies and Insects

Biting flies inflict painful bites, can transmit viruses and other diseases and can spread the worm larvae that cause summer sores. Some horses become hypersensitive (allergic) to their bites.

Stable flies to the naked eye look almost identical to face flies and house flies. Instead of vacuuming-type mouthparts, these flies give a painful bite. Stable flies prefer to feed on the legs of horses and humans. In horses they cause foot stomping and leg shaking that can be severe enough to wear hooves and shoes, or even dislodge shoes. Stable flies also feed on the lower abdomen of horses.

Horn flies are primarily an annoyance to cattle, but may attack horses pastured with or near cattle. They are small—less than $1/2$ inch long—and resemble stable flies. They feed in aggregates on the neck, shoulders, withers and abdomen and can cause skin crusting and ulceration. They are carriers of onchocerca, a worm that inhabits and migrates in the skin tissues of the head and in the deeper tissues of the neck. Along with fly control, treatment with ivermectin to kill the onchocerca worms may be necessary.

Black flies are the scourge of the Adirondacks and other wooded areas of eastern North America. They are only about $1/4$ inch long, but their bite packs a wallop. Some animals become hypersensitive to their bites. They resemble large gnats with small wings. These flies hatch in rapidly flowing streams and are most commonly a problem during spring. Swarms of black flies emerge to feed on humans and livestock during daylight hours. Favored feeding sites on horses are inside the ears and the head, neck, chest, groin, medial thighs and abdomen. Large linear welts may appear on the chest (brisket) and in the groin and medial thighs, and crusts with blood occur inside the ears.

Deer flies are primarily a problem in the wooded areas of the eastern United States. They are about $1/2$ inch long and have obvious large wings. They are active during the day and seem to prefer to bite the topline, head and ears. Because of their propensity to attack ears we often call them ear flies. They circle human and horse heads like small satellites and inflict painful bites. When you work near or in wooded areas apply a fly repellent and ear masks on your horses, wear a hat and carry a fly whisk. Move at a brisk pace through infested areas.

Horse flies are a diverse group of flies ranging from $1/2$ inch to more than 2 inches long. They feed during the day and at dusk. Their bite is painful and may leave a noticeable lump in the skin. They are most commonly found near wooded areas and only rarely enter stables.

Gnats are tiny flies—variously known as midges, sand flies, and no-see-ums—that are active at dusk and in the evening. They transmit the skin parasitic worm onchocerca. Individual horses may develop an allergy to the gnat bites, resulting in an itchy skin disease variously called sweet itch, Queensland itch or culicoides hypersensitivity. The most affected areas may be the topline, the base of the mane and tail, over the withers and the midline of the bottom of the abdomen. Affected skin becomes rough and scaly, with hair loss from rubbing to relieve itching. Control involves using fly repellents and stabling horses during the dusk and early evening when these flies are most active. If flies continue to be a problem for a stabled horse, placement of fans blowing into the stall may be effective because gnats are weak fliers and prefer not to venture into, and cannot successfully navigate through, turbulent air.

Mosquitoes are most active in the first two hours after sunset. They are, in general, not a big worry to horses unless an individual horse becomes allergic to their bites. Their main

A properly fitting fly mask stays off the horse's eyes; this mask has Velcro top and bottom fasteners for maximum adjustability.

Courtesy of Stitch 'n Hitch

danger is in the transmission of serious viral diseases such as the encephalitis viruses.

Fly and Insect Control

The frequent application of effective fly repellents such as oil-based wipes and roll-ons, as well as protective masks, nets and sheets are effective measures against flies. Stabling horses or allowing them access to shaded shelters during peak times of fly activity helps reduce exposure. For flies in the stable, hang flypaper outside stalls to reduce the fly population.

Some horse owners use an electrified insect zapper. Zappers can be unpredictable and noisy and may result in horses spooking,

possibly resulting in injuries in a stall or causing horses to leave a run-in barn, which defeats the purpose of the apparatus. We suspect the notion that pathogen-filled zapped flies spread disease over a wide radius around the zapper is a figment of someone's imagination, as we have never seen scientific studies of this. Zapped flies drop quickly, with no evidence of splattering that we can see.

In addition to fly control, corticosteroids to control itching may be necessary for horses that are allergic to certain insects. Products are also available that are fed to horses and that pass in the manure and decrease the breeding population of flies. Consult your veterinarian before using any such products.

Masks, Nets and Sheets

Fly masks are necessary in areas with abundant face flies, house flies and other annoying insects. In places with healthy populations of black flies and deer flies, we prefer masks with ears. The overall best turnout mask we have found is Farnam's SuperMask, which comes in sizes from pony and foal size up to XX large. The extra large sizes are big enough for most draft horse heads. Ample room is furnished over the eyes, with no dangerous seams that could damage the cornea. An under-the-chin Velcro fastener allows for an adjustable fit. This mask is not indestructible (particularly for draft horses), but does hold up well, and its brightly colored trim makes the mask easy to spot when it is laying out in the pasture. A separate ear mask is also available, but unfortunately it does not come close to fitting a full sized draft horse.

To keep flies off a horse's body you might use a fly net or a fly sheet. A net consists of nylon strips that buckle onto the harness and sway as the horse moves, discouraging flies from landing. A sheet is made from mesh fabric with a weave that is tight enough to keep out flies, but open enough to allow air to circulate.

You can fashion an inexpensive homemade fly sheet by cutting open a burlap bag and adding two holes for the hames. *Photo by Bonnie Nance*

Natural Controls

Some folks feel that adding natural products such as garlic-based compounds to their horse's feed cuts down on fly problems. These products may make the horse distasteful to certain insects, much as some people are bothered by gnats, fleas and mosquitoes more than are others. Studies on the use of garlic-based products fed to dogs and cats, however, have shown that they are ineffective against fleas and we are skeptical that they work for horses. Although we appreciate the efforts of the natural food and herbal remedy companies, in some cases you'll just have to resort to chemicals. If your fly repellent is effective, be aware that the flies will remain hungry and you may need to employ similar measures to protect yourself.

Some horses become allergic to the chemical compounds in the most common fly wipes and sprays, and some folks just prefer the idea of natural products. One formula that has been suggested is as follows: In a gallon jug combine four 16 ounce bottles of Avon Skin-So-Soft and 40 cc (about 5 tablespoons) of eucalyptus oil (available from a natural food store or pharmacy). Fill the jug with white vinegar and shake well before using. We have no personal experience with this formulation, so we cannot comment on its effectiveness except to say that some folks swear by it.

The most natural fly control is a horse's tail. You will often see a horse in a pasture or paddock with its head up against its buddy's rump to take advantage of the tail fly whisk. Many drafts have bobbed (docked) tails that are not effective fly whisks. Bobbing involves removal of the end of the tail bone in a draft foal, and is not without risk of infection that could spread up the tailbone to involve the spinal cord. This procedure is supposed to ensure that a long tail does not get caught up in harness or machinery. We do not advocate this procedure and prefer to see a draft with a long, full tail. If the tail needs to be shortened, trimming the long hairs with scissors is more humane and allows the horse to have an effective fly whisk when it is no longer working or showing. Tail hairs grow slowly, though, and if your horse's tail has been trimmed short by either yourself or another horse in the pasture, or by rubbing an itchy butt or tailhead, months to years will go by before it grows out again. We have seen advertisements for horse tailpieces that might be useful for a short-tailed horse that is being tortured by flies.

Lice

Lice are microscopic insects that can affect a horse's skin and hair. They spread by contact with affected horses, tack, or grooming tools. Lice seem to be more common in draft horses than in others, but whether this is due to an inherent susceptibility or to environments where large numbers of drafts are housed close together is not clear.

Lice can affect the body, the legs, the mane and the tail. The haircoat of a horse with lice is usually dull and dry, with patches of hair loss and possibly patches of irritated skin. Lice do not, however, seem to cause the horse to be particularly itchy. The haircoat may have a sour or mousy odor. The adult lice and the eggs attached to the hairs may be visible as tiny white to gray specks when the hair is examined in direct sunlight, but identification of lice often requires microscopic examination.

If one horse in the barn has lice, all horses must be treated as some may be carrying lice even if they appear to be normal. Sponge-on insecticidal dips work better than other methods of control. Clipping the feathers of an affected draft results in a more rapid cure for that horse and helps keep the lice from spreading to other horses. Treat all tack and blankets with insecticide, and spray the barn and paddocks with a product designed to kill fleas. Worming with ivermectin every two weeks for three doses is another effective treatment for the horses, but you will still need to treat the environment.

Ticks and Mites

Additional insects that affect our horse's health and well-being are ticks and mites. Both of these insects have eight legs and are related to the spider family.

Ticks

Severe tick infestations may result in blood loss. Many horses born and raised in tropical climates such as the

On a summer day horses will stand head to rump to take advantage of each other's natural fly whisks.

Photo by Bonnie Nance

Dominican Republic, although not always in the greatest of physical condition, can carry a tremendous tick load apparently without danger of dying. A heavy tick load, however, is certainly not desirable for any horse. Some ticks prefer to attach to skin at the base of the mane and the groin area, where they may be difficult to see. Tick bites may result in large skin bumps in sensitive horses. If these reactions are itchy and bother your horse, apply corticosteroid cream to the area once or twice a day until the horse seems more comfortable. Under the microscope, persistent insect bite reactions can mimic tumors of lymphocytes or lymph nodes, a condition known as pseudolymphoma.

Horse ear tick
(Otobius megnini)

Ticks

Ticks responsible for spreading
Lyme disease:
East coast—Deer tick *(Ixodes dammini)*
West coast—Western black-legged tick
(Ixodes pacificus)

How to remove a tick

If you find a tick on your horse, remove it by grasping the body and pulling it out. If the tick is engorged with blood, wrap the body in a tissue to make removal more pleasant. Leaving mouth parts in the skin is not dangerous because they will be broken down and expelled from the skin and will not result in serious complications.

Unless ticks are present in large numbers in a debilitated animal, their major danger is in the transmission of diseases like Lyme disease in areas where both the bacteria and the deer tick (in the East) or the black-legged tick (in the West) are present. Some ticks infect the inside of the horse's ear, resulting in a potential source of continued irritation and head shaking.

---

pseudolymphoma
    pseudo   = false
    lymphoma = a malignant tumor of
                        lymphocytes or lymph nodes

Tick control involves mowing pastures, as well as avoiding tall grass and overgrown forest where ticks are most likely to be found. Insect repellents or residual insecticides may be of some use.

Mites

Mites are similar to ticks but are much smaller and are not visible to the naked eye. The two mites most likely to cause problems in horses are the straw itch mite and the chorioptes mite. Despite its name, the straw itch mite causes outbreaks of usually non-itchy skin disease of the neck and withers in stabled horses.

Chorioptes mites cause a severe itchy and irritating skin disease of the lower legs or the coronary band. Chorioptes mite infection is more common and severe in horses with heavy feathering, such as Clydesdales and Shires. A moist and dirty environment add to the probability of infestation. In horses with heavy feathering this problem is difficult to see in its early stages.

If you suspect a mite infection, treatment with ivermectin may cure the problem. Draft horses with severe infection may need their hair clipped and the skin treated with an insecticidal dip. If straw itch mites are present in straw bedding or hay, replace the bedding or feed with non-infested material.

Vaccinations

Draft horses, like other animals, should be given only the essential vaccines. Careful evaluation of your horses and their situation is better than just blindly vaccinating every horse for every possible disease.

Vaccines are of two kinds:

1. those prepared from killed (inactivated) infectious organisms or inactivated toxins. These vaccines have no risk of causing infection.

2. those containing live organisms that are modified (modified live vaccines) to result in minimal to no infection but good immunity. These vaccines may be more effective but may also be more dangerous.

Vaccine reactions are fairly common in horses and may range from a slight swelling and soreness at the site to a large swelling accompanied by fever and malaise, to a severe allergic response that can cause collapse and death. Fortunately serious reactions are rare. Severe swelling and pain from a vaccine site in the neck can interfere with the horse's ability to bend its neck for food and water and may require several days of lay-up and special care.

Vaccines for strangles, influenza and rhinopneumonitis may cause a more severe reaction than other vaccines. Although vaccines containing several different compounds in the same dose (multivalent vaccines) are economical and convenient, giving only the necessary vaccines, and separating out the more irritating vaccines may help prevent severe reactions. For a sensitive horse, an anti-inflammatory medication such as phenylbutazone (bute) given at the time or after vaccination may be necessary.

After receiving a vaccination, you likely have experienced a day or so of not feeling right. A horse may feel the same way. Vaccines are designed to boost the body's immune response to the agent in the vaccine. Stress can interfere with the body's immune response to a vaccination. Shipping or a hard workout soon after vaccination just doesn't make sense. Avoid stress to the horse at the time of vaccinations.

Besides the vaccines mentioned below, others are available for protection against Potomac horse fever, strangles, equine viral arteritis, botulism and anthrax. Consult your veterinarian for advice about the needs of horses in your area and in your situation.

Although many vaccines are available through catalogs or feed and tack stores, an appropriate and safe vaccination procedure for your horses can be determined *only* through consultation with your veterinarian.

Tetanus

Tetanus vaccine is essential for all horses. Tetanus is caused by the toxins of the bacterium called *Clostridium tetani*, which is present in the soil and can infect wounds. Tetanus toxin affects nerve activity by blocking the parts of the nervous system that help control nervous system function, causing the muscles to go into severe spasms. Horses with tetanus overreact to noises and other external stimuli, and die due to spasm of the diaphragm and other muscles involved in breathing.

Foals should receive their first vaccination before reaching four months of age, with a second dose at five months. A booster vaccination is required every year, as well as any time a horse is injured with a deep puncture wound. Pregnant mares should receive a tetanus booster four to six weeks before foaling.

Rabies

Horses in barns and at pasture have a high risk of exposure to wildlife and bats with rabies, a fatal disease. Rabies vaccine is administered to foals between three and six months of age, with a second dose at six to seven months, and must be boostered on a yearly basis in areas in which the rabies virus is present. With a high risk of spreading rabies to humans and other animals, a horse that has not been adequately vaccinated for rabies and develops any sort of unexplained nervous disease may be immediately euthanized for examination of the brain, even though a potentially treatable disorder may be mimicking rabies infection. Keep your horse's rabies vaccinations current by vaccinating every year.

Encephalitis Viruses

Eastern equine encephalitis (EEE), Western equine encephalitis (WEE) and Venezuelan equine encephalitis (VEE) are carried by mosquitoes and cause inflammation of the brain of horses and people. Vaccination is an effective control. Vaccinate foals at three to four months and again at four to five months, followed by an annual booster. Give the booster in spring to protect your horses during the mosquito season. In most areas of North America, vaccination for EEE and WEE is enough, and most vaccines contain both. In the Southwest VEE is also a problem. West Nile encephalitis virus has caused disease and death in horses and humans in the northeastern United States. Although West Nile virus is also carried by mosquitoes, at the time of this writing no vaccine is available.

---

encephalitis
encephal   = brain
itis   = inflammation

Influenza

Influenza (flu) is a viral disease that is rarely fatal, but can cause outbreaks of respiratory disease in exposed horses. It is particularly a problem in horses traveling to shows, sales and other public events. Vaccinate foals at three to six months of age and again at four to seven months.

Vaccination does not always confer complete protection against influenza. Repeated vaccination is a useful practice for horses with a high risk of exposure, such as show horses during showing season. For such situations, repeating vaccination at four- to six-week intervals may be advisable. Newer vaccines in development at the time of this writing may confer immunity for longer periods of time. Please consult your veterinarian for advice.

Rhinopneumonitis

Rhinopneumonitis, or equine herpesvirus, is a viral infection that commonly causes abortion, stillbirth or death of newborn foals and mild respiratory disease in adults. Protection following vaccination is short-lived. Many veterinarians therefore advocate repeat vaccination of pregnant mares with inactivated vaccines at five, seven, and nine months of pregnancy. Vaccination of foals is started at two to three months of age, and repeated at two- to four-month intervals until the age of one year.

Because the respiratory disease of rhinopneumonitis is not a big problem in adult horses, continued re-vaccination of geldings, stallions and non-breeding mares may not be essential. Although vaccination is an effective control of the respiratory and reproductive disorders caused by equine herpesvirus, this vaccination unfortunately affords little or no protection against herpesvirus myelitis, the form affecting the spinal cord.

---

rhinopneumonitis
rhino   = nose
pneumo   = lung
itis   = inflammation

Equine Protozoal Myeloencephalitis

EPM is a protozoal disease that affects a horse's central nervous system, sometimes with devastating consequences. The disorder can be difficult to diagnose, as the testing available at this time results in many horses testing positive that do not have the disease. A vaccine is being marketed that is said to protect horses against EPM infection, but at this time absolutely no evidence exists that this, or any other vaccine, will ever be effective against EPM or any other protozoal disease.

Any company requesting a license to sell a vaccine for horses needs prove only that the vaccine is safe when administered to horses, not that it is effective. We cannot recommend the use of this vaccine and we are willing to bet your veterinarian feels the same way. Please do not pressure a vet into giving your horse an untested vaccine that could cause the horse to test positive for EPM, not because the horse has been exposed to the disease but because the vaccine has caused your horse to produce antibodies to the organism. Testing for EPM in horses is already difficult enough without the added task of trying to distinguish between antibodies due to exposure and antibodies due to vaccination.

> *myeloencephalitis*
> myelo = spinal cord
> encephal = brain
> itis = inflamation

Coggins Testing

At least once a year ask your veterinarian to draw bloodsample to send for Coggins testing. Horses that are being shipped, sold or entered into show competitions are usually required to provide proof of a negative test within the past year. Some states and shows require a negative Coggins test within the past six months.

This test, invented by Dr. Leroy Coggins, looks for antibodies in a horse's blood that indicate the presence of infection with the viral disease equine infectious anemia (EIA), sometimes called swamp fever. Although this disease may be carried by horses showing little or no clinical problems, it may cause sudden disease characterized by fever, depression, weakness, weight loss, edema and anemia. The virus is carried from an infected horse to other horses through hypodermic needles or biting insects. Some people say EIA is the horse equivalent of AIDS. This belief is not true, although the causative virus of EIA is a retrovirus, as is the virus that causes AIDS.

No vaccination is available to prevent EIA and no treatment has been found. An infected horse must be either kept in an isolation facility for the rest of its life or destroyed. This measure may seem extreme, but testing and removing infected horses from the equine population has turned a once common and devastating

Disease Prevention by Vaccination		
Vaccine	*Seriousness of Disease*	*Need for Vaccination*
Tetanus	Serious	Absolutely necessary
Rabies	Serious	Variable*
EEE/WEE	Serious	Variable*
VEE	Serious	Variable*
Influenza	Mild	Variable*
Rhinopneumonitis (equine herpesvirus)	Serious in fetus and newborn; can cause serious spinal cord disease in adults	Necessary for pregnant mares and foals; will not protect against spinal cord disease
Potomac Horse Fever	Mild to moderate	Variable*
Strangles	Mild to moderate	Variable*
Equine Viral Arteritis	Serious in breeding horses	Variable*
Botulism	Serious	Variable*
Anthrax	Serious, but rare	Rarely necessary
EPM	Serious	Not recommended

* Need depends on the potential for exposure to these diseases. Exposure risk involves factors such as prevalence of the disease in your area and whether your horse travels to other areas or is exposed to horses traveling from other areas. Broodmares and foals require vaccinations that may not be necessary for adult non-breeding horses.

Horses that are shipped, sold or entered into shows usually must have proof of a negative Coggins test within the past year.

Photo by Phil Krahn

disease into a rarity. The virus still exists, however, and testing of wild horse populations in the United States has revealed a small number of infected horses. Some of the western states and Canadian provinces do not require annual Coggins testing for show horses, which may be why EIA-positive horses have been detected in those areas. The test is not expensive and is well worth performing every year, even where it is not required.

Medical records

Keep a medical record on each of your horses. Note the dates and kinds of vaccinations and wormers administered, as well as any illnesses and lameness problems. Ask your veterinarian for copies of blood tests or pathology reports. Having complete records will help you and your veterinarian maintain proper health care for your horse, and may be invaluable if you change veterinarians or if your horse is referred to a specialist.

Cleaning Genitals

A horse's genitals accumulate excessive secretions (smegma) that result in skin irritation and predispose horses to the development of skin cancer (squamous cell carcinoma). These areas must therefore be kept as clean as possible. Accustom your horse to being handled in these sensitive areas.

The cleaning procedure is not for the faint-hearted, and you may want to wear latex gloves. Clean the areas with a mild detergent solution and scrub with a soft sponge. You may use any of a variety of cleaning products including commercial products designed for the purpose, standard issue green soap or Ivory dishwashing liquid.

Although regular hosing will help clean the area, once or twice a year perform a thorough cleaning followed by a thorough rinse. Some horses require cleaning more often, and the procedure is easier to do on some horses than on others. With gentleness, time and patience a horse rarely requires serious restraint or sedation.

Have someone hold the horse's head and carefully proceed with the cleaning while standing at the horse's side, well away from the kick zone and as close as possible to the horse's thigh. Remember, horses can kick to the side (called a cow kick). If you have trouble with or are unsure about the cleaning procedure, ask your veterinarian to demonstrate.

Cleaning Stallions and Geldings

Get the horse used to a forceful stream of hose water on the area, especially the insertion of the hose into the sheath (prepuce) of male horses. In stallions and geldings, reach deep into the sheath to scrub the insides free of accumulated material, which is greasy, sticky and smells bad.

The penis is difficult to clean, except in a horse that willingly drops the penis and leaves it dropped for cleaning. A thorough scrub up inside the prepuce (also called the sheath, which is the skin into which the penis retracts when it disappears), with the penis retracted, will result in a cleaner penis. Take every opportunity to examine the surface of the penis and get the horse used to its penis being gently handled. Some horses will give you more opportunities than others.

At the end of the penis next to the irregularly ruffled, pink tissue surrounding the urethra is a cavity. Secretions can accumulate and harden in this cavity and form what is known as the bean of the penis. Check this area regularly and remove any accumulated material. If your horse does not allow you to examine this area, get your veterinarian to assist you.

Cleaning Mares

Using the sponge with soap and water, scrub the mare's perivulvar area, the area directly around the vulvar lips. As with stallions, get the mare used to a forceful stream of hose water directed on the area. *Never* place a hose into the mare's vulva and vagina.

If you notice any indication of a growth, swelling, or irritation of the vulva, penis, or sheath call your veterinarian.

Future Outlook

Routine care of our draft horses has become easier and safer in recent times. The economic impact of the equine industry is such that we anticipate even better treatments and preventive medicines in the future. Many disorders that plagued horses over the years are now readily preventable or treatable.

Photo by Vickie Darnell

Foot and Hoof Care

Draft horses are particularly predisposed to problems with their feet and hooves. For some horses poor hoof quality results in an increased chance for infection or bruising. Even in a horse with excellent hooves, the large surface area of the draft foot may be part of the reason drafts have frequent problems.

Since drafts often go barefoot, their owners may not be as conscientious about regular hoof care as are other horse owners. Lack of regular hoof care can lead to serious problems. Always remember the saying, "No hoof, no horse." All draft horses deserve regular attention to their feet.

Hoof Quality

Genetics play a large role in hoof quality. Draft horses are descended from diluvial coldbloods, horses that survived the last ice age. For centuries these horses were bred for adaptation to a specific climate and soil. In modern times draft horses have been imported to all parts of the world.

Clydesdales, for example, were developed to work in soft, boggy soils and therefore required a large, flat foot to prevent sinking and avoid compacting the soils. Their hooves are adapted to a soggy environment. When we move the Clydesdale to an area with hard, rocky soil, the horse develops problems.

By way of contrast, Percherons, Ardennes and Suffolks were developed to work on compacted or rocky soils and therefore have harder, more durable hooves.

Breed Origin and Soil Type		
Breed	*Origin*	*Soil Type*
Ardennes	Ardennes region of France and Belgium	hard, rocky mountainous soils
Belgian	Belgium	heavy rich soils
Clydesdale	Clyde Valley of Scotland	soft, boggy soils
Percheron	La Perche region of France	compacted clay soils
Shire	The Fens of England	marshlands
Suffolk	East Anglia region of England	heavy clay soils

Flattened Hooves

The heavy horse's flattened hoof is a consequence of breeding and has nothing to do with evolution. Humans, not nature, developed these animals. Breeding for appearance has, in some cases, resulted in horses that are dramatically different from their ancestors. The American Belgian, for example, no longer resembles the original breed. The original Belgian was similar to what today we call the Brabant Belgian.

Building Better Hooves

Good nutrition is essential to good hoof quality. Although some owners think draft horses don't need anything more than good quality forage, in many draft breeds forage alone is not enough to maintain hoof quality.

If your draft horse's hooves are less than ideal, include in the horse's diet a supplement containing high levels of methionine and biotin. Methionine is an essential amino acid that is a building block of hoof protein. Biotin is made by bacteria in the horse's intestine, but feeding additional biotin can improve hoof and sole growth.

The more hoof growth, the stronger the hoof. The faster the hoof grows, the more likely a nail will be driven into solid, healthy hoof when shoes are reset.

Getting the Horse to Stand

According to common knowledge, draft horses have difficulty standing for trimming and shoeing. Shoeing stock advertisements may be found in any draft horse publication and some farriers carry a portable stock. We do not use stocks for any horse. We have heard too many stories of broken stocks and frightened horses to advocate their use. In some problem cases, owners have resorted to tranquilizers to make handling the horse easier for the farrier.

The belief that draft horses cannot stand for hoof care is unfounded. A healthy draft horse can stand on three legs long enough for a hoof trim or shoeing. If you have problems, either your horse has not been properly trained to stand, something is wrong that makes it difficult or uncomfortable for the horse to stand for hoof care or your farrier is not attuned to the special needs of a draft horse.

Studies of imprinting indicate that the first six weeks of a foal's life are critical for getting a foal accustomed to having its feet handled. If this training is not done early, time, patience, blood, sweat and tears are needed to get the horse used to having its feet handled. If you are physically unable to work with your horse's or foal's feet, get help.

Standing on three legs and having the fourth lifted and bent may be uncomfortable for a horse, and is probably the primary reason why some horses give the farrier and owner trouble during hoof cleaning, trimming and shoeing. The person handling the feet must recognize when the motion of a joint is being limited by a joint injury or disease. Pulling the hind leg back behind the horse may result in resistance and discomfort. In such a case, try a different angle or find a more comfortable position for the leg. Draft horses are built with their legs well under their bodies (base narrow) and often travel a narrow path. Although this conformation is ideal for working in a furrow, it can make pulling a leg to the side uncomfortable.

A horse does not want to stand on a sore leg. Horses with scratches or leg mites may not stand well because of skin irritation. Letting the horse frequently put the foot down requires more time for trimming and shoeing, but will save time in the long run. Shoeing or trimming may be easier after a horse has been worked or exercised because its energy level will be lower.

Trimming and shoeing should not become traumatic experiences for the horse. Horses with shivers and other manifestations of equine polysaccharide storage myopathy (EPSM) may have difficulty standing. Their muscles are weak and may undergo painful cramping. They may have decreased bend in their hocks. If a draft horse with problems standing for foot care has an unknown history, or had no foot care problems at an earlier age, consider the possibility that you may be seeing the early signs of EPSM.

A draft horse may stand better for resetting if both shoes on one side are pulled and replaced before removing and resetting the other side.

Hoof Anatomy

The hoof is a uniquely designed structure that absorbs and distributes concussive forces when the horse's foot hits the ground. The hoof wall and sole are the most visible parts of the hoof and are made of a protein known as keratin, similar to the keratin your fingernails are made of. The hoof is actually an adapted fingernail. Neither hooves nor fingernails contain calcium; feeding additional calcium will not strengthen either hooves or fingernails. The hoof wall bends in at the heels to form ridges—known as the bars of the hoof—on the sole surface.

The hoof wall and sole may be pigmented, partially pigmented, or lacking any pigmentation. The belief that a white (non-pigmented) hoof is weaker than pigmented hoof is untrue. Melanin granules (pigment) within the keratin do not change the hoof's biomechanical nature. The hoof wall of the draft horse is thicker than that of a light horse, allowing a larger safe zone for placing nails in the hoof.

The hoof's sole meets the outer wall in a linear non-pigmented zone known as the white line. This zone is less impenetrable than other parts of the sole and can allow dirt and bacteria to gain access to the foot, causing problems such as gravel and abscesses. It can also allow infection of the hoof wall by fungi, causing white line disease.

This Clydesdale demonstrates the base-narrow stance common in many draft breeds. *Photo by Mike Wildenstein*

A postmortem specimen cut through the hoof and shoe to show the proper placement of a nail in the hoof—the thickness of a draft hoof offers a relatively wide safe zone for nail placement.

Photo by Mike Wildenstein

Hoof Growth

The hoof grows from the soft tissue of the coronary band just above the hoof. Damage to the coronary band results in defects in hoof growth, which may be either temporary or permanent, depending on the severity of the injury. Hoof growth is usually about one-half inch or less per month. Hoof growth is often slightly slower in cold months and slightly faster in warm seasons, mostly due to changes in diet and exercise.

Slight irregularities in hoof growth or quality may result in concentric rings in the hoof wall. A change in diet or previous stress, such as might be caused by illness or a change in weather, may cause these variations. Small rings are usually nothing to worry about if the hoof is otherwise intact and healthy. Severe ridging of the hooves occurs in horses with chronic laminitis and founder.

The inner wall of the hoof contains the laminae (also called lamellae), which are microscopic finger-like extensions of tissue that interdigitate (intertwine) to hold the hoof wall firmly to the underlying coffin bone. Between the coffin bone and the hoof wall is the blood and nerve supply to the hoof, the laminae, and the bone. The hoof wall and insensitive sole contain neither blood vessels nor nerves, allowing these tissues to be trimmed and to hold shoe nails without pain to the horse.

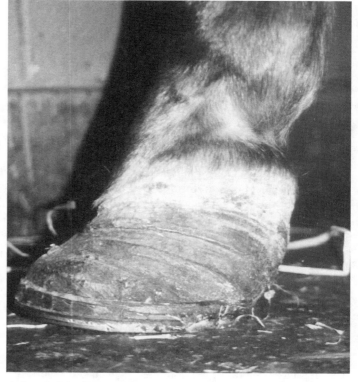

A hoof showing the obvious laminitic rings and distorted shape of a horse with chronic laminitis. *Photo by Mike Wildenstein*

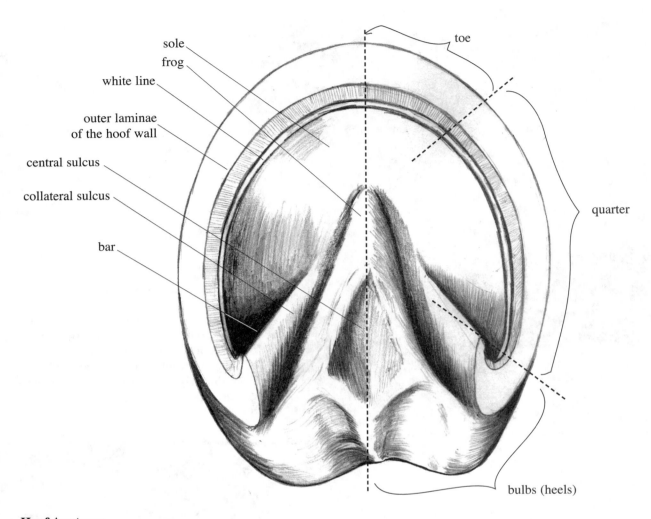

sole

frog

white line

outer laminae
of the hoof wall

central sulcus

collateral sulcus

bar

toe

quarter

bulbs (heels)

Hoof Anatomy

The Frog

Like the wall and sole, the frog is also made of keratin, but is softer and more pliable. The frog extends from the back of the hoof to form a point slightly more than halfway to the toe. A t the back of the foot, the frog merges with the bulbs (heels), which are made of a similar pliable keratin.

The shape of the frog has little resemblance to the animal of the same name. Why it's called the frog was a mystery to us until we learned (from the book *On the Horse's Foot*) that the words frog and thrush both originate in the same word, frush, which is a corruption of the French word *fourchette* or *fourche,* meaning fork, and is indicative of the way the frog divides into two parts toward the heels.

The frog cushions much of the hoof and is subject to infection. The frog has a central depression, the sulcus, and two grooves, the collateral sulci, on the outsides between the frog and the bars of the hoof.

Angle, Shape and Size

The angle where the toes meet the ground is about 50 degrees in the forefeet and 55 degrees in the hind feet. This angle increases toward the heels, where it is about 100 degrees.

The curvature of the wall is wider on the outside than on the inside, which helps you tell which shoe is left and which is right. The slope of the hoof's medial quarter (inner side) is steeper than that of the lateral quarter (outer side). The base-narrow build of many draft horses causes more wear on the outer lateral wall of the hoof. This wear can result in a bending outward (flaring) of the outside wall.

The forefeet bear more weight than the hind hooves. The front hooves are usually more round than the hooves of the hind feet and may require a larger shoe. In contrast to the hind feet of light horses, which are usually more elongate than the forefeet in the toe-to-heel axis, the hind feet of drafts and draft crosses are often shaped more like an equilateral triangle when viewed from the bottom.

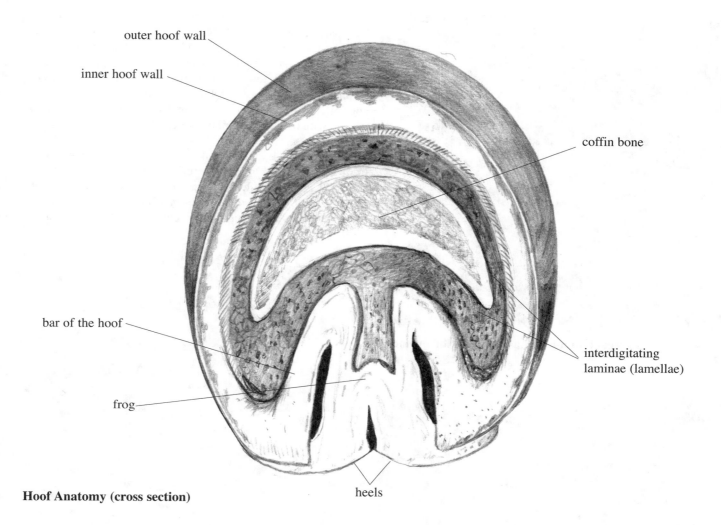

outer hoof wall

inner hoof wall

coffin bone

bar of the hoof

interdigitating
laminae (lamellae)

frog

heels

Hoof Anatomy (cross section)

The hoof's size is directly related to the size of the coffin bone, also called the third phalanx or pedal bone, which is within the hoof. A horse said to have good bone is likely to have a larger than normal hoof. A well-formed hoof is slightly concave on the sole surface, which helps reduce injury to the sole and increases the support structure for the coffin bone. Clydesdales and other draft horses that have been bred to have flat soles are predisposed to sole injuries.

Hoof Care

Proper care and maintenance of the hoof includes providing the horse with a clean and dry environment, as well as regularly cleaning and examining its hooves. The hoof and frog must be trimmed regularly.

Hoof trimming and shoeing are best left to those who are skilled in these procedures. Depending on where you live, you may have a difficult time finding a farrier willing to work on drafts, and many draft owners would prefer to do their own

trimming and shoeing. With some instruction it is possible to do a reasonable job. Before you attempt to trim or shoe your horses, please get training from an experienced draft horse farrier. Many excellent books and videotapes are available, but hands-on experience has no substitute. Maintaining proper hoof balance is vital to ensuring that your horse's hooves and legs remain healthy.

Protect your back

Working on a horse's feet is hard on the human back. Use your legs instead of your back as much as possible to avoid strain on your lower back. A high and solid-based hoof stand makes work easier on tall, long-legged draft horses.

After a session of cleaning, trimming or shoeing stand straight with your hands on the back of your hips. Bend and stretch backward to help keep your disks in place so they won't bulge backward between your vertebrae and cause back pain or more serious consequences.

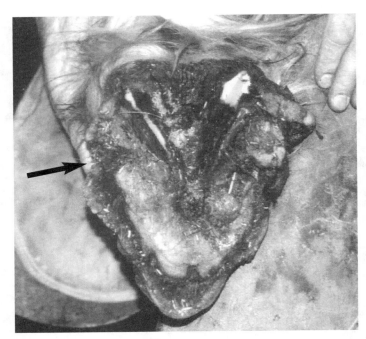

This severely neglected hind hoof has a split at the quarter.

Photo by Mike Wildenstein

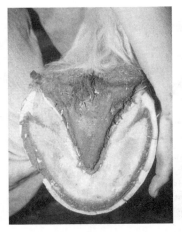 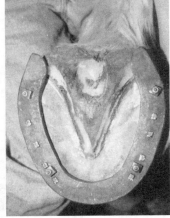

Left: Hind hoof, trimmed but unshod; notice the slightly triangular shape.

Right: Hind hoof wearing a properly fitting shoe with studs for traction.

Courtesy of Mike Wildenstein

Picking the Hoof

In contrast to trimming and shoeing, picking is a procedure that should be performed regularly by all horse owners. Begin by standing beside either the horse's shoulder or thigh facing the tail. While leaning into the horse's body, run your hand down the back of the leg, which should result in the horse shifting its weight and lifting its hoof. Use voice commands or grasp the feathers to make sure the horse knows what you want.

Once the hoof is in the air, turn your back against the horse's body and, if you are working on a front hoof, bring the hoof between your legs. If you are working on a hind hoof, rest the hoof on your inside thigh. These positions help support the horse and make holding up the hoof more comfortable. A farrier's apron or other protective clothing is useful to prevent injury to yourself, as well as cut down on laundry bills. We sometimes ask a horse with muddy feet to hold up one leg without support, but not for long.

Use a hoof pick to clean out embedded dirt and rocks. Work from heel to toe to reduce the chance of injury to the frog's collateral grooves. After picking the hoof you may use a stiff brush to remove embedded dirt. Dirt should be brushed away whenever shoes are being reset or if the hoof is to be medicated.

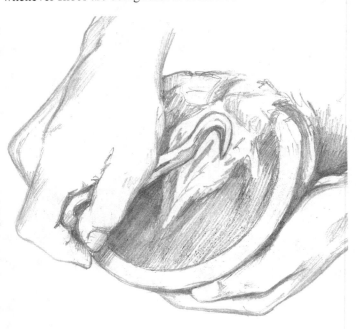

Frequently clean out dirt and rocks with a hoof pick.

Trimming and Shoeing

Regular attention to hooves is particularly important in the draft breeds because they are susceptible to developing hoof problems or lameness from poor hoof care. Even the unshod horse, unless it is working regularly on a hard surface, needs trimming at six- to eight-week intervals. Although this interval may be extended if hoof wear is equal to hoof growth, rebalancing is as important as removal of extra hoof because horses rarely wear down their feet in a balanced manner.

Other than obtaining shoes that are large enough, and finding a farrier willing to work on drafts, no shoeing problems are unique to heavy horses. Trim or reset shoes on your horses every six to eight weeks, both for the horse's welfare and because a regularly maintained hoof requires less human energy to remain healthy and balanced.

Draft Horse Shoes

Shoes protect a horse's hoof from excessive wear. If the horse has good hoof quality and does not work on hard surfaces, shoes may not be necessary. Unshod hooves tend to spread somewhat and may require a larger shoe if the horse is shod after going barefoot.

The shoe style you use will depend on your purpose for shoeing. Flat shoes protect the hooves from wear. Rubber or urethane shoes are used to reduce concussive damages to the horse's hooves, such as road founder, that may occur when the horse is worked on hard ground or pavement.

Traction Shoes

Traction shoes have caulks, borium, Drill-Tek, or studs added to the bottom to improve traction on ice, mud or snow, and for competitive pulling.

Caulks are either built into the shoe or welded onto the shoe. They are generally placed on each heel, with a broader caulk across the toe. Never put a horse with caulks in a field hitch. The soft footing and tight turns make it likely that a horse may step on its partner's feet, and the caulks would increase the chance of injury.

Borium is soft steel with tungsten carbide pieces and is gas welded onto the shoe.

Drill-Tek is bronze with tungsten carbide that is braised (the welding process used with bronze) to the shoe.

Studs may be either threaded or nonthreaded. The shoe is drilled and may also be tapped to receive the studs. The advantage of threaded studs is that they may be changed or removed as conditions require.

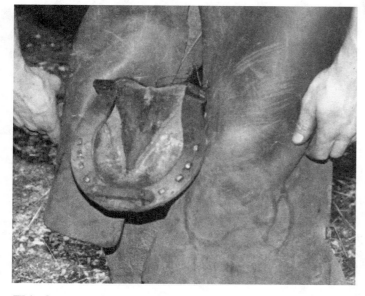

This front hoof has been trimmed and shod with a well-fitting shoe with heel and toe caulks to provide traction.

Courtesy of Mike Wildenstein

Show Shoes

When it comes to shoeing show draft horses, a farrier's loyalties are often divided between the customer's satisfaction and the horse's well being. Methods and techniques of shoeing show horses have their origins in the late 1950s and early 60s when showing drafts in the United States began to rise in popularity.

Scotch Bottoms

Show shoes, or so-called Scotch bottoms (a term we find insulting to the people of Scotland), are weighted and shaped to enhance the horse's gait or movement. Bevels may be added to enhance the hoof's size. Because of attempts to increase hoof size and change the gait in the show draft, shoeing the show horse may cause problems. An increase in the weight of the shoe creates an exaggerated gait that puts stress on muscles, tendons, ligaments, and bones. The increased weight of the shoe also increases the force of the hoof hitting the ground, creating concussion injuries.

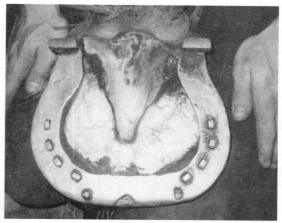

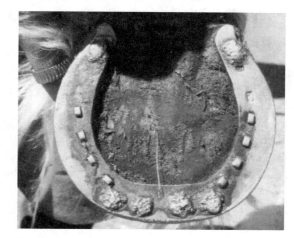

Show Plates (Scotch Bottoms)
Top: Hoof shod with a show plate with heel caulks and borium for traction.
Bottom: Show plate with Drill-Tek for traction and a pad to protect the sole.

Photos by Mike Wildenstein

The original beveled shoe (Scotch bottom) complemented the Clydesdale's foot. The shoe was full and had a slightly square toe and a well-defined toe clip. It had a gentle slope to the outer edge of the shoe to follow the natural slope of the hoof wall. These shoes came either with or without heel caulks.

Our current style of shoeing show drafts consists of an oversize shoe on an overgrown hoof. Flares of the hoof are exaggerated and promoted, resulting in tearing of the hoof laminae. This trend results in a greater incidence of navicular fractures and degenerative joint problems. The hoof of the show draft is no longer natural in form or function, often leading to early retirement of the horse.

We discourage oversize show shoes, designed to exaggerate the size of the horse's hoof, as they result in improper hoof balance.

Going Against Fashion

Many heavy horses today are kept to be looked at, and fashion plays a greater role than it should in the way they are shod. A regional draft horse show is a good place to check out what's popular in shoeing in your area. Once a fashion becomes accepted it may quickly become the norm. The fashion we have seen develop is for overgrown feet with built-up outside heels and exaggerated square toes on the forefeet. This fashion has been encouraged to the point of crippling horses.

To stand in the way of fashion takes a brave person, but the hooves of show horses can be brought back to a normal shape and balance. Debilitating fashion trends may be addressed by suggesting classes for Best Shod and an award for Best Shod in Show, to be judged by a knowledgeable draft horse farrier and not the horse owners.

Hospital Plates

For some problems, such as canker or a puncture of the sole leading to infection of the coffin (pedal) bone, your veterinarian or farrier may suggest the use of a shoe called a hospital plate. The removable flat plate on the bottom of the shoe allows ready cleaning of the bottom parts of the hoof, as well as placement of medications that may be packed under the plate to continuously expose affected tissues to the medications. A hospital plate may also be used as support and protection for flat-soled horses or those with chronic laminitis.

The removable bottom of a hospital plate supports the sole and hoof and also gives you a way to keep medications in contact with the frog and sole. *Photo by Mike Wildenstein*

Pulling a Loose Shoe

Always remove a loose shoe before it damages the hoof wall. Use a clinch cutter or solid straight-edge screwdriver, a hammer, and a pair of extra-large hoof pullers. Loosen and straighten the clinches of the nails by hammering the screwdriver head edge or the clinch cutter edge up against the clinch, hammering in the direction of the coronary band. After the clinches are loosened, grasp the shoe with the pullers and pry between the shoe and the hoof at the heels, prying down and toward the toe.

Always pry down and toward the toe to reduce the risk of breaking the hoof wall.

As the nails become loose, use the pullers to pull them out, again prying down and toward the toe. Continue to pry the shoe and the nails, working from both sides toward the toe until the shoe is off. Leave the dirt and debris in the hoof to protect the sole from injury until the hoof can be reshod.

Health Clues

To the casual observer a sick or lame horse may look healthy, but when you know your horse's normal, healthy appearance you are able to quickly spot a problem when something starts to go wrong. Daily examination of each horse will help you discover small problems before they turn into serious injury or disease.

Appetite

The expression to "eat like a horse" didn't come to be for no reason—horses are adapted to be almost continuous grazers. A healthy horse rarely turns away from additional food. If it has nothing to eat, a horse will look for something to nibble on. One of the first signs that a horse is not feeling right is refusing grain, since grain is usually a horse's highlight of the day. Even apples and carrots may be refused.

A normal horse enjoys nibbling all day long.

Photo by Dusty L. Perin

Although feed refusal may be the first clue something is wrong, it may also occur when a horse is nervous or anxious. A horse that doesn't feel quite right, or is under stress, generally still goes for grass and hay. A cold horse may leave the grain to eat hay because hay provides internal heat through fermentation in the gut. When a horse stops eating hay or grass, you have a serious problem and need veterinary assistance.

In contrast, a horse that eats everything in sight and still loses weight is in a catabolic state, which means that for some reason its body is breaking down fat and muscle to use as a source of energy. Your veterinarian should carefully evaluate the animal for underlying disease such as a tumor (pituitary or otherwise), intestinal disease that results in poor absorption of feed, or a condition that causes muscle wasting, such as equine polysaccharide storage myopathy (EPSM) or equine motor neuron disease.

Eating dirt may be nothing more than a bad habit, but if it occurs, evaluate your horse's diet to ensure that all the minerals and vitamins are at adequate levels. Dirt eating may also be a sign of boredom, easily resolved by giving the horse a companion or play toy.

Attitude

As a prey animal, the horse has evolved to be on the alert for predators. A healthy horse, even while relaxed, is constantly aware of its surroundings. When a horse is alert, the eyes are bright, the head is up and the ears turn in response to any movement or sound. Although some horses are naturally more alert than others, a horse that continuously hangs its head, with ears constantly at half mast or pinned back, feels discomfort or lacks energy. The horse could be ill.

Fever is the number one cause of a dull attitude in a previously healthy horse. If the temperature is normal, check pulse and respiration rate, and evaluate the gait for the ouchiness of laminitis or other causes of painful lameness. Listen for the presence of normal gut sounds.

If temperature, gut sounds, pulse, respiration and gait are all normal and the horse is shivering, the horse could simply be cold and miserable. Cover the horse with a warm blanket and move it to a warm, dry environment.

Tack Discomfort

Attitude in harness or under saddle is an important indicator of how a horse feels and how your equipment fits. A horse that pins its ears or wrings its tail is not a happy horse. An anxious, fretful horse is fearful of something bad happening, a stark contrast to the attitude of a horse that is excited about working.

Is the horse trying to tell you it feels some pain or discomfort with the harness or tack, or does the work itself cause discomfort? Although some horses have bad attitudes caused by bad experiences, try to figure out the problem before forcing the horse to perform. A draft horse may merely whisper to you that something is wrong and may continue to work despite pain or discomfort. A light horse, in contrast, may throw itself to the ground or buck, rather than keep working in an uncomfortable or painful situation.

Well-trained horses will settle down as soon as they recognize the task they are harnessed to perform.

Photo by Vickie Darnell

A horse's attitude is an important indicator of how the horse feels and how the equipment fits. *Photo by Phil Krahn*

The Runaway

One attitude of particular concern is the runaway. When a horse that has shown good manners and attitude in early groundwork training becomes a runaway in harness or a rearing and bucking bronco under saddle, several reasons could be possible. The horse may have been pushed too fast in training. Experts like John Lyons, Pat Parelli, and Ron Meredith know how to communicate with horses and can often saddle and ride them within a few hours. If you are not such an expert, you must be an investigator and figure out why your horse is acting badly. Perhaps as the horse's new owner you may not be aware of some bad experience in the horse's past.

Running away may be a horse's response to pain or discomfort. We have heard many stories of drafts that were runaways early in training and later proved to have muscle pain. Another reason a horse may try or succeed at running away may be that it is being asked to pull too much weight. The idea that an anxious horse should pull the heaviest possible weight until it has settled down to work suggests that only a tired horse will obey. An excited horse and an anxious horse are two different things. It's up to you as the owner to figure out which is which. A well-trained draft horse may be excitable in harness, but will still listen and should settle down as soon as it has recognized the task you desire.

Low Energy

A horse that's quiet all the time, almost to the point of semi-consciousness, may be considered gentle, but a knowledgeable handler will realize that something is wrong. A horse should not need constant urging and should be able and willing to pull its weight in a team. The quiet, easy-going manner of a draft horse does not equate to a low energy level. A healthy draft has plenty of energy, but shouldn't waste it in unproductive behavior.

In the wild, predators would immediately pick off a low-energy horse. As domesticated as horses have become, they have not come so far as to forget the instinct for survival. Look for problems in the too-quiet horse. It may have an energy problem, perhaps caused by inadequate or improper feeding. Low feed is a common ploy of horse traders to make horses appear quiet and well mannered. The horse could be ill or could have a metabolic problem that does not allow it to derive sufficient energy from its feeds.

Horses that suddenly become dull and depressed, particularly if they have a normal temperature, may have an infection involving the brain (encephalitis), or may have severe liver problems resulting in high ammonia levels in the blood that affect brain function. Horses with severe liver disease may be found pressing their heads into walls. This severe depression may alternate with episodes of excitability. Excessive yawning may be seen in horses with liver disease, although plenty of healthy horses do a lot of yawning. Some horses start yawning at mealtime—just hope it's not a commentary on your choice of feeds.

> *encephalitis, myeloencephalitis*
> encephal = brain
> myelo = spinal cord
> itis = inflammation

Excitability

A horse that has become excitable, sometimes to the point of maniacal behavior, has a serious problem. Various diseases should be considered, including severe liver failure or inflammation of the brain caused by viral infection (such as encephalitis viruses, rabies, or herpesvirus) or protozoal infection (such as equine protozoal myeloencephalitis). In such a case you must call a veterinarian.

Some folks swear feed can affect a horse's behavior, and the idea has truth; thus the expression "feeling your oats." High soluble carbohydrate feeds such as grains and sweet feeds may cause susceptible horses to have something akin to a hyperactive child's sugar high.

Protein, especially from alfalfa, also has a bad reputation for causing horses to get high. This idea has no scientific basis. Under many circumstances we favor feeding alfalfa and clover products. The high protein content of alfalfa and clovers is not the problem; the problem comes from the feed's total calorie (energy) content.

As a rule, 7 pounds of alfalfa hay have as many calories as 9 pounds of timothy or other grass hay.

Alfalfa hay has more calories than grass hay, when both are of equal quality. Concentrated feeds that are high in protein are often also high in calories, containing calories from both protein and higher levels of carbohydrates. Before you decide that a particular feed is adversely affecting your horse's behavior, make sure you're not feeding extra calories that, in some horses, result in extra activity.

Some horses with EPSM go through a period of increased activity when their diet is adjusted to provide the energy they need. This period of "Yahoo—I feel great!" passes quickly, and most owners report that it is a joy to see their draft horses kicking up their heels, running, and high-tailing it around for the first time in a long while, or ever.

Exercise Tolerance

Exercise tolerance and performance problems are difficult to evaluate, especially if your veterinarian can find nothing obviously wrong with your horse. General fitness, health and conformation each play a role in exercise tolerance and performance.

When a horse owner recognizes that a horse is not performing as well as or as long as it should, the veterinarian must listen carefully to the owner—even if little or nothing is found wrong with the horse—and try to think of possible problems that may not be obvious with a physical examination. A common cause of exercise intolerance and poor performance in draft horses is EPSM, a muscle metabolic problem that can usually be controlled by diet change.

Another big question concerns exercise and tying up, also called Monday morning disease. Can a normal horse that is not well conditioned be overworked to the point that massive muscle damage becomes life threatening? We cannot rule out this possibility, but we believe any episode of tying up is due to an underlying problem. Although severe electrolyte imbalance may cause tying up, in draft-related horses EPSM is the most common cause of tying up.

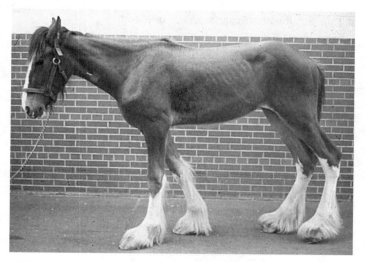

Although starvation or chronic illness can cause poor condition, all this young Clydesdale with EPSM needed was a high fat and low soluble carbohydrate diet.

Photo by Tom Divers

Body Condition

The healthy draft horse has full and well-defined muscling and a shiny haircoat. The haircoat should shed out rapidly and completely each spring. Delayed or incomplete shedding may be an indication of a pituitary tumor. Shedding usually occurs over several weeks, and often proceeds from the front of the horse to the back.

Body Contour

Although a draft has a lot of area to cover, be totally familiar with your horse's normal contour and have a mental map of all the bumps and divots. Some owners consider daily grooming essential to the health of a horse's hair and skin. One good reason for regular grooming is to find wounds, growths, or skin infections before they get out of control. If your horse is otherwise healthy and happy, however, do not feel guilty about not grooming daily. Sporadic grooming is not dangerous, provided the horse's environment is healthy. In an unhealthy environment, a horse's coat may be constantly wet or matted with manure.

Regularly clean and examine your horse's feet for loose shoes or infections. Remove stones or other objects that may become jammed and cause damage. Check the feet and legs for areas of injury, swelling or heat.

Often-neglected areas that require regular examination are the groin, penis and sheath, perianal area, tailbone, underside of the tail, and perivulvar area in mares. These areas may develop tumors that, if left too long, cannot be removed. We have seen cases of old horses with malignant tumors along the tailbone and sometimes at the end of the tail. Found earlier, such tumors may have been successfully treated by tail amputation. The procedure is difficult for many light horse owners to contemplate, but does not drastically alter the appearance of a draft.

Laying-On Hands

A hands-on examination of your horse is easily done. During feeding, for example, you may be able to handle various body parts while the horse is distracted by its meal. Handling is good for your horse, as it helps establish and maintain the lines of communication and trust between the horse and you. Feeding

time is also a good time to clean hooves, apply fly wipe, or administer various medications on the skin or hoof. Doing these procedures during the horse's feeding time diminishes the emotional trauma that might occur if the same procedures were done with the horse in cross-ties.

Some horses are overly defensive during feeding, especially when eating concentrates such as pellets or grain, and may feel threatened if you are in the area. If yours is such a horse, wait until after it has finished eating. Having a helper hold the horse while you examine its body, clean its hooves, or apply medications may be safer than using ties or cross-ties.

Most of a healthy draft horse's body mass is in muscle. The muscles should be full and rounded, have definition and be resilient to the touch, not rock hard. No bones should be obvious to either the eye or the hand. Ribs should not be visible, but you should be able to feel the ribs by putting a bit of hand pressure on the area. Some folks unreasonably swear that the ribs of a healthy draft should be visible once a year. In the past horses at the end of a cold winter looked thin because they hadn't had enough to eat; owners may have needed a justification for their poor condition.

Thick layers of fat are as undesirable as visible ribs. Increased weight from fat may put extra stress on joints and hooves. If you have to push hard to feel the ribs, your draft may be too fat. No scientific evidence has been found, however, showing that obesity in horses represents a serious health risk. That thought makes the owners of overweight horses, including ourselves, sleep a bit more peacefully.

The horse should appear balanced, with the muscling of the shoulder matching that of the rump. If bones—such as the ridge of the shoulder, withers, backbone or rump—start to stand out, the horse is not in good body condition; the horse may have poor feed intake, internal parasites, or some systemic problem. If one horse in a herd is in poor condition and the others look great, that

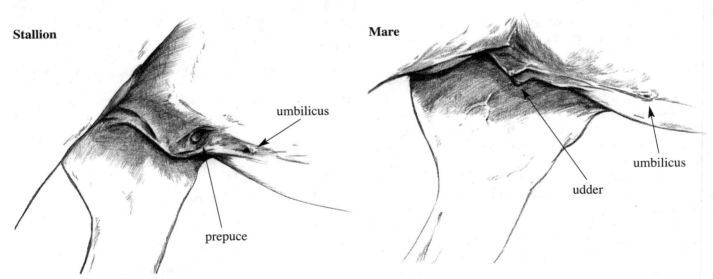

Stallion

umbilicus

prepuce

Mare

umbilicus

udder

A horse has a small lump on the midline of the bottom of the abdomen, just in front of the udder or prepuce. This lump is the umbilicus, similar to a human's navel or belly button, and should not be mistaken for a tumor or skin reaction.

Photo by Debby Peterson

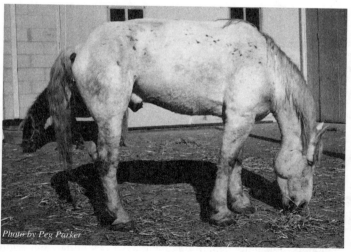

Photo by Peg Parker

The muscles of a healthy draft horse (left) are full and rounded; if bones stand out at the shoulder, withers, backbone or rump (right) the horse is not in good body condition.

horse may be a hard keeper or may be at the bottom of the pecking order. You may need to change feeding practices so it can get enough feed. If you are thinking of buying a poorly conditioned horse that is among healthier horses, don't assume it has been mistreated. It could have a health problem.

Gauging Changes

Unless you regularly lay-on hands, weight loss may be hard to detect during winter when the horse sports a heavy coat. A horse may lose 100 pounds or more before the weight loss becomes obvious to the eye. None of the measuring tapes designed to estimate a horse's weight fit around a full-sized draft horse. If you have a tape that fits your smaller draft or draft pony, it will underestimate your horse's weight.

You might design your own measuring tape, use the accompanying formula for estimating weight, or make a point of remembering which hole the harness girth buckles to. Even if you don't know your horse's exact weight, using a tape or harness as your guide will let you know when weight has been gained or lost around the girth.

Loss of muscling is a more difficult determination than weight loss, as it may occur slowly and be neither obvious to the eye nor detectable by a girth measure. Your best indication of changes in muscle mass is to notice any dramatic differences in the fit of the collar and harness.

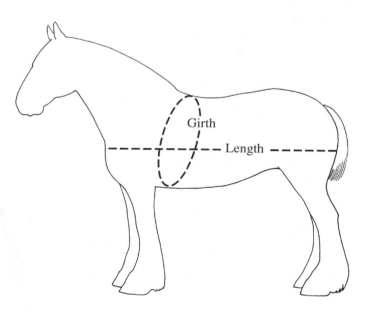

You can estimate your horse's weight in pounds by measuring its girth and length in inches, then multiplying girth x girth x length and dividing the result by 330.

What Goes in Should Come out

The horse has a long gastrointestinal tract with a large volume. The small intestine of a large draft horse is about 90 feet long and the large intestine is about 27 feet long. The stomach itself, which is unusually small for such a large animal, does not expand much and therefore cannot hold high volumes of concentrated feeds. A 2,000-pound draft horse's stomach may hold only four to five gallons of digesting material.

The kidneys filter out many potentially dangerous breakdown products of digestion and drug metabolism. The kidneys are, in addition, the primary organs responsible for maintaining normal fluid and electrolyte balance.

You can learn a lot about the health of your horse's gastrointestinal and urinary systems by keeping a close eye on what goes in and what comes out.

Digestion Basics

Digestion starts in the mouth with the breakdown of food by salivary enzymes. Food passes rapidly from the mouth to the stomach, through a tube called the esophagus. The esophagus lies in a groove on the lower left side of the neck, along with the jugular vein and carotid artery. The esophagus is often visible as swallowed food or water passes through it, but may be hard to see in a thick-necked draft horse.

Digestion continues in the stomach. No nutrients are absorbed into the bloodstream until the food gets to the intestinal tract, which has many loops and is supplied by a large number of blood vessels in the intestinal lining. In the small intestine the more easily digested nutrients are absorbed into the blood

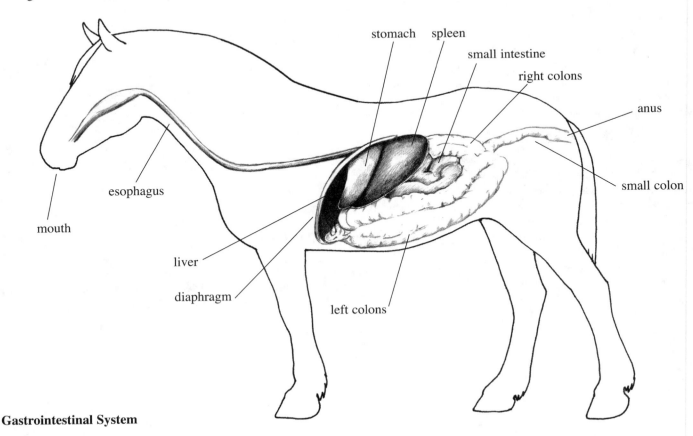

Gastrointestinal System

stream. The fiber, mixed with water, is not broken down until it reaches the bacteria and other microorganisms in the large intestine, which is designed to break down the cellulose of forages for energy.

The large intestine starts on the right side with a blind-ended sac called the cecum and continues with two U-shaped loops of large colon that occupy much of the space in the horse's abdomen. The volume of the cecum and large colons is tremendous. The large colon ends in the small colon, where water is absorbed and fecal balls are formed.

The abdomen is nearly filled by the large colon and the cecum; the small intestine, small colon, and other anatomical parts are squeezed in between. Movements of ingested feed are well regulated to allow the maximum breakdown of digestive material and the absorption of nutrients and water. As you can imagine, feed takes a long time to move through this complicated system. Some feeds take one to two days to traverse the system, depending on the feed's type and amount.

Monitoring Manure

An important part of evaluating the health of your horse's gastrointestinal system is evaluating what comes out. Manure should be passed regularly, without undue strain, and should be moist but well formed. A horse normally passes manure 6 to 12 times per day, depending on the type and amount of feed. A draft horse may produce up to 50 pounds or more of manure each day.

The absorption cycle is sometimes shortened in a nervous horse, allowing moist or liquid manure to pass. Unfortunately for the farrier, a horse often gets nervous when its hind feet are worked on. Soft manure may also occur after a change in feed, such as when a horse is first put on grass, in which case the manure will be quite green. A day or two of soft manure is usually not a problem, provided the horse otherwise maintains its normal alert attitude, good appetite, hydration, temperature, and rates of pulse and respiration.

If the manure contains whole grains, a qualified individual (veterinarian or equine dentist) should check the condition of the teeth. You may need to switch to a feed that requires less vigorous chewing. If you see a lot of sand in your horse's manure, feed off the ground or in a different area to keep your horse from developing sand colic.

Horses may pass immature forms of intestinal parasites that are not visible to the naked eye, but after you have wormed a heavily parasitized horse you may see bots and adult worms in the manure. Although a horse with tapeworms may pass segments of worms that are visible in the manure, never seeing these segments does not necessarily mean your horse does not have tapeworms.

If diarrhea occurs and persists for several days or more, or the diarrhea is accompanied by increased body temperature, pulse, or respiration or a decreased intake of food or water, get your veterinarian to evaluate the horse, and possibly the manure, for parasites, bacteria or other intestinal problems. Sometimes the

problem is solved just by changing to feed that includes plenty of quality fiber.

A horse with watery or foul-smelling diarrhea should be immediately examined by a veterinarian. Various bacteria, including salmonella and clostridia, cause life-threatening intestinal infections requiring intensive medical care. Diarrhea in individual horses may be caused by a reaction to drugs, including phenylbutazone (bute) and some antibiotics. Potomac horse fever causes systemic illness and diarrhea, which often is not fatal if treated early and aggressively.

Colic

Colic is the most common and severe gastrointestinal problem. It involves gastrointestinal pain due to spasm, obstruction, displacement, distention or other problem with the viscera. A horse with colic shows obvious signs of discomfort, goes off feed, often paws or shifts weight from limb to limb, may sweat profusely, may turn its head as if to look at its flanks and may kick at its abdomen. A horse with severe colic pain may go down and roll violently.

A horse can't tell you what hurts. The signs of distress that accompany gastrointestinal pain are similar to those accompanying the sudden onset of muscle pain or muscle weakness. If you find your horse with these signs of distress, call your veterinarian immediately. While waiting for the vet's arrival, carefully evaluate the horse for what is going in and what is coming out. If the horse still passes manure and eats hay, even if not in normal amounts, the distress may not be gastrointestinal.

Monitor the horse's pulse and respiration. A horse experiencing any pain or distress often has a slightly increased heart rate, up to about 60 beats per minute.

A high heart rate accompanied by a purplish color of the gums and conjunctiva (mucus membranes) indicates severe toxic changes in the horse's system and constitutes an emergency.

Be particularly concerned about a horse that was showing violent pain but suddenly relaxes and is more comfortable. A sudden end to violent pain could be a good sign, but in some instances could indicate a rupture of an impacted and extremely painful organ, such as the stomach. Such a rupture only temporarily decreases pain, and the resulting infection in the abdomen is almost always fatal.

A horse with an intestinal blockage has few or no abdominal sounds and should be examined immediately. Your veterinarian will use the parameters of pulse, respiration, temperature, intestinal sounds and mucous membrane color to evaluate the horse's status. Your veterinarian will also evaluate capillary refill time—a crude measure of blood circulation, which may be decreased due to shock or reduced blood pressure. Capillary refill time is evaluated by pressing the gums and observing how long the pink color takes to return to that area; up to two seconds is considered normal. Passing a stomach tube, doing a rectal examination, and tapping the abdomen with a needle to evaluate abdominal fluid are other methods the veterinarian may use to determine the nature of the problem, where it is, and how bad it is.

The gums turn pale when pressed; in a normal horse the pink color will return within two seconds.

Gut Sounds

An important part of evaluating the gastrointestinal system is listening for sounds. You can hear some of these sounds with your ear to the horse's side. You may hear distant gastrointestinal sounds while listening to the horse's heart. If you listen with a stethoscope over the flanks and sides of a normal horse you will hear a cacophony of squeaks, rumbles and gurgles, collectively called borborygmi, which is Greek for "rumbling in the bowels."

Belching

The passage of gas through the esophagus to the mouth (burping or belching) is uncommon in horses and may be a sign of a stomach ulcer. In one case we saw, a Clydesdale had distinct burping, in addition to poor appetite and mild depression. We found no gastric ulcer or other obvious problem in the abdomen. The horse eventually perked up following a change to a pelleted feed with added vegetable oil. The relationship of the diet change to the burping in this horse in unclear, but does reinforce the concept that the right diet is important for each horse.

Passing Gas

A subject that doesn't gets much mention, but that every horse owner knows about, is the passage of gas, commonly known as farting. An old saying about draft horses (and teamsters) goes, "A farting horse will never tire; a farting man's the man to hire." We're not sure about the human aspects of this expression, but it is true that healthy horses regularly pass gas.

Diet affects the amount of gas produced. Poor quality roughage contains large amounts of fermentable substances and may cause increased gas production. Following a feed change, a horse's production of intestinal gas may change until the intestinal microorganisms adjust to the new feed. The gas produced by the fermentation of fiber in the horse's intestines needs to pass or the horse will have gas colic.

The gas passed by healthy horses may emerge relatively quietly or with a loud noise. The loudest eruptions may occur during exertion such as bucking and jumping or during the deep coughs of a horse with allergic bronchitis or heaves. Although the amount and nature of this farting varies from horse to horse, the regular passage of gas is indicative of a healthy bowel. Some horses pass gas more often and louder than others—that's just the way they are.

Gelding Sounds

A sound heard only in male horses, most often while trotting, seems to come from the abdomen. It is a low-pitched squeak or groan that occurs in rhythm with the horse's trot. It seems to be more common in geldings, but may also occur in stallions. We have heard several explanations for this sound.

At one time it was thought to occur in the intestine, possibly the cecum, but that would not explain why only males make the sound. Another explanation is that the sound is caused by the horse's thighs rubbing together, since this sound is common in geldings and geldings are said to have fatter thighs than other horses. We have trouble with this one, as we don't believe the thighs of geldings are fatter than those of mares. Yet another explanation is that this sound is emitted by the horse's penis moving up and down in the sheath, which doesn't explain why it is more common in geldings than in stallions.

A veterinarian finally solved this small mystery to our satisfaction: The sound is caused by air moving through the inguinal canal. This area is nearly empty following the removal of the testes during the process of gelding, and a stallion's testicles move up and down somewhat, leaving room in the inguinal canal for air. This explanation makes sense and fits all the facts.

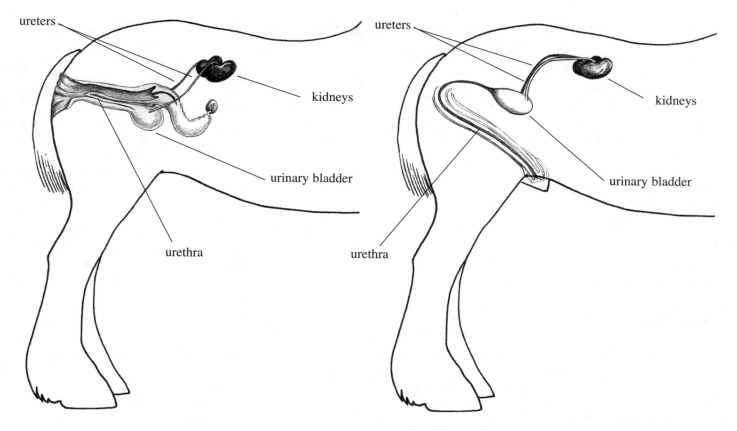

Urinary System of the Mare

Urinary System of the Stallion or Gelding

Urine

Evaluation of urine volume and frequency of urination is difficult, especially if the horse is on pasture. Normal daily urine output varies somewhat, but is generally no more than four gallons per day. If the horse is kept in a stall, you may be able to detect increased volume from the wetness of the bedding. Increased water intake will accompany increased urine production. Increased volume of drinking and urinating not associated with heavy work or hot weather commonly indicate either a problem with the kidneys or a pituitary tumor.

Occasionally a horse gorges on salt, which results in increased drinking and urinating. For such a horse, replace free-choice salt with small volumes of salt mixed with the feed. Horses that consume salt to excess are rare, and determining how much salt any horse needs is difficult. Err on the side of too much salt and make plenty of water available.

Some horses, particularly young horses, develop a drinking problem if they are bored or stressed. The excess water they drink can cause washout of the parts of the kidney that would normally reabsorb water from urine. These horses continue to drink and urinate large volumes. Careful water restriction under veterinary supervision will correct the problem.

Urine Color

The normal color of equine urine varies with its degree of concentration. Horse urine should be a pale to dark yellow, or occasionally light tan. Numerous crystals in equine urine give it a slightly cloudy appearance, especially toward the end of the stream.

Reddish Urine

Some urine, when exposed to sunlight, turns red-orange to bright red, which may be mistaken for blood or muscle pigments in the urine. This orange or red urine is most visible when the urine pools in snow. Stall bedding may become discolored if urine is allowed to stand and the stall is open to sunlight. This poorly understood but normal phenomenon is caused by compounds called pyrocatechins (pronounced pie-row-CAT-eh-kins) that some horses pass in their urine. These compounds may relate to the level of adrenal hormones (catecholamines) passed in the urine.

Urine that is discolored at the time of passage, rather than after it pools on the ground, is cause for concern. Urine that is bright red or port-wine colored may be a sign of bleeding from the kidneys, bladder, or urethra. It may also be caused by either red blood cell breakdown products (hemoglobin) resulting in hemoglobinuria or pigmented protein (myoglobin) released into the blood from damaged muscle resulting in myoglobinuria. Although these pigments are filtered out of the blood by the kidneys, their presence may result in severe injury to the kidney cells. A bright red color that occurs at the end of urination may indicate bleeding caused by bladder or kidney stones. Any of these conditions necessitate careful examination by your veterinarian and should never be ignored as something that will pass (no pun intended).

```
hemoglobinuria, myoglobinuria
   hemo   = blood
   myo    = muscle
   globin = protein
   uria   = urine
```

Black Urine

Black pigments in the urine of a gray horse generally indicate that melanomas are present somewhere within the urinary system, which may be either internal or external, for example around the urethra of a stallion or gelding. Provided urine is still passing easily, melanomas do not constitute an emergency situation. Unfortunately we do not have a good treatment for these tumors in older gray horses, but examination by a veterinarian to determine if any of these tumors may be removed is in order.

Stream Quality

The urine stream should pass easily without excessive showering of adjacent skin. If the horse appears to have problems urinating, is straining, or is unable to pass a good stream of urine, an examination for blockages should be done by a veterinarian as soon as possible. Possible causes of interference with a horse passing a steady urine stream are:
- infection or swelling of the sheath,
- inflammation of the tail end of the spinal cord (neuritis of the cauda equina),
- growth of tumors such as squamous cell carcinoma or melanoma,
- nerve damage from sorghum toxicity,
- obstruction by stones.

Urine that does not pass in a strong, steady stream may dribble down the horse's legs. Constant exposure of the skin to urine results in severe irritation called urine scald. Although urine scald may be treated with the frequent application of petroleum jelly or Desitin (sold for diaper rash), it is always important to try to find the cause and, if possible, correct it.

Kidney and Bladder Stones

Kidney and bladder stones are not terribly common in horses, draft or otherwise, but they do occur. Stones in the urinary system may result in blood in the urine, either periodically or all the time. Take the opportunity to carefully observe your horse's urine flow and color whenever it presents.

Diet does not seem to be a factor in the formation of stones in a horse's urinary system. Stones may form in either the kidney or bladder following infection or other damage to the tissue of these two organs. Traumatic damage may occur during passage of a urinary catheter used to relieve an obstruction or to obtain a sample of urine, or following surgical repair of some damaged part of the urinary system. Certain medications, including phenylbutazone (bute), may cause damage to tissue of the kidneys, and the damaged tissue may mineralize to form a stone. Stones may form in horses of any age, but must become fairly large before they cause problems, so are more commonly found in adult horses.

The word urolith refers to a stone anywhere in the urinary system. Stones in the urinary bladder are called cystoliths or urinary calculi. Stones in the kidneys are nephroliths. Stones in the ureter—the tube from the kidney to the bladder—are ureteroliths.

```
cystolith, nephrolith, ureterolith, urolith
   cysto     = pertaining to the
               urinary bladder
   nephro    = kidney
   uretero   = ureter
   uro       = pertaining to the
               urinary system
   lith      = stone

cystic calculi
   cystic  = bladder
   calculi = mineralized concretions (stones)
```

Stones within the urinary system are more of a problem in stallions and geldings than in mares, as stones have more difficulty passing through the male's longer, narrower urethra. Large stones occurring within the urinary bladder may not appear to bother the horse. The only indication that a stone is present may be the appearance of blood at the end of the urine stream. Of course having a large stone in the bladder cannot be comfortable for the horse, and may predispose the horse to developing infections due to the constant rubbing of the stone against the bladder lining.

Uroliths may be successfully treated with either surgery or the use of devices designed to break up larger stones so the smaller fragments can pass on their own.

Analyzing Movement

The old saying "a horse is only as good as its legs" is a wise one. For centuries humans have depended on the horse for transportation and work. If a horse cannot move well, it is of little use for the purpose for which it has always been intended.

Gait

Gait analysis is critical to an evaluation for possible lameness, as well as for detection of incoordination caused by spinal cord disease. A horse that is in pain because of lameness alters its gait to try to take weight off the painful limb. Gait analysis is used to judge the overall quality of a horse and is particularly important for show and hitch horses.

Reflexes that are controlled through the spinal cord regulate a horse's movements to keep its gait smooth and fluid. Length of stride and action vary among horses and may be influenced by conformation, but may also be affected by problems in the nerves, muscles or spinal cord.

A horse should appear to always know where its feet are.

The gaits of many drafts and draft crosses, like this Belgian-Thoroughbred, are ideally suited to dressage training.

Photo by Barry Cooper

Lameness Tests

A lame horse limps with its head—the head drops or nods when the opposite normal leg bears weight, and the head is thrown up when the painful leg is down. This behavior is an attempt to take some weight off the lame leg to reduce the pain.

Although a horse that is in severe pain may be obviously lame at the walk and may hold the painful leg off the ground while standing, the head limp behavior (called head nod) is most readily apparent at the trot. A lameness evaluation therefore usually involves trotting the horse in a straight line on a loose lead on a flat, smooth surface.

Some drafts, especially working drafts, are not accustomed to trotting in hand, which can make a lameness examination difficult. For this reason alone, train your draft horse to trot on a loose lead line. Having someone behind to urge the horse on by clapping or clucking may help. A nod down when the right front and left rear leg are on the ground indicates lameness in either the left front or the right rear leg.

Flexion Test

With the exception of Standardbreds the majority of equine lamenesses, including those in draft horses, involves front legs. Lameness commonly involves the lower joints or hoof. Most lameness examinations start with hoof testers—pincers that look for areas of sensitivity indicative of pain in the hoof—and checking for heat in the hoof. The examination also includes feeling for heat or swelling in the pastern, fetlock, tendons, splint bone areas, knee or hock and elbow or stifle. The joints may be flexed to look for evidence of pain or decreased range of motion.

anesthetic	
an	= lack of
esthesia	= sensation

The flexion test involves holding the leg up with the suspect joint bent tightly (flexed) for a minute or so. This maneuver may be difficult to perform in a draft horse that is not willing to stand on three legs. The horse is then trotted to check for exaggeration of the lameness that might indicate pain in the joint that was flexed. If necessary the veterinarian will block nerves or joints with injections of short-acting local anesthetic to see if the pain is diminished or eliminated.

Effects of EPSM

In checking for lameness, make sure you are not looking at the early signs of muscle and joint stiffness caused by equine polysaccharide storage myopathy (EPSM). Consider EPSM if the horse is reluctant to back, sinks down in the rear while backing, has an occasional hitch in the hind stride or waddles in the rear like a duck or goose. EPSM has been seen, too, in drafts with a peculiar backing action in which the hind leg swings back from the hip, the hoof is placed on the ground, and the hock and stifle snap down into position in an action resembling Michael Jackson's moon walking.

Other conditions that cause gait abnormalities include shivers, stringhalt, and fibrotic myopathy.

Incoordination

Damage to the spinal cord affects limb reflexes. Since we cannot tap a horse's stifle with a hammer or pick the horse up to evaluate limb placement, as we can with a cat or dog, gait analysis is the key to detecting equine spinal cord disease. The gait is evaluated at the walk, during tight turns, and while backing.

Severe incoordination may appear as weakness. Pulling the tail to the side may cause an affected horse to swing its rump toward the pull, instead of resisting it. Since a positive tail pull may also be caused by weakness from nerve or muscle disease, it must not be used alone to diagnose spinal cord disease.

A critical part of diagnosing spinal cord disease is evaluating how the horse places its limbs. A horse with spinal cord disease cannot control the carefully timed placement and lifting of its feet, and may show a delay in lifting its feet off the ground, which may be followed by overcompensation in the form of widely swinging the limbs. These problems are more obvious in the hind limbs than in front, especially when the horse is turned in a tight circle around the handler, which forces the animal to pick up its feet quickly and put them down underneath itself to accomplish the tight turns.

Exaggerating action

Different kinds of training and shoeing are designed to exaggerate action. Any attempt to change the natural action of a horse by means other than proper hoof care, conditioning and health will, in the long run, do more harm than good.

A horse with severe incoordination will have an uncontrolled body sway when turned, may occasionally cross its limbs and may be in danger of falling. Subtle problems that could be caused by spinal cord, nerve, muscle or joint disease are difficult to distinguish from one another, and you may need a

veterinarian with specialized expertise to diagnose the problem. Videotaping your horse's gait will allow you and your veterinarian to analyze the gait during playback. The video may be sent to distant consultants for analysis and comment.

Action

As with many subjects related to horses, opinions differ about equine conformation and how it relates to a horse's movement. A normal, well-built and sound horse swings its shoulders and hips freely and symmetrically. The hind limb gait has a long stride at the walk, with the hind foot extending into or forward of the mark left by the corresponding front hoof. Stride length is easily seen while walking the horse on a soft, moist surface. The hock joints should show a smooth and obvious bend (flexion). The degree of bend of the different leg joints varies among breeds and individual horses, and determines the horse's natural action.

Stiffness in the muscles or joints is often pronounced in the rear limbs, which have a unique link between the hock and stifle called the reciprocal apparatus. You cannot bend a horse's hock without also bending the stifle, even after the horse has died, because these joints are linked by tendons, ligaments and muscles.

A horse that swings the hind leg from the hip with little or no bend in the hock or stifle may have an exaggerated flip of the hind foot. This subtly abnormal gait may resemble a duck or goose waddle. This waddling gait may be due to damage in the hock or stifle joint, but may also be caused by muscle stiffness due to EPSM, especially in a draft.

The degree of bend of the different leg joints has determined the natural action of this pair of Hackney-Clydesdale crosses.
Photo by Susan Greenall

Stumbling

Horses stumble mostly on their front feet. Stumbling may be readily resolved if it is due to something simple like overgrown feet, poor trimming and shoeing, or lack of condition. Draft horses that get lazy may stumble on rough terrain simply because their feet are large and they don't pick them up high enough.

If your draft horse is in regular work and continues to stumble, or if the horse stumbles so badly that it falls to its knees, have it evaluated for possible spinal cord or muscle disease. In a draft that is otherwise not obviously uncoordinated, stumbling is more likely to be due to EPSM than to spinal cord disease.

Resting

The horse has evolved a mechanism called the stay apparatus that allows it to doze standing up. The horse has three separate tendons in the stifle joint, the middle, medial (inside) and lateral (outside) ligaments, that allow the kneecap (patella) of a hind leg to slide into a resting position on the femur (the bone from the hip to the stifle), effectively locking the patella into position.

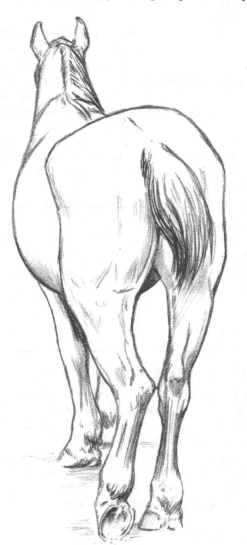

The stay apparatus allows a horse to stand for long periods with minimal muscular effort.

With the stifle stabilized, the actions of the reciprocal apparatus mean the hock is also stabilized, letting the horse stand for long periods with minimal muscular effort. You can see this stay apparatus in action in a horse standing at rest: one hip is higher than the other and the leg with the lower hip is resting on the toe while the other hind leg holds up most of the weight.

You can feel the changing position of the kneecap by placing your hand on the front and a little toward the inside of the stifle joint of the leg your horse is standing on. Push the horse over so he stands on the leg he had been resting, and the kneecap will move out of its resting position back into the position that allows the joint to bend. In the resting leg you should be able to feel at least two of the three patellar ligaments. Take care, though, as some horses are sensitive about having their stifles palpated.

Lying Down

Individual horses vary in the time they spend lying down. Some horses go for weeks at a time without lying down, whereas others lie down for a while everyday. As long as the choice is left to the individual, standing for long periods may be normal for that particular horse.

If a horse is confined where it is unable to lie down, it may lack the period of sleep known as rapid eye movement (REM) during which dreams occur. Although no one knows for sure if horses have dreams, it is known that a horse deprived of REM sleep may periodically collapse to its knees. This occurrence, documented in studies by Dr. Katharine Houpt at Cornell University, indicates that horses should have the opportunity to lie down if they so choose. A horse that either lies down more than usual or doesn't seem to ever lie down may have a problem.

Getting Up

Unlike cattle, which stand in the rear first, horses prop their front legs in front of them, then rise from the rear. To stand, a large heavy horse requires a tremendous muscular effort in the thighs and back. Difficulty rising may be caused by muscular weakness or painful injuries in the joints of the back or legs. A horse that has trouble standing back up may be reluctant to lie down. A weak horse may be reluctant to lie down for fear of getting into trouble upon rising.

A horse with equine motor neuron disease has profound weakness of the postural muscles and therefore prefers to lie down rather than stand. Such a horse generally has no difficulty rising. Constant or frequent lying down may also be caused by painful feet (perhaps due to founder), painful joints or overall weakness from illness, poor nutrition or EPSM.

Carefully observe your draft horse for frequent lying down and be especially observant of how the horse places its limbs in order to rise. You may need to help the horse place its limbs

In contrast to cattle, which rise from the rear first, horses stand up front first.

properly if the horse falls or becomes trapped in a position where it cannot get its rear legs under itself or prop its front legs for support.

Rolling

As with lying down, some horses roll more frequently than others. All horses want to roll at some time; if not, something is wrong. Rolling is a way of grooming during shedding season and of scratching areas—such as the crest, withers and top of the back

A normal horse enjoys an occasional roll.

Photo by Debby Peterson

and rump—that are difficult to scratch any other way. Rolling in mud helps protect the horse from flies and provides insulation against cold or hot weather. A horse that never rolls may have problems similar to those of a horse that never lies down.

Some people believe that a horse capable of rolling from one side to the other is worth more than a horse that can't. Although a horse that is stiff from side to side and has difficulty bending its back is less likely to be capable of a full rollover, don't use rolling as a major criterion of value.

Sudden Collapse

Sudden collapse is a well-known problem in Quarter horses with hyperkalemic periodic paralysis (HYPP). These horses have a genetic defect affecting sodium ion transport in their muscle cells. Collapse is often associated with increased blood levels of potassium (hyperkalemia). All HYPP horses are related to the Quarter horse stallion Impressive. Affected horses need only have one affected parent to have HYPP. So, although we have never heard of a case, it is possible that a draft bred to an affected Impressive-line Quarter horse could have an HYPP foal.

Narcolepsy is a sleep disorder in which affected individuals periodically fall asleep and collapse. This condition occurs in horses and ponies as well as in people and dogs. Although we haven't seen it ourselves, narcolepsy is supposedly an inherited problem in Suffolks. Affected individuals have no problem standing up again and are normal between episodes. Fortunately medical therapies are available. If you have a draft with narcolepsy, we would love to see a video.

---

hyperkalemia
  hyper = increase
  kal   = potassium
  emia = blood

narcolepsy
  narco = numbness
  lepsy = seizure

Unable to Rise

A horse that is unable to rise has a far more serious problem than a horse that does not get its REM sleep. A horse that is unable to rise is the nightmare of any veterinarian involved in general anesthesia and surgery on draft horses, as well as of the draft horse owner who comes home to find a horse down. Inability to rise is far too common in drafts. A 2,000 pound draft horse needs quite a bit of strength to stand up and any weakness, pain or incoordination may result in a down horse.

Getting the Horse Up

A horse may jam itself against a wall or fence and not be able to position its front and hind legs properly to allow it to rise. This predicament is referred to as being cast. Pulling or rolling the horse into the open using ropes and/or heavy equipment may help a cast horse get up. The horse may require help placing its forelegs in front of it with the hind legs bent underneath. Take extreme care when working around a down horse because a sudden fit of struggling and thrashing could result in severe injuries to anyone in the way.

If the horse is in a reasonable position to rise, but is still unable to stand, a little encouragement with voice and hands may help. Harassing such a horse with whips and prods is more likely to cause exhaustion than the desired result. If the horse can prop up on the front legs, but cannot rise in the rear, the horse needs assistance. The help of a veterinarian may be invaluable.

A sturdy sling placed under the horse's belly may help if a strong supporting beam or branch above is available to which to fasten it. Ropes or a sling attached to a front-end loader or other heavy lifting equipment may help. Some folks have used a team of horses to get a down draft horse up. A horse may be lifted using a rope tied securely to the tail (but don't try this with a bovine or you may break the tail off).

Once the horse has been helped to its feet, it may seem fine or it may try to go down again. The horse could be exhausted from struggling after being cast or trapped under a fence. If so, continued support from a sling or several hay or straw bales under the horse's belly may help it recover. Horses with spinal cord disease may go down due to severe incoordination. If the horse's weakness and inability to rise has no apparent cause, the down horse could be in serious trouble.

Underlying Cause

The most common underlying reason a draft goes down—whether it occurs out of the blue, after anesthesia, after foaling, after shipping, after strenuous exercise or in association with dark red or red-brown urine (the hallmark of Monday morning disease)—is the muscle problems that occur with EPSM. Even if EPSM is the underlying problem, however, studies have not revealed what exactly pushes the horse into going down.

We have traced an "outbreak" of down drafts to changes in their feed, in which additional corn was used to compensate for low quality hay. Low selenium may or may not affect the incidence of EPSM horses going down. Several EPSM drafts we have seen repeatedly went down, but could stand and stay up for varying amounts of time following

assistance. Without dietary treatment, and sometimes even with dietary treatment, such severely affected horses eventually go down for good.

The most common underlying cause of down drafts is EPSM

Going down because of muscle cramps, pain and the damage of tying up may look like colic. These signs in an EPSM draft indicate a severe problem in muscle function, even if the horse looks normal while standing and may be capable of light work.

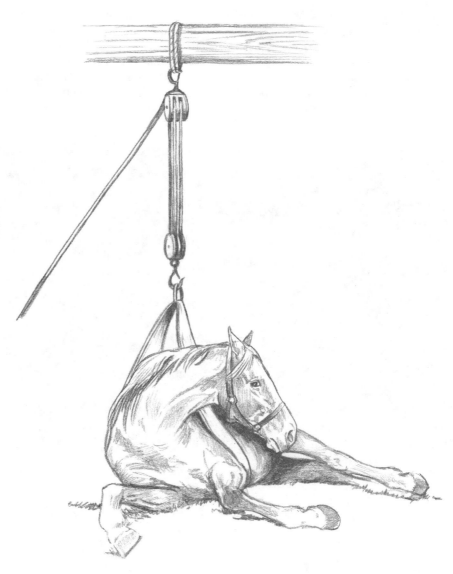

If the horse is in a position to rise but can't get up, it may be lifted using a sturdy sling attached to a strong beam or branch.

Survival Tactics

If your horse goes down for any reason, and you are not able to help it stand, you and your veterinarian can at least improve its chance of survival by using the following suggestions:

● Pad the surface where the horse is lying with plenty of straw or other bedding. If the horse does not panic when rolled from side to side, pad one side and then the other.

● If the horse is on its side (lateral recumbency), roll the horse regularly to help prevent pressure injury to muscle and pressure sores in the skin.

● If the horse can lift itself into a sternal position (lying with the bottom of its chest on the ground and its legs tucked underneath), use hay or straw bales to prop it in that position so the horse can breath more easily, as well as eat and drink while in sternal recumbency.

● If the horse is eating and drinking, provide plenty of fresh water and good quality hay. If you have any suspicion that the horse might have EPSM, feeding or intravenous administration of fat may provide enough energy for the horse to stand within a day or two. Up to 4 cups, or even more, of vegetable oil per day may be administered by stomach tube, dose syringe or turkey baster. Intravenous fat solutions may be obtained from a veterinary or human medical supplier.

● If the horse is drinking little or not at all, intravenous fluids along with electrolytes such as calcium may be necessary.

● If you suspect that pain is contributing to the horse's inability to stand, a pain reliever such as banamine or phenylbutazone (bute) may be helpful.

A horse that appears comfortable may remain down for up to two days as it regains its strength. A horse that is down for longer than two days or a horse that is down and in distress has a poor outlook for survival.

Getting a Load Off

Fortunately most horses that lie down are simply taking a load off or basking in the sun. A draft lying flat out in the pasture may resemble a beached whale. A group of drafts lying flat out is quite a sight to see, although it may cause the owners or their neighbors a moment of concern for the herd's health. A flick of the tail or ears, or a repositioning of the head or legs, will assure you that your "down" horses are just taking a well-earned rest.

Photo by Barry Cooper

Vital Signs

Being able to check your horse's vital signs and knowing what is normal for your horse will help you determine when something is wrong. When something does go wrong, if you are prepared to act as a first-responder by checking and recording your horse's vital signs, the information will help your veterinarian understand what is going on and how serious it may be. Monitoring any changes will help you and your veterinarian know when a horse is recovering from an illness or problem.

Breathing

A horse's respiratory rate is easily counted by watching the flanks move in and out. The rate of an adult horse at rest is usually 12 to 20 breaths per minute. Foals normally breath 20 to 40 breaths per minute. A healthy horse breathes easily and deeply, without sucking up its abdomen.

Breathing Patterns

Each horse has a characteristic pattern of breathing while exercising. With exercise the respiratory rate goes up rapidly, increasing to 100 breaths or more per minute in a galloping horse. Within 30 minutes of ceasing exercise, the breathing rate of a fit horse will decrease nearly to resting level. A horse that is overheated, however, needs to be cooled in order to help bring the respiratory rate back to normal.

A distressed horse takes rapid, shallow breaths and flares its nostrils. Normal breathing is usually not noisy except for the sound of exhaling during exercise, which is most audible during a canter.

Breathing Sounds

A horse with a laryngeal problem—a common condition in the taller draft breeds—cannot tolerate strenuous exercise. When stressed by exercise such a horse produces a unique roaring sound. If the problem is severe, the horse may require surgery to open the laryngeal passage and allow sufficient air movement.

We have noticed a distinctive snort in draft horses, particularly when something makes them nervous. We call this sound the Belgian blow, but admit that it may not be confined to Belgians.

Coughing may mean the horse has an allergy or infection such as allergic bronchitis or pneumonia. Short sporadic coughs occurring while the horse is feeding may indicate that the horse has briefly inhaled a bit of food or dust.

bronchitis	
bronch	= bronchi and bronchioles, the airways of the lungs
itis	= inflammation

Heart Rate

The resting heart rate of a healthy adult horse is normally between about 30 and 45 beats per minute. Count the heartbeats for 10, 15 or 30 seconds and multiply by 6, 4 or 2 to get the heart rate. The resting heart rate of large draft horses is often in the lower end of the range; the resting heart rate of light horses is often in the higher end. The resting heart rate of well-conditioned horses is lower than that of unfit horses. Foals normally have a higher heart rate than adult horses, about 70 to 100 beats per minute.

Draft Horse Vital Signs	
Sign	*Normal Range*
Temperature	
newborn foal	99-102°F
adult draft	99-101°F
Respiration	
foal at rest	20-40 breaths/minute
adult at rest	12-20 breaths/minute
adult at gallop	60-100 breaths/minute
Heart rate	
foal at rest	70-100 beats/minute
adult at rest	30-45 beats/minute
adult at gallop	200+ beats/minute

A horse's heart is large and has the ability to pump huge volumes of blood during exercise. With exercise the heart rate may increase to 200 or more beats per minute. The heart rate of a well-conditioned horse decreases rapidly after exercise and should return to normal within 30 minutes. A good way to evaluate your horse's fitness is to check its heart rate at rest and again 30 minutes after exercise, parameters that are part of evaluating horses competing in trail riding and endurance.

Checking Heart Rate

The only practical way to determine a horse's heart rate is to use a stethoscope and listen to the heart. You may purchase a stethoscope from a medical supply dealer or pharmacy, or through an equine supply catalog.

Seek a quiet area for listening. The heart is easier to hear on the left side, just behind the point of the elbow. Move the stethoscope around to find the spot where the heart sounds are loudest, listening in each spot for several seconds before trying another.

Heart Sounds

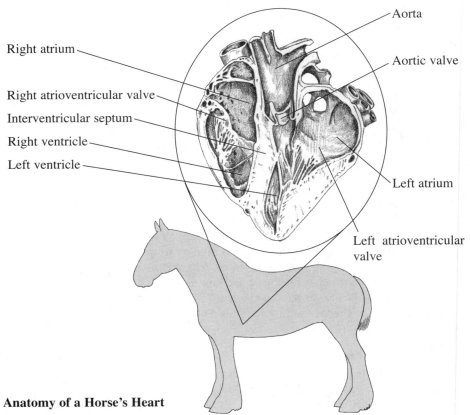

Right atrium

Right atrioventricular valve

Interventricular septum

Right ventricle

Left ventricle

Aorta

Aortic valve

Left atrium

Left atrioventricular valve

Anatomy of a Horse's Heart

As in all mammals, the heartbeat of a horse makes two distinct sounds, the "lub-dub" of the valves as blood moves from the atria to the ventricles and from the ventricles to the arteries. Occasionally a normal horse has a third

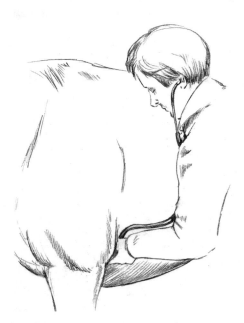

To hear the characteristic heart sounds, place a stethoscope on the left chest wall behind the elbow and look for the spot where the sounds are loudest.

heart sound: "lub-dub-dub." Because the draft horse has a thick chest wall, these sounds may be muffled. You're likely to hear some breathing and gastrointestinal sounds, as well.

A normal horse, especially a fit horse, may have a slightly irregular heart rate that slows down when the horse inhales and speeds up when the horse exhales. This irregular rhythm, called sinus arrhythmia, is common in people and dogs as well as in horses and is nothing to worry about.

A rapid-fire rate without two distinct sounds could indicate that the atria are beating rapidly and not allowing the ventricles to fill sufficiently with blood. This condition, called atrial fibrillation, appears to be more common in draft horses than in light horses and requires medical attention from a veterinarian.

If you are worried about anything you hear, have your veterinarian check it out. Although heart disease is generally uncommon in horses, some veterinary clinicians feel it may be more common in drafts than in light breeds.

Checking Pulse

The pulse is the wave of increased pressure of blood in the arteries that follows each heart beat. You can feel a horse's pulse on the lower edge of the mandible (lower jaw), where the facial artery is close to the surface. Checking the pulse here can be frustrating because any movement of the horse's head or jaw throws off the count.

Another place where the pulse may be found is at the digital arteries on both sides of the pastern. The digital pulse is easiest to find in horses with laminitis or other infection within the hoof, which markedly increases the pulse's force (bounding pulse) and makes the arteries easier to palpate. If you can't feel your horse's digital pulse, it is likely normal.

The digital artery (marked by white tape) is found on each side of the pastern, toward the back. *Photo by Beth A. Valentine*

Temperature

A horse's normal internal body temperature is maintained at a relatively steady level when the horse is at rest, but horses in the same barn won't necessarily have the same base temperature. It's a good idea to take each horse's temperature at rest on several different days to get an idea of the normal temperature so you can readily determine when it has changed significantly.

Marked increases may occur during heavy exercise, especially in hot, humid weather. Mild increases in temperature may occur when the horse is excited or in pain. Increased temperature for no apparent reason indicates fever, which may be caused by infection, tissue damage, pain, or a combination of factors.

The body temperature of draft horses is not noticeably different from that of light horses. The body temperature of any horse is slightly more variable than a human's, and ranges from 99ºF to 101ºF. A newborn foal's temperature is between 99ºF and 102ºF. Unless a horse shows other signs of problems, we would not get overly excited about a temperature below 102ºF.

Taking Temperature

Some folks are sure they can tell a horse's body temperature by touching the skin. We do not believe this is possible. Monitor your horse's temperature accurately by investing in a large animal rectal thermometer, which comes with a hole at the top to attach a string.

Lubricate the end of the thermometer with petroleum jelly or saliva before inserting it into the rectum. Stand to the horse's side, facing the rear, with one hand on the horse's rump. Gently insert the thermometer with a slight twisting motion to help it slide. Make sure the thermometer is inserted as fully as possible. To keep the thermometer from being lost into the horse's rectum or on the ground, either tie the string to the tail hairs or attach a small alligator clip to the string and clip it to the tail hairs.

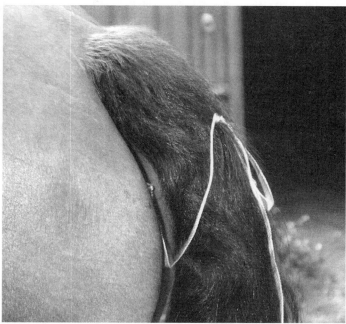

Tie or clip the thermometer to the horse's tail to ensure that the thermometer doesn't get lost in either direction.
Photo by Beth A. Valentine

Cold Horse

If the weather is chilly and the horse is wet, it will lose essential body heat. Muscle trembling creates heat, but also uses essential muscle energy for heat instead of work. Any horse, but especially a draft horse, requires adequate strength to stand and to carry its own weight. A chilled horse needs a warm dry blanket and a warm dry environment until it returns to body-heat balance.

A dry horse with a thick haircoat, adequate roughage to produce internal heat and a place for shelter out of chilling winds will be comfortable even in sub-zero weather without added blankets. Providing heavy blankets during cold weather may, however, decrease the length and thickness of a winter coat, which may be desirable if the horse is being worked or shown in an indoor environment.

Hot Horse

A horse that is hot from exercise is probably sweating and possibly taking rapid, shallow breaths (panting). Sweating and panting are two ways for the horse to try to cool down. The best thing to do is cool the horse with cool, or ice cold, water. Hose or sponge water onto the horse until the water drips off cool. Leaving water on the horse will allow further cooling through evaporation. The idea that cooling a horse too fast can bring on muscle cramps, colic or laminitis is absolutely wrong.

Give the hot horse water to drink. Drinking water helps to cool the horse and replaces fluids lost in sweat. Profuse or prolonged sweating may cause dehydration and an imbalance of electrolytes.

Although some folks believe in giving only a gallon or two of water at a time, we can find no scientific evidence to suggest that letting a horse drink more is dangerous. Allowing a severely dehydrated horse only sips of water, however, may cause problems.

A horse that is severely dehydrated and refuses to drink, even after it has been cooled with water spray, may need to be rehydrated with intravenous fluids administered by a veterinarian.

> *intravenous*
> intra = into
> venous = vein

Sweating

Sweating is the process by which a horse cools itself. The amount of sweat varies depending on heat, humidity, degree of fitness and body mass. A large draft horse has a smaller skin surface-to-muscle mass ratio than a light horse or a small draft such as a Suffolk. This large heat-producing muscle mass sometimes results in difficulty controlling excessive heat during intense exercise.

Carefully watch your horse for attitude and respiration so you can tell when its ability to regulate body temperature is in trouble. If the horse seems overheated, stop working immediately and rapidly cool the horse by hosing or sponging it down until the water running off its body is cool.

A sweating horse loses electrolytes (primarily salts), as well as protein. Protein causes the foaming you see on a horse's skin during heavy exercise or while the horse is being hosed down. Being a little hot under the collar is normal for a horse during heavy exercise. Become concerned if the horse is anxious or reluctant to move, or develops respiratory distress.

Horses that are nervous or in pain may sweat profusely. If you find your horse in a lather while it is standing in the stall or pasture, do not hose or otherwise cool it down. If the horse seems at all distressed or uncomfortable, or does not eat, call your veterinarian immediately—the horse may be in pain from tying up, colic or other serious problem.

Lack of Sweating

Lack of sweating, known as anhidrosis, is a problem that may develop in hot, humid climates. A horse's inability to regulate body temperature through sweat is a serious condition that may mean the end of the horse's athletic career.

> *anhidrosis*
> an = lack of
> hidro = sweat
> osis = condition of

Because of variations in the degree of sweating between horses, you may not notice when sweating is insufficient. The horse may appear to be exercise intolerant or may breathe hard during exercise, suggesting a respiratory problem. With longstanding anhidrosis, the horse may develop a dry, sparse haircoat. The best treatment is to move the horse to a cooler climate, where sweating will likely resume. Since moving a horse to a different climate is not always feasible, ask your veterinarian about new treatments or feed supplements that may be available for this condition.

Localized Sweating

Localized sweating that is not related to an obvious cause for increase in skin temperature (such as areas in contact with tack) and that occurs almost continuously is a curious response to a localized injury to nerves in the skin known as autonomic nerves. These nerves are not under the brain's control but respond to circulating hormones such as the stress hormone adrenaline.

No evidence suggests that letting a hot horse drink will cause colic, founder or other problems.

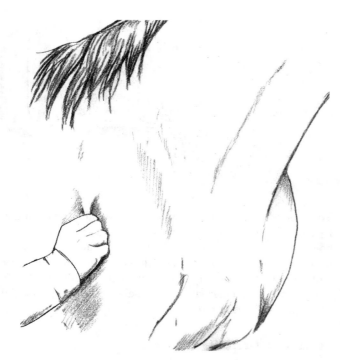

You can judge a horse's hydration status by how long a pinch of skin takes to flatten out when you let go.

An injury to one of the nerves that plays a role in regulating circulation of blood and temperature in the skin will result in a peculiar pattern of sweating in one area. The injury may be from trauma or a previous infection, or may have no obvious cause. Localized sweating is not a serious condition, but makes a dandy conversation starter.

Dehydration

Dehydration means the body tissues do not contain enough water to maintain normal function. Sweating can lead to dehydration, as can the simple lack of sufficient water intake. Sweating and lack of water intake together may lead to severe dehydration. The nervous and gastrointestinal systems are particularly sensitive to malfunctions caused by dehydration.

The easiest test of hydration status in a horse is to take a pinch of neck or shoulder skin between your thumb and forefinger to form a small crease of skin. Let go and see how long the skin takes to flatten out again. Normally hydrated skin snaps back into place quickly, the exact time depending on where you pinch and how much you pinch up. By practicing this check for hydration, you will know what is normal for your horse. If you find a slowed flattening time, your horse is dehydrated and needs water.

This test is insensitive, which means that if you see evidence of dehydration on the pinch test, the dehydration may be approaching a danger zone. A seriously dehydrated horse may need frequent drinks or even intravenous fluids to bring it back to normal hydration.

Awesome Sight

A healthy draft horse in its prime is an awesome sight. We often see folks who are driving along the road stop to watch when they see a draft horse in harness or in a paddock or pasture near the road. If you take a draft or draft cross to a non-draft competition, you'll have lots of comments and questions. Many folks are ignorant about drafts. People can ask the strangest questions, such as "Is that [16.3 hand, 1,600-pound Belgian cross] a Haflinger?" or "Is that a *real* Clydesdale?"

People may suggest that you are asking your carriage horse to work too hard. If you are a carriage operator, or you bring your drafts to any public events, your horses must present the healthiest possible attitude and condition to avoid inviting bad publicity. We believe the public can be educated about draft horses that are just doing their jobs.

Children are usually the first to approach a draft, and even the largest and most energetic draft horses seem to recognize the special qualities of a child. We are often amazed by the gentleness and patience our drafts exhibit toward children.

Photo by Phil Krahn

The Head

A draft horse's head is second only to its well-rounded rump in focusing our attention and eliciting our admiration. Some drafts have more refined heads than others, and people who favor the chiseled features of an Arabian may not fully appreciate an honest draft horse head. Since the horse's head is so visible, problems involving the head and face are often recognized sooner than those involving other parts of the body.

Ears

The part of the ear we can see is called the pinna and is formed primarily by skin over cartilage. A horse's ears are sensitive.

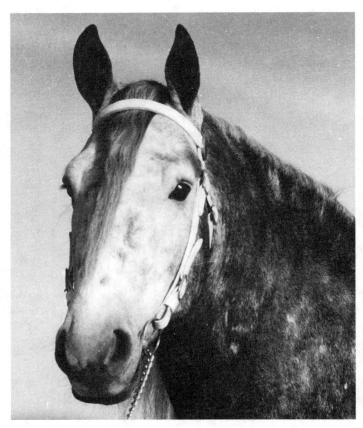

The visible part of the ear, formed by skin over cartilage, tends to be quite sensitive. *Photo by Debby Peterson*

Your horse may be reluctant to let you examine its ears or apply fly repellent, especially if the horse once had someone use an ear hold to keep it still during a painful or frightening experience. Be patient and work quietly and slowly. Eventually your horse will learn not to pull away when you touch its ears. Horses often enjoy having the inner surface of their ears rubbed, especially when flies have been biting.

Aural Plaques

The inner skin surface of the ear may develop slightly raised white growths known as ear (aural) plaques. Although they may look like a fungus growing in the ear, these thickenings of the skin are similar to warts and are caused by a viral infection (papillomavirus). They may affect one or both ears and may be multiple. They never resolve on their own. The only cure is surgical removal.

The virus is most likely carried to the skin by biting flies. The plaques may be annoying to the horse when they first occur, but eventually they stop growing and usually stop being irritating. Ear plaques are unsightly but not dangerous.

Ear Ticks

Ear ticks may be present in or on the ear. Ticks in the ear are irritating, causing the horse to toss its head. Occasionally the presence of ear ticks results in a bizarre rippling of the skin of the horse's neck and body, along with trembling, which resolves once the tick is removed.

A tick on the skin may easily be removed by grasping the tick's body and pulling it out. A horse with a tick deep in the ear may require sedation for tick removal, or the tick may be killed by an insecticidal dip or drops, or by treatment with ivermectin. If persistent irritation occurs where a tick has been feeding, treatment with a topical anti-inflammatory medication such as cortisone and tincture of time should resolve the problem.

External Ear Infections

The skin inside the ear may be slightly rough, especially when bitten by flies. It should be dry with no material building up or spilling out of the base. Any such material may indicate an infection that requires medication. If the infection involves only the outer portion, or external ear (external to the ear drum), it is called otitis externa. A horse with an ear infection may toss its head from the irritation.

otitis externa, media and interna
oto	= ear
itis	= inflammation
externa	= external or outside
media	= middle
interna	= internal or inside

Middle and Inner Ear Infections

Infections of the middle ear (otitis media) and the inner ear (otitis interna) often occur together. Discharge of infected material from the outer ear may not be obvious. The horse may suddenly start tilting its head to one side or may shake its head. Because of the danger of permanent damage to the middle or inner ear, the horse should be examined immediately. Infections of the inner ear can cause the horse to lose its balance and fall to one side.

Nerves to the face are close to the middle and inner parts of the ear. They may be damaged by infection, which may cause paralysis of one side of the face (facial palsy). Such an infection must be controlled with systemic antibiotics. Fortunately ear infections are not nearly as common in horses as they are in cats, dogs, and children.

Guttural Pouches

The horse has a unique structure on each side of its head called the guttural pouch, which is an expanded pouch off the tube leading from the middle ear to the throat. The function of these two pouches is unknown. They may have developed to create a large airspace to decrease the weight of the horse's head. A recent theory suggests that air flow through the pouches during exercise helps cool the blood flowing to the brain through the internal carotid artery.

Distention

Two conditions commonly affect the guttural pouches. One is distention by air occurring in foals, in which an abnormality causes air to be trapped in the pouches. The

affected foal has pouching out of the jowls, similar to a hamster or chipmunk with a mouth full of food. Treatment involves a simple surgical procedure to correct the anatomic problem.

Infection

More commonly the guttural pouches become infected by bacteria, fungi or both. Infection may occur on one or both sides and is a serious condition. The carotid artery—the main artery to the head—and several important nerves to the face and eye are present in the guttural pouch wall and may be damaged by infection. Guttural pouch infection may cause a discharge from one or both nostrils, a swelling in the throatlatch region, difficulty breathing, or bleeding from the nostril.

Depending on which nerves are damaged, you may see facial paralysis or closing down (constriction) of the pupil in one eye. Pupil constriction in one eye due to nerve damage is called Horner's syndrome. The eyelids of the affected eye may droop and the third eyelid may become more visible. The horse may sweat only on the affected side of its head. If the infection

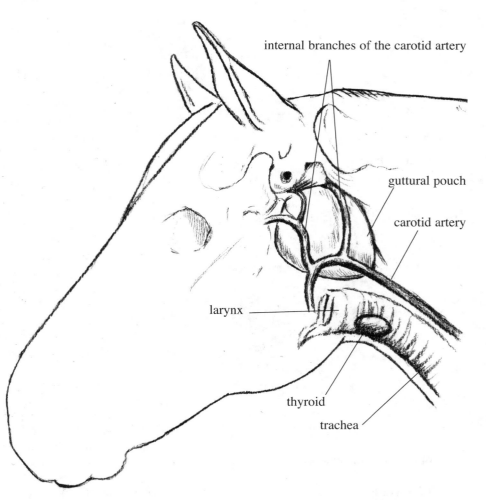

internal branches of the carotid artery

guttural pouch

carotid artery

larynx

thyroid

trachea

The guttural pouches lie just above and behind the jowls, where the bottom of the jaw meets the neck.

damages the carotid artery, periodic bleeding from the nostril may occur or the horse may die suddenly due to massive blood loss.

Eyes

Normal eyes are wide open, clear and bright. A small amount of gray gelatinous mucus accumulated at the medial (towards the midline) corner is normal. If you look into the eye you are looking through the cornea, the clear membranous covering of

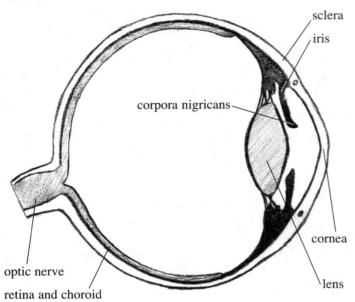

Side view of a horse's eye.

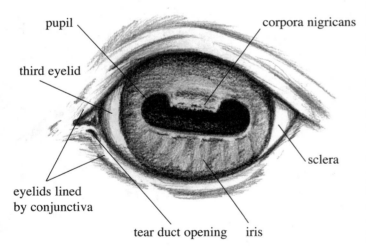

Parts of the eye you can see.

the eye that normally has no blood vessels. You can see the iris surrounding the central black opening of the pupil, through which light passes to the back of the eye.

Although the iris of most horses is brown, one or both eyes may be blue. Blue eyes are uncommon in the draft breeds, except in Clydesdales. One of the most striking horses we know of is a Belgian-Appaloosa cross, a tall, well-built chestnut with a flaxen mane and tail and two blue eyes. Eye color is present at birth and does not change.

> *corpora nigricans*
> corpora   = bodies
> nigricans   = black

Examining the Eyes

Use a flashlight with a narrow, intense beam to look inside your horse's eyes. As with a human eye, the horse's pupil will dilate in low light and constrict in bright light to regulate the amount of light getting to the retina lining the back of the globe. A horse's pupil response is slower than the response of a human, dog or cat. You will have to shine the light for several seconds to see a decrease in the pupil opening. The pupil should be the same size in both eyes.

The horse's retina, like that of many animals and unlike that of humans, has a layer called the tapetum (pronounced tah-PEA-dumb) that reflects light. The tapetum is the reason you see an eerie green, orange, gold or brown glow when a bright flashlight or headlights shine into a horse's eyes.

Look carefully at the upper edge of the pupil and you will see a unique anatomical feature of the equine eye growing off the top part of the iris and hanging down into the pupil opening. These growths, consisting of either several nodules or one nodule with several lobes, are the corpora nigricans, or black bodies. Don't mistake them for tumors in the eyes. Black bodies supposedly act as a sunshade for the horse, although no one knows for sure.

Behind the pupil is the lens, which is clear and therefore difficult to see. The lens gets slightly cloudy when a horse reaches about 20 years of age. A cloudy lens is an aging change similar to that in old dogs. It is not a cataract and does not interfere with the horse's ability to see.

Horses are occasionally born with true cataracts in one or both eyes. An unproven theory is that cataracts are an inherited problem in Belgians and Morgans. Surgical removal of a cataract is possible; whether surgery is performed will depend on the severity of the cataract and the budget of the owner. Small cataracts may not seriously interfere with the horse's vision. Horses with severe inflammation within the eye, such as from equine recurrent uveitis (moon blindness) may have damage to the lens and develop cataracts. Surgery in these cases is not useful, as other portions of the eye are likely to be damaged and surgery may cause increased inflammation and further damage.

The eyelids are lined with the conjunctiva, which are normally pale pink. Like many animals, but unlike humans, horses have a third eyelid at the medial corner of each eye. Powerful muscles control the horse's eyelids, especially the upper eyelids. Under circumstances only of weakness caused by nerve damage (facial palsy) can you easily lift a horse's upper eyelid manually.

Signs of Eye Problems

A horse that squints in one eye, or holds the eye tightly closed, has a painful eye. The eyelid may be swollen and warm to the touch. The horse may pull away if you try to touch the eye. An excessive amount of tears may flow or a discharge may come from the eye. A clear, gray gelatinous mucoid discharge may occur with any irritation.

A discharge that is yellowish or yellow-tan means an infection is producing pus. If your horse has this kind of eye problem, and it does not open the eye enough for you to see the cornea and inside the lids, try to gently pull open the lower lid by pulling down with your fingers. The conjunctiva will often be bright red, swollen and unusually wet. More discharge may be present in the lower lid.

Look for a bit of plant or other foreign material that might be causing discomfort to the eye. Examine the normally clear cornea for a white or opaque zone, indicating a corneal injury or infection causing an ulcer. If you cannot open the eye, or you see foreign material or an opaque area on the cornea, stop looking and call a veterinarian. If possible move the horse to a dark area away from flies until the veterinarian arrives.

Do not attempt to remove foreign material embedded in the conjunctiva or cornea.

Conjunctivitis

If you see no foreign material and the cornea appears normal in the eye of a squinting horse, it may have severe conjunctivitis. This inflammation of the conjunctiva may be caused by allergic irritation, with contributions from ever-present bacteria. Although flies may carry bacteria that cause conjunctivitis, the common conjunctivitis (pink eye) of cattle that is spread by flies does not occur in horses. Equine conjunctivitis generally occurs only in individual susceptible horses.

The inflammation may be readily treated with eye ointments that contain a mix of antibiotics and a small amount of corticosteroids. Placing a small amount in the affected eye two or three times a day for a few days generally cures conjunctivitis. Consult your veterinarian before administering any eye treatment.

Corneal Injuries

If you cannot see into the eye, do not treat it with any eye ointment that contains corticosteroids. Using corticosteroids to treat a horse with corneal injury increases the chances of infection with bacteria or fungi. In addition, even one treatment with corticosteroids will slow the growth of blood vessels that are necessary to heal the corneal wound.

Your veterinarian will use a local anesthetic for the eye and may need to sedate the horse to open the lids, flush the eye, remove any foreign material and locate any corneal damage. The veterinarian may instill a fluorescent green dye into the eye, using dye-impregnated paper, and shine a light to look for damaged areas of the cornea that hold the dye and shine bright green.

A corneal injury or infection is an emergency.

Only aggressive, appropriate therapy may allow the eye to heal without loss of sight. A corneal injury necessitates placing antibiotic ointments into the eye multiple times per day. Atropine ointment is often given to dilate the pupil to try to avoid pupil

Fit blinders so they do not touch the eyelids or eyelashes, otherwise they might cause rubbing and damage to the cornea.

Photo by Debby Peterson

scarring from the inflammation that occurs inside the eye. A low dose of phenylbutazone (bute), such as one gram per day, has a remarkable effect on the swelling and the associated pain, and simplifies treating the eye, even in a 2,000-pound draft.

Depending on the severity of the injury, treatment may be for days to weeks. Superficial corneal damage may heal quickly, whereas deep areas require growth of blood vessels from the sclera (the white part of the eye that surrounds the cornea and contains blood vessels) and gradual replacement of damaged tissue with healthy tissue.

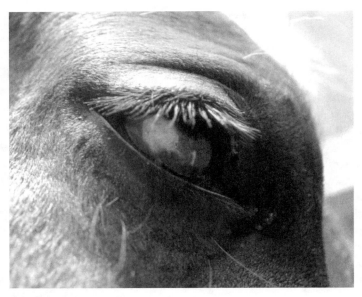

The opaque white area on this horse's cornea indicates a large, deep injury; the dark area at the lower edge is due to the growth of blood vessels to the site of injury to allow healing. *Photo by Barry Cooper*

The cornea is normally a low maintenance tissue that contains no blood vessels, but derives nutrition from the fluids bathing both its outer and inner surfaces. For repair of damage, particularly deep injury, blood vessels must grow from the surrounding sclera of the eye to provide the nutrients required for regeneration of tissue. The ingrowth of blood vessels and the inflammation that accompanies tissue damage results in fluid accumulation in the cornea (corneal edema) and imparts a hazy appearance to the normally clear surface of the eye. In some cases flaps of damaged tissue may need to be removed or allowed to slough off before tissue repair can be completed.

Once blood vessels have reached the damaged area and no secondary infection by bacteria or fungi has appeared, the wound will heal rapidly, although deep wounds may leave a small scar. Since the blood vessels grow at the rate of about one millimeter (less than 1/16th of an inch) per day, you can estimate the time required to reach this rapid healing phase by measuring the distance between the blood vessels and the area of corneal injury.

Blocked Tear Duct

If the horse has an otherwise healthy eye but tears are continuously flowing down the horse's face, it may have a blocked tear (lacrimal) duct. Tears normally drain into an opening in the lower eyelid that leads through a small-diameter duct to just inside the nostril. Constant tearing can cause moisture-associated skin irritation. If this condition occurs your veterinarian can sedate the horse and pass a flexible tube into the duct at the nostril opening and flush out the plug of mucus or other material blocking it.

Moon Blindness

A horse that squints or appears to have a painful or hazy eye without much swelling of the conjunctiva should be examined for signs of equine recurrent uveitis, also called moon blindness. This inflammation of the iris, which is part of the uveal tract of the eye, involves internal parts of the eye and may cause reddening or a haze within the inner portion of the eye. The pupil and/or iris may be obscured.

Move the horse to a shaded area and *call your veterinarian immediately* because only prompt and aggressive therapy with anti-inflammatory drugs can save the horse's eyesight. Uveitis usually affects one eye at a time, but horses may later develop a similar problem in the other eye. Although uveitis is often seen in Appaloosas, it may occur in any breed including the drafts.

The cause is not entirely understood, but evidence suggests that previous exposure to the bacterial organism leptospira in certain horses sets up a change in the eye and causes episodic flare-ups of inflammation. The horse's body fails to recognize tissues of the eye as *self* and reacts to the tissues as if they were foreign invaders. This response, known as an immune-mediated disease, requires corticosteroids for therapy to calm the inflammation.

conjunctivitis, uveitis

conjunctivia	= the moist mucous membrane lining the eyelids
uvea	= the portion of the eye that includes the iris
itis	= inflammation

Other Causes of Uveitis

Direct trauma to the eye may result in damage to internal structures and uveitis. Treatment is similar to the treatment for moon blindness. Foals with systemic bacterial infections (septicemia) often develop uveitis and may require eye medications as well as systemic antibiotics.

Blindness

What happens if, despite your best efforts and those of your veterinarian, your horse goes blind in one eye? A horse's normal field of vision is wide—from the front to behind, and loss of vision in one eye reduces this wide field of vision. Loss of eyesight on one side, however, is not as bad as it sounds; you might never notice the horse is blind in one eye.

Uveitis is the number one cause of blindness in horses.

A horse that suddenly goes blind in one eye may be spooky when approached from its blind side, especially early on. Always maintain voice and hand contact with a blind or partially blind horse. Be careful when leading a partially blind horse. Even when the horse has adjusted well to the loss of sight in one eye, in following your lead it may find itself walking into doorways or obstacles it would otherwise have seen and avoided. When hitching a team, put the horse's blind eye to the inside.

Horses can adjust remarkably to being blind even in both eyes, provided they are in familiar surroundings and are well trained. A completely blind horse that is of good temperament and well trained to voice and line commands can sometimes continue to work in a team.

Eye Tumors

Tumors, called neoplasms, are common in the conjunctiva, the eyelids, the cornea and the white area around the cornea (sclera). Tumors involving structures within the eye are uncommon in horses. The most common tumor around a horse's eye is squamous cell carcinoma, a skin cancer that is at least partially triggered by sunlight.

Apply sun block to any non-pigmented (pink) skin—most common in Clydesdales—around the eyes of horses that are exposed to sunlight. Although some fly repellent ointments contain sun block, if the horse has already shown signs of chronic skin irritation around the eyes, a 19 or higher spf (sun protecting factor) sun block designed for humans may be more effective for protecting the skin. A water repellent sun block is ideal for horses. Take care not to get sun block into the eyes because it may be irritating.

> *neoplasm*
>   neo   = new
>   plasm = tissue
>
> *squamous cell carcinoma*
>   squamous   = scale like
>   carcinoma   = cancer

Squamous Cell Carcinoma

Belgians tend to develop squamous cell carcinoma, not on their pigmented outer eyelids but on the conjunctiva and the adjacent sclera. Squamous cell carcinoma in its early stages may look like a scratch, wound or infection that won't heal, or like something stuck on the surface of the eye. The surface is often rough and may be scabby or oozing, as if infected.

Because squamous cell carcinomas cause a break in normal skin, they are often secondarily infected. Treating the infection may cause some improvement, but won't cure the problem. If you see the signs of a squamous cell carcinoma ask your veterinarian to check it as soon as possible. In some cases removal of all or part of the lesion and submission to a veterinary pathologist may be necessary for a confirmed diagnosis.

The sooner you treat a squamous cell carcinoma the better, because the tumor will continue to grow and invade tissues. Such tumors don't usually spread rapidly to other parts of the body, and in early stages may be completely removable. A more advanced tumor or a tumor that is not entirely removable because of its location may be successfully treated with various therapies, including radiation, laser therapy, cryotherapy (freezing) and topical chemotherapy.

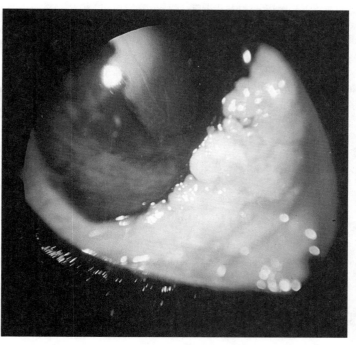

The raised rough-surfaced growth on this Belgian's third eyelid, typical of squamous cell carcinoma, was surgically removed to effect a cure. *Photo by Dr. Bill Rebhun*

Melanoma

In Percherons and other gray horses melanomas may occur in the eyelids (as well as other places). Compared to squamous cell carcinoma, these tumors rarely have surface irritation and grow as nodules covered by smooth, often hairless, skin. Having the tumors removed when they are small may solve the problem.

Given time, these tumors grow and not only invade the adjacent tissue, but spread to internal structures. Gray horses frequently develop more than one melanoma, often in the same area, and surgical removal is not always possible.

No effective cure exists for multiple melanomas. Melanoma of mature gray horses is much less aggressively malignant than melanoma in humans. Horses with melanomas, even that have spread internally, often die of something else. A melanoma that spreads to a vital area such as the heart, brain or spinal cord, though, certainly compromises the horse's health.

Mucous Membrane Color

Mucous membranes are the moist non-haired skin that line the mouth, nose, prepuce, vagina, eyelids and part of the sclera. Learn to recognize their normal color.

Conjunctiva and Gums

The conjunctiva are normally pink to pale red. Excessive redness may indicate irritation and is usually accompanied by swelling and tearing or discharge.

Conjunctiva that appear pale may indicate anemia; check the color of the gingiva (gums) for paleness, as well. Anemia is best determined from a count of the circulating red blood cells. Significant anemia is a rare condition except in a horse that has

experienced a serious loss of blood or damage to red blood cells.

A purplish color to the conjunctiva and gingiva may occur in a horse with circulating bacterial toxins in the blood, such as occurs in severe colic or generalized infection. Prompt veterinary attention is vital.

Sclera

The sclera is normally white with fine blood vessels. The vessels may become engorged with blood (congested) if the eye has been irritated. If the sclera appears blotchy red, bleeding (hemorrhage) has occurred, the cause of which will need to be investigated.

If the sclera takes on a yellow tinge (jaundice or icterus), call a veterinarian immediately. Various conditions cause yellow jaundice in horses. Any horse that has not eaten for several days will develop mild jaundice. Since lack of appetite indicates a serious problem, the cause must be investigated. Liver disease and certain diseases causing a breakdown of red blood cells may cause jaundice and are serious problems requiring veterinary attention.

Teeth

The teeth continue to grow throughout a horse's life. In the first five to eight years tooth eruption and wear may be used to tell a

Progression of the lower teeth showing the age of a horse up to 8 years old.

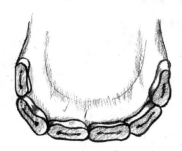

2 years
all temporary (baby) teeth are present

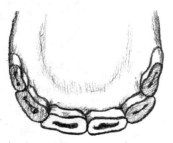

3 years
first two permanent teeth are present

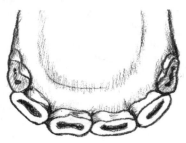

4 years
first four permanent teeth are present

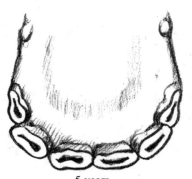

5 years
all six permanent teeth, and canine teeth, are present

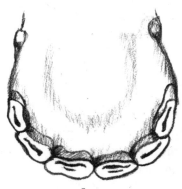

8 years
wear begins on first two incisors

Tooth Eruption	
Tooth	*Eruption Time*
Baby teeth:	
1st incisor	birth-1 week
2nd incisor	4-6 weeks
3rd incisor	6-9 months
Permanent teeth:	
1st incisor	2.5 years
2nd incisor	3.5 years
3rd incisor	4.5 years
canines*	4-5 years
*In mares the canines are small or absent.	

horse's age. After the horse reaches eight years of age, tooth wear is inaccurate for estimating its age other than to suggest the horse is either old or not so old—perhaps the reason so many horses are sold as eight-year-olds.

Looking at the angle of the horse's front teeth, or incisors, will help you determine if the horse is in the old or not-so-old group. As a horse ages the incisors grow long and meet at a sharp angle. A younger horse's incisors meet in a more upright or vertical position.

Floating

The most important aspect of the continuous growth of a horse's teeth is that the grinding teeth, the premolars and molars, are slightly offset on top compared to the bottom. As a result uneven wear occurs and sharp points and hooks form on the outsides of the upper teeth and the insides of the lower teeth.

You can feel the points by grasping the horse's tongue out to one side of its mouth and placing your hand inside the cheek on the opposite side—although we don't recommend you actually do this. Let the professional veterinarian or equine dentist, who is both experienced and insured, perform this task.

Regularly rasping down the sharp points, a procedure called floating, is a part of good horse care. For most horses, floating once a year is enough. Teeth occasionally develop such large points that they need to be cut off, rather than rasped. Teeth that are infected or cracked may have to be pulled.

Bad Teeth and Weight Loss

The impact of bad teeth on a horse's general health and body condition is overrated. Rarely will a horse's teeth be so bad that the horse loses weight. Weight loss in a draft horse is much more likely to be caused by some other problem.

When an aging horse starts to drop weight, a general rule of horse owners and veterinarians is to have the horse's teeth floated. While once-a-year examination and floating are important, because any severe problems can be corrected early, regular tooth care won't necessarily correct poor overall condition. Drs. Sarah Ralston and Harold (Skip) Hintz have found that digestibility of feed in mature horses was not altered significantly by floating the teeth.

Geriatric horses, or horses with parrot mouth—where the lower jaw is shorter than the upper jaw so the incisors don't meet—may lose weight due to bad teeth. They may have difficulty grazing and may find whole grains difficult to grind. Feeds such as pellets or extruded feeds that are more easily chewed, as well as fat added to the diet, are helpful to the aging horse and to horses with dental problems.

Ear Tooth

Occasionally a horse is born with a developmental abnormality known as an ear tooth, or dentigerous cyst, in which tissue destined to form a tooth is displaced to the bone at the base of

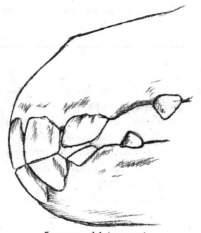
5 years old (young)

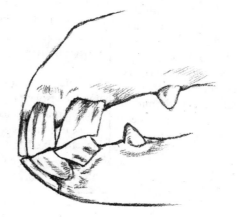
10 years old (not so old)

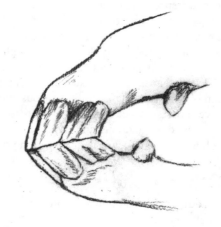
20-25 years old (old)

Comparison of incisors as a horse ages.

the ear. The bony cavity around this poorly formed tooth structure may communicate with an opening to the skin of the face, which may continuously drain a small amount of fluid. Surgical removal of the tooth structure and the tissue around it solves the problem.

```
dentigerous cyst
    denti        = pertaining to teeth
    gerous       = growth
    cyst         = a thin-walled,
                   fluid-filled structure
```

Lymph Nodes

Lymph nodes are small glands occurring throughout the horse's body; many are present just under the skin. Several lymph nodes are in the throatlatch region of the jaw, as well as under the jaw in the narrow space between the jawbones (intermandibular space). These glands are normally not readily apparent. If you can easily feel one, it is probably enlarged.

The lymph nodes may enlarge as a reaction to infection or inflammation in the area, a condition known as reactive lymph nodes. Enlargement may also occur due to either a tumor—whether primary in the node or spread to the node from another site—or infection within the lymph node, most commonly strangles.

Lymphoma

Lymphoma, also called malignant lymphoma or lymphosarcoma, is a primary tumor of the cells (lymphocytes) within the lymph node that causes slow to rapid enlargement of multiple lymph nodes. Other tissues, such as skin or internal organs, may be involved.

Lymphoma in horses is generally less aggressive than lymphoma in other species. In early stages the presence of these multiple lumps may be the only sign of cancer. In later stages affected horses begin to lose weight and condition. Swelling (edema) may occur in the legs due to blockage of lymphatic drainage.

Diagnosis is best made by the removal of an enlarged lymph node or other involved tissue and its submission to a veterinary pathologist for examination. Various modes of chemotherapy have proven successful for the treatment of lymphoma in humans, dogs and cats and have been used with some success in horses. The expense is great and the outcome is uncertain.

Other Tumors

In addition to lymphoma, two other kinds of tumor affect the lymph nodes:

Melanomas in mature gray horses often spread from the skin surface to lymph nodes in many parts of the body. They may be seen, for example, as nodules under the skin at the base of an ear.

Squamous cell carcinoma in advanced stages may spread to lymph nodes, usually those in the region where the tumor originated.

Your veterinarian may be able to determine the cause of lymph node enlargement by using a needle placed into the enlarged node to pull out some of the cells and spread them onto a glass slide or by removing a portion of tissue for microscopic examination. Unfortunately, little can be done to treat cancer that has spread (metastasized) to a horse's lymph nodes.

Strangles

The most common cause of lymph node enlargement in the horse is infection by *Streptococcus equi,* the bacterial organism that causes strangles. The most commonly affected lymph nodes are those in the throatlatch area, which may become so large they appear to strangle the horse, hence the name for this condition. The bacteria infect the horse's nose and throat as well, potentially causing breathing difficulties.

Signs and Treatment

An infected horse usually runs a fever, goes off feed, becomes depressed and has a nasal discharge that contains pus. The large pockets of pus and bacteria that form abscesses in the lymph nodes heal rapidly following rupture and drainage. This disease generally runs its course within three to six weeks.

Treatment with penicillin or other antibiotics is controversial. The best cure is by rupture and drainage of affected lymph nodes; antibiotic treatment may slow the development and rupture of the abscesses. Penicillin treatment is usually most useful in early stages of the infection, before enlargement of the lymph nodes is apparent. Once the lymph nodes enlarge, antibiotic treatment should be stopped and hot compresses applied to encourage the affected lymph nodes to rupture. Rupture usually happens spontaneously, but in some cases your veterinarian may need to use a lance to hasten the process. Once the lymph node is opened, daily flushing of the area with an antibacterial solution such as Betadine or chlorhexidine (Nolvasan) enhances healing.

Controlling strangles

Strangles is a highly contagious infection. Its containment involves isolation of affected horses and the meticulous use of decontamination techniques prescribed by your veterinarian. These techniques will likely include using a solution of chlorine bleach, mixed 1:10 with tap water, to scrub stalls, instruments and any other equipment that came into contact with the infected horse, as well as washing all clothing and tack.

Complications

Two serious problems may be associated with infection by *Streptococcus equi.* One is post-streptococcal blood vessel inflammation, known as vasculitis, but also called purpura hemorrhagica because of the small blotches of hemorrhage appearing in the gums and other tissues. The problem is not contagious but occurs only in the individual horse that has an abnormal immune system response to the bacterial infection, resulting in an attack on the horse's own blood vessels.

Such a horse may develop edema from fluid leaking from the damaged vessels. The process may involve muscle and internal organs, as well as skin. Damage to intestinal blood vessels may result in death of affected intestine and death of the horse. Treatment of a horse with purpura hemorrhagica involves high doses of corticosteroids in an attempt to stop the immune response.

The second devastating consequence of *Streptococcus equi* infection is bastard strangles. A horse with bastard strangles may apparently recover or be recovering from a typical strangles infection but then suddenly become ill or die. Postmortem examination of such cases often reveals previously undetected involvement of internal lymph nodes, or development of abscesses within critical parts of the body such as the brain.

---

vasculitis
vasc	= blood vessel
itis	= inflammation

purpura hemorrhagica
purpura	= purple
hemorrhagica	= areas of bleeding

Nostrils

The upper part of the horse's nostril is not connected to the rest of the airway, but is a blind sac called the false nostril. As with several other parts of the horse's anatomy, this structure has no known function, other than to occasionally develop cysts that may need surgical removal. Horses generally don't react violently to the probing of this cavity with a finger. We know of one horse in which such probing causes lip movements resembling an imitation of Mr. Ed, the talking horse.

The real airway is below the false nostril, and is surrounded by bone and cartilage throughout its length, except at the true nostril opening. Despite a common belief among horse owners, no noseband—no matter how low or tight—is likely to interfere with a horse's ability to breath. The increased control you achieve with a dropped or tight noseband is most likely caused by decreasing the horse's ability to open its mouth to avoid the bit or by pressure on sensitive parts of the nose.

Head Carriage

The way a horse carries its head while in harness or under saddle can affect the horse's breathing. A horse forced to hold its head high with its chin tucked has decreased airflow through the nostrils and the airways of its head and larynx. Try this position yourself and you'll feel the difference.

Forcing an abnormal head carriage is not a problem for working draft horses, but could be a problem for hitch horses, where high head carriage is favored. A horse should be allowed to maintain a head carriage that is as close as possible to normal for whatever activity it is doing.

Nasal Discharge

Material draining from the nostrils is common in horses. Some discharges are nothing to worry about, others indicate a serious problem. You must be observant and aware of various signs and their causes.

Clear watery (serous) fluid at the nostril is not always indicative of an infection. It could indicate increased watering of the eyes or nose due to irritation. If accompanied by fever and malaise, however, it may be a sign of a viral infection such as influenza (flu) or rhinopneumonitis (herpes) virus.

Mucus is a gray gelatinous material some horses seem to delight in sneezing all over unsuspecting humans. Mucus is present in airways as a protective substance that traps dust and other foreign material, including potentially harmful bacterial and fungal organisms. Mucus flow may increase during irritation of the airways but does not, in itself, indicate infection. A horse with allergic airway disease may have more obvious mucus discharge, which often increases after exercise. Unless the horse has other problems, treatment is not usually required.

Blood occasionally trickles from a horse's nostrils, usually after exercise. If the bleeding occurs infrequently and in a small amount the condition may not be serious. A small amount of bleeding into the airways may occur because of increased pressures in the lungs during strenuous exercise. Affected horses are referred to as bleeders. Bleeding from the nostrils is less common in draft horses than in race horses. If your horse develops a nosebleed ask your veterinarian to evaluate its nasal passages, sinuses and guttural pouches for infection or tumors.

Feed material or fluid in the nostrils of an adult horse is indicative of a serious problem, which may involve blockage of the esophagus, stomach or intestines. Milk in the nostrils of a foal may indicate a birth deformity in which the ledge separating the mouth from the nasal cavity (the palate) is incomplete. In either case immediately call your veterinarian to investigate.

Pus anywhere is never normal. A nasal discharge containing pus is called a purulent (pronounced PURE-you-lent) discharge. Pus is distinguishable from mucus by its color and texture. Pus is yellow or tan and the consistency of a thick fluid or paste. A purulent discharge may contain various amounts of mixed mucus (mucopurulent discharge) or blood.

A purulent nasal discharge always indicates infection, but does not distinguish between an upper airway infection in the head or neck and a lower airway infection in the lungs. An affected horse should be evaluated immediately to determine site, cause and proper treatment of the infection. Because the roots of the cheek teeth are close to the internal sinuses of the head, an infected tooth may result in discharge of infected material through the nose.

Face and Lips

The horse uses its lips like fingers, exhibiting labial dexterity where a human would use manual dexterity. Horses vary in their ability to perform fine movements such as opening stall gates with their lips. Draft horses seem to have more lip area, more power and more range of motion than other horses.

Bitting

A bit should properly fit the horse. A too-small bit causes pinching of the lips. A too-large bit may not function properly, although a bit that is too large is probably better than one that is too small.

A properly adjusted bit makes one or two wrinkles in the horse's lips. A bit that is too tight puts pressure on sensitive tissues of the mouth and lips. A bit that is too loose can cause discomfort by moving against sensitive tissues. A too-loose bit also will not function effectively. For a horse with a sensitive mouth, a bitless or hackamore bridle may be best.

For a horse with a sensitive mouth, try a hackamore bridle— either the bosal style (top) or the English style (bottom) with a mechanical, or hackamore, bit.

A properly fitting bit makes one or two wrinkles in the corner of the horse's mouth.   *Photo by Debby Peterson*

Flehmen Response

The curling up of the upper lip, with head raised, is known as the flehmen response (pronounced FLAY-men). A stallion usually shows this expression after investigating a mare that may be receptive to breeding. In such a case the action causes fluid from a small gland located above the hard palate of the mouth (the vomeronasal gland) to enter the nose. Although this fluid must be important for something, its exact effect on a stallion is not known. The flehmen response may occur in any horse that senses an unusual taste or scent, or in a horse experiencing pain.

Suffolk stallion demonstrating the raised head and curled upper lip characteristic of the flehmen response.

Photo by Sarah Fryer

Drooping Lips

Sometimes a horse lets its lower lip droop, especially when at rest. Some horses flap their lips under saddle or in harness. As long as the horse can use its lips normally when it wants to, you need not be concerned if its lip flaps or droops.

Facial Palsy

The large nerve to the lips, ears and eyelids is the facial nerve. This nerve emerges from the base of the brain through tiny openings in the bones of the skull, and provides several branches to reach the many structures of the face that it controls. The facial nerve has a superficial branch running across the side of each cheek. In some horses you may see it as a thin flat cord and feel it by gently rolling the cord under your fingers.

Damage to the facial nerve causes one side of the horse's face to be partially or completely paralyzed (facial palsy). The most obvious sign of facial palsy is the pulling of the upper lip toward the side with the normal nerve. The ear on the affected side often droops. The eyelid on that side may also droop and will be

relatively easy for you to lift; in a normal horse the muscles to the upper eyelids are powerful, as you will see if you try lifting a normal upper eyelid with your fingers.

Severe facial nerve damage is often not repairable, but less severe damage may resolve with time. The facial nerve may be damaged by pressure from a halter buckle, for example if the halter becomes caught in a fence or branch, or if the horse becomes ill and lies down on a hard surface. For this reason among others, remove the halters from your horses whenever possible. A horse that is anesthetized and laid on its side is provided with padding under its head in an attempt to avoid damage to the facial nerve.

Facial palsy causes the ear on the affected side to droop, the upper eyelid on the same side to droop slightly, and the upper lip to pull toward the opposite (normal) side.

With thanks to Alexander de Lahunta

In horses with equine protozoal myeloencephalitis (EPM) the facial nerve may become damaged where the nerve begins in the brain. Other causes of facial nerve damage include trauma, the nerve disease equine polyneuritis, and guttural pouch or middle/inner ear infections.

If the branches of the facial nerve to the eyelids are damaged the horse may not be able to blink properly and tear production may decrease, causing the surface of the eye to become dry and leading to eye damage. Your veterinarian will likely prescribe medications to maintain moisture and lubrication while you wait to see if the nerve damage will resolve.

Head Swelling

Swelling of the head may be caused by faulty nutrition, infection, fluid build up (edema) or tumors. Depending on its cause the swelling may be either symmetric (occurring equally on both sides) or asymmetric (occurring only on one side or more severely on one side).

Symmetric Swelling

Symmetric swelling of the bones of the head is the hallmark of big head, a bone disease seen in horses fed an improper calcium-to-phosphorus ratio. The disorder occurs when horses are fed a diet that is high in phosphorus and low in calcium, such as poor quality grass hay and high levels of corn, bran or other whole grains. The condition is potentially reversible with the addition of calcium to the diet. The loss of mineralization of the bones that results in their replacement by fibrous tissue, however, causes increased fragility in all bones, making affected horses more prone to fractures.

Severe selenium deficiency may cause serious sudden damage and swelling of the muscles of the head and jaw. Affected horses may have difficulty eating. Prompt treatment with selenium and anti-inflammatory medications usually resolves the problem.

> *tracheostomy*
> tracheo = trachea, also called the windpipe
> stoma = mouth or opening

Symmetric head swelling may occur due to fluid build up (edema), usually in a horse with low blood protein, vasculitis or obstruction to blood flow in both jugular veins.

Asymmetric Swelling

A condition that looks like bone swelling over the nasal or sinus areas may be an expansion of the facial bones because of pressure from an underlying infection or tumor. A veterinarian should investigate immediately. Tumors may cause large localized swelling of the jaw. If such tumors are present near the incisors they may be treated by surgical removal and are generally not the kind of tumors that spread.

Infection of a cheek (molar) tooth or root can cause painful swelling of one side of the face or jaw. Treatment may include removing the infected tooth and administering antibiotics.

Fractures of the head bones may occur, most often due to a kick. The diagnosis is generally confirmed by radiographic (X-ray) studies. Anti-inflammatory medication and time may be all that is needed for a facial fracture to heal.

Snake bites and bee or wasp stings often occur on a horse's face, because horses are likely to encounter these creatures while grazing. If you believe your horse is having a reaction to a bite or sting, and the area is large, enlarging rapidly or causing discomfort to the horse, call a veterinarian immediately. Your horse may need medications to combat shock and to treat damage and inflammation at the site. If swelling interferes with the horse's ability to breath, your veterinarian may need to make a temporary airway into the trachea by performing a procedure known as a tracheostomy. Fortunately most horses recover from such experiences with little or no permanent damage.

Photo by Vickie Darnell

Skin and Hair

A horse's skin and haircoat provide protective barriers against infectious agents and damaging sunlight. They also play an important role in regulating body heat during hot or cold weather.

Numerous bacteria and fungi are always present on the skin surface. Most of them are harmless and some may even help protect the horse against infection by harmful organisms. Potentially harmful bacteria and fungi are also always present in the horse's environment, often on the skin and hair.

Skin Infections

Horses are much less susceptible to bacterial and fungal skin infections than are dogs. Cats are like horses in being resistant to bacterial skin infections, which may be because of their meticulous grooming habits. That can't be the whole story, though, since horses delight in dust and mud baths and yet are resistant to most skin infections.

As an unfortunate exception, draft horses are susceptible to skin infections of their pasterns and lower legs, which are difficult to prevent and control. Whenever a skin problem does not respond to seemingly appropriate medication, get a veterinarian to examine the horse. A biopsy of the affected skin, sent to a veterinary pathologist, can help sort out the cause of the problem and indicate the best approach to treatment.

In many skin problem cases, one cause may start the problem, then bacteria get involved secondarily. A reaction to medications, especially those applied on the skin surface, may further complicate matters. Sorting out a chronic (long-standing) skin problem is often challenging. In a complicated case, after examining biopsy samples the veterinary pathologist or dermatologist may advise your veterinarian to treat for one or more of the most obvious problems. If the skin fails to completely heal, a repeat biopsy may be necessary to see what problems are left.

The general rule of antibiotic treatment for bacterial skin disease is to continue treatment for 10 days to two weeks after the infection appears to clear.

Bacterial Infections

Bacteria are often involved in causing secondary infection (occurring as a result of decreased immunity from some other cause), but bacteria may also be the primary cause of a skin disease such as scratches or rain scald.

Scratches

Scratches, also known as greasy heel, is most often caused by bacteria. Mites and fungi cause a condition that looks similar, so the cause of the skin irritation must be ascertained before an appropriate treatment can be determined. Signs are a roughened and irritated skin surface on the lower legs that is most severe on the backs of the pasterns and fetlocks. The hind legs are more commonly and severely affected than the forelegs. Some horses seem unaware of the infection, others may be sore to the touch and even lame.

Susceptibility

Shires and Clydesdales, with their long flowing feathers, are particularly susceptible to this infection because their thick, long leg hair tends to retain moisture and dirt, thus providing a good environment for bacteria. Muddy pastures and wet stalls may sufficiently irritate the skin for the bacteria to take hold. Geldings and stallions in tie stalls, where the bedding around their hind feet becomes wet with urine, have more problems with scratches than do mares, because mares urinate behind themselves.

We know of several owners of draft breeds with heavy feathering that swear by the daily application of a layer of mineral oil to their horse's feathers as a way to prevent scratches, although we worry that this practice will attract dirt and moisture.

Treatment

Treating scratches involves clipping the hair, including the feathers, cleaning the skin surface with an antibacterial soap such as Betadine surgical scrub (available through your veterinarian or pharmacy) and applying antibiotics to the skin surface. In a mild case, scrubbing the surface with medical gauze sponges soaked in Betadine surgical scrub may clear the infection. We keep a small jar of Betadine-soaked gauzes in our barn for such use. Treatment at least twice a day is best.

Many antibiotic creams and ointments are available. Antibiotic tube medications designed for treating the mammary glands of a cow with mastitis work well because the contents remain clean, the application is less messy than applying antibiotic pastes from a jar and the tube's nozzle lets you direct the medication to exactly the right spot, including into cracks and crevices.

If the infection clears but comes back, you will need to continue treatment for a longer period. If the infection never really clears or gets worse, consult your veterinarian. Your veterinarian may have a favorite recipe for treating scratches, or your horse may need oral or injected antibiotics to reach the affected skin through the bloodstream.

Sometimes the addition of DMSO to any recipe helps, as DMSO has an anti-inflammatory action and can also carry antibiotics deep into the tissue. Always wear gloves if you are applying a medication containing DMSO, which penetrates human skin as well as horse skin. Although no adverse effects have been seen in horses, possible risks to humans remain in question.

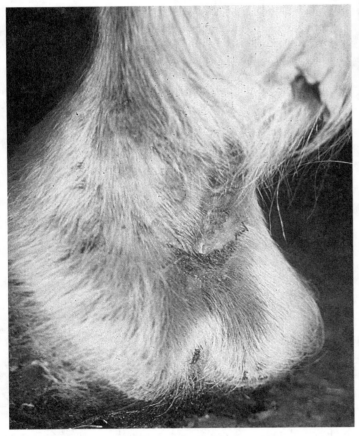

The skin on the back of this horse's pastern is rough and crusted due to the bacterial infection known as scratches or greasy heal. *Photo by Mike Wildenstein*

Draft horses tend to get a severe form of scratches that may require both corticosteroid therapy to reduce inflammation and high doses of antibiotics to treat the infection. If the infection is especially severe, do not stop treatment as soon as the skin looks normal. The bacteria may still be present deep in the tissue and can begin to grow again if you stop treatment too soon.

Scratches in a draft horse can be a frustrating disease to treat. You may have to try several different treatments before finding one that works for your horse. Give any treatment at least two weeks before you decide it's not working.

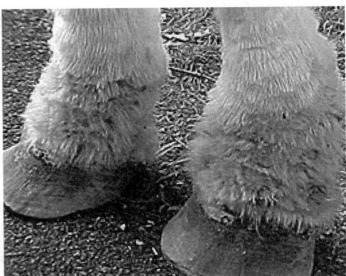

A severe and longstanding case of scratches may involve extensive areas of the lower legs, including the front of the pastern as well as the back, and can result in growths of abnormal skin in the affected area. *Photo by Brittany Love*

Rain Scald or Rain Rot

Dermatitis caused by dermatophilus bacteria may occur in a horse with reduced immune system function, such as may be caused by poor nutrition, stress, corticosteroid therapy or Cushing's disease. It may occur in horses kept in stalls or paddocks that are not regularly cleaned and become heavily contaminated with dermatophilus bacteria, or in a horse that has a constantly moist skin surface because it lives in a rainy climate and has no dry shelter, hence the common names for this condition: rain scald and rain rot. Filthy or constantly moist environments cause a horse's normal skin barriers to break down and allow the bacteria, which are commonly present in the soil, to take hold in the form of an infection.

Dermatophilus infection often involves the top of the back, but may spread to most of the body. It causes rough, raised clumps of hair and skin that may ooze fluid. When you pull gently on the affected hairs they come out, along with a patch of skin, and leave a red, raw oozing sore. The individual horse's immune system plays such an important role in susceptibility to dermatophilus infection that in a group of horses kept in a dirty, wet environment fostering this infection, only one or two horses may become infected.

An affected horse may benefit from being bathed with an antibacterial shampoo, and a mild case may be cleared by once or twice daily scrubbing of the affected area with Betadine scrub or chlorhexidine (Nolvasan) solution. Owners of gray horses may prefer to use chlorhexidine, as Betadine has an orange-red color that stains the haircoat.

The control of a severe infection often requires systemic antibiotics, either oral or by injection. Keep the horse's environment as clean and dry as possible. Discard all removed crusts well away from any horses. Keep affected horses and the equipment used to groom them away from other horses. Disinfect brushes and stalls with chlorine bleach diluted 1:10 with tap water to kill the bacteria.

If a horse develops recurrent dermatophilus infection for no apparent reason, have the horse tested for problems such as pituitary tumors causing Cushing's disease that may decrease the horse's immune system function.

> *dermatitis*
> dermat = skin
> itis = inflammation

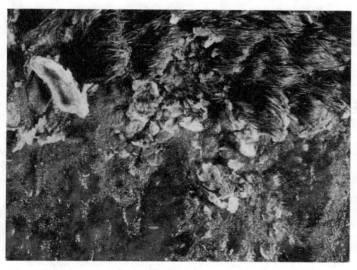

Rain scald (dermatophilosis) affects the skin of many areas, particularly the top of the back and rump. The crusted tufts of hair are easily pulled out leaving raw, moist areas of skin.

Photo by Beth A. Valentine

Ringworm

Many problems, including allergic and bacterial disease, resemble ringworm, a fungal infection that is relatively uncommon in horses. Ringworm results in hair loss caused by damage to the hair follicles. The haircoat may look moth eaten, but infected horses are not usually itchy so they do not rub off hair. The fungi that cause this condition are often present in the soil and on the horse's skin, usually without causing a problem. Infection and hair loss occur when the horse's natural immunity is altered, allowing the fungi to penetrate deep into the hair follicles.

Diagnosis is usually based on identification of the fungi, either by growth in the laboratory from hair samples or by an examination of affected skin biopsy samples. A topical antifungal treatment will clear the infection. The most commonly recommended treatment is a once daily total body lime-sulphur sponge-on dip (4 ounces lime-sulfur mixture in 1 gallon of water).

The fungi that cause ringworm in horses can affect humans. Wear gloves while treating or handling an affected horse, and wash your hands in an antiseptic solution such as Nolvasan to minimize the risk of human infection. If one horse in the barn develops ringworm, the infection may spread to other horses. If possible isolate the affected horse from other horses and disinfect brushes, blankets and stalls with a 1:10 solution of chlorine bleach. As with dermatophilus infections, a horse with recurrent fungal skin disease should be tested for underlying problems affecting its immune system.

Other than ringworm, fungal skin disease is relatively uncommon in horses. Occasional skin lumps may be localized reactions to fungi, most likely introduced through minor skin wounds. In most cases, removal of these lumps resolves the problem.

Lymphangitis

Draft horses seem particularly susceptible to lymphangitis, which affects the lower legs and can extend up the legs toward the body. Strictly speaking this disease is not a skin infection, but an infection of the lymphatic vessels under the skin. The result is the appearance of thickened, twisting cords that extend up the horse's lower leg, similar to the distended surface blood vessels visible in the inner thigh of a horse after heavy exercise.

The reduced movement of fluids that lymphatic vessels normally carry from the tissues back to the heart may result in severe swelling of the lower legs from fluid accumulation (edema). Lymphangitis may be caused by bacterial or fungal infection and requires serious long-term attention. In some cases the infection may be controlled, but permanent damage to lymphatics may result in persistent or recurrent limb edema. Regular exercise may help improve circulation in the lower legs, but this problem may never be completely controlled.

Parasites

A variety of parasites affect the skin and hair of draft horses. Lice, ticks and straw itch mites can cause skin problems, as discussed in Chapter 4.

Fortunately for draft horse owners fleas are rarely a problem for horses. The fleas that torment dogs and cats do not affect horses, but poultry fleas can occasionally be a problem. Treating the horse with an insecticidal dip and the environment with an insecticidal spray will kill the fleas.

A tiny worm, onchocerca, is transmitted to horses by the bite of infected mosquitoes or gnats. The worm migrates through the skin of the crest and face, causing itchy scaly areas to appear around the face and eyes. Some horses are more sensitive to these worms than are others. An antiparasitic treatment for onchocerca, such as ivermectin, will solve the problem, although repeated treatment may be necessary.

Summer Sores

Larval worms (most often habronema larvae) carried by flies may be deposited on the horse's skin and cause irritation (habronemiasis). This problem is most common in the summer months—hence the name summer sores—and often disappears in winter. It occurs most often on the legs, the underside of the belly, the inner corner of the eye, the penis and prepuce, and at wound sites.

Examination of a skin biopsy reveals intense inflammation surrounding worm larvae. Ivermectin kills these larvae, and summer sores have become much less common since it has been available. In some cases the inflammation is severest after the worm has died, in which case the use of corticosteroids, either orally or injected at the site, is necessary for the sores to heal.

Mange

The tiny insects that cause leg mange in horses are chorioptes mites. Shires and Clydesdales are more susceptible to mite infection than other draft breeds because of their heavy

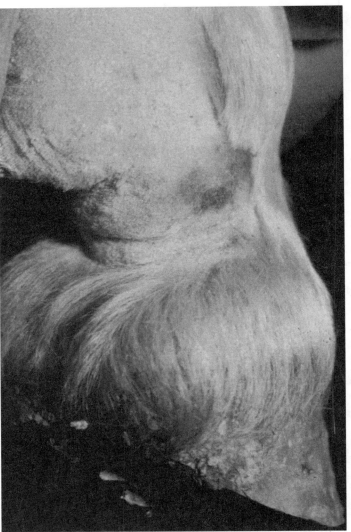

The crusting skin and hair loss on the lower legs due to leg mange mites (chorioptes) may resemble bacterial infection (scratches). *Courtesy of Danny Scott and Bill Miller*

feathering. Affected skin is thickened, may be raw and crusted, and is intensely itchy. A secondary bacterial infection is often present that may clear with antibacterial therapy, but the skin will not completely heal unless treated with an antiparasitic medication. Mange mites may also infect the coronary band skin, resulting in a profound thickening and roughening of the infected area. Horse leg mange mites do not affect humans, as do some of the mites that cause mange in dogs.

Treatment with ivermectin paste wormer two to three times at two-week intervals may effectively kill chorioptes mites on horses, but some draft horses are resistant to this therapy. Affected drafts may need the use of topical insecticides such as a pyrethrin dip, in addition to ivermectin treatment. The use of a dip may necessitate clipping the feathers to allow the insecticide dip greater access to the affected skin.

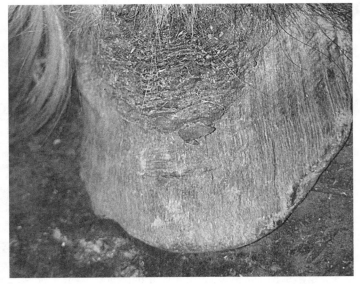

Leg mange mites (chorioptes) infecting the coronary band can cause abnormal hoof growth. *Photo by Mike Wildenstein*

Rubbing: Normal or Allergy?

All horses like a good rub, especially of their faces, chins and rear ends. Any posts, doors or other structures they may want to use to rub themselves need be either sturdy or protected by electric wire. An occasional rub, such as head rubbing after work, is normal.

All horses, but especially draft horses, must be taught at an early age that their owners are not head scratching posts. Keeping a rough towel or cactus cloth groomer in the area where you remove tack, and teaching your horses to wait for you to offer it as something to rub their faces on, will help keep you the draft horse owner intact and healthy.

A horse that rubs excessively may have a persistent itch due to an allergic skin problem. In summer months excessive rubbing is a common reaction to biting insects. Excessive rubbing results in areas of hair loss. A horse can reach even a difficult-to-scratch place, such as the underside of its belly, with a carefully placed hind hoof or by using a bush or small tree of the right height.

The same things that cause hives (discussed in the next chapter) can cause itchy, rough allergic skin disease. As with hives, the allergen must be identified so exposure may be limited or stopped. Identifying and removing the cause is always better than continuous treatment with corticosteroids, because these drugs adversely affect the immune system.

The affected skin surface of an itchy horse is usually rough and scaly, and may become secondarily infected by bacteria. Recognizing where the skin is affected and the time of year when the reaction occurs may help you determine the cause. Some allergic skin diseases have a characteristic pattern and occur in certain seasons. Biting gnats, for example, may cause horses to rub out their manes and tails and cause an itchy, scaly dermatitis on the midline of the bottom of the abdomen, because these areas are where gnats tend to bite. Tail rubbing is more likely to be due to an allergy than to pinworms. Apply fly repellent and keep the horse inside at dusk, when gnats are active.

Haircoat

A foal's haircoat is soft and fuzzy. By the time the foal reaches the age of about six months its foal coat is replaced by a sleeker haircoat. Although some horses inherently have shinier coats than others, a high fat diet makes any horse's haircoat shine.

Except for the hairs of the forelock, mane and tail the horse's haircoat grows and sheds in cycles. These cycles are directed by temperature and day length, and are influenced by hormones from the thyroid, adrenal and pituitary glands.

Winter coats are long and fine, providing an insulating layer. Some horses have longer, thicker coats in winter than do others. A horse with a good layer of insulating fat under its skin may not grow as long a winter coat as a thinner horse, but this occurrence is not always predictable. Horses in milder climates do not develop as thick a coat as those in frigid areas. The coat of a horse kept indoors or blanketed in winter will not grow as long or as thick as the coat of a horse kept outdoors without blankets.

Muscles in the skin let a horse raise the hairs to increase cooling in summer and increase heat retention in the winter. Each horse sheds its winter coat at a slightly different rate from other horses. Once shedding starts, the coat of a healthy horse will rapidly shed over several weeks, aided by rolling and rubbing. Using a shedding blade or a rubber curry comb on your horse can help out, as well, although do not use a metal curry comb—it is designed for cleaning a softer-bristle body brush and should never be applied to the horse's body.

Too Much Hair

A mature horse that does not properly shed its winter coat and that develops a long, often slightly curly haircoat, may have a tumor of the pituitary gland causing Cushing's disease. This small gland in the skull at the base of the brain directs and controls the activity of many other glands, including the thyroid and adrenal glands. Pituitary tumors often cause increased activity of the adrenal gland, where substances such as corticosteroids and other important regulators of the body's functions are made.

Affected horses often drink more water than usual and urinate excessively. They are not itchy and do not appear to be susceptible to overheating. Why the hair growth cycle changes is not clear, but affected horses should be evaluated and treated, since other more serious problems—such as laminitis, muscle loss and blindness—may occur because of pituitary tumors.

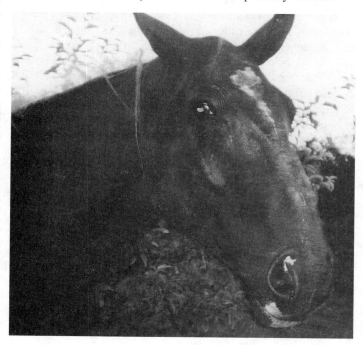

Harry the hairless Percheron has been bald since shedding his foal coat; the areas of white skin on his face have been irritated because of sun exposure. *Photo by Beth A. Valentine*

Baldness

If a horse develops a bald area that is not itchy and shows none of the crusting or roughened skin surface caused by infection, the horse may have a condition known as alopecia areata. An affected horse may have small to large areas of bald skin, which may or may not grow back the next season. The diagnosis should be confirmed by a veterinary pathologist or dermatologist after examination of a skin biopsy. No treatment is available. The bald areas are usually small but may spread with time and can get quite large.

The most unusual case of equine baldness we have seen is a blue roan Percheron that has been completely bald all over his body since he shed his foal coat. Horse baldness is rare and is considered a hereditary problem. As you might imagine, a completely bald horse requires extra care, including protection from wet, cold and excessively hot weather, as well as sunblock on white areas in sunny weather.

Loss of Color

Gray horses are born dark and gradually lose hair pigment. As they age their hair may turn completely white, while the skin remains pigmented. The speed at which gray horses turn white is extremely variable, and we know of no way to accurately predict whether or when a black or gray horse will change color. The pattern of graying with age predisposes these horses to melanin-pigmented skin tumors (melanomas) that are different from melanomas in any other species.

Some non-gray horses may lose pigment from only patches of hair, which may occur under areas of harness or tack. Perhaps continuous pressure causes damage to the hair follicles. At any rate, since no loss of hair usually occurs in these areas, it's difficult to understand why only the pigmentation is lost. Loss of hair color in patches may also occur outside of harness and tack contact points, possibly the result of a biological change similar to the graying horse, but on a smaller scale.

A horse's haircoat may fade somewhat in the summer sun. Fading may be a problem for owners of black draft horses that are on the show circuit, but it hardly seems a good reason to deny a black horse a good bask in the sun. Some horses have winter coats that are obviously lighter or darker than their summer coats.

Regardless of a horse's color, the hair over skin that has been wounded may or may not grow back white. We do not recommend any of the various remedies used to keep the hair from growing back gray. If the hair is going to grow back a different color, it usually does so no matter what you do.

An examination of skin samples from areas where skin and hair have lost color confirm a lack of pigmentation at the site, without suggesting a cause or treatment. In people as well as horses this condition is called vitiligo (pronounced vit-el-EYE-go), which is a great word to know, but doesn't tell you the cause. A lot remains to be learned about changes in the color of a horse's skin and hair.

The possibility of fading hardly seems a good reason to deny black horses their time in the sun. *Photo by Susan Greenall*

Sun-Related Skin Disease

Most horses seem to enjoy basking in the sun, especially when few flies are around to annoy them. Under some circumstances, though, exposure to the sun can result in skin problems. Percherons and other all-gray or all-white horses generally have pigmented skin and are therefore not as likely to experience sun-related problems as do darker horses with poorly or unpigmented (pink) skin under white markings of the face, legs or body.

Percherons have pigmented skin and therefore rarely have the sun-related problems experienced by darker horses with patches of unpigmented skin under white hair.

Photo by Claude J. Sinnen

Sunburn

Skin that is nonpigmented may be sensitive to sunburn, especially on the face around the eyes and on the muzzle. Sunblock may be needed because the irritation of sunburn is not

The pink skin under the near horse's white muzzle is more likely to get sunburned than the darker skin of the off horse's muzzle.

Photo by Bonnie Nance

only unsightly but also painful and could lead to skin cancer. This problem is common in Clydesdales and Belgians with extensive white markings on their faces.

The application of an SPF (sun protection factor) 19 or higher sunblock sold for use on people will help protect a horse's sensitive areas of skin if applied at least once daily. A sunblock that is water resistant provides longer protection than one that is not water resistant.

Photosensitization

Plants such as St. John's wort and buckwheat contain compounds that build up in the skin and react with sunlight to cause a skin irritation known as photosensitization. Liver damage may also result in a build up of compounds in the skin that are normally cleared by the liver and that can cause photosensitization.

Photosensitization most often targets areas of the horse where the hair is white, such as the face and lower legs. As you can imagine, paints or Clydes with large areas of white hair can have tremendous skin damage due to photosensitization. Damaged skin often peels off, sometimes severely enough to be life threatening because of dehydration and secondary infections. Treatment may involve removing the horse from the area containing the plant causing photosensitization or treating the cause of the liver disease. In either case, such a horse must be kept away from the sun during healing.

photosensitization	
photo	= light
sensitization	= becoming sensitive to

Pressure Sores

Horses that lie down more than usual may develop pressure sores, which are the equine equivalent of human bedsores. These sores occur in the skin over prominent bones, and therefore appear most often in horses with severe overall weight loss or muscle atrophy. Draft horses with muscle atrophy and weakness due to EPSM tend to spend more time than usual lying down and often develop pressure sores.

To prevent these sores from developing, keep the bedding as soft and deep as possible. If a horse is down and unable to rise, frequently change its position. These procedures, along with topical treatment with antibacterial ointments or ointments containing aloe, may aid healing. In any case, you must identify the cause of the weight loss and weakness that led to development of pressure sores so you can provide appropriate treatment.

Congenital Skin Disease

A devastating disease of the skin and hooves occurs in Belgians. Affected foals are born normal, but within hours of birth areas of their skin and hooves begin to break down and fall off. Entire hooves are lost due to changes in the coronary band.

The disorder is known as a mechanobullous disease, which means that under pressure, such as rubbing, the affected skin forms blisters and falls off. The condition is sometimes called junctional skin disease, because the changes occur at the junction of the non-vascular and underlying vascular portions of the skin. Two other names for this disease are epidermolysis bullosa and epitheliogenesis imperfecta.

By whatever name, this fatal disease is known only in Belgians and is inherited. The means of inheritance is not clear. In one study a mare produced affected foals when bred both to a stallion that was related to her and to a stallion that was apparently unrelated. Any horse that has been a parent to such a foal should not be bred. Fortunately for Belgian breeders, this problem is not particularly common.

mechanobullous	
mechano	= mechanical, as in pressure
bullous	= blister-like
epidermolysis bullosa	
epidermis	= the top layer of the skin
lysis	= breakdown
bullosa	= blister
epitheliogenesis imperfecta	
epithelio	= epidermis
genesis	= production or origin
imperfecta	= imperfect or abnormal

Immune-Mediated Skin Disease

Horses may develop one of several severe total body skin diseases caused by an abnormal immune reaction against their own skin. These diseases, such as pemphigus, are often characterized by blisters that rupture to form open sores. Affected horses do not itch, but may get secondary bacterial infections. Treatment may involve either high doses of corticosteroids or gold-containing compounds. Since these latter medications are not cheap, their use to treat a draft horse could get quite expensive.

Wounds

Horses tend to get wounds no matter how safe their environment and how careful their owners. Most skin wounds are caused by other horses or sharp objects in the environment, such as branches, wooden boards, wire fence, nails and other metallic objects. Maintaining an environment that is free of such objects is ideal, but horses always seem to find ways to injure themselves.

Most superficial (shallow) wounds heal rapidly. Keep the wound clean by hosing it or cleaning it with Betadine surgical scrub or other antibacterial soap. Treating a wound with a topical antibiotic to decrease surface infection also helps promote rapid healing. Do not clean wounds with hydrogen peroxide, which causes tissue damage and delays healing. If you are uncertain about the severity of your horse's wound or what to treat it with, call a veterinarian.

Deep or large wounds require veterinary attention, which may include suturing (stitching) and possibly the placement of a drain to keep infected material from building up behind the damaged skin. Any horse with a deep wound should be given a tetanus booster.

Malignant Edema and Tetanus

Punctures and other deep wounds have a decreased oxygen level deep in the tissue that can allow growth of clostridial bacterial organisms, such as those that cause malignant edema and tetanus. These organisms are often present as inactive spores in the soil and can produce powerful toxins.

Painful swelling of the affected tissue may occur in horses with malignant edema, but only if the horse lives long enough. The toxins produced by the clostridial organisms that cause malignant edema are so powerful that often the first clinical sign is death. Unfortunately no vaccine has been developed for this problem. Aggressive surgery to open up the wound and clean out the affected area, as well as high doses of penicillin, *may* save the horse's life.

Tetanus affects the nervous system and causes painful muscle spasms, which in the respiratory muscles can result in death. Keep your horses current on tetanus vaccinations. As a precaution your veterinarian may want to administer a tetanus booster following any serious injury. For the draft horse an ounce of prevention is worth several pounds of cure.

The swelling and pain of malignant edema, and the painful spasms of tetanus, are life-threatening situations that require immediate veterinary attention.

Proud Flesh

Wounds below the knees and hocks are particularly susceptible to the development of excessive scar tissue growth known as proud flesh. The overgrowth of the underlying tissue does not allow the skin to close over the wound and can present a tough challenge for the owner and veterinarian.

Surgical removal of excess tissue, and surface treatment with compounds to decrease irritating infection and discourage the growth of excess tissue, are often necessary. Enzymes that dissolve proteins in tissue (such as Adolf's meat tenderizer), corticosteroids and light wraps are often useful treatments. A large, non-healing wound in the lower leg or elsewhere may heal best if small pinches of skin from the neck are planted in the wound area, a procedure known as skin grafting.

A wound that is more than skin deep—such as one involving joints, tendons, ligaments, muscle or blood vessels—requires veterinary attention. Never give up on a wounded horse until you have consulted with a veterinarian. Even serious wounds to skin and muscle, such as from a motor vehicle or farm equipment, may heal if given time and proper attention.

Photo by Bonnie Nance

Lumps and Bumps

Lumps and bumps are common on a horse's skin and occur for many different reasons. Some come and go without appearing to bother the horse. Some are itchy and some are painful. Tumors involving skin may grow only to a certain size or may continue to grow and invade into deeper tissues. The observant horse owner who spots these lumps and bumps early on and watches them carefully will be in the best position to get veterinary assistance when needed. Early treatment of a lump due to an infection or malignant tumor may save the horse's life.

Trauma

A bump may occur following trauma, such as a kick or a bite. Such wounds may be slightly warm to the touch and the horse may be sensitive to pressure on the area. Warmth and sensitivity especially occur in a swelling that appears at the site of a vaccination.

Other traumatically induced swellings may not be apparently painful, especially to a stoic draft horse. These lumps may be soft to the touch because they contain a lot of fluid, or they may be quite firm. Any swelling that is hot to the touch, that grows, or that bothers the horse should be examined by a veterinarian.

Infection

An abscess due to bacteria, or a reaction to a bit of foreign material such as a stick or plant awn, can appear similar to a tumor. Your veterinarian may make the diagnosis of abscess after inserting a needle to pull out cells to spread on a microscope slide, or after removing a portion of the abscess for microscopic examination. The veterinarian may culture the bacteria to determine which antibiotic to use. Most bacteria causing abscesses in horses still respond well to treatment with penicillin.

Bursae

Bursae are fluid-filled sacs, some of which occur under the skin over pressure points such as the point of the elbow and the hock. According to anatomists these bursae are not present at birth, but may develop following trauma to these areas. Bursae that are associated with tendons or ligaments, such as at the poll and withers, are present at birth.

Bursitis

A bursa is difficult to detect unless it swells and fills with fluid or becomes infected (bursitis) or ruptures, causing inflammation in the adjacent tissue. Although bursitis is non-life threatening and usually not painful, some bursae do cause pain, and occasionally horses develop persistent inflammation or progressive scarring of the affected area following bursal rupture.

The opening of (or an injection into) a fluid-filled bursa subjects the horse to the risk of infection. A bursa that ruptures on its own may result in continued irritation, in which case surgical removal may be necessary.

Capped Hock and Capped Elbow

The conditions known as capped hock and capped elbow are due to increased fluid in the bursae. These conditions do not seem to bother the horse, but they are unsightly.

A capped elbow, also called a shoeboil, may be caused be the horse's hind shoe hitting the back of the elbow as the horse lies down and stands up. Refitting the horse with shoes that have shorter heels may help. More often, though, a shoeboil forms because the horse is lying down on a hard surface.

Sometimes the swelling decreases in size with time. A large or persistent bursal swelling may need to be treated by draining the fluid or injecting an irritating material (such as iodine) to cause reduction in size by scarring. If shoes or hard surfaces are the real problem, these swellings often recur.

Allergies

Many bumps that occur on a horse, especially bumps formed by contact with the harness or saddle, have been called protein bumps. The term is inappropriate because diet has no effect on the formation of skin bumps, unless the horse is allergic to something in the feed. Such bumps may also be caused by allergy to biting insects or to inhaled substances, similar to hay fever in humans.

Eosinophilic Granulomas

The most common bump caused by an allergy is usually covered by normal skin and hair and is not apparently itchy, but does not

Fly nets help reduce the incidence of skin bumps due to biting insects.

Photo by Claude J. Sinnen

go away. Typically this area is no more than a couple of inches around. Examination of the area under a microscope will reveal many cells, known as eosinophils (pronounced EE-oh-sin-oh-fills), that stain red in blood smears and tissue samples. These cells accumulate in areas in which an allergic reaction or parasite is present. Eosinophils often surround areas in which the fibrous part of the skin, the collagen, has degenerated. Collagen is a tough substance that forms most of what we know as leather.

Such bumps are often called eosinophilic granulomas or nodular collagenolytic granulomas. The word granuloma refers to the other cells in the lesion, called macrophages, which are capable of ingesting broken down cells, organisms, and foreign material. Cure may be either by removal or by treatment with corticosteroids, which may be administered systemically or by injection into each bump.

eosinophilic granuloma
eosin	= a red stain
phil	= liking
granuloma	= an inflammatory reaction containing many macrrophages

nodular collagenolytic granuloma
nodule	= roundish, firm bump
collagen	= fibrous tissue
lytic	= breakdown
granuloma	= an inflammatory reaction containing many macrophages

macrophage
macro	= large
phage	= eating

Hives

Some horses have allergies that cause them to develop hives. The hives may appear rapidly, involve many parts of the body, and irritate the horse. If you have ever developed hives, you can understand what the horse is going through. Hives are both itchy and painful. A horse with hives near the udder, prepuce or groin may kick at its belly as if it had colic. Hives may be large and appear as skin swellings that are slightly flattened, and may rapidly increase and decrease in size, and appear and disappear on different parts of the body. Hives are soft due to fluid build up in the skin. Horses with long-standing problems with hives lose hair, but the skin surface generally stays smooth.

The allergen causing hives may be a substance that is on the skin, such as pollens, molds, fly wipes, blankets, saddle pads or other substances applied to the skin. The allergen may be in the feed and may affect the horse following either ingestion or inhalation, or it may be in the air. A horse sometimes develops an allergy to a substance that never bothered it before.

Your veterinarian may prescribe corticosteroids to reduce the irritation of hives; antihistamines are not particularly effective for treating hives and other allergic skin diseases in horses. If the hives continue, the horse is still being exposed to an offending substance. Carefully examine the horse's environment. To identify the cause, you may need to remove or change the grain, straw, hay and blankets one by one until the hives disappear.

If your horse develops hives after you have acquired new feed or bedding, remove the feed or bedding immediately. If a new product is the cause, the hives should disappear within a day or two after the product is removed.

Bites and False Tumors

In regions with biting flies and ticks, large firm lumps from insect bites may suddenly appear anywhere on the horse. When they occur in the groin area or inner thigh they are difficult to see, but you can feel them.

Such lumps may have small surface crusts and be slightly irritating to the horse. The bumps do not enlarge after the first few hours or days, but may persist for months. They should, however, decrease in size and eventually disappear.

Like people, some horses are more sensitive than others to fly and tick bites. Some flies, such as black flies, are more likely than other flies to create an obvious skin reaction at the site of a bite.

A swelling at the site of a tick bite is not from parts of the tick's mouth left in the skin. Any tick parts left in the skin do not create a problem; they are eventually expelled from the site as the skin heals.

If reaction to an insect or tick bite obviously bothers your horse, the application of corticosteroid skin cream once or twice a day should help make the horse more comfortable and may result in more rapid healing.

A fly or tick bite reaction may occasionally be so large, and remain for so long, that the owner and veterinarian become concerned enough to remove it. Learning that the bump is not a tumor is always a relief. A persistent insect bite reaction is called pseudolymphoma because the large number of lymphocytes in the tissue resemble a malignant tumor of lymphocytes and lymph nodes. The cost of surgical removal and determining the nature of the bump is never money wasted because the horse's life may be saved by early diagnosis if it turns out to be a real tumor.

> *pseudolymphoma*
> pseudo = false
> lymph = lymph nodes
> or lymphocytes
> oma = tumorous swelling

Tumors

A tumor is a swelling that results from new growth of tissue composed of a single kind of cell, rather than from inflammation or the accumulation of fluid. Tumors are also called neoplasms. A tumor may be benign, meaning it remains in one place, or malignant, meaning it can spread into adjacent or distant parts of the body.

Tumors	
Tumor	*Appearance*
carcinoma	skin appears angry, red and often ulcerated
melanoma	dark colored, usually smooth
papilloma	wart-like
sarcoid	may be wart-like or smooth and flat
mole	nodular growth that may cause skin ulceration, usually dark colored
lymphoma	multiple smooth nodules or swellings

> *neoplasm*
> neo = new
> plasm = tissue

Benign Tumors

Although a benign tumor may grow until it is quite large, it does not spread like a malignant tumor, but remains in one area. Removal of a benign tumor by surgery usually results in a cure.

Warts

In young horses tumors caused by viruses, or viral papillomas, may occur around the head, especially on the lips and muzzle. In older horses they may occur on the penis or on the sheath. Commonly called warts, these benign tumors are often multiple and unsightly.

Warts in young horses usually resolve on their own as the horse matures and develops a strong immunity to the virus. Possible treatments to speed the process include removal of one or more of the warts, which may trigger an increased immune response that causes the remaining tumors to resolve, or injection of compounds known to incite an immune response.

In older horses warts on the penis or sheath are persistent and can develop into skin cancer (squamous cell carcinoma). They should be treated promptly by surgery or medical therapy.

> *viral papilloma*
> viral = caused by a virus
> papilla = nipple or pimple
> oma = tumorous swelling

Sarcoids

Equine sarcoids can look like warts or can appear as areas of thickened skin. Although they may occur in a horse of any age, sarcoids usually appear in horses one to four years of age. Under the microscope they look like malignant tumors (sarcomas), hence the name sarcoid (sarcoma-like). They are a problem for horse owners and veterinarians because they may become large and may regrow following removal. They do not, however, spread to internal tissues.

The cause of sarcoids was recently recognized to be infection by bovine papillomavirus. This association had been suspected for years based on observations that equine sarcoids are most common where cattle and horses are pastured together or in close proximity. Sarcoids are rarely or never seen in Japan and other countries where horses and cattle are widely separated.

The virus is likely spread by biting flies. Various therapies, including removal, injection of immune-stimulating agents and the use of topical anti-tumor medications all have some success.

> *sarcoid, sarcoma*
> sarco = fleshy
> oid = like
> oma = tumor

Moles

A horse is sometimes born with a birthmark or mole called a melanocytic nevus. Such a mole may also develop after birth, usually in a young horse up to about six years of age. The mole

A sarcoid may resemble a large wart on the horse's head, body or leg.
Photo by Stan Snyder

may grow rapidly and cause a breakdown (ulceration) of the overlying skin, thereby becoming worrisome to the horse's owner.

Moles may be white, gray, or black. A black mole may resemble the melanoma that occurs in mature gray horses. Moles, however, may appear on horses of any color and most often in places not typical of the melanoma occurring in mature gray horses. Moles are most common on the body, neck and legs. Although their initial growth is often rapid, these benign tumors generally stabilize and just sit quietly on the horse.

We recommend surgical removal and microscopic examination of any mole, because occasionally one grows into the underlying tissue. If spreading occurs on the lower part of the leg and involves tendons, the mole may become impossible to remove. Furthermore, what looks like a benign tumor sometimes turns out to be malignant. The sooner you get the tumor removed and analyzed, the better.

> *melanocytic nevus*
> melano = black
> cytic = cells
> nevus = mole

Malignant Tumors

With the exception of gray horses that develop melanomas, horses are less likely to develop dangerous malignant tumors of the skin than are dogs, cats and people. Malignant tumors invade deeply into adjacent tissue, have the ability to spread through the body, and are often known collectively as cancer, the Latin word for crab—the spread of cancer is likened to the spreading of a crab's legs.

Various therapies, including surgical removal and chemotherapy, may be effective against tumors. When it comes to fighting cancer, some horses seem to be inherently stronger than others. Dr. Bill Rebhun, late of Cornell University College of Veterinary Medicine, observed that the Clydesdale with a

malignant tumor, even a tumor that is potentially treatable, is more likely than other draft breeds to succumb to the cancer.

Gray Horse Melanomas

Any horse with a coat color that changes to gray or white with age is subject to melanomas. Common wisdom is that every gray horse will develop at least one melanoma if it lives long enough.

Although melanomas grow slowly, they eventually invade underlying tissue and may spread internally. They are covered by sparsely haired or hairless smooth black skin and are most

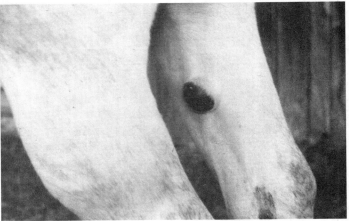

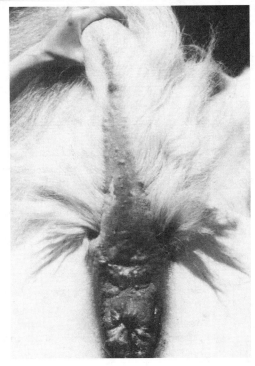

A mole (top) is likely to be a single structure on the horse's body, neck or leg, in contrast to a gray horse melanoma (bottom) which is more likely to be multiple and appear in other areas, like these multiple melanomas on the underside of the tail and around the anus.
Photos by Betsy Graham

Mole or Melanoma?		
Typical	*Mole*	*Melanoma*
Horse color	any color	matures to white or gray
Horse age	newborn foal or young adult	more than 6 years old
Location on horse	on the body on the neck on the legs	underside of tail around anus and vulva in or on sheath around lips on eyelids in the throatlatch area at base of ears
Growth rate	rapid then stabilizes	slow but often continues
Skin surface	may be rough	typically smooth

common on the underside of the tail, around the anus and vulva, in or on the sheath, around the lips, on eyelids, in the throatlatch area or at the base of the ears.

If the tumor occurs as a single isolated mass, surgical removal may be the best option. Removal in the early stages may cure the problem. Unfortunately gray horses often develop multiple melanomas, which may merge to form a large area of small to large lumps and bumps that are impossible to remove. Fortunately a horse with melanomas may live many years without apparent discomfort.

Gray horses that are more than six years old are most susceptible to developing melanomas. Although melanomas do occur in Percherons and other gray draft horses, and we have seen a seven-year-old Percheron with several large melanomas, they do not appear to be as great a problem in drafts as they are in gray light horses such as Arabians and Thoroughbreds.

Lymphoma

A lymphoma is a malignant tumor of lymphocytes, cells that are important to the body's immune system. Also called malignant lymphoma or lymphosarcoma, this tumor commonly affects the lymph nodes, but may involve the skin or internal organs. In a horse's skin the tumor causes multiple swellings that do not bother the horse. Although the swellings rarely go away, they may vary in size or location over time.

An examination of the cells under a microscope is necessary to confirm this diagnosis. The cells are taken either by suction applied to a needle placed into one of the masses and spread onto a glass microscope slide, or from tissue samples obtained by surgical biopsy. Even though lymphoma is a malignant tumor, it is usually not as aggressive in horses as it is in dogs, cats, cattle or humans. Horses may live for many years before

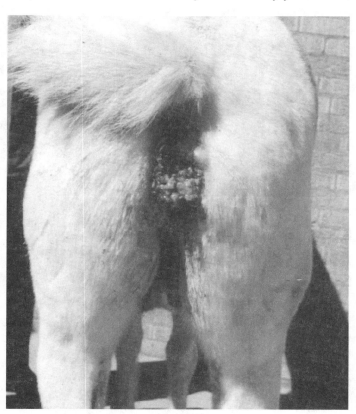

This mare has an advanced case of squamous cell carcinoma of the vulva.

Photo by Stan Snyder

lymphoma
  lymph = lymph nodes or lymphocytes
  oma   = tumorous swelling

succumbing to the cancer. Although chemotherapy is costly, especially for a large draft horse, its use has recently enjoyed some success.

Skin Cancer

Squamous cell carcinoma is a common skin cancer that may occur in sun-exposed non-pigmented or poorly-pigmented skin, such as around the eyes. Squamous cell carcinoma also occurs commonly on the penis, sheath, and vulva because of irritation from the secretions (smegma) that accumulate in these areas. Belgians are more likely than other drafts to develop squamous cell carcinoma. To help prevent this tumor apply sunblock to susceptible skin and frequently cleanse the skin around the vulva, and of the penis and sheath.

Often raw and angry looking, these tumors resemble wounds that will not heal, but rather continue to spread. The affected skin ulcerates (breaks down), often with associated surface infection. On rare occasions squamous cell carcinoma will develop at the site of a large poorly healing wound.

Squamous cell carcinomas are hard to detect if they begin to grow in areas that are difficult to examine, such as on the penis or sheath. When they are present in these areas they may result in discharge, urination difficulty, pain and swelling.

Although these tumors may spread into adjacent tissue, they generally spread slowly. Surgical removal when possible, along with various treatments such as freezing, radiation or laser therapy, or the application of topical anti-tumor agents often results in a cure. A horse that has developed a squamous cell carcinoma tends to develop other similar tumors, requiring constant vigilance to detect the growths in early stages.

> *squamous cell carcinoma*
> squamous   = scale like
> carcinoma   = cancer

Other Tumors

Other tumors that affect a horse's skin are much less common that those described here. Fortunately most skin tumors in horses are benign, and even some of the malignant tumors may be cured through early detection and treatment.

Photo by Barry Cooper

Breathing Hard

A horse that breathes hard at rest has a problem. Airway infection, allergy or fluid build up in the lungs can cause an increased respiratory rate, usually associated with a cough. Lung tumors can also affect breathing, but are quite uncommon in horses.

A horse that breathes hard (blows) following exercise could have an airway or a cardiac (heart) problem, but may be suffering from other causes including poor condition, overheating and muscle disease. A horse with a fever or pain may have an increased respiratory rate. These other causes, however, are not associated with coughing or abnormal respiratory noises.

Unlike most species, a horse cannot breath through its mouth, only through its nose. When a horse has difficulty breathing you will often see flaring of the nostrils, increased breathing rate, and increased abdominal wall movements during breathing; you will not see the horse trying to breath through an open mouth.

The respiratory rate increases when horses work hard, but if the horses are well conditioned their breathing rate will drop to normal within 30 minutes after work stops.

Photo by Susan Greenall

Coughing

A deep cough means the horse has a problem deep in the smaller airways of the lungs. A shallow cough may accompany either a lung problem or something higher in the respiratory system, such as a foreign object or irritation in the upper airways (larynx or trachea). A persistently coughing horse, or one that is off feed or has an increased temperature, should be examined by a veterinarian.

The veterinarian will perform a physical examination, including carefully listening to the lungs to determine where the problem is and how bad it is. The veterinarian may also perform a transtracheal wash, in which a small amount of sterile fluid is injected into the trachea then withdrawn back into the syringe. Microscopic examination and culture of the contents can help determine if bacteria or fungi are present or if the horse has an allergy or other problem affecting the lungs.

transtracheal	
trans	= across
tracheal	= pertaining to the trachea (windpipe)

Heart Failure

The condition known as heart failure is due to a dysfunctional heart, but is not necessarily immediately fatal. By way of contrast, any heart condition in which the heart's electrical activity is disrupted can result in sudden death (cardiac arrhythmia). Heart failure is uncommon in the general horse population, but veterinary clinicians have told us they suspect that, for unknown reasons, heart failure is more common in drafts.

The failing heart cannot pump blood properly. A backup of blood trying to return to the heart may result in fluid accumulation in the lungs or abdomen. Fluid in the lungs causes an increased resting respiratory rate, and may be associated with difficulty breathing and/or coughing and exercise intolerance.

Specific treatments may vary somewhat, depending on exactly what has caused the heart failure. Digoxin to improve heart muscle function and furosemide (Lasix) to help remove fluid buildup are the mainstays of treatment for heart failure in horses and other species. Treating a horse for heart failure makes sense only if the animal is either a pet or valued for breeding (most heart problems are not inherited). Such a horse will not be able to perform, and the longterm outlook (prognosis) is not good. Treatment may be effective for only a few months to a few years.

Heaves

A horse with respiratory allergies may have severe bouts of deep coughing during exercise. The allergens are usually pollens and/or mold spores in feed, bedding or pasture. Exposure to the allergens causes the lung's small airways, the bronchioles, to close down, resulting in difficult breathing similar to that in people with asthma. Allergic bronchitis, which causes a horse to cough after exposure to the allergen, is sporadic and the horse may have few or no problems breathing most of the time.

If the horse with allergic bronchitis continues to have a high exposure to the allergens, it may go on to develop heaves, also known as broken wind or technically as chronic obstructive pulmonary disease (COPD). A horse with heaves is always uncomfortable breathing; exhaling air is more difficult than inhaling.

Horses with allergic bronchitis or heaves may be treated with various medications. Do not confine an affected horse to a stall or other enclosed area; 24-hour turnout with adequate shelter is a must. The exception is the occasional horse that is allergic to plant pollens in the pasture. Removing such horses from the pasture to a well-ventilated barn or a dirt paddock may solve the problem.

If the horse is fed hay, soak it thoroughly to keep the pollens and mold spores from being inhaled. Hosing or dumping buckets of water on the hay at feeding time are not adequate. The best method is to completely immerse the hay in a water tub for at least an hour, but preferably all day or overnight, before feeding it.

Another important place to decrease pollen and mold dusts is in the horse's concentrated feed, whether it is grain or pellets. Either soak the feed in water or mix it with one cup or more of

The increased effort of breathing out enlarges the muscles at the base of the ribs (muscle hypertrophy), causing what's known as a heave line.

vegetable oil to keep the dusts from getting into the air. Dr. David Kronfeld, an equine nutritionist at Virginia-Maryland College of Veterinary Medicine, has reported that a high fat diet results in less carbon dioxide production within the body cells. Since carbon dioxide must be exhaled from the lungs, reducing carbon dioxide production may be beneficial for horses with heaves and difficulty exhaling.

> *hypertrophy*
> hyper   = increased
> trophy   = growth

Lungworms

Infection with parasitic lungworms in horses, although relatively uncommon, can result in clinical signs similar to heaves. The horse lungworm *Dictyocaulus arnfeldi* is carried by donkeys and mules. Donkeys and mules do not show any clinical signs of infection with this parasite. Horses and ponies housed with donkeys or mules eat the infective larvae that pass in manure, and the larvae migrate to the horse's lungs where they develop into adult worms.

Horses infected with lungworms cough frequently and make an increased effort to exhale. A stethoscope may be used to listen for abnormal lung sounds described as crackles and wheezes. Worming horses, mules and donkeys with ivermectin effectively controls lungworms, and seems a more reasonable approach than not pasturing horses with mules or donkeys.

Keys to a healthy respiratory system

Key components to helping maintain the health of your horse's respiratory system are:
- a clean environment
- good ventilation
- regular removal of urine, which produces airway irritants such as ammonia.

Pneumonia and Pleuritis

Pneumonia is an inflammation of the lungs, which in the horse is most often caused by bacterial infection. All foals, and adult horses that are shipped long distances or subjected to other stresses, are most susceptible. An unclean or otherwise unhealthy environment plays a large role in the development of pneumonia.

Allergic bronchitis or heaves makes a horse more susceptible to bacterial infection of the lungs, but treating allergic horses with antibiotics is not usually useful unless you have clear-cut evidence of infection, such as fever or yellowish nasal discharge.

Signs of pneumonia include:
- an increased rate of respiration at rest
- fever
- lethargy
- lack of interest in eating

Horses with pneumonia generally cough, but may not. They may or may not have a nasal discharge indicative of infection.

Aggressive treatment of pneumonia is imperative because the infection may spread to other parts of the horse's body (septicemia) or may result in serious and permanent damage to lung tissue. Infection of the membranous tissue lining the chest cavity and covering the lungs is called pleuritis, as painful a disorder in horses as it is in people.

septicemia
    septic = infection
    emia = blood

pleuritis
    pleura = the membranous lining of the
             chest cavity that also covers
             the lungs
    itis   = inflammation

Foal Pneumonia

To prevent lung infection, a foal should be born in and kept in an environment that is as clean and well ventilated as possible. Foals are particularly susceptible to pneumonia caused by *Rhodoccous equi,* a bacterium found in the soil that can cause infection of the lungs after either being inhaled directly into the lungs or swallowed and brought to the lungs through the bloodstream. On farms in which a large number of these bacteria reside in the soil, greater exposure and more risk of infection exist.

A foal is more likely to become infected if it has decreased immunity, due either to inadequate ingestion of the mare's first milk (colostrum), which contains large amounts of antibodies to help protect the foal, or to an inherent problem in the foal's immune system. An inherited immune system problem has been recognized in Arabians for many years, and a similar problem has been recently identified in Fell ponies. Since inherent immune system problems have not been recognized in draft horses, the best protection is to see that the newborn foal gets plenty of the dam's first milk.

Infection with *Rhodococcus equi* may allow overgrowth of the fungal organism *Pneumocystis carinii,* which is common in small numbers in the lungs of healthy horses and people. Overgrowth of this organism is difficult to treat. Streptococcal infection is another cause of pneumonia in foals, as well as in adult horses. A foal is occasionally born with pneumonia caused by herpesvirus, a virus that is more likely to cause abortion in the later stages of pregnancy. If a foal infected with

herpesvirus is born, it will be obviously distressed and won't survive. Various other bacteria, such as the Gram-negative bacteria that are normally passed in manure, can cause pneumonia in foals exposed to high numbers of these bacteria in the environment or in foals whose immune systems are not operating at peak efficiency.

A foal that gets plenty of its dam's first milk (colostrum) will have a healthy immune system. *Courtesy of Beaver Dam Farm*

Pneumonia in Adult Horses

Pneumonia is much less common in adult horses than in foals. When it does occur, it is usually caused by stress such as long-distance shipping (shipping fever) during which the horse's head has been tied in an upright position. This position compromises the horse's ability to remove infectious organisms from its respiratory tract through snorting, coughing and gravity. Stress decreases the function of the horse's immune system, so bacteria in the environment can more easily take hold.

Viral infection of the airways, such as may occur due to influenza (flu) virus or rhinopneumonitis (herpes) virus is generally a mild disease in adult horses that clears rapidly. Viral infection does, however, compromise the horse's immunity and can predispose the horse to secondary bacterial infection.

Sudden onset of bacterial pneumonia in an adult horse may be due either to a recent infection with strangles or to the breakdown of a walled-off infection (abscess). Abscesses may persist following apparent recovery from foal pneumonia or strangles. Stress compromises the horse's immune system and allows the bacteria to spread.

Fungal infection is a less common cause of pneumonia in horses, which is good since treatment of fungal pneumonia is difficult.

Tying a horse's head upright (left) during long-distance travel can lead to pneumonia (shipping fever); leave enough slack in the rope to allow the horse to drop its head (right).

When shipping a horse over a long distance, maintain the best possible ventilation in the trailer and make plenty of overnight stops where the horse can be released at least into a box stall.

Aspiration Pneumonia

Damage and infection of the lungs may occur if material meant to go to or stay in the stomach is inhaled (aspirated) into the lungs. Aspiration may occur when:

- medications or other substances are forced too rapidly into the horse's mouth or throat
- muscles involved in closing off the airways during swallowing are weak, such as in horses with botulism, selenium deficiency or protozoal myeloencephalitis
- colicky horse has digestive material from its stomach moving up into its mouth and nose, caused by pressure (reflux)
- a horse has developed choke—obstruction of the esophagus by feed material.

Medications, feed and stomach contents are damaging to lung tissue. The damage creates a favorable environment for bacteria to grow. Make sure pregnant mares and foals have adequate selenium so they avoid developing weakness of the laryngeal muscles, and be careful when administering liquids or pastes by mouth. If your horse develops choke, call a veterinarian immediately.

Aspiration pneumonia is one of the most serious infections of the lung and is often fatal.

Silica inhalation

Horses in the Monterey and Central Peninsulas of California may develop lung disease due to inhaled silica particles present in the soil. No symptoms are apparent other than breathing problems, and no cure is available.

Roaring

A horse that makes a loud roaring sound while exercising has laryngeal paralysis, also called laryngeal hemiplegia, a condition in which the nerves to the muscles of the larynx are damaged, resulting in poor opening of the larynx during inspiration (inhaling). This condition usually affects only the left side of the larynx, but both sides may be involved. The sound is unmistakable and unlike the expiratory (exhaling) snort some horses make during the canter. Roaring is caused by air being forced in through a collapsed laryngeal opening, instead of through a wide open one. The reason this nerve problem occurs is not entirely known.

Susceptibility

Tall horses are most prone to laryngeal hemiplegia, which is a common problem in big draft horses but virtually never seen in ponies. Draft horses may be more susceptible because the nerve to the left side of the larynx, the left recurrent laryngeal nerve, is one of the longest nerves in the horse's body (the sciatic nerves

Horses that are asked to exert a maximal effort, such as in pulling competitions, need wide airways for maximum breathing capacity.   *Photo by Vickie Darnell*

in the hind legs are the other long nerves). Long nerves may be more subject to damage. In young growing drafts and other tall horses the nerve growth may not be able to keep up with the neck's growth rate.

Treatment

A veterinarian can determine the degree of severity by passing a flexible tube, called an endoscope, through the nose to watch the larynx during breathing. A mildly affected horse that isn't asked to gallop or pull heavy loads may never appear to have a problem. Some horses may have noisy respiration, but still not have enough interference with their breathing to require surgery.

In a more severe case, or in a horse that is asked to exert maximal efforts such as engaging in pulling competitions, surgical correction may be required to widen the airway through which to breathe. Occasionally both sides of the larynx are affected, in which case the horse may need to be fitted with a permanent tube opening directly into the trachea (windpipe), through which it can breath and which requires continuous monitoring and care by the owner.

Two surgical procedures are done to correct roaring. One is the quick and simple removal of a portion of the laryngeal tissues that obstruct the opening. This procedure has a higher success rate in draft horses than in light horses.

> *laryngeal hemiplegia*
> laryngeal = pertaining to the larynx
> hemi = partial
> plegi = paralysis
>
> *endoscope*
> end = inside
> scope = device used to see things

A more complicated procedure is tieback surgery, which involves the placement of sutures to hold the larynx in an open position. Tieback surgery takes longer, and veterinary surgeons and anesthetists are always worried about keeping a draft horse under general anesthesia for long periods. Anesthesia problems with drafts, however, may change as we begin to understand the underlying muscle metabolic problem (EPSM) that may be the cause of unexpected difficulties in standing up experienced by some draft horses following general anesthesia.

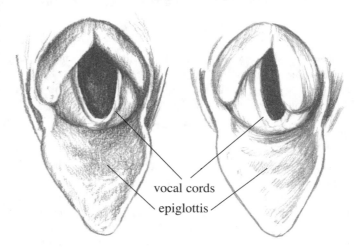

vocal cords
epiglottis

The larynx of a normal horse (left) as viewed through an endoscope, compared to the larynx of a roarer, in which the paralyzed left side does not open during inspiration.

Breathing Easy

Although a horse's respiratory system can develop a variety of problems, good management—including providing plenty of fresh air, maintaining a reasonably clean environment, and using common sense—go a long way toward keeping our horses healthy.

Photo by Claude Sinnen

Gastrointestinal Problems

14

Many horses remain apparently healthy their entire lives, perhaps due in large part to good horse management. If horses have an Achilles' heel, though, it is their susceptibility to disorders affecting the esophagus, stomach and intestines.

Choke

A horse with choke has a blockage of the esophagus, the tubular organ leading from the back of the throat to the stomach. Sometimes the blockage is visible on the left side of the horse's neck—where the esophagus lies under the groove bearing the jugular vein, carotid artery and some of the major nerves to the head. You may merely see or feel a thickening in this area, but even that can be difficult in a thick-necked draft horse. The blockage may instead occur lower down, where the esophagus is inside the chest wall and cannot be seen or felt.

A choked horse will stop eating and drinking, although it may appear hungry or thirsty. The horse will generally be quite distressed, and may appear to be trying to cough up or regurgitate something. The blockage may cause fluid and feed to be expelled through the nostrils. Fluid noises may be heard coming from the neck or throatlatch area.

Treatment

The blockage must be resolved quickly, as the esophagus may become permanently damaged or the horse may inhale regurgitated feed and develop a severe pneumonia. Because it is not possible to perform a Heimlich maneuver on a draft horse, if your horse chokes, call a veterinarian immediately—don't wait to see what happens.

While you are waiting for the veterinarian to arrive, gently massage the area of the jugular groove on the left side of the horse's neck, trying to break up the blockage and move it toward the stomach. If you have to ship the horse to a hospital don't tie its head upright, or you will increase the risk that the horse might inhale food.

Your veterinarian will most likely use a stomach tube to gently flush water into the area to try to break up the blockage. Sometimes just sedation with something like acepromazine allows the muscles of the esophagus wall to relax and let the normal contractile waves of the wall (peristalsis) move the material down to the stomach.

If the choke has resolved by the time your veterinarian arrives, your horse will be drinking and trying to eat again. Initially offer the horse only water. The veterinarian will likely treat the horse with a medication like banamine or phenylbutazone to decrease inflammation, and may also treat the horse with antibiotics to avoid infection. The first few meals after a horse has choked should consist of feed mixed with water to make a mash or gruel.

Prevention

Horses on pelleted feeds may have a slightly increased chance of developing choke, possibly because they are able to eat large amounts more quickly. The benefits of pelleted feeds, especially those that are low in soluble carbohydrates, vastly outweigh the disadvantages. You can easily design a program that allows feeding a relatively small volume of pelleted feed, which should minimize the risk of choke. Two draft horses we know of surprised us by choking on pelleted feed with large amounts of added vegetable oil.

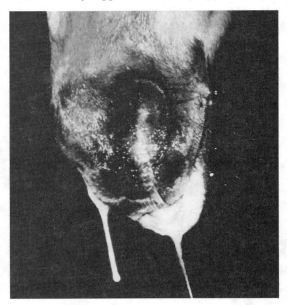

A horse with choke may have mucus, saliva and sometimes food material draining from its nostrils and mouth.

Courtesy of Jill Parker

Horses that gulp their food too rapidly are at a higher risk for choke. Owners of such horses may find that placing large rocks or other smooth objects into the horse's feed bucket causes the horse to eat more slowly because it has to eat around the non-food objects. Soaking feed in water to form a damp mash prior to feeding is the most effective way to prevent choke in a horse that has developed this problem, and is the safest way to feed a horse that has choked, even if it has occurred only once.

Horses with a form of rabies infection may have problems swallowing and appear to have choke, although this sign is more common in rabid bovines.

Bacterial Infections

Infections of the small or large intestine may occur in adult horses, sometimes for no obvious reason, although under most circumstances such an infection is relatively uncommon. A previously healthy adult horse with symptoms of an intestinal bacterial infection may have another underlying problem affecting its immune system or intestinal movements, or may have infection of an area previously damaged by parasites.

Salmonella

Salmonella infection is a serious concern of veterinarians at equine hospitals. A horse carrying salmonella organisms without any problems may, under the stress of hospitalization, break out with intestinal damage and severe diarrhea, and pass the bacteria in its feces to infect other stressed horses. Such an outbreak is a nightmare for the equine veterinarian.

Most hospitals where several horses are under treatment use footbaths and other decontamination procedures designed to minimize this hazard. Ideally the hospital should maintain isolation facilities for horses with infectious diseases.

Salmonella infections may occur in horses that are shipped or stressed in other ways.

Clostridia

Stressed horses may develop a sudden severe and generally fatal inflammation of the colon known as colitis X. Severe clostridial infection is thought to be the most likely cause.

Horses being given systemic antibiotics, especially by mouth, may develop an intestinal bacterial infection due to *Clostridium dificile* or *Clostridium perfringens*. These organisms are often present in the intestines of healthy horses but may become damaging when antibiotics have altered the normal gastrointestinal bacterial populations that help keep potentially dangerous bacteria at bay.

Various compounds known as probiotics may be given to horses being treated with high levels of oral antibiotics or that have developed antibiotic-related diarrhea. Probiotics often contain the bacteria known as lactobacillus that help promote a healthy intestinal bacterial population. Your veterinarian may suggest one of the commercial products designed for horses, or may recommend feeding your horse plain yogurt.

Potomac Horse Fever

Potomac horse fever is an infectious disease caused by rickettsial organisms, which are microscopic and related to bacteria. Potomac horse fever appears to occur only in certain areas of the world, such as along the Potomac River in Maryland, areas of northern California and southern Oregon, and parts of Canada, France, Italy, Venezuela, India and Australia.

Transmission to horses involves flukes that parasitize fresh water snails. Horses drinking from streams and ponds in areas where the organism is present are at risk of infection, but the infection does not spread from one horse to another.

This infection causes fluid thickening (edema) of the bowel wall, but is much less damaging to the tissue compared to bacterial infections. Signs in affected horses include:
- fever, which may be as high as 107°F
- depression and going off feed
- signs of colic
- edema of the lower legs and abdomen
- diarrhea
- dehydration.

With proper nursing care, most horses with Potomac horse fever survive. They may, however, develop severe, life-threatening laminitis.

Colic

Pain, stress and other problems can affect the normal movement of the contents of a horse's stomach and intestine. These normal movements, collectively known as gastrointestinal motility, ensure that food continues to pass through, with the proper breakdown of feed into nutrients that are absorbed into the blood stream. These movements also ensure that water added during the process is eventually absorbed and re-used.

Horses cannot vomit to relieve any irritation or overload of the stomach. At the first sign of colic, a veterinarian often passes a nasogastric tube into the horse's stomach in an attempt to release the increased pressure. The tube may also be used to administer necessary treatments, such as water to rehydrate a dehydrated horse and mineral oil or other compounds designed to help soften the intestinal contents and lubricate the intestinal walls to keep things moving.

The material that spontaneously comes up from the horse's stomach through the nasogastric tube is known as gastric reflux. Its presence indicates increased volume and pressure in the stomach caused by decreased gastrointestinal motility. The increased volume and pressure may be caused by obstruction due to:

- gas
- feed
- intestinal stones
- tumors of or around the intestines
- a twist or displacement of either the small or large intestine.

The horse's stomach wall is not able to stretch far before it breaks down (gastric rupture). Relieving pressure in the stomach as soon as possible may be critical to the horse's survival.

Signs of colic

A horse with colic pain:
- shows obvious signs of discomfort
- may repeatedly curl its upper lip (flehmen response)
- goes off feed
- does not pass normal amounts of manure
- may paw the ground
- may shift its weight from limb to limb
- may sweat profusely
- may turn its head as if to look at its flanks
- may kick at its belly
- may go down and roll violently.

Draft horses, because of their naturally stoic nature, don't always show classic signs of colic. Evaluating a draft horse with colic to confirm the correct diagnosis requires careful observation by you and a careful examination of the horse by your veterinarian.

Medical or Surgical?

Veterinarians classify equine colic into two categories, medical and surgical, based on the results of their evaluation of the horse. Your veterinarian will assess the status of a horse with colic by evaluating various body parameters: the color of its gums and conjunctiva, heart and respiration rates, body temperature, and gastrointestinal sounds. If you are able to assess your horse's vital signs and relay them to your veterinarian when you call, you will help the veterinarian decide how best to manage your horse.

A horse with vital signs indicative of serious trouble, such as a high heart rate and dark purplish gums, may need to be transported for treatment in a hospital setting. In many colic cases time is of the essence. A horse requiring surgery has a better chance of recovery if the surgery is performed before intestinal breakdown occurs. Some colics that, if treated immediately, might have been treated medically may end up requiring surgical correction.

All horse owners should have ready access to transportation for their horses in case of emergency. In some colic cases the bouncy trailer ride is all it takes to resolve an intestinal displacement. This phenomenon is the basis for the often-repeated recommendation to load a horse with colic into a trailer and drive on a bumpy road. Given the possibly life-threatening nature of colic, we recommend that the road you take leads directly to an equine hospital. Don't be embarrassed if your horse is apparently normal when you get there. The costs of gas and keeping the horse at the hospital overnight, to confirm that it is not in trouble and to administer fluids or other useful medications, is money well-spent. Your veterinarian's evaluation may include palpation of the intestines by rectal examination, an examination of the consistency of any manure in the rectum, and evaluation of abdominal fluid by obtaining a small sample through a needle (abdominal tap).

A trailer ride on a bumpy road may benefit a horse with colic, but make sure the road leads directly to a veterinary hospital.

Surgical Colics

The small and large intestines are attached to the body wall and other organs within the abdomen in only a few places, and therefore have plenty of freedom to move around, which can allow displacement and twists to occur. Displacement of the large intestine means a portion of the large intestine has moved and become trapped in an abnormal position within the abdomen. Twists of the intestine are more serious than displacements.

Depending on exactly how the intestine is twisted, the condition may be referred to as a torsion or a volvulus. Although sometimes a cause cannot be identified, some of the known reasons for intestinal displacement and twisting are known:

● Feeding large amounts of grain may result in increased gas production in the intestines that may lead to intestinal displacements or twists.

● The small intestine of mares may become trapped in the birth canal during foaling.

● Mares are susceptible to displacement or twisting of the large intestine during the first few months after foaling.

Twisting or trapping of the intestines constitutes an emergency, because the blood supply to the affected intestine can become cut off and cause the death of intestinal tissue.

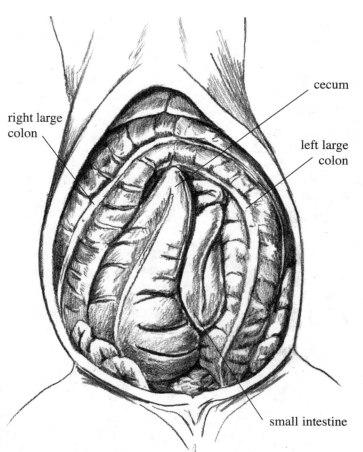

Surgeon's view of the horse's intestines.

right large colon

cecum

left large colon

small intestine

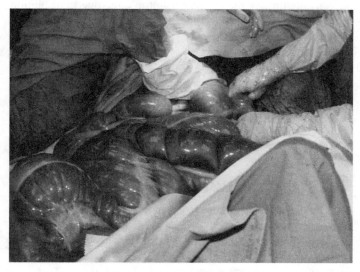

Colic involving a twist or displacement requires surgical correction.
Courtesy of Jill Parker

---

lipoma
lip = fat
oma = tumorous swelling

Fatty Tumors

In geriatric horses fatty tumors (lipomas) of varying sizes growing in the tissue around the intestines are common. The intestine may suddenly twist around one of these tumors, leading to a compromise of the blood supply and severe colic. Although this condition may occur in both males and females, it is more common in males. Obesity does not appear to be a factor; the development of lipomas seems to be purely a function of age.

Enteroliths

Enteroliths are stones that may occur in the large intestine of horses. They may form around bits of hair, metal or gravel within the intestine. Enteroliths may continue to grow and become quite large. They may also be multiple. When they get big enough to obstruct the intestine, the horse shows signs of colic.

Sometimes these stones may be felt during a rectal examination. Surgical removal of enteroliths is associated with a good recovery rate, provided the surgery is the performed before a large stone has resulted in breakdown of the intestinal wall.

In California, horses that eat significant amounts of alfalfa hay or pellets may be predisposed to developing enteroliths, possibly because of the high level of magnesium in California alfalfa. Preventive measures include feeding less alfalfa and adding vinegar to the horse's feed to cause the content of the large intestine to be more acidic (have a decreased pH), because intestinal stones do not form in an acidic environment.

> *enterolith*
> entero = intestine
> lith = stone

Enteroliths—stones that form within the large intestine— may become quite large.

Photo by Beth A. Valentine

Parasite Load

Blockage of intestinal contents occasionally occurs at the ileocecal junction, where the last part of the small intestine (the ileum) meets the first part of the large intestine (the cecum). Blockage may also result from an inversion or telescoping (intussusception) of the ileum into the cecum. Both conditions are associated with a heavy tapeworm load.

Other intestinal parasites, especially the small worms known as strongyles, are also a problem, although colic caused by damaged blood vessels and intestinal obstruction due to the migrations of these worms has become less common now that effective and easily administered horse wormers are available.

> *intussusception*
> intus = within
> susception = to take up or receive

Medical Colics

A sudden change of feed may cause colic or diarrhea in horses, especially if the change results in a high intake of soluble carbohydrates such as are found in grains, sweet feeds and spring grass. An unintentional feed change may occur when a horse gets into the grain bin, a storm causes a large windfall of apples or other fruit, or a horse unaccustomed to grass gets into lush pasture.

All changes in feed should be made gradually. Horses being introduced to rich pasture should be given limited grazing time for several days until their intestinal bacteria adjust to the new diet. Although pasture colic is often given as the cause of a horse going down on pasture colic in horses adjusted to pasture is quite uncommon.

A horse that becomes dehydrated for any reason may develop impaction colic because of decreased moisture in the contents of its large intestine. Horses should always have continuous access to good clean water. For a horse with impaction colic, water given through a stomach tube or intravenously may solve the problem. If the horse does not respond to medical therapy, surgery may be required.

Increased gas production or reduced gastrointestinal movements for any reason may result in colic due to distention of the intestine by gas. This type of spasmodic, or gas, colic may respond to medical therapy.

Rapidly cooling down a hot horse will not cause colic, although muscle pain following exercise may mimic colic.

Gastric Ulcers

Gastric ulcers are common in foals and are often related to stress caused by illness, weaning or change of feed. Foals should eat every few hours; foals that are fed less often may develop ulcers.

Signs of early stomach ulceration in foals include:
- grinding the teeth
- colic
- excessive salivation
- decreased appetite
- lying on the back (presumably to help relieve pressure and pain).

Long-standing problems may result in:
- diarrhea
- poor growth and haircoat
- potbelly.

The diagnosis may be confirmed by viewing the ulcer through a flexible tube (endoscope).

Ulcers in Adults

Gastric ulcers are less common and less obvious in adult horses. They tend to be common in racehorses, in which they are generally associated with poor racing performance. They may occur in any adult horse, including drafts, being treated with nonsteroidal anti-inflammatory medications such as phenylbutazone (bute) or banamine.

Signs of gastric ulceration in young adult and adult horses include poor performance, poor appetite, poor condition and depression. These signs are non-specific, meaning they could be caused by a wide variety of problems, and therefore a thorough examination by a veterinarian is needed. Unfortunately many endoscopes are not long enough to allow a veterinarian to look at the entire stomach of a large adult draft horse. In such cases, the diagnosis of gastric ulcer can be suspected based only on clinical signs and a positive response to therapy.

An adult horse with gastric ulcers rarely grinds its teeth. If your adult horse grinds its teeth, it is probably unhappy for some other reason.

Treatment

Severe ulcers in a horse of any age may progress to involve the entire thickness of the stomach wall, resulting in perforation and infection of the abdomen (peritonitis). Prompt attention to ulcers, however, generally results in healing with no long-term consequences. Several effective medications are available from your veterinarian to treat gastric ulcers.

A high soluble carbohydrate (grain) diet and strenuous exercise contribute to the development of gastric ulcers in adult horses. Gastric ulcers may be induced by feeding a high grain diet and running the horse on a treadmill. Treatment of a horse with confirmed or suspected gastric ulcers involves both stomach protection medication and a change in husbandry.

peritonitis	
periton	= abdomen
itis	= inflammation

Prevention by Good Nutrition

Esophageal, gastric and intestinal problems in the horse are often associated with the horse's diet. Horses on pasture rarely choke, colic or develop gastric ulcers. Good quality roughage, and plenty of it, are vitally important to maintaining a healthy horse.

Concentrated feeds high in carbohydrates are not good for any horse, and especially not draft horses. Instead, feeding a high fat and low soluble carbohydrate diet to drafts and other horses makes sense for a number of reasons, not the least of which is preventing gastrointestinal problems.

Photo by Pat Evia

15

Back and Spinal Cord

A healthy back and spinal cord are essential for equine performance. A horse with a weak or painful back is unwilling or unable to perform hard work. A draft horse with incoordination due to spinal cord disease may be willing to work but unable to coordinate the movement of its legs and body, and may be dangerous to both itself and the people around it.

Structure

The back is supported by bones, ligaments, tendons and muscles. The back's bones are the vertebrae. The vertebrae of the neck, back, rump and tail form the vertebral column, also called the spine. The tips of the spinous processes of the vertebrae are what you see or feel when a horse (or other animal) has a prominent spine. The intervertebral disks form cushions between the vertebral bones. Between the spine and the surface of the back is a thick cushioning layer of muscle, fibrous tissue and fat.

The spinal cord is encased in the vertebrae, in a space called the spinal canal. The spinal cord extends from the base of the brain to the rump. Small nerves from the spinal cord merge to form the larger nerves responsible for sensation and for muscle activity of the neck and body (the nerves to the head start in the brain). Some nerves, such as those to the larynx and to the hind legs, are particularly long.

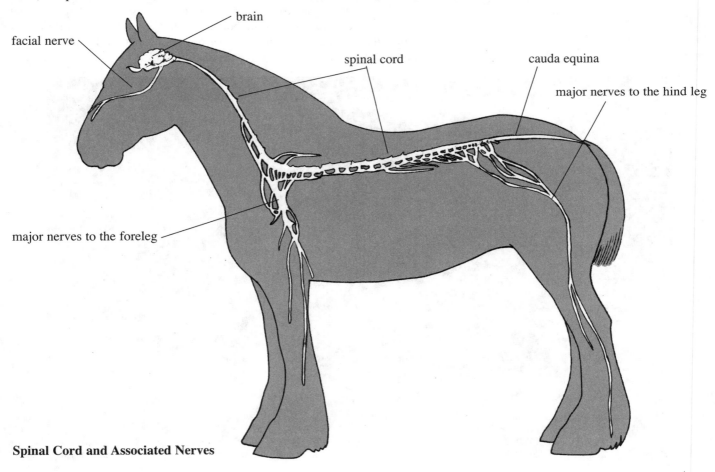

Spinal Cord and Associated Nerves

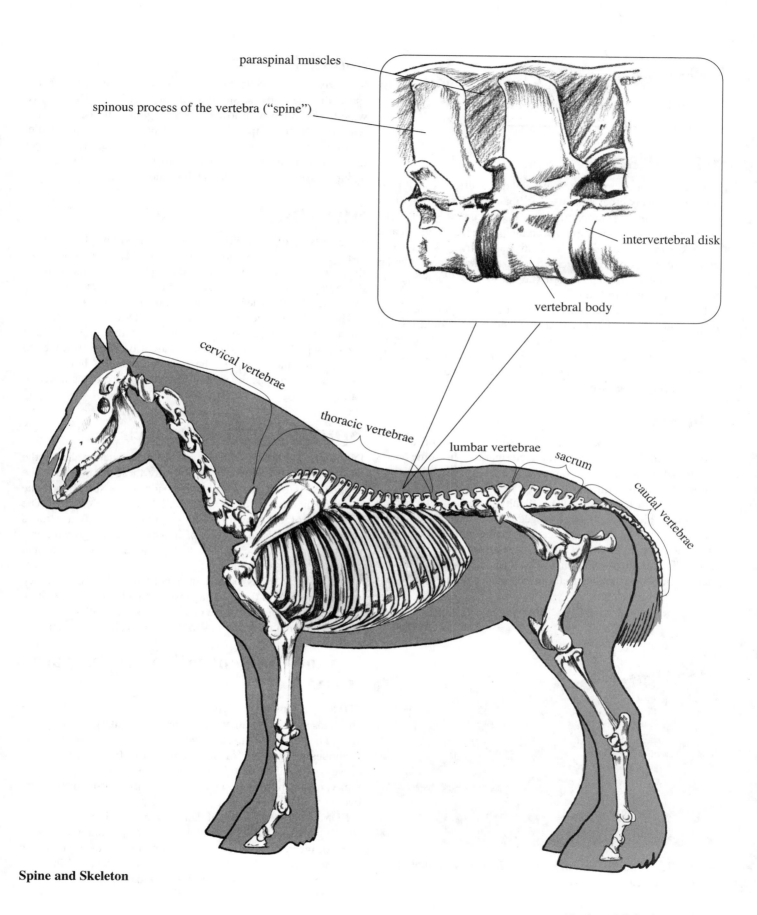

paraspinal muscles

spinous process of the vertebra ("spine")

intervertebral disk

vertebral body

cervical vertebrae

thoracic vertebrae

lumbar vertebrae

sacrum

caudal vertebrae

Spine and Skeleton

intervertebral
    inter   = between
    vertebral   = pertaining to vertebrae

Back Pain

The structure of a horse's intervertebral disks differs from that in people and many other animals. The horse's intervertebral disks never protrude or rupture to cause back pain or spinal cord problems. They may, however, become inflamed and cause pain.

Back pain may cause a horse to have an ouchy back that sinks when you put pressure or tack on it, or the horse may have an abnormal hunched-up posture. The muscles surrounding the bones may spasm and be painful.

Fractures and dislocations occur, but rarely. Muscle strain may occur in an overworked harness horse, but should resolve quickly with rest. If a draft horse shows signs of recurrent or persistent back pain, the possibility of underlying muscle disease, such as equine polysaccharide storage myopathy (EPSM), should be investigated.

Therapies

Determining and treating the underlying cause of a back problem requires the help of a veterinarian. In some cases inflammation of the back's joints may be relieved by injection of corticosteroids into the site.

Having learned first hand the difficulty of separating a horse's vertebrae, which are held tightly together by an intricate design of tendons and ligaments, we cannot believe the practice of chiropractic manipulation to realign the spine is possible in horses, especially draft horses. Certain forms of acupuncture and massage therapy, however, may be useful in treating a painful back.

A well-fitted saddle for a draft or draft cross will likely have a wide or extra wide tree. *Photo by Barry Cooper*

Saddle Fit

A poorly fitting saddle can put pressure on the horse's back, especially the withers, and may cause back pain. Drafts have wide backs, often with low withers, so you will need a saddle with an extra wide tree. Don't settle for an almost-fits saddle. You may need to work with a professional saddle fitter to get tack that is right for your horse. We have heard good things about adjustable tree saddles such as those made by Orthoflex.

Swayback

An excessive dip in a horse's back is called swayback. Some swaybacked horses are born with improperly formed bones of the spine, but most swaybacks develop with age and may be caused by weakening of muscles, tendons or ligaments around the spine. The disorder does not appear to be painful.

The condition is not well understood, but seems to occur most often in hard-working drafts. We've heard that a swaybacked horse can pull more weight than a straight-backed horse. We are not sure whether a dip in the back results in a horse being stronger or occurs as the result of a strong horse being asked to pull more.

Spinal Cord Diseases

Disease of the spinal cord results in incoordination, hence the term wobbles or wobblers. Technically these terms should be applied only to horses with compression of the spinal cord due to osteochondrosis dissecans (OCD) of the vertebra. The evaluation of a horse for signs of spinal cord disease relies almost entirely on an analysis of its gait. In a full-grown horse no other way may be used to test the reflexes controlled and coordinated by the spinal cord.

The spinal cord is bathed in a normally clear fluid called cerebrospinal fluid (CSF). Diagnosing spinal cord disease often involves examining a sample of CSF to look for either evidence of inflammation or antibodies to disease-causing organisms.

Equine Degenerative Myelopathy (EDM)

EDM is a disease of young growing horses. Evidence of problems with incoordination is usually present by six months of age. The incoordination generally comes on slowly and continues to worsen, distinguishing this disease from other causes of spinal cord problems such as herpesvirus infection or injury, in which the signs come on suddenly, worsen over one or two days and then stabilize.

EDM is related to insufficient vitamin E intake in young growing horses. This preventable disease was common 20 years ago. An increased awareness of the importance of vitamin E in pregnant mares and young growing foals has resulted in EDM being an uncommon disease in horses today.

EDM occurred on a Percheron breeding farm where grass hay was fed, no pasture was available, and vitamin E supplements were not given. Successive generations had more and more problems due to progressive depletion of the dams' stores of vitamin E.

When EDM is caught in the early stages it may be treated successfully by feeding megadoses of 10,000 IU or more of vitamin E per day. Preventing the disease is much better than treatment.

Vitamin E deficient adult horses do not get this disease, but may be susceptible to developing a different spinal cord problem, a muscle wasting condition called equine motor neuron disease (EMND). This disabling condition affects the nerves to the muscles and is similar to Lou Gehrig's disease in humans.

> equine degenerative myelopathy
> equine = horse
> myelo = spinal cord
> pathy = disease

Green grass is a good source of vitamin E, which is important for maintaining a healthy spinal cord.

Photo by Ruth Freeman

Cervical Stenotic Myelopathy

Cervical stenotic myelopathy, commonly called wobbles, is a compression of the spinal cord due to an abnormality of the bones forming the spinal canal. Its most common cause is osteochondrosis dissecans (OCD), a form of developmental orthopedic (bone) disease.

Radiographs (X-rays) usually show a narrowing of the spinal canal due to bone changes at the intervertebral joints. These radiographs are often done with the horse standing and sedated. In some cases, to confirm spinal cord compression, the horse is given a general anesthetic and a dye is injected into the cerebrospinal fluid for a procedure known as myelography. The dye outlines the spinal cord on the radiograph, creating X-ray film called a myelogram.

Multiple factors may predispose the spinal canal of a young growing horse to fail to widen properly. The two main factors are genetics and nutrition.

Nutrition plays a large role in causing or preventing growth problems. Even in a horse that is genetically predisposed to wobbles, the problem can be either prevented or alleviated through proper diet. Since the feed companies have increased the amount of copper in commercial equine feeds, the possibility has been reduced that low copper in the diet contributes to the development of OCD. Recent focus has been on the role of high soluble carbohydrate diets in causing OCD of the leg or spine joints.

Ongoing studies suggest that young growing horses should not be fed large amounts of high soluble carbohydrate feeds such as sweet feed or grain. Plenty of fiber in the form of hay or pasture is the mainstay of the diet, but additional energy and protein are needed for growth.

The ideal diet for a young growing draft horse is low in soluble carbohydrates, high in fat and fiber, and moderately high in protein with plenty of vitamins and minerals.

> osteochondrosis dissecans
> osteo = bone
> chondro = cartilage
> osis = condition of
> dissecans = drying out
>
> cervical stenotic myelopathy
> cervical = neck
> stenotic = reduced diameter (in this case of the spinal canal)
> myelo = spinal cord
> pathy = disease
>
> myelography
> myelo = spinal cord
> graphy = writing

Degenerative Joint Disease

Aging adult horses may develop a progressive spinal cord disease similar to wobbles due to degenerative joint disease (arthritis) of the intervertebral joints. Radiographs often show degenerative changes in the vertebrae at affected joints. As with wobbles in youngsters, myelography may be necessary to confirm this diagnosis.

In some cases surgery may be possible to remove the affected bone and stabilize the joint. Unfortunately the outlook for such cases is quite uncertain. If the horse has problems at more than one joint, surgery is not an option, and little can be done to alleviate the spinal cord damage.

Equine Protozoal Myeloencephalitis (EPM)

EPM is caused by the protozoal organism *Sarcocystis neurona*, which are slightly larger than bacteria. These protozoa are carried in the feces of North American opossums and are present only where the North American opossum is present. Unfortunately for horses and horse owners the 'possum lives happily in many parts of North America. EPM does not occur in horses born and raised in Europe, Asia, Australia or New Zealand.

Horses most likely ingest the protozoa in feed or pasture that has been contaminated by opossum fecal matter. Keeping all feeds secure from wildlife is ideal, but for most horse owners protecting hay is not easy. Keeping concentrated feeds in containers with tight lids may help decrease exposure. We would rather attempt to protect feed from opossum fecal contamination than declare all-out war on 'possums.

Keep concentrated feed in a container with a tight lid to prevent contamination by marauding 'possums.

Susceptibility

Surveys of levels of antibodies to the organism in the blood of North American horses show a high rate of exposure in draft horses, but the incidence of infection appears less in drafts than in light horses such as Standardbreds or Thoroughbreds. The disease is more common on some farms than on others, most likely because of a higher exposure to opossum contamination. The fact that many exposed horses do not become infected suggests that the horses' immune systems may be able to prevent damage following exposure.

This apparent immunity to EPM is another good reason to ensure that your horses' diet contains plenty of the vitamins and minerals that help make a healthy immune system. Good quality forage, plenty of green grass and/or vitamin E supplementation, and selenium supplementation when needed will ensure adequate levels of these important vitamins and minerals.

EPM infection generally occurs in multiple sites in the spinal cord. It often causes damage to one or more nerves leading to the muscles, as well as incoordination from spinal cord dysfunction. Typical cases of EPM may show rapid loss of one or more muscle groups, usually on only one side (asymmetric muscle atrophy). This condition may involve muscles of a limb or the face. Affected horses may show depression, partial paralysis and incoordination. The disease does not spread from one horse to another.

No evidence exists that any vaccine is effective against EPM.

Blot Test

The Western blot test looks for the presence of antibodies to the organism in the cerebrospinal fluid. This test has resulted in large numbers of horses being diagnosed as positive for EPM. Unfortunately the test often identifies as positive horses that do not have EPM (false positive tests).

The treatment is lengthy and expensive, especially for a draft horse, and therefore is sometimes infeasible. Before you invest time and money into treatment for EPM, or decide to put your horse down, seek the opinion of a veterinarian who is capable of accurate gait analysis for signs of incoordination, or who is willing to send the horse or a videotape of the horse to a consultant for analysis. The muscle wasting and hind limb gait problems of EPSM may easily be mistaken for EPM, especially in a draft horse.

equine protozoal myeloencephalitis	
equine	= horse
protozoal	= caused by protozoa
myelo	= spinal cord
encephal	= brain
itis	= inflammation

Neuritis of the Cauda Equina

The cauda equina is the hind-most portion of the spinal cord where the long nerves in the spinal canal resemble a horse's tail. The degeneration of these nerves occasionally occurs in mature horses because of inflammation. The cause is unknown and no treatment or cure has been found.

Affected horses develop hind leg incoordination and the progressive loss of urinary bladder function. The penis and tail may be partially or completely paralyzed. The facial and other nerves are occasionally affected, hence the other common name for this condition, polyneuritis equi.

neuritis of the cauda equina	
neur	= nerve
itis	= inflammation
cauda	= tail
equina	= horse
polyneuritis equi	
poly	= many
neur	= nerve
itis	= inflammation
equi	= horse

Herpesvirus Myelitis

Herpesvirus, also known as equine rhinopneumonitis virus, commonly causes a mild infection of the lungs and nasal passages. This same virus may infect a fetus and cause abortion, stillbirth or a sick foal that dies soon after birth. This virus can also infect the spinal cord of adult horses, causing herpesvirus myelitis.

Vaccinating a mare during pregnancy is effective in protecting the foal from infection. Vaccination of adult horses prevents respiratory disease but is not effective against infection of the spinal cord.

The conditions under which this virus can infect the spinal cord are not well understood. The virus often causes an outbreak of spinal cord infection in multiple horses in the barn or at the farm. Onset of the paralysis caused by infection of the spinal cord may be preceded by mild respiratory disease or may occur with no other signs of a problem.

Donkeys and mules do not seem to be susceptible to herpesvirus myelitis, but horses exposed to donkeys and mules carrying the virus may be at a higher risk for developing this problem.

Equine herpesvirus myelitis usually causes a sudden onset of severe incoordination that may worsen over the first one or two days and then stabilize. The nerves to the urinary bladder, penis and anus may be affected, resulting in partial to complete paralysis that may cause the horse to have difficulty urinating, holding urine or defecating.

Paralysis of the hind legs, which may progress to complete paralysis, looks similar to one of the forms of rabies in horses. The cerebrospinal fluid may be tested for high levels of antibodies to equine herpesvirus and other changes suggestive of this infection, but no one wants to handle cerebrospinal fluid that *may* be infected with rabies virus. If rabies virus is present in your area, keep your horse's rabies vaccination up to date.

Herpesvirus infection has no specific treatment, but generally runs its course in a few days. Given good nursing care some horses with herpesvirus myelitis recover to a remarkable degree. Fortunately spinal cord disease due to herpesvirus is relatively uncommon.

herpesvirus myelitis	
myel	= spinal cord
itis	= inflammation
equine rhinopneumonitis virus	
rhino	= nose
pneumo	= lung
itis	= inflammation

A healthy back helps provide the power to pull.

Photo by Beth A. Valentine

Basis of Power

A horse's back is its basis of power for pulling a load or carrying a rider. To keep your horse's power base healthy, make sure all tack fits well, feed your horse a healthy and balanced diet, work your horse sensibly, observe carefully and, when needed, provide prompt veterinary attention.

Muscles

We value a draft horse for its strength, and we admire its large well-rounded muscles. If the muscles fail to function properly, however, the horse may not have sufficient strength to stand, much less to perform work. Loss of muscle mass in the heavy draft may be difficult to detect in the early stages, but eventually becomes obvious—often more so to the owner than to the veterinarian.

Loss of muscle function may be even more difficult to detect. An affected horse may have only a subtle performance or gait problem, or may develop sudden severe muscle damage or weakness.

Asymmetric Atrophy

Muscle atrophy (wasting away) may or may not be associated with obvious weakness or interfere with the horse's movement. Whether the muscles atrophy on one side (asymmetrically) or on both sides (symmetrically) gives you a clue to the underlying cause.

A horse's loss of muscle on one side may be caused by injury to the associated nerve or to the muscle itself. Occasionally a horse is born with a divot, or depression, where part of the muscle failed to form, usually in the neck. A similar depression in the muscle of the neck may occur, but rarely, following a reaction to a vaccination or other injection.

Asymmetric muscle atrophy is often the hallmark of spinal cord damage with involvement of the nerves to the muscles originating in the spinal cord. Disease from the spinal cord infection equine protozoal myeloencephalitis (EPM) is associated with incoordination due to spinal cord damage and often also causes an asymmetric muscle atrophy. Migrating parasites that lose their way may occasionally enter the spinal cord and cause severe damage that may involve the nerves to the muscles.

atrophy	
a	= lack of
trophy	= growth
asymmetric	
a	= lack of
symmetry	= balance

Denervation Atrophy

When a muscle loses the input from its associated nerve, atrophy occurs rapidly and is known as denervation atrophy. Depending on which nerves and muscles are affected, an obvious or a more subtle problem may occur with bearing weight on, or movement of, the affected part. Denervation atrophy of a gluteal (rump) or thigh muscle results in an obvious sunken appearance in that area. Denervation atrophy of the shoulder muscle may cause the shoulder blade to appear more prominent.

To prevent sweeney, make sure your horse's collar conforms to both sides of the neck and allows enough room at the bottom for you to slide your fingers between the collar and the horse.

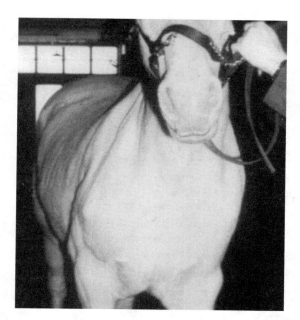

The prominent shoulder blade on one side of this horse is due to sweeney—muscle loss caused by damage to the nerve to the shoulder muscles. *Photo by Alexander de Lahunta*

Sweeney

Sweeney is a condition first described in draft horses, but which occurs in other breeds as well. Please don't ask us why it is called sweeney. It is an atrophy of the shoulder muscles, usually on one side, due to nerve damage.

Damage to the nerve to the shoulder muscle may be caused by pressure from the collar. Preventing sweeney is a good reason to ensure that collars are well-fitted and well-padded, especially for hard-working horses.

This condition may also be seen following trauma to the front of the shoulder region, such as may occur if a horse runs into a fence or other immoveable object or is at the receiving end of a well-placed kick.

Causes of Muscle Wasting	
Asymmetric	*Symmetric*
nerve injury	starvation
muscle injury	cancer
genetic divot	intestinal parasites
reaction to injection	pituitary tumors
spinal cord damage	advanced heart disease
	liver disease
	kidney disease
	generalized nerve disease
	equine motor neuron disease
	equine polysaccharide storage myopathy

Symmetric Atrophy

Muscle atrophy that occurs to a similar degree on both sides of the body is unlikely to be caused by nerve injury or EPM. Profound muscle atrophy may accompany starvation or a severe systemic disease, especially one that either causes a lack of appetite or feeds on the horse's system, such as cancer or severe intestinal parasite infection.

Mature horses are susceptible to developing pituitary tumors (equine Cushing's disease) that cause overall muscle wasting as well as increased frequency of drinking and urinating, growth of a persistently long haircoat, founder, and sometimes a potbelly.

If your horse experiences total body muscle atrophy, call your veterinarian. In some cases the cause may be readily apparent following a careful physical examination and review of the horse's management and medical history. In other cases extensive testing may be necessary to determine the cause. Severe and total body muscle atrophy and weakness may occur with advanced heart disease, liver disease, kidney disease, diseases that affect nerves such as equine motor neuron disease (EMND) and diseases that affect muscles such as equine polysaccharide storage myopathy (EPSM).

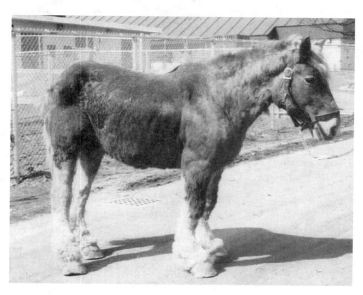

This aged Belgian mare has overall muscle atrophy, a long and slightly curly haircoat and founder due to Cushing's disease. *Photo by Tom Divers*

EMND

Equine motor neuron disease (EMND) is the equine equivalent of the human disease amyotrophic lateral sclerosis, or Lou Gehrig's disease. A horse with EMND rapidly loses weight, despite a good appetite, because of muscle atrophy. The affected horse soon becomes weak and stands with all four legs held well underneath itself. The muscles often tremble and the head is held low. Weakness is severest in the muscles used by a horse to maintain posture, and the affected horse usually spends a lot of time lying down. Such a horse appears to be more uncomfortable standing in one place than walking, trotting or cantering.

This disease is associated with low levels of vitamin E and occurs in horses without access to pasture, alfalfa products or supplemental vitamin E. To our knowledge EMND has not yet been diagnosed in a draft horse, perhaps because most owners of drafts recognize the importance of making pasture available to their horses. We do not, however, believe that draft horses are immune to EMND. We are particularly concerned about urban carriage horses that do not have access to green grass pastures.

The clinical signs of EMND may appear similar to the weakness and muscle atrophy that may occur in horses with equine polysaccharide storage myopathy.

Urban carriage horses without access to green pasture may be fed alfalfa hay or a vitamin E supplement to prevent EMND.

Photo by Dusty L. Perin

EPSM

Equine polysaccharide storage myopathy—variously known by the acronyms EPSM, PSSM, or EPSSM—seems to be the most common cause of symmetrical muscle atrophy in draft horses. EPSM is a metabolic disorder that affects many breeds. It is common in draft horses and ponies, and occurs in draft crosses including mules. More than half the draft horses and ponies studied in North America have EPSM, and affected horses have been identified in Europe and Australia.

The muscle atrophy of EPSM is severest in the rear, involving the rump and thighs. Muscle atrophy may also involve the top line, neck and shoulders. Affected horses may appear tucked up in the abdomen or crouched in the rear, as if from a back injury.

The cause of EPSM may be that the affected horses are maladapted to properly utilizing soluble carbohydrates (starches and sugars) in their diets. Instead of being broken down for energy, these carbohydrates build up to high levels in the

muscle. The resulting energy deficit may eventually lead to a break down of muscle protein for energy, as well as causing muscle damage, weakness, cramps or stiffness.

A veterinarian who is not aware of the existence of EPSM may think you are talking about EPM, a disease about which more is known and which sometimes looks similar. A draft horse with an energy deficit due to EPSM may be mistakenly assumed to be a low-energy horse by nature.

polysaccharide storage myopathy	
poly	= many
saccharide	= sugar
storage	= refers to carbohydrates stored in the muscle
myo	= muscle
pathy	= disease

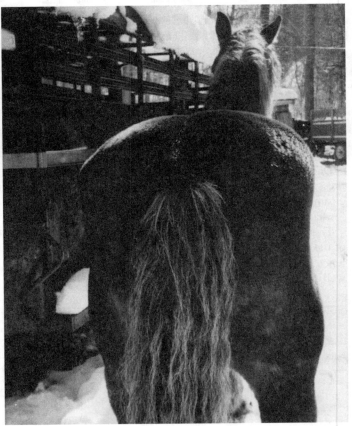

This Belgian mare with EPSM has lost muscling in her rump and has a caved-in appearance to her thighs.

Photo by Beth A. Valentine

Hereditary Nature

We believe the condition is inherited. One case of EPSM in a Belgian mule suggests that the disorder may be passed on through dominant genes, meaning that to produce the condition in the offspring, only one parent need carry the gene or genes. All draft breeds, including Norwegian Fjords, Haflingers and other draft ponies, are susceptible. We have seen problems appear in EPSM drafts from one and one-half to 21 years of age.

The question of whether or not to breed a mare or stallion suspected or known to have EPSM is a tough one. EPSM horses often have many other desirable traits, and you may have a hard time finding an unaffected horse you like. We therefore cannot consider the breeding of these horses to be unethical. Changing to a diet that will prevent or effectively control the problem (as outlined in Chapter 3) and weaning offspring onto the same diet is the most rational approach.

This Belgian-Percheron cross lacked energy until he was diagnosed with EPSM and was switched to a diet that is low in soluble carbohydrates and high in fat. *Photo by Barry Cooper*

Metabolic Disorder

The disorder is metabolic in nature. Affected horses are apparently unable to obtain adequate energy from soluble carbohydrates, such as those present in grains and sweet feeds. These horses may live for many years without apparent problems, or may from an early age be poor keepers with a lack of proper weight, muscling and strength. Some behavior problems occurring in younger drafts in training may be due to EPSM; the runaway horse or one that balks at working may be trying to tell you something is wrong.

In a mature draft EPSM may cause a subtle but progressive stiffness of the hind legs, which may be worse on one side than on the other, and may be mistaken for degenerative changes in the joints (arthritis). Draft horses with EPSM may develop peculiar hind limb gaits, such as shivers (which can be mistakenly called stringhalt) and locking stifle.

No one knows how this disease has become so common and widespread in the draft breeds. It is probably not a new disease, and perhaps was more difficult to recognize as an entity when its

signs were given such widely different names as shivers, Monday morning disease, post-anesthetic myopathy, locking stifle and stringhalt. While rebuilding draft breed populations after the Depression, breeders may have inadvertently concentrated the responsible gene or genes; or draft horses may have always been metabolically different and no one had either the knowledge to recognize this difference or the means to control the problem with diet.

Many drafts live with this problem and deal with it in some way, showing little or no obvious signs. The EPSM horse is probably aware of the problem, even if the owner is not. The previous owner of one of our EPSM drafts had noticed that the horse resented pressure on the back of his thighs during grooming, and always pushed off with both hind legs at once when pulling up a hill, long before he became obviously stiff and muscle wasted. A tribute to the draft breeds is their willingness to continue to train and work for us despite weak muscles that possibly undergo repeated injury and painful cramping during exercise.

Checklist of EPSM signs

Draft-related horses with EPSM often have one or more of the following signs:

- symmetric loss of muscling, especially of the rump, shoulder, or topline
- weakness, especially in the rear
- trembling, especially after exercise
- difficulty backing or reluctance to back
- poor performance
- lack of energy
- stumbling
- reluctance to pick up feet for trimming
- slightly stiff, awkward or short-strided gait in one or both hind limbs
- shivers, locking stifle or stringhalt in one or both hind limbs
- episodic colic-like signs, especially after exercise
- tying up.

Diagnosing EPSM

Muscle atrophy is only one manifestation of EPSM, which may result in a wide variety of problems. The onset of EPSM problems may be either:

slow and subtle, with progressive loss of muscling, especially over the rump and thigh, and an increasingly stiff gait

sudden and catastrophic, in which the horse:

- undergoes massive muscle damage during or after work, a problem known in drafts as Monday morning disease,
- goes down and is unable to rise, or
- dies suddenly.

In a draft-related breed, having one or more of the characteristic clinical problems may be enough to make a diagnosis. Higher than normal blood levels of the muscle enzymes CK and AST, especially if blood is drawn four to six hours after exercise, is also highly suggestive of EPSM, even if the horse appears clinically normal. Normal enzyme levels, however, do not rule out this problem. A more definitive diagnosis may be made by examining a muscle biopsy.

Examining a muscle biopsy can help determine the cause of symmetric or asymmetric muscle atrophy. In a normally muscled horse with unexplained hind limb gait problems or problems with tying up, a muscle biopsy may be examined for evidence of EPSM or other problems. Taking a muscle biopsy is a relatively simple procedure your veterinarian can perform at the barn, using sedation and a local anesthetic. A pathologist who is familiar with equine muscle problems will examine the sample to determine if it contains evidence of denervation atrophy, muscle damage or stored carbohydrates to explain the horse's problem.

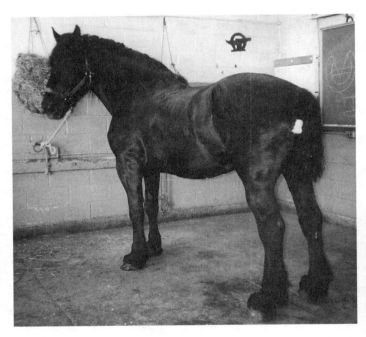

A muscle biopsy (bandaged site on gelding's rump) can help determine if muscle loss is due to EPSM or some other problem.

Photo by Beth A. Valentine

Monday Morning Disease

Monday morning disease (MMD), a manifestation of EPSM, was prevalent when horses were more commonly used as a source of power. MMD occurred most often in hard working horses on a high grain ration. The horses were rested on Sunday and developed severe muscle injury when put to work on Monday morning.

This problem is variously known as tying up, azoturia, black water and setfast. The more technical term is exertional rhabdomyolysis (usually pronounced RAB-doe-my-oll-eh-sis). The resulting massive muscle injury causes:

- pain and swelling, usually severest in the rump and hind leg musculature
- reluctance to move (hence the terms setfast and tying up)
- passage of damaging muscle pigments (myoglobin) through the kidneys into the urine, giving the urine a port-wine color (hence the terms azoturia and black water).

Affected horses often go down. Blood testing reveals high levels of muscle enzymes released into the blood from damaged muscle. The many names for the syndrome of muscle damage associated with exercise reflect the fact that little was known about the cause of the problem.

Monday morning disease and being down are life-threatening situations for a draft horse. Saving the horse's life requires immediate and continued attention.

A horse that tied up was previously considered to have been the victim of mismanagement, such as being fed too much grain or not being given enough exercise or warm-up before a hard workout. Although these factors affect a horse's chances of tying up, veterinarians recognize that only horses susceptible to muscle injury will tie up under these circumstances. A normal horse will not have the problem no matter how much grain it is fed or how little warm-up exercise

The Percheron in this team had severe episodes of tying up and (as you can see) did not pull as hard as his Belgian teammate; a change in diet stopped the tying up and improved his performance.

Courtesy of Helen Harrington

it performs before a hard workout. Predisposed horses can tie up with minimal exercise, even if they have been fed only grass or pasture.

azoturia	
azo	= nitrogen-containing compounds, including red-purple dyes
turia	= pertaining to urine
rhabdomyolysis	
rhabdo	= striated
myo	= muscle
lysis	= breakdown

Monday morning disease is less of a problem in today's drafts that lead more relaxed lives, but is still a problem for horses used for farming, logging and pulling competitions. It is even more common in light horse-draft crosses trained for dressage, eventing, jumping and fox hunting.

Muscle Pain vs. Colic

An affected horse that is not obviously tied up after exercise may still show signs of pain due to muscle cramps that may be misinterpreted as colic. A careful evaluation of the gastrointestinal system, as well as an evaluation of the blood levels of muscle enzymes by your veterinarian may be necessary to distinguish muscle pain from gastrointestinal pain.

A horse with muscle pain may also have an associated slowing of gastrointestinal movement, resulting in gas colic or stomach rupture as a secondary problem. Localized muscle cramps, especially if they occur in the hind legs or back, are often a manifestation of EPSM, and may be mistaken for a lameness problem or for muscle strain caused by overexertion or poor conditioning. Affected horses may go down while in harness. For the carriage operator such an incident only feeds the flames of the often horse-ignorant public, which may believe the horses are being inhumanely treated.

Fortunately for draft horses and their owners, feeding the horses a diet that is low in soluble carbohydrates and high in fat appears to effectively control signs of EPSM. A diet change prior to onset of any serious problems is much preferred and is part of good draft horse management.

Photo by Bonnie Nance

Joints and Legs

17

From foaling to old age, the draft horse may be affected by various joint and leg problems. Knowing the normal characteristics of your horse's joints and legs, along with close and regular observation, will help you notice any problems that arise.

Chestnuts and Ergots

Chestnuts and ergots are horny growths of soft keratin that are normal structures of the horse's legs. The chestnuts occur just above the knee on the inside of the fore legs and just below the point of the hock on the inside of the hind legs. They are supposedly evolutionary remains of the first toe from when ancient horses had five toes. Donkeys do not have chestnuts on the hind limbs. Owners of donkeys may wish to use this fact as evidence that donkeys are more highly evolved than horses. Mules may have only small hind limb chestnuts.

Ergots are the growths on the backs of the fetlock joints and may be the remains of the second and fourth digits of the ancient five-toed horse. Ergots can make trimming the hair in the fetlock area difficult. Ergots on the hind legs are usually larger than those on the fore legs.

Draft horses tend to develop excessive chestnuts and ergots that may require trimming for cosmetic purposes. The superficial layers of chestnuts and ergots often loosen and may

fall or can be pulled off. Drafts kept in tie stalls may not have the opportunity to rub off excessive tissue, and chestnuts and ergots may get large.

Trimming them with hoof nippers is safer than using a hoof knife or other knife. Soaking the tissue with mineral oil helps soften it to make trimming easier. Like the outer hoof, these structures have no blood supply until you reach the skin surface. Be careful not to trim too deeply. If you have doubts about trimming chestnuts or ergots, check with your farrier or veterinarian.

Developmental Orthopedic Disease (DOD)

Rapidly growing youngsters are prone to developing a variety of problems involving the conversion of cartilage into bone and the proper balance between bone growth and tendon and ligament growth. These problems, collectively known as developmental orthopedic disease (DOD), are common in young draft horses, perhaps related to their rapid growth.

Although genetics likely play a role, proper nutrition may help prevent these problems. Excessive total daily calories, high soluble carbohydrate feeds, inadequate calcium intake or a low calcium to phosphorus ratio and a deficiency of trace minerals such as copper, manganese and zinc may be involved in DOD.

Osteochondrosis Dissecans (OCD)

OCD is a disorder of the joints. It most often affects the shoulder and hock joints, resulting in a loss of the normal cartilage that allows smooth, pain-free joint movement. Affected joints may be lame and swollen, especially in the hocks. Bending the joint causes pain, and small fragments of cartilage and bone, called joint mice, may break off and float freely in the joint, creating further degeneration of joint surfaces. A similar process occurring in the bones and joints of the spine may put pressure on the spinal cord, resulting in a condition of incoordination called wobbles or wobblers.

To reduce the risk that horses might develop this bone and joint disorder, feed a well-balanced low soluble carbohydrate and low total energy feed to young growing horses to allow

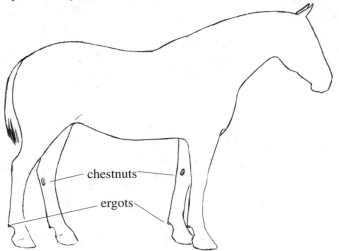

chestnuts

ergots

Locations of chestnuts and ergots

them a more controlled growth. A controlled weight gain of one to two pounds per day is far safer than a gain of two-and-a-half to three pounds or more per day that youngsters on high energy diets sometimes achieve. Feeding weanlings a high fiber, low soluble carbohydrate and high fat (but not high energy) diet may help prevent OCD.

Controlled growth in a youngster will not adversely affect its eventual adult size.

Mild cases of OCD may be treated conservatively with rest and anti-inflammatory medications. Severe cases often require surgery to scrape off the affected cartilage and remove any bone fragments. A newly developing procedure involves the implantation of normal cartilage grafts to promote healing. A mature horse that had OCD as a youngster may be predisposed to severe degeneration of joints and to bone fractures.

osteochondrosis dissecans	
osteo	= bone
chondro	= cartilage
osis	= condition of
dissecans	= drying out

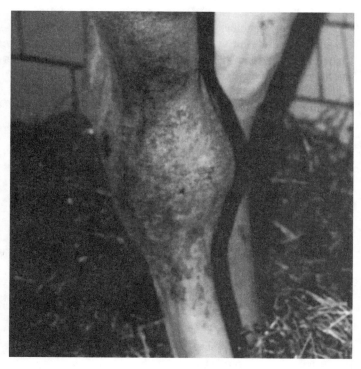

Hock swelling, especially in a young horse, may be due to OCD.
Courtesy of Jill Parker

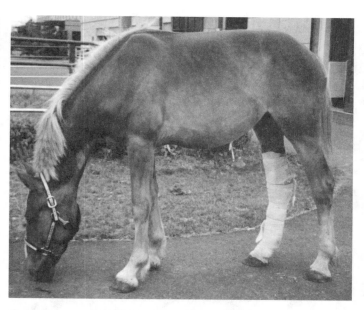

Surgery may benefit a youngster with joint problems due to OCD.
Photo by Beth A. Valentine

Physitis

The epiphysis and physis are the parts of a bone near each end that allow the bone to grow. The epiphysis is the top of the bone; the physis is the growth plate. Inflammation in these areas is often called epiphysitis, but the correct term is physitis. Lameness and swelling of these regions of the long bones of the legs may occur in rapidly growing foals. Swelling near the knees (carpi) is most common.

If your foal develops swollen knees, call your veterinarian immediately. The diagnosis of physitis is confirmed by radiographic findings of widening and irregularity of the physeal region and increased density of adjacent bone. Most foals recover with treatment, which includes anti-inflammatory medications such as phenylbutazone (bute) or banamine, rest and a decrease in total daily calories.

epiphysitis, physitis	
epi	= upon
physis	= the growth plate of the bone
itis	= inflammation

Contracted Tendons in Foals

A foal born with contracted tendons may reflect abnormal positioning or activity as a fetus in the uterus. Such foals often correct themselves once they gain strength and begin to exercise.

Shortening (contraction) of the flexor tendons on the backs of the legs may occur months after birth in rapidly growing foals.

These foals may begin to walk on the tips of their toes, resembling ballerinas. Contracted tendons may lead to the development of a hoof with an abnormal shape and angle, known as clubfoot.

Treatment includes a decrease in total daily calories, controlled exercise, and hoof trimming and shoeing to extend the toe and lower the heels to allow for a more normal hoof angle. In severe cases surgery may be necessary to release tension on the affected tendons.

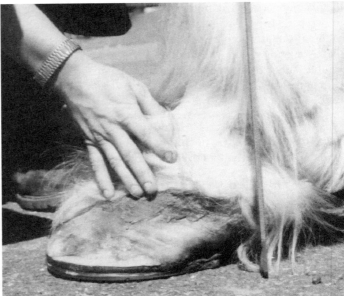

A show horse with overgrown hooves and oversize shoes has abnormal angles and stresses that can lead to degenerative joint or hoof problems. *Photo by Mike Wildenstein*

Exercise helps a foal develop strong, healthy legs.
Photo by Ruth Freeman

Problems in Adult Horses

Joint problems in adult horses may develop due to years of joint stress. Severe joint disease may effectively end the working life of a draft horse.

Degenerative Joint Disease (DJD)

Heavy horses can put a lot of strain on their joints. Keeping your draft horse's hooves properly trimmed and shod goes a long way toward maintaining healthy joints. Oversize shoes on an overgrown hoof over-stresses the bones, joints and the hoof wall. Draft horses should be allowed to adopt a natural gait. The use of devices such as weighted shoes or chains around the pasterns to force the horse to adopt an unnatural exaggerated gait will likely lead to joint problems later in life.

Arthritis

Degenerative joint disease (DJD) is often referred to as arthritis or osteoarthritis, but it is not a true arthritis because it involves little or no inflammation. The condition causes degeneration of joint surfaces and the growth of painful bony spurs. It may develop gradually and may start with changes caused by OCD or may occur due to years of stress on the joints, following injuries, or when another problem such as a tendon or ligament injury makes the joint unstable. Conformational defects in the legs may result in increased stress on joints and subsequent degenerative joint disease.

Degenerative changes most commonly occur in mature horses in the joints of the lower legs. Because the horse carries most of its weight on its fore limbs, the front leg joints are more commonly affected than are the hind joints. Beware, therefore, of making the diagnosis of degenerative joint disease in a mature draft horse if the pain or stiffness appears to involve only the hind limbs.

The diagnosis of arthritis has often been applied to drafts that are instead developing signs of equine polysaccharide storage myopathy (EPSM). Your veterinarian can perform a careful lameness examination that may include palpation for swelling, bending the joints (flexion tests) to look for pain, radiographs (X-rays), ultrasound, and nerve blocks. If a definitive cause for

arthritis, osteoarthritis	
arthro	= joint
osteo	= bone
itis	= inflammation of

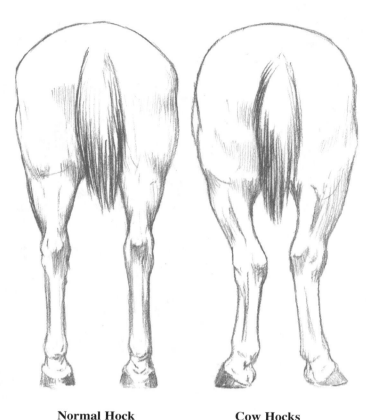

Normal Hock   **Cow Hocks**

Normal Hocks   **Sickle Hock**

hind-limb stiff gait or discomfort cannot be found in your draft horse, suspect EPSM.

In mature horses degenerative joint disease may affect the joints of the spine, resulting in spinal cord disease and incoordination caused by pressure on the spinal cord.

Spavin

Spavin is a degenerative disease of the hock joint. It may be a soft swelling of the hock joint capsule, in which case it is called bog spavin or thoroughpin, or a hard bony swelling known as bone spavin.

Bog spavin is typically considered a cosmetic defect and is rarely associated with lameness. It may occur due to excess stress on the hock joint resulting from conformational defects such as cow or sickle hocks. Bog spavin may also occur following excess strain on the hock joints, such as occurs when a horse is worked in heavy, wet soils (bogs). Although the injection of corticosteroids into the affected joint capsule may relieve the excess fluid and swelling, the problem often recurs.

Bone spavin is caused by abnormal bone proliferation involving the joints of the hock and is usually accompanied by some degree of lameness. We believe bone spavin results from abnormal stresses on the bones of the hock joint, which may be exacerbated by poor conformation or improper hoof care.

Both bog spavin and bone spavin are common problems in drafts. Certain breeds, especially Clydesdales, tend to be somewhat cow hocked, making them more susceptible to these hock disorders. Underlying OCD may also be a predisposing factor.

Treatment of DJD

Treating degenerative joint disease often involves rest and anti-inflammatory drugs such as phenylbutazone (bute). Various compounds may be injected directly into the affected joints to ease pain and aid healing. Proteoglycan treatments have been developed that may be injected or fed as supplements to help rebuild damaged cartilage and joints. Glucosamine and chondroitin sulfate are two such compounds that show promise.

> *proteoglycans*
>   proteo   = protein
>   glycans   = carbohydrates and
>   related compounds

Lyme Disease

Lyme disease, caused by a bacteria carried by deer ticks in the East and black-legged ticks in the West, is still poorly understood in the horse. Studies have shown that many horses have been exposed to the organism, but few cases have been documented of horses having clinical disease. Ponies that have been experimentally infected with the Lyme organism have failed to demonstrate any lameness or other illness.

In areas with a high incidence of Lyme disease, horses with unexplained illness or lameness may be diagnosed and treated for Lyme disease because of a positive blood test, which may or may not relate to their problem. Blood testing must be done by a laboratory that understands how to interpret the results.

Make sure no other problem, such as EPSM, is causing a draft horse's stiffness, lameness and general malaise.

If Lyme disease is confirmed to be the cause of a horse's total body pain and stiffness, improvement may occur after aggressive treatment with antibiotics. As with people, the treatment of horses with chronic Lyme disease can be discouraging. A better course of action is to diagnose and treat Lyme disease as soon as possible.

Windpuffs

Windpuffs are soft puffy swellings of the fetlock joint capsule and may occur on one or both sides of the leg just above the fetlock. Although they are common in the legs of heavily-built horses, they are not usually a cause of lameness. They may increase or decrease in size depending on the level of exercise. Like bog spavin, this condition is typically considered a cosmetic defect of little significance, although a horse with obvious windpuffs may not be a good prospect for showing in halter classes.

Tendons, Ligaments and Splints

Tendon, ligament and splint injuries are not as common in draft breeds as they are in high performance horses such as racehorses and jumpers. Among drafts, pulling competition horses are the most likely candidates for these types of injury. Of course, as more drafts and draft crosses are being trained for dressage and jumping, these problems may become more common. A diagnosis involves careful examination, palpation and radiographs (X-rays) aided by ultrasound and other newer imaging procedures.

Bowed Tendons

Bowed tendon is caused by the overstress and breakdown of the flexor tendon at the back of the fore leg cannon bone, resulting in swelling, pain and an outward bow or bend in the affected tendon. Bowed tendons are more common in racehorses and jumpers than in draft horses, but since more and more drafts and draft crosses are jumping in eventing, the hunt field and the show ring we may begin to see this problem more often in these breeds.

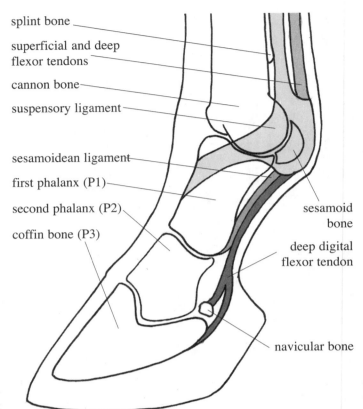

splint bone
superficial and deep flexor tendons
cannon bone
suspensory ligament
sesamoidean ligament
first phalanx (P1)
second phalanx (P2)
coffin bone (P3)
sesamoid bone
deep digital flexor tendon
navicular bone

Some Important Tendons and Ligaments

Treatment involves rest and anti-inflammatory medications while the tendon heals. Horses with strongly healed bows, especially bows high on the leg, often have no subsequent problems. The outward bend of the affected tendon, however,

Among the draft breeds, those engaged in competition pulling are the most susceptible to leg ailments.

Photo by Dusty L. Perin

will be evident for life. Fortunately the relatively short and sturdy cannon bones of draft-related horses helps protect them from tendon injury.

Draft horses can make willing and able jumpers, and their sturdy build helps protect their legs from injury.

Photo by Margaret Delehanty

Contracted Tendons in Adults

The development of contracted tendons in adult horses is much less common than in youngsters. A contracted tendon in an adult horse means something is interfering with normal weight bearing and the action of the limb. Painful joint problems, tendon injuries and muscle disease may all cause a tendon to gradually shorten. This problem in drafts is seen more often in the hind limbs than in the front limbs. If no injury has occurred and no joint problems are identified, underlying muscle disease (EPSM) should be considered.

Suspensory Ligament Desmitis

The suspensory ligament is part of the apparatus that helps support the fetlock joint. It is part of the sling across the back of the fetlock and pastern. Two small bones, the sesamoid bones, are embedded in the ligament at the back of the fetlock.

Inflammation of the suspensory ligament, or suspensory desmitis, is similar to bowed tendon and splint bone injury in being more common in racehorses and jumpers than in working draft horses. It does, however, occur in drafts and draft crosses involved in other disciplines. Besides becoming inflamed, the suspensory ligament may also be damaged by a fracture at the end of the splint bone.

Treatment involves rest, anti-inflammatory medications and shoeing to relieve pressure on the ligament. Lameness may recur, however, if heavy exercise is resumed. Full recovery from suspensory desmitis is much more likely if the problem involves a fore leg rather than a hind leg.

> *desmitis*
> desm = fibrous tissue
> itis = inflammation

Splints

The splint bones are remnants of ancestral toe bones. Splint bones may become damaged from stress or trauma, and the fore legs are the more often affected than hinds. The horse becomes noticeably lame on the affected leg and pressure applied over the splint bone causes pain. Swelling may or may not be evident.

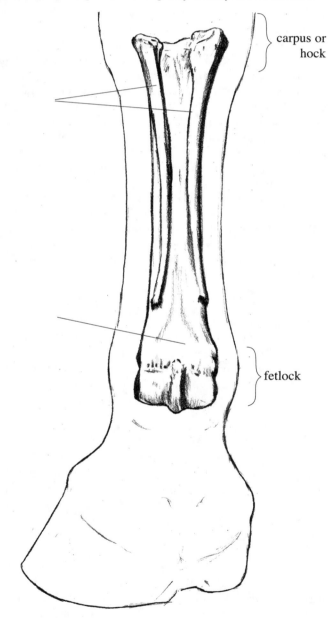

carpus or hock

fetlock

Splint bones as viewed from the back of the leg.

This injury is uncommon in working draft horses but, as with bowed tendon, may occur in drafts training and competing in dressage and other disciplines that are less traditional for the heavy breeds. Splint bone injuries may occur in any horse due to trauma, such as from a kick.

Splint injuries usually respond well to rest and anti-inflammatory treatments. When a splint bone is fractured the horse may heal faster if the affected bone is surgically removed.

Abnormal Gaits

An abnormal gait may result from a painful lameness; your veterinarian will use a variety of tests to try to pinpoint the source of pain. The abnormal gaits described here are not associated with joint, tendon or ligament pain, and may be perplexing to both the owner and the veterinarian.

These gaits are classified as mechanical lamenesses, which means something is affecting the biomechanics of the horse's gait. Due to the complex biomechanics of the equine hind legs, these abnormal gaits most commonly affect the rear limbs. Horses with mechanical lameness generally do not appear to be in pain, but they may appear to be somewhat uncomfortable or distressed.

These gaits have been given various interesting names. Shivers, stringhalt, springhalt, being stringy and stifle locking are the gait problems most often described in draft horses. They also occur with some frequency in Warmbloods, perhaps reflecting the heavy horse ancestry of these breeds.

The abnormal action in one or both hind legs, which usually disappears at the trot or canter, becomes most obvious when a horse is:

- walking
- backing
- turning in a tight circle.

The abnormal action may be caused by the failure of individual muscles to stretch properly. To bend a joint, the muscles inside the bend contract and the muscles outside the bend must stretch. Muscle cramps and abnormal nerve activity are also potential causes.

Shivers vs. Stringhalt

Shivers causes an abnormal action in one or both hind legs and is a progressive problem that will eventually affect both hind limbs. It can progress to involve the fore limbs and is associated with eventual muscle wasting and weakness. We believe shivers in draft horses, and probably in other breeds, is due to the underlying metabolic problem known as equine polysaccharide storage myopathy (EPSM).

We have heard that shivers in draft horses may begin after a systemic illness such as a viral or bacterial infection. In one case a Belgian began signs of shivers following an illness that was (probably erroneously) identified as equine herpesvirus infection. We do not believe an infection can cause shivers, but the stress of an infection may be enough to push an EPSM affected horse over the edge to show signs of shivers.

The farrier may initially diagnose shivers when the horse develops difficulty lifting its feet for hoof care. The limb may jerk up or the joints may be difficult to bend. The horse may object, sometimes emphatically, to standing on three legs. In some cases the horse refuses to lift its legs. The owner and farrier may resort to using a shoeing stock or tranquilizer.

In its early stages shivers may cause a horse only to appear stringy, or to have stringhalt. Dr. A.J. Neumann has described shivers as an abnormally exaggerated flexion of the hind limb followed by movement of the limb out to the side before placing it on the ground, whereas horses with stringhalt move the raised limb inward before placing in on the ground. Clearly these two disorders may be easily confused, particularly in early or mild cases.

We are less dogmatic about definitions based on specific actions of the legs. Instead we consider these problems to be types of mechanical lameness that may involve problems in the muscles or nerves of the hind limbs. In our experience true stringhalt is a problem in the nerves to the limb muscles. The abnormal hind limb action of horses with stringhalt occurs with almost every walk step, and the hind hoof comes close to hitting the abdominal wall. In Australia, New Zealand and the Pacific Northwest outbreaks of stringhalt occur in horses on pasture bearing large numbers of dandelions (Australia and New Zealand) or false dandelions (Pacific Northwest). In such cases removing the horses from the pasture may result in their gradual recovery. Surgery to remove a portion of muscle and tendon may also be useful.

Shivers, by contrast, is a muscle problem. The abnormal gait of shivers occurs only occasionally, usually when turning, backing, in the first walk stride and in the last walk stride before halting. The abnormal action of shivers is often most obvious when the horse walks or backs after standing still for some time, or can occur while the horse is standing still. In our experience a stringy draft horse is more likely to have muscle disease (EPSM) than a nerve problem. We agree wholeheartedly with Dr. Neumann that heredity plays a role in the development of both shivers and stringy horses, and also with his observation that we are seeing more stringy draft horses now than we did years ago.

Locking Stifle

Locking stifle, also called upward fixation of the patella (kneecap), is most evident when a horse first moves out of a stall or after standing still for some period. The stifle joint appears to lock up and not allow free movement of the stifle or, due to the connection between the hock and the stifle, of the hock. The horse drags the affected leg on the toe. Your veterinarian can show you where to put pressure to help your horse unlock the joint. In a young horse this condition may be due to an inherited abnormal formation of the stifle joint.

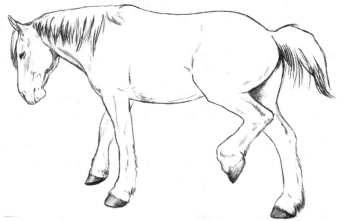

Shivers: The leg is hiked up and out, especially when the horse turns or backs; the tail may be raised and may quiver.

Stringhalt: The leg is hiked up and the hoof comes forward under, and sometimes almost hitting, the belly.

Locking stifle: Neither the stifle nor the hock can bend, causing the horse to drag the affected leg behind on the toe.

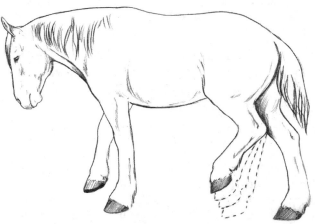

Fibrotic myopathy: The horse pulls the affected leg backward before slapping the hoof down on the ground.

An intermittent form of stifle lock may occur, causing the stifle joint to catch only briefly. The abnormal gait in such a horse resembles shivers or stringhalt.

Various surgical procedures and joint injections are used for the treatment of locking stifle. In some cases an exercise conditioning program to include work on hills may help. Locking stifle that develops in an adult horse, especially a draft horse, may be due to muscle tightening or weakness resulting from EPSM.

Fibrotic Myopathy

Fibrotic myopathy is a rare condition in draft horses. It is most commonly seen in Quarter horses that perform sliding stops, which are considered undesirable for a draft horse. The gait abnormality involves a shortened forward swing phase of one or both hind legs, followed by an abrupt slapping of the hoof onto the ground as if something has mechanically caught up the leg joints during the swing.

Fibrous tissue may develop behind the stifle joint on the back of the leg and may be felt as a thickening where the hamstring muscles end. The gait abnormality is most obvious at the walk and does not appear to be painful to the horse. Although in some cases muscle damage from undue stress may be the cause, in other cases the damage is in the nerves to the muscle. Surgery to relieve the tension on the muscle sometimes improves the gait.

Although true fibrotic myopathy is rare in drafts, the abnormally stiff hind limb gait of a draft horse with EPSM may be mistaken for fibrotic myopathy.

fibrotic myopathy
    fibro = fibrous (scar) tissue
    myo   = muscle
    pathy = disease

Leg Swelling

Any sudden appearance of severe lameness and swelling in a leg should be evaluated immediately. Causes of leg swelling include:

- fracture
- bacterial infection of the muscles
- trauma resulting in bruising
- a tumor within the muscle.

Fractures result in severe swelling and lameness. In the past euthanasia was the only option for a horse with a broken leg. Many fractures are still impossible to repair, but some may be successfully repaired using new techniques.

The most common bacterial infection causing swelling is due to clostridial organisms that proliferate in a wound or traumatized area, including a contaminated injection site. These bacteria produce powerful toxins and cause the disease known as malignant edema. Affected horses are depressed, have a fever and go off feed. This disease is serious—affected horses are often found dead.

> *euthanasia*
> eu = good
> thanasia = death

Treatment includes antibiotics and surgically opening the affected area to remove the dead tissue, drain the fluid and get oxygen into the tissue. Oxygen decreases the growth of these bacteria, which grow best in areas with little or no oxygen.

Trauma that results in bruising of muscles can cause swelling with only mild lameness. Rarely a malignant tumor (cancer) of blood vessels within the muscle will result in swelling. Bleeding from the tumor into the muscle may mimic a large bruise.

Stocking Up

Stocking up is a condition in which excess fluid accumulates in a horse's lower legs, usually in the tendon sheaths. Gravity causes fluid to tend to naturally accumulate in these tissues. Stocking up may occur when the horse has been standing in one place too long and has not had enough contraction of the muscles to help pump fluid back up the legs. Stocking up may be more difficult to see in a draft with heavy feathering, but if you feel the lower leg you will find that the leg feels thicker than usual and the tendons at the back of the cannon bone are more difficult, or impossible, to feel. If you push on the affected areas, you will find them to be fairly soft and squishy due to the build up of fluid.

The problem may occur in horses shipped long distances in tie stalls, or confined to stalls for any reason, and in mares standing in tie stalls for urine collection for medical use. Stocking up is generally not a serious problem. The excess fluid will usually resolve once the horse begins moving around.

Stocking up can occur in a leg that is taking excessive pressure, such as the opposite leg to one that is severely lame. For this reason, and to help relieve pressure on the tendons, the opposite leg to one that is injured may often be wrapped to help support tendons and prevent fluid build up.

Heart failure, post-streptococcal vasculitis (blood vessel inflammation), Potomac horse fever, lymphangitis and eating hoary alyssum may also cause stocking up. A few owners have reported that their horses stocked up after beginning an alfalfa pellet and vegetable oil diet. We have no explanation but are happy to report that the stocking up problem resolved quickly as the horses continued on the diet.

Photo by David Wisnieski

18

No Hoof, No Horse

When a draft horse develops hoof problems, your veterinarian and farrier should work together so your horse receives the most appropriate treatment. Some veterinarian-farrier combinations work better than others; keep looking until you find the right team.

Hoof Cracks

Hoof cracks are common in draft horses, especially when their hooves have not been trimmed at regular intervals or have been trimmed so the hoof is unbalanced. Some drafts are amazingly sound with feet that are spread and split, but don't risk trouble by allowing feet to overgrow and counting on a draft horse's sturdy nature.

Cracks may be superficial and require little treatment other than trimming to rebalance the hoof, or they may be deep enough to cause pain or become infected. The most common hoof crack occurs on the side of the hoof and is known as a quarter crack.

For severe and deep cracks, clean the hoof and eliminate any infection with medication recommended by your farrier or veterinarian. Stabilize the crack using shoes with clips, the application of acrylics or fiberglass, a mechanical device to bridge the gap, or a combination of these techniques. In such cases you'll need the attention of a good farrier.

The hooves of newborn foals are soft and may appear split or

A newborn foal's hooves are soft and may appear frayed or split, but will soon harden.

Photo by Mike Wildenstein

frayed, which is nothing to worry about. They will quickly harden and become smooth.

Sole Bruises and Abscesses

The thickness or thinness of a horse's sole is determined mostly by genetics, but diet and overall health can affect the thickness and strength. Sole bruises may be painful. Affected horses may

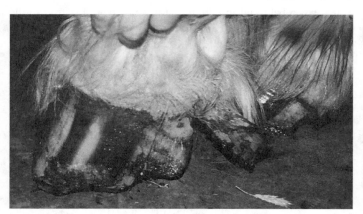

The severely neglected hind hoof of this Belgian has developed a large quarter crack.

Photo by Mike Wildenstein

Hoof cleaning solutions

Any of the following solutions may be used to thoroughly clean a hoof before applying medication:
- 1 pint (2 cups) Epsom salts mixed with $1/2$ gallon water
- 1 part 3% hydrogen peroxide (drugstore strength) mixed with 1 part water
- Betadine solution, straight from the bottle
- Clean Trax or White Lightning (our favorite commercial products).

---

show lameness for weeks afterward. Bruises appear as a discoloration of the sole after it has been trimmed with a hoof knife. Horses that go barefoot after a long time of being shod, or are put on hard, dry ground after a long period of being on soft, boggy soil, may be prone to bruise development. Placing a pad under the shoe helps relieve some of the pressure until a bruise heals.

Sole abscesses are common in drafts. They may cause sudden and severe lameness that can look like a broken leg, and the horse may hold up the affected leg. The hoof wall often feels warm or hot, and the digital pulses may be prominent.

The same conditions that cause a horse to develop a sole bruise can predispose the horse to develop a sole abscess, and a bruise may develop into an abscess. We knew one horse that routinely developed a sole abscess within days of having thrown a shoe.

A good farrier may be more useful and less expensive than a veterinarian for the diagnosis and treatment of sole abscesses. Successful treatment may involve simply opening the affected area to relieve pressure and allow it to drain. Some abscesses need to be treated medically with hoof soaks or wraps containing antibacterial medications. Stubborn abscesses may be successfully treated with a paste made from sugar mixed with povidone-iodine (Betadine).

A sole abscess may require treatment with hoof soaks containing antibacterial medications.

Photo by Bonnie Nance

Diseases of the Frog

Sloughing off of the frog tissue in almost a complete piece is a normal process in horses, but not in those that enjoy regular hoof and frog trimming. New frog tissue is always beneath the sloughed-off part.

Between trims, the tissue forming the frog often becomes tattered and pieces may begin to break off. Remove these flaps by pulling on them or cutting them off with scissors or a hoof knife.

Thrush

Thrush is a bacterial infection of the frog that most often occurs in horses exposed to persistently wet environments. We have seen thrush develop also during overly dry periods. Some horses seem more susceptible than others to having problems with this bacterial infection. The infection can be destructive, but does not result in the proliferation of dead and dying tissue that occurs in canker. Thrush causes a foul odor, and the horse often has pain in the affected feet.

Treat thrush by thoroughly and regularly cleaning the frog, trimming excess tissue and applying medication. Successful therapies include Betadine solution or scrub, or products such as Thrush Buster applied once or twice a day until the hooves are healed. Antibiotics that are active against Gram-positive bacteria, such as mastitis treatment tubes for cows, are often effective. In some cases a combination of these therapies results in rapid healing.

We have heard of a therapy that involves igniting iodide crystals with turpentine. We recommend treatments that result in less pain and discomfort, since painful treatments may cause the draft horse to become reluctant to pick up its feet for you or the farrier.

Keep the stall and turnout area as clean and dry as possible to promote healing and to help prevent recurrence of thrush.

Canker

Canker is a bacterial infection that extends from the frog to the adjacent sole and heels, causing the growth of abnormal infected tissue, the surface of which is dead or dying. Canker, more properly called necrotic pododermatitis, is common in draft horses, occurring especially in those without regular hoof care and kept on wet and contaminated soil or bedding. Canker produces an extremely foul odor, and may be caused by any of a number of gram-negative bacteria that live in the soil.

Lameness may initially be mild, but will get worse if the infection is not treated promptly and aggressively. Although most texts recommend the removal of all dead and proliferating tissue, which in some cases requires general anesthesia, we find that the best approach is less aggressive excision of affected tissue and more aggressive medical therapy. We remove only the most superficial of dead tissue, then thoroughly clean and pack the hoof with medication. Placement of a hospital plate or

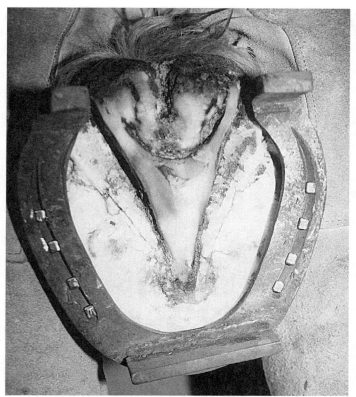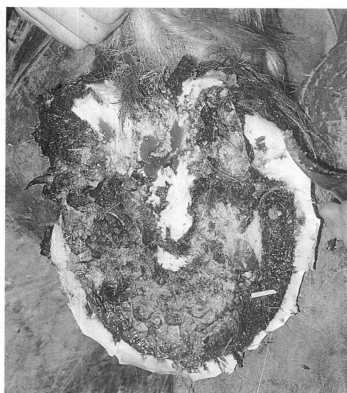

The frog of the hoof on the left has been partially eaten away by thrush. Canker (right), a much more serious infection, results in severe, deep damage and proliferation of abnormal tissue involving the frog and heels.   *Photos by Mike Wildenstein*

similar apparatus allows for ease of treatment and keeps the foot protected from further contamination during treatment.

Although canker treatment recipes abound, the following is our favorite: Thoroughly clean the hoof and pack it with a mixture of Terramycin antibiotic powder (available at farm supply stores) and DMSO gel (available from your veterinarian), a compound that has anti-inflammatory action and also acts as a penetrant to convey the medication into the tissues. Mix enough antibiotic powder into the gel to make a thick paste.

This medication, combined with systemic antibiotics and moving the horse to a clean, dry environment, greatly facilitates healing, as well as reduces the chance of canker developing in other feet. This treatment causes the death of affected tissue. Remove the black and foul-smelling parts and repeat the treatment until a healthy frog and sole remain.

Canker is a challenging disease to treat, and some folks just plain give up, but with proper attention it can be cured.

necrotic pododermatitis	
necrotic	= dead
podo	= foot
derma	= skin
itis	= inflammation

Coronary Band Problems

The coronary band is the soft tissue forming the crown around the top of the hoof. It is the area where new hoof is produced; the hoof wall grows down from the coronary band. Injury to the coronary band requires immediate attention because coronary band damage can result in permanent disfigurement of the hoof. For coronary band problems you may need to consult both your veterinarian and your farrier.

Mange mites (chorioptes) can infect the coronary band and alter hoof growth.

Diseases of the Hoof Wall

The equine hoof wall is composed of a combination of nonvascular tissue, similar to fingernails, and vascular tissue that is essential for maintaining the connection between the hoof wall and the underlying coffin bone (also called the foot bone, hoof bone, pedal bone, third phalanx, or P3).

White Line Disease

White line disease affects the inner hoof wall. Its exact cause is controversial, but we believe it is due to an infection by fungi that are present in the soil. Some horses are more susceptible than others. The fungus causes extensive damage to the hoof wall, which may result in the complete separation of the hoof wall from the foot. Treatment includes removal of the affected hoof wall (hoof resection) to eliminate the infected tissue, allow oxygen to get to the area (oxygen decreases the growth of the fungus) and provide access to the infected tissue for treatment.

White line disease causes the separation and partial detachment of the outer hoof wall, illustrated in this severe case by the depth a knife may be inserted between the separated wall and the sole.
Photo by Mike Wildenstein

Treatment includes cleaning, soaking the hoof in antifungal solutions and providing a clean, dry environment. For the treatment of white line disease, we recommend Clean Trax for cleaning and antifungal medications such as itraconazole, miconazole or clotrimazol (available from your veterinarian).

Under especially hot, dry conditions the white line may normally become prominent and flaky or crumbly, which may cause concern about possible disease. In such a case, many or all of your horses will have the same condition and will not show signs of lameness or hoof wall problems. If you are at all concerned about the condition of your horse's hooves, consult your veterinarian or farrier. The early treatment of white line disease or any other hoof disorder is always preferable to trying to salvage a horse with advanced disease.

Gravel

Gravel is an infection of the hoof wall that starts at the sole. It may be caused by dirt and bacteria getting into the hoof through

---

Hoof soaking boot

When a hoof must be soaked, getting your horse to stand with its foot in a bucket may be a problem. Before spending a lot of money on any of the numerous treatment boots available on the market (which usually don't fit draft horses anyway), try placing the horse's foot in a length of rubber truck tire inner tube.

A piece of truck inner tube makes an inexpensive device that provides both protection and continuous soaking to an infected foot.
Photo by Mike Wildenstein

Tape the end onto the horse's leg with duct tape. Fold up the other end, pour the soaking solution into the tube, and tape the loose end around the horse's leg. Instead of using tape, you could design a harness that goes over the horse and acts like suspenders in holding up the ends of the inner tube.

With this inexpensive and durable device the horse can be turned out to a pasture or paddock. The continuous sloshing of fluid as the horse walks aids in getting the solution deep into the hoof.

---

the white line. The infection often travels up the hoof to break out at the coronary band. It may or may not result in lameness, but often causes temporary defects in the hoof wall because of the involvement of the coronary band. The best treatment is to soak the hoof in antibacterial solutions.

Laminitis and Founder

Laminitis is an inflammation of the interdigitating laminae (lamellae) that attach the hoof wall to the underlying coffin bone. Laminitis is common in drafts and may be caused, in part, by the heavy weight of the hoof.

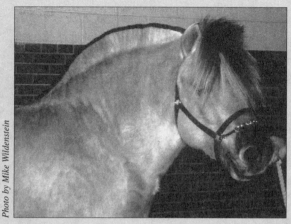 
Laminitis is a potentially life-threatening problem. The inflammation occurs following a reduction of blood flow to the hoof, which may result from:

- carbohydrate (grain) overload
- an infection, including a uterine infection from retained placental tissue
- exposure to the toxins in black walnut shavings
- a tumor of the pituitary gland in a mature horse
- repeated concussion on hard surfaces (called road founder).

Although carrying excessive weight increases the concussion on the hoof, excess weight alone does not lead to laminitis.

Laminitis most commonly involves the front feet, but severe cases may involve the hind feet as well. The affected hoof becomes extremely painful and walking becomes difficult. Affected horses are often reluctant to pick up their feet. To take weight off its front feet, the affected horse may stand with its forelegs placed well in front (camped out). The horse may appear to be walking on eggshells. The arteries to the foot have a markedly increased blood flow resulting in a pulse that is readily felt (bounding pulse), even though the laminae of the hoof are not receiving enough blood because the blood is being shunted away from the deeper parts of the hoof. The hoof walls of affected feet are often warm.

Treatment

The treatment of laminitis in its early stages often includes rest on soft bedding, anti-inflammatory medications and such medications as acepromazine to increase blood flow. Nitroglycerine patches, like those commonly used for human heart disease patients, may be placed at the coronary band to dilate blood vessels and increase blood flow to the hoof. A footing of blue clay, red clay or sand helps support the entire sole and often makes a laminitic horse more comfortable. Standing in mud, a springfed pond or a stream also reduces the inflammation and helps ease the pain of laminitis.

> *laminitis*
> laminae = the fingers of tissue that hold the hoof wall to the underlying bone (also called lamellae)
> itis = inflammation

A horse with laminitis may stand camped out to try to take weight off the painful front feet.

Laminitis vs. Founder

Founder is the most serious complication of laminitis. The words laminitis and founder are often, and incorrectly, used interchangeably. Chris Gregory, owner of Heartland Horseshoeing School and the virtual farrier at ruralheritage.com, offers this easily understood explanation of the difference:

- Laminitis is an inflammation of the laminae that connect the hoof wall to the coffin bone.
- Founder refers to sinking, as in "the ship foundered off the coast of New England."

Damage to the laminae connecting the hoof to the underlying bone may or may not result in partial sinking (rotation) or total sinking of the coffin bone. All foundered horses have had laminitis, but not all horses with laminitis will founder.

The sinking of the entire coffin bone is more serious than rotation of the toe alone, because it indicates a more extensive loss of connections. Radiographs (X-rays) can detect the presence of rotation or sinking of the coffin bone. Either change is permanent, necessitating the placement of shoes to support the hoof and relieve the painful pressure on the abnormally located bone.

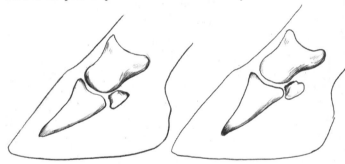

The front edge of the normal coffin bone (left) is parallel to the hoof wall. Laminitis causes a breakdown of the connections between the coffin bone and the hoof wall. If the connections become weak enough, the tip of the coffin bone rotates toward the sole and the horse founders (right).

Bones, Joints and Cartilages

The bones, joints and cartilages of the foot are subjected to continuous stress and concussion. Poor conformation, or poor trimming and shoeing, can predispose these structures to permanent damage. Some horses may be genetically predisposed to developing problems in these areas.

Navicular Disease

Navicular disease is an inflammation and degeneration of the navicular bone and its associated tissues, which are the tendons attaching the coffin bone to the adjacent pastern bone. These structures, deeply embedded in the hoof, absorb some of the concussion of the foot hitting the ground. Navicular disease is less common in drafts than in Quarter horses, most likely because drafts are bred for hooves that are proportional to the horse's size and weight. Many Quarter horses have small feet in relation to their body size; small feet cannot absorb concussion as well as large feet.

Draft horses are bred for hooves that are proportional to their size and weight, making navicular disease uncommon in these breeds. *Photo by Dusty L. Perin*

We have seen severe navicular disease causing chronic lameness in a Percheron. This horse also had muscle weakness and atrophy of the hind limbs due to EPSM. We speculate that this muscle disorder may have caused the horse to shift weight to the front, resulting in more concussion on the fore feet.

Navicular disease is not curable, but the pain may be controlled with proper hoof care, the placement of shoes designed to reduce pressure on the affected parts and periodic treatment with anti-inflammatory medications such as phenylbutazone (bute).

Pedal Osteitis

Pedal osteitis is an infection of the coffin bone, known also as the pedal bone. This infection is most often the consequence of a penetrating wound to the sole. Infection in any area of the coffin bone is difficult to treat because of the difficulty of getting high levels of antibiotics into the blood supply to the affected bone. Treatment includes attempting to remove the infected bone, applying antibiotics to the hoof, and giving the horse systemic antibiotics. The use of a hospital plate shoe will protect the foot and allow continued contact and easy placement of hoof packing medications.

> *pedal osteitis*
> pedal = foot
> osteo = bone
> itis = inflammation

Quittor

Quittor is the infection and degeneration of hoof cartilage, resulting in a draining abscess. It stems either from a coronary band injury over the area of the cartilage of the hoof or from a deep penetrating wound through the sole. The origin of the name for this disease comes from a Middle English word meaning boiling. Quittor is more common in drafts than in light breeds, probably because the hoof cartilage in drafts tends to harden (a condition known as sidebone).

Working draft horses in teams makes them susceptible to hoof injuries that may lead to the development of sidebone and quittor.

Photo by Bonnie Nance

Drafts working in teams, especially when shod with caulks or other traction devices, may step on the side of their hooves or be stepped on by a teammate during tight turns, which can injure the coronary band and/or cartilage. This combination of circumstances and the degenerative changes in the hoof cartilage create an environment that is favorable to bacterial growth. Opportunities for injury while working in teams make this problem almost exclusive to drafts.

Treatment involves opening the abscess, removing damaged tissue including affected cartilage, and using suitable antibiotics recommended by your veterinarian. If the damage is severe and the joint becomes involved, chronic lameness may result.

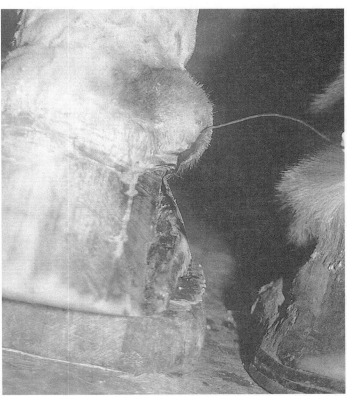

This swollen and draining abscess is characteristic of quittor, an infection of the cartilage of the hoof.

Photo by Mike Wildenstein

Sidebone

Sidebone involves ossification (hardening) of the cartilages of the coffin bone, and is common in drafts. Since this disorder is not exclusive to mature hard working drafts, but also occurs in young draft horses, its exact cause remains a bit of a mystery. Suspected causes include poor conformation and poor trimming and shoeing. Another cause may be repeated concussion on the hoof from the weight of the horse, made worse if the hoof is repeatedly traumatized by being stepped on by a teammate or by another of the horse's own hooves (interference).

No Hoof, No Horse **137**

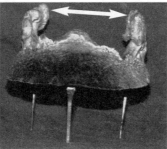

In this side view (left) and front-on view of the coffin bone from a horse that had sidebone you can see that the cartilages (indicated by arrow) have hardened and resemble wings attached to the coffin bone.

Photos by Mike Wildenstein.

In support of the concussive force theory, sidebone is most common in the fore limbs, where it most often affects the cartilages on both sides of the hoof. In support of the trauma theory, sidebone of the hind hoof usually involves only the lateral (outside) cartilage. Many draft breeds appear to have a genetic predisposition to developing sidebone, which may or may not produce pain and lameness.

A diagnosis is made by direct examination, nerve blocks, and radiographs (X-rays). Pain and swelling may be evident on either side of the top edge of the affected hoof. The cartilage, which should be soft and pliable, tends to break when it is hardened by bony transformation. Damaged cartilage may become infected.

Treatment includes proper trimming and shoeing, rest, and the use of anti-inflammatory medications such as phenylbutazone (bute). Shoes should be padded to reduce concussion. A rocker (rolled) toe on the shoe will improve breakover and put less stress on the cartilages.

> *ossification*
> ossi   = bone
> ossify = become bone-like

Ringbone

Ringbone, or osteoarthritis, is a degenerative joint disease leading to the proliferation of bone around the pastern joints. It may be high or low or both, depending on which ends of the pastern bones are involved. The causes include poor conformation and improper hoof care, improper shoeing, and an unbalanced hoof leading to increased concussion on the pastern joints. Lameness is most severe in the early stages and may diminish with time. Treatments include rest, the use of anti-inflammatory medications such as phenylbutazone (bute), and trimming to achieve a properly balanced hoof.

> *osteoarthritis*
> osteo = bone
> arthr = joint
> itis   = inflammation

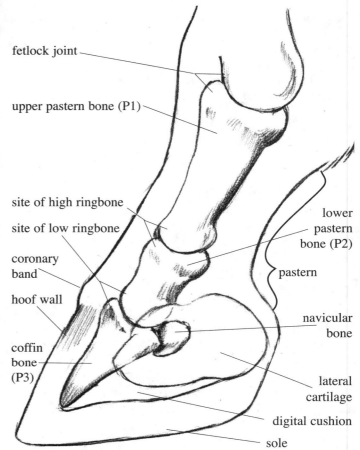

Parts of the foot showing sites of high and low ringbone.

Clubfoot

A foot with abnormally upright angles of the lower pastern joints can lead to a condition called clubfoot. The hoof angle at the toe of a clubfoot exceeds 60 degrees, in contrast to the normal toe angle of about 50 to 55 degrees. Clubfoot seems to be most common in Arabians, where heredity may play a role. In most cases clubfoot develops due to a conformational problem within the leg, such as contracted tendons or an injury to the leg that leads to abnormal weight bearing in that leg.

Although clubfoot is uncommon in drafts, it does occur. A horse with a clubfoot may be perfectly sound, but will require regular attention from a knowledgeable farrier to maintain a hoof balance that is as close as possible to normal.

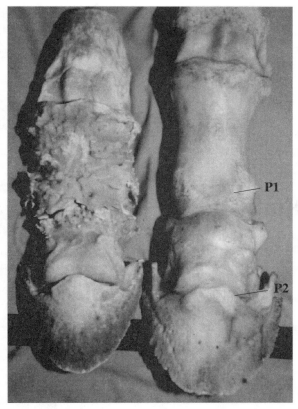

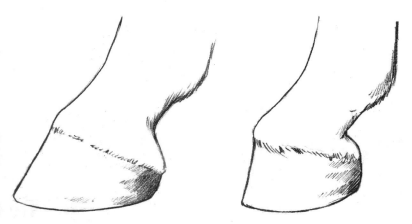

Compared to a normal foot (left), a clubfoot has an abnormally upright angle at the toe.

In contrast to the normal leg bones on the right, the leg on the left has severe irregular bony enlargements on the first pastern bone (P1) and the upper part of the second pastern bone (P2), including the joint; involvement of the P1-P2 joint is characteristic of high ringbone. *Photo by Mike Wildenstein*

Healthy Feet

Many factors contribute to the health of a draft horse's feet. Genetics, conformation, environmental conditions, nutrition, hoof care and shoeing all play a role. A healthy environment, good nutrition, a good farrier and prompt attention to any problems that arise go a long way toward ensuring healthy feet on our draft horses.

Photo by Richard S. Swinney

Stallions and Mares

When it comes to conflicting information and opinions, breeding draft horses is second only to feeding draft horses. Unfortunately for the draft horse breeder, few scientific studies have been done to help sort fact from fiction. Of the available studies, many were conducted in the 1930s and may or may not be applicable today.

Draft Horse Fertility

Breeding horses is always tricky business. The stallion and the mare must both be fertile and the mare must be able to maintain a healthy, growing fetus for more than 11 months. As tricky as horse breeding is, breeding draft horses can be particularly vexing. Fertility problems are often attributed to the draft breeds, supposedly due to their small genetic pool, especially since the middle of the 20th century when industrialization and economic disasters nearly wiped out many of the heavy breeds.

Dr. Sarah Fryer, while a senior veterinary student at Oregon State University, presented results of an extensive study of fertility in Suffolks and could find no basis for the belief that this breed experiences reduced fertility. Similar studies in draft mares at pregnant mare urine (PMU) farms have shown no evidence of reduced fertility in draft mares.

Contrary to popular belief, draft mares are no less fertile than light horse mares. *Photo by Ruth Freeman*

The Stallion

The most important attribute of a draft stallion is manageability. Whether the stallion provides natural cover of the mare or is collected for artificial insemination, ease of handling is essential. Fortunately draft stallions are typically far more manageable than many light horse stallions. Many draft stallions are capable of working in a team alongside a mare in heat and still maintain good manners.

Brabant Belgian stallion quietly working alongside a Brabant mare in heat. *Photo by Sam Moore*

Sperm Quality

A breeding stallion must have good sperm quality and quantity. The stallion's overall health and the health of his reproductive system affects sperm production. Sperm quality is highest during the breeding season, usually from April to September. A pre-breeding evaluation of the semen from a potential breeding stallion will include a total sperm count, as well as an evaluation of motility and the presence of abnormally formed sperm. The examination will also look for blood or urine in the semen, either of which markedly decreases sperm quality.

In some cases of poor sperm quality or quantity a specific problem—such as malnutrition, an infection or tumor in the testes, or a lack of normal hormone production—is identified and can be corrected. In other cases the testes have failed to form normally, in which case nothing can be done. When the cause of poor sperm quality is not apparent, it may possibly be the result of the small gene pool from which the draft breeds draw.

A stallion's overall health affects sperm production.

Photo by Pat Evia

Testis Size

Sperm count is linked to the size of a stallion's testes. Stallions with larger testes produce more sperm. A stallion with small testes is not necessarily infertile, but he will have a lower rate of successful breedings.

One testis may be noticeably larger than the other for several reasons:

- testicular tumor—A tumor generally results in a progressive testicular enlargement without obvious discomfort. The testis must be removed, but a stallion that has had a testis removed for whatever reason may still be fertile.
- infection—The infected testis may be warm and the horse will likely resent your attempts to feel it.
- testicular torsion—A twisted testis can be extremely painful, but may possibly be untwisted by a veterinarian.

Any of these conditions may occur in a stallion of any age. Sometimes what looks like an enlarged testis turns out to be a scrotal hernia, where portions of small intestine have passed into the scrotum, or the pouch of skin containing the testes. Scrotal hernias require surgical repair, and soon, as the small intestine trapped in the scrotum could become twisted and lose its blood supply.

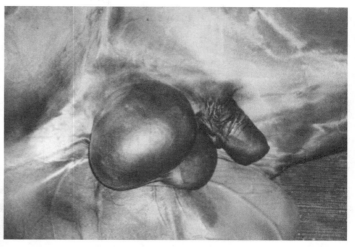

Enlargement of one side of the scrotum may be due to a testicular tumor, infection, torsion or a scrotal hernia.

Courtesy of Beth A. Valentine

Sexual Drive

A stallion may be capable of breeding a mare by the time he is two years of age. The number of mares a stallion can cover by natural service varies tremendously. Although we do not have good figures for draft stallions, Thoroughbred stallions have covered more than 100 mares per season, which we assume to be the maximum. A young stallion should be bred to only a small number of mares, half a dozen or so, which will allow you to evaluate his fertility as well as help protect his libido (sexual desire). Overuse of young stallions can lead to loss of libido.

Muscle Problems

After breeding, a draft stallion may develop muscle cramps and damage that may result in tying up. Stallions that show muscle problems or any signs of weakness or stiff gait following breeding should be checked for equine polysaccharide storage myopathy (EPSM).

The Mare

Yearling mares have occasionally become pregnant, and delivered and raised healthy foals with no apparent adverse effects. Most mares, however, are not sexually mature until they reach about two years of age. Since two-year-olds are still growing and maturing, a mare should be at least three years of age before she is bred.

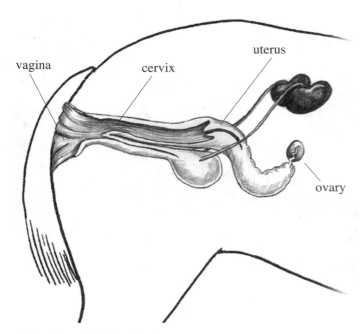

Mare Reproductive Anatomy

Heat Cycles and Breeding

A healthy uterus and ovaries, good conformation of the vagina and vulva and good nutrition all play important roles in the ability of a mare to conceive and carry a foal to term. Successful broodmares may produce healthy foals year after year until well into their twenties.

Estrus

Mares are seasonally polyestrous; seasonally refers to the fact that increasing day length induces ovarian activity, and polyestrous means that during the season of increasing day length they experience repeated estrus (heat) cycles. The estrous cycle of a mare is about 21 days. The time during which she is receptive to breeding (when she is in estrus, or in heat) is during the last five to six days of the cycle. Ovulation, or release of the ovum (egg), occurs 24 to 48 hours before the end of estrus.

Although some mares continue to cycle year around, the ovaries of most mares in the northern hemisphere become active in April and become inactive when day length shortens, usually in September. The widespread belief that breeding a draft mare after July is usually unsuccessful has not been supported by scientific studies.

You may induce your mares to begin cycling earlier in the season by providing them with artificial light to ensure they get 16 hours of light per day starting late in the fall. Ovarian activity may also be manipulated by various hormones administered by your veterinarian.

Mares in estrus often show obvious behavioral changes, especially in the presence of a stallion. Behavior may include winking of the clitoris—a small organ usually hidden in the folds of the bottom portion of the vagina—and squatting, raising the tail and spurting small volumes of urine. Some mares in estrus are less obvious about it, having what are known as silent heats. Suffolks may be more likely than other draft mares to have silent heats.

polyestrous
  poly = many or multiple
  estrus = heat cycle

In the presence of a stallion, a mare in heat may squat, raise her tail and spurt small volumes of urine.

Photo by Peter Rolfe

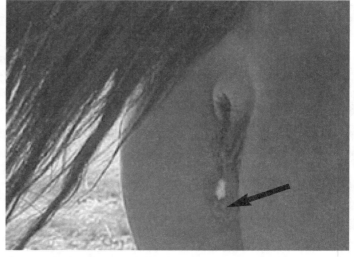

A mare in heat may wink her clitoris, a small organ that is usually hidden. *Photo by Peter Rolfe*

When to Breed

During the latter part of estrus the ovary develops a fluid-filled structure called a follicle, containing an ovum, or egg. Rectal palpation (feeling with the hands and fingers) or transrectal (through the rectal wall) ultrasound is used to determine when an ovarian follicle is developing such that the mare is ready to breed. Palpation and ultrasound both require a veterinarian or highly trained equine reproduction technician. Rectal palpation involves the careful insertion of a well-lubricated hand and arm into the mare's rectum to palpate the ovaries. For an ultrasound examination the probe is carried into the rectum and used to image the ovaries.

Rule of thumb: Begin trying to breed the mare on day two after you observe signs of estrus or when the ovary contains a 30 mm follicle.

Repeat breeding every other day from the second day you notice signs of heat until the end of estrus. If only limited breedings are possible, breeding is best done when a large follicle is present that is beginning to soften. The softening of the follicle indicates impending ovulation, or release of the ovum to travel down the oviduct to the uterus. During ovulation the follicle ruptures and is gone.

The size a follicle reaches before ovulation depends on the mare's body size. Light horse mares up to 1,300 pounds typically ovulate when their follicles are about 35 to 50 mm in diameter. Large draft mares may develop follicles that are 50 to 60 mm or more. Individuals vary, even among mares of the same size, and each mare has her own fairly consistent ovulatory follicle size. Once you have this information for each mare, keep a careful record so you can look it up when necessary.

Foal heat

During the foal heat, or the cycle occurring about a week after the mare foals, follicles are often larger than usual. Breeding during this foal heat cycle is possible, provided the mare's uterus has recovered quickly and has no residual infection, but the chance of a successful breeding during the foal heat is less than for later cycles.

Cycling Problems

A mare that cycles abnormally or not at all may have a tumor or other problem in the ovary. The most common ovarian tumor is a granulosa cell tumor. This tumor often produces various hormones including the male hormone testosterone and can result in stallion-like behavior in a mare. Surgical removal of the affected ovary usually cures the problem, and the mare may still be fertile.

Behavior Problems

The behavior of some mares during estrus detracts from their training and performance. Breeding may or may not help settle down such mares.

Various hormones may be used to suppress estrus. If the mare is not a potential broodmare, removal of her ovaries (ovariectomy) may be useful. This surgery is sometimes performed with the mare standing, through an incision in the flank or using a flexible endoscope (laparoscope) inserted in a smaller incision. The procedure carries potential risks, so think carefully and discuss your mare's problems with your veterinarian before deciding to remove her ovaries. In a mare with tying up problems, removal of the ovaries is not particularly useful.

Removal of the uterus is rarely attempted in horses, as the procedure is extremely difficult and dangerous.

> *ovariectomy*
> | ovari | = ovary |
> | ectomy | = excision or removal |
>
> *endoscope, laparoscope*
> | endo | = inner |
> | laparo | = flank |
> | scope | = device for viewing things |

Mare Fertility

A mare is considered fertile if she conceives and is able to successfully carry a foal to term. Statistics regarding fertility in mares vary greatly depending on the many factors that influence fertility including the mare's age, condition and level of nutrition.

Conception occurs when the ovum has been fertilized by the stallion's sperm. The developing embryo remains unattached in the mare and migrates through the uterus for about a month, after which it attaches to the uterine wall. If the uterine lining has infection or scarring, the embryo will die and be absorbed. The mare may have successfully conceived, but the resulting embryo did not continue to develop because it could not establish a healthy connection with the uterine wall.

Various hormonal abnormalities and problems such as tumors within the ovary interfere with conception, and various uterine problems interfere with the continued development of the embryo or fetus. Given the extremely complicated processes involved in ovulation, conception, implantation in the uterus, and the formation and maintainence of the placenta, it is a wonder that so many healthy foals are born.

Condition

A mare's body condition is linked to fertility. A mare in poor condition due to inadequate nutrition is far less likely to conceive and carry a foal to term than is a mare in good to excellent body condition. Maintaining good condition in harsh climates means mares must be well fed through the winter months to ensure that they are ready for breeding in the spring.

A mare that is gaining weight at the time of breeding is more likely to conceive than one that is losing weight. Careful studies have disproved the common wisdom that excessive body fat interferes with fertility. Fat mares are just as fertile as trimmer mares, and are just as able to successfully carry their foals to term.

A fat mare is just as fertile and able to carry a foal to term as a trimmer mare.

Photo by Sarah Fryer

Uterine Infection

Infection of the uterus, or endometritis, is the most common cause of infertility in mares. Bacterial infection that results in filling of the uterus with pus, a condition called pyometra, may cause an obvious thick yellow vaginal discharge. In other cases the infection is less obvious and may be apparent only after an examination of the uterine fluid and endometrial samples. Culturing for the presence of bacteria and yeast may be useful.

A uterine infection generally does not threaten the mare's life, only her ability to conceive and carry a foal to term. Older broodmares often have a decreased ability to clear the mild infection of the uterus that almost always occurs after foaling. Therapy may include uterine flushes, antibiotics and various hormones that help empty the uterus.

> *endometritis*
>   endo = inner
>   metri = uterus
>   itis = inflammation
>
> *pyometra*
>   pyo   = pus
>   metra = uterus

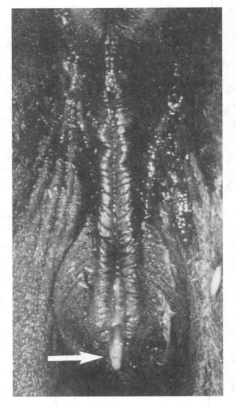

A vaginal discharge most often means the mare has a uterine infection.

Photo by Jim Brendemuehl

Windsuckers

The conformation of the mare's vulva and vagina can affect her fertility. Some mares, particularly older broodmares, develop a sinking and tipping of the vulva such that feces, urine and air may enter the vagina and affect the cervix and uterus. Such mares, referred to as windsuckers, are especially susceptible to uterine infections.

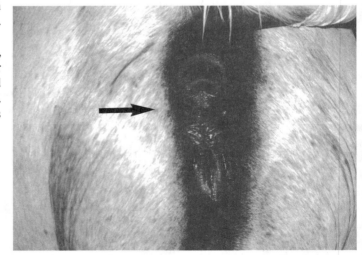

The top of this mare's vulva is severely sunken, resulting in the tipped vulvar conformation of a windsucker.

Photo by Jim Brendemuehl

Provided the uterus is not severely damaged, these mares may benefit from a surgical procedure known as a Caslick's operation, in which all but the lower portion of the vulva is sutured (stitched) closed until the mare is ready to foal. For severe cases a relatively simple surgical procedure can be done to rebuild the area and give it a more normal vulvar conformation.

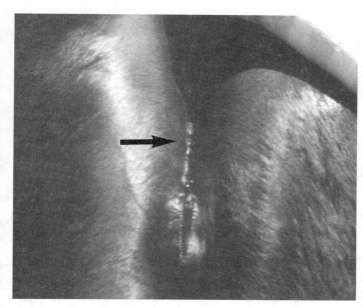

Suturing the upper portions of a windsucker mare's vulva decreases the risk of uterine infection from manure contamination. *Photo by Jim Brendemuehl*

Pregnancy Detection

Whether or not your bred mare is pregnant can be determined in three ways:

Rectal palpation will detect enlargement of the uterus and may detect the presence of fetal membranes (the placenta) lining the wall of an enlarged uterus. Palpation is, by definition, somewhat traumatic and is accurate only after about 28 days of pregnancy.

Ultrasound testing has largely replaced rectal palpation. Transrectal (across the rectum) ultrasound testing can detect pregnancy earlier (from day 10) and is a non-traumatic way to monitor fetal health and development. In most cases a single confirmation of pregnancy by ultrasound is sufficient. Repeat ultrasound evaluations are important only when a previously pregnant mare shows signs of returning heat cycles or displays external indications of problems such discomfort or vaginal discharge.

Measuring increased blood levels of estrogens can detect pregnancy starting at about day 35.

Embryonic Death

Regular ultrasound of bred mares has shown that early death of the fetus when it is still an embryo, known as early embryonic death, is common. Such mares are shown to be pregnant when ultrasound is performed early on, but later show signs of heat cycles with a negative ultrasound. The mare has lost and resorbed the embryo.

This occurrence is also called slipping the fetus. The developing fertilized egg technically changes from an embryo to a fetus when development has advanced to the point that the new lifeform is recognizable as a horse. This transition occurs at about one month of development.

The potential causes of early embryonic death are many. The embryo could have an abnormality that is incompatible with life. The uterus may be infected or scarred, leading to poor placental formation. Nutrition must play some role, since the addition of fat to the diet of an older mare can result in a dramatic increase in fertility.

As far as we know, early embryonic death is no more common in draft mares than in other breeds. Whether or not rebreeding will be successful, and whether or not the mare should be immediately rebred, depends on the cause of the early embryonic death.

Abortions and Stillbirths

Abortions and stillbirths occur later in pregnancy than embryonic death, and are relatively common in all horse breeds. Abortion is the loss of a dead fetus before it reaches full term—you will find the aborted fetus, along with the fetal membranes. Stillbirth is the birth of a full-term dead fetus.

Both abortion and stillbirth may be caused by infections. Bacteria or fungi may spread from the vagina through the cervix to infect the placenta and/or the fetus. Viruses, such as equine herpesvirus, may spread through the blood to the fetus.

In a case of abortion or stillbirth, the placenta and fetus should be submitted to a veterinary pathologist for evaluation. In some cases the examination indicates no evidence of infection but may find a poorly formed placenta incapable of supporting continued growth of the fetus. Causes of poor placental formation are not well understood, but a combination of good nutrition and a careful evaluation of the uterus before breeding may enhance the chances of producing a healthy placenta and a healthy foal. Possible causes of poor placental formation include:

- nutritional factors
- uterine scarring
- premature separation of the placenta from the uterus
- loss of blood supply due to umbilical twisting.

Horses have a long umbilical cord, which is always twisted. Before attributing the death of a fetus to twisting of the umbilicus and loss of blood supply, your veterinarian will examine the number of twists and look for evidence of bleeding (hemorrhage) or fluid build-up (edema) in the umbilical cord. Since the umbilical cord also carries the waste products of the fetal urinary bladder, a fetus that dies because of twisting of the cord may have a full bladder.

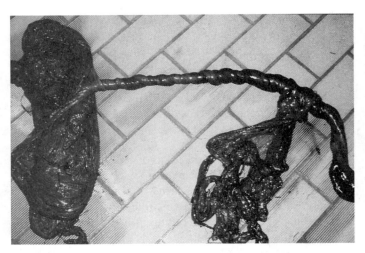

Although some twisting of the umbilical cord is normal, this cord has too many twists, causing reduced blood flow and an aborted fetus.

Courtesy of Rob Bildfell

Uterine Biopsy

Mares that apparently fail to conceive or that lose the foal due to early embryonic death, abortion or stillbirth may benefit from having a uterine biopsy examined by a veterinary pathologist. This procedure is performed with uterine biopsy forceps, a small scissors-like instrument that is passed through the cervix and is used to pinch off small samples of the uterine lining, or endometrium. The mare's cervix relaxes during estrus, easing the passage of the forceps, but opening a mare's cervix at any time is relatively easy, so this procedure need not to be done during a heat cycle. The pathologist will examine the samples for infection and scarring that may be interfering with the mare's ability to carry a foal to term. The biopsy classification used by pathologists ranges from 1 (normal) to 3 (severely damaged), with two grades in between.

> *endometrium*
> endo = inner
> metrium = uterus

Gestation Length

The common belief that the gestation (pregnancy) of a draft mare is longer than that of a light horse has not borne out under careful scrutiny. The gestation length ranges from 321 to 365 days, averaging about 342 days or a little more than 11 months. This, of course, is what the books say and some mares apparently have not read that particular chapter. A mare carrying a male foal may have a slightly longer gestation than one carrying a filly foal. Mares foaling in late winter have longer gestation periods than those foaling in spring or early summer.

Prolonged gestation, longer than 370 days, may occur for several reasons. The date of conception may have been miscalculated. The mare may be among the one percent of pregnant mares that normally have longer gestations. In most such cases, if the mare and the fetus are apparently healthy your veterinarian will not intervene. Mares on endophyte-infected fescue grass pasture or hay may have prolonged gestation because of placental damage, and their foals are often weak or dead at delivery.

Pregnant mares should not eat fescue grass or hay, especially in the last two months of gestation.

Twins

Mares frequently ovulate more than one ovum at a time, which can result in twin pregnancies. Double ovulations are more common in draft mares (about 32 percent of ovulations) than in light mares (about 20 percent of ovulations). Mares that conceive twins once are likely to conceive twins again.

A mare's uterus is generally not capable of supporting twin pregnancies to term, due to its inability to develop sufficient placentation for both fetuses. In many cases one fetus spontaneously dies and is resorbed. In other cases one or both

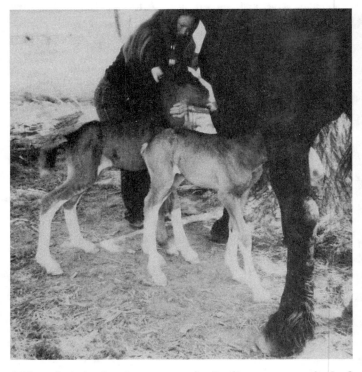

Although twinning is common in draft mares, survival of both twins is not; these two-day-old Shire fillies have beaten the odds.

Photo by Dave Daniher

twins die at a later stage, often resulting in abortion. If your veterinarian detects a twin pregnancy at an early stage you may be advised to opt for the elimination of one fetus to allow the other to develop properly.

Dr. O.J. Ginther at the University of Wisconsin reports that of 403 births from 102 draft mares, 13 (approximately 3 percent) of births were twins. Only two pairs of twins (about 15 percent) survived. One twin survived in two cases, and both twins died in nine cases. Most known cases of surviving twins in draft mares have occurred in Belgians, which may merely represent the popularity of the breed in this country rather than an increased likelihood of the survival of twins in Belgians.

Foaling Time

Signs of impending foaling in a mare include:

- distention of the milk veins on the belly just in front of the udder
- the presence of a waxy material on the teats
- enlargement of the udder with the production of milk
- elongation and relaxation of the vulva
- a slight sinking of the muscles of the hips and at the base of the tail
- an apparent dropping of the back part of the abdomen due to the relaxation of abdominal muscles.

As foaling time nears, do not wrap the mare's tail or wash her vulva or udder. These often-recommended procedures have no medical basis and may serve only to disturb the mare at this critical time.

When you are sure your mare is ready to foal, provide a clean environment for the foaling. A large foaling stall (12'x15'or larger) is ideal and should be bedded with a thick layer of clean straw. We do not recommend shavings as they are often dusty and may clog a newborn's nostrils and mouth.

Although mares may successfully foal at pasture, you will have much less control over where the foal is born. We would prefer to avoid such situations as the newborn draft foal found in a ditch on the other side of the pasture fence. Fortunately this foal survived. A foal that is stressed following birth and does not get adequate colostrum—the first milk produced by the mare

Induced foaling

A mare may be induced to foal by the administration of hormones such as oxytocin and estrogen that can cause relaxation of the cervix and contractions of the uterine wall. Induced foaling may be necessary for a mare with severe problems such as previous vaginal or rectal tears or pelvic fractures that narrow the birth canal. Induced foaling ensures that you have the veterinarian on hand for the birth. Inducing foaling does not have any adverse effects on the mare's future fertility. The timing of induced parturition has to be correct, however, or you may end up with a premature foal.

that is highly enriched in antibodies for protection against disease—is susceptible to developing neonatal infections.

Foaling

A mare that is ready to foal will often appear anxious, become restless, stop eating for periods of time, and may appear to have episodes of mild colic-like pain. She may sweat and switch her tail. Milk may spurt from her teats.

Uterine contractions are intermittent and typically last from about one to 20 minutes. This period of intermittent contractions usually lasts from one to four hours. A mare typically foals at night, and if you attempt to remain with her during this time she will quite likely choose to foal as soon as you leave to get another cup of coffee.

Red Bag

In a normal birth, the clear membranous amnion is seen first, followed by the foal. If the thicker, red (allantochorionic) membrane that contains the placental blood vessels presents first, the condition is known as red bag. Red bag indicates premature separation of the placenta and means that the foal is in trouble. *You must break this membrane immediately*, as the continued separation will cut off the foal's oxygen supply.

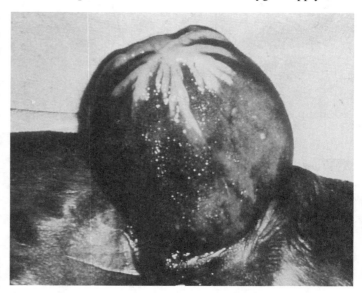

The cervical star, the pale zone of the placenta with the radiating arms, should break during delivery; the appearance of the allantochorionic membrane with an intact cervical star indicates premature separation of the placenta—the membrane must be broken immediately.

Courtesy of Jim Brendemuehl

Birth Position

Once the placenta has broken down to allow the foal to begin passing through the birth canal, the birth should occur within about an hour. Any longer may indicate a delivery problem and require the assistance of your veterinarian. Mares usually lie down to foal, but may choose to foal while standing.

Normal presentation of the foal at birth is right side up, front feet first, with the head resting on the foal's knees. One front leg is usually just ahead of the other, which helps the foal's shoulders pass through the birth canal. If the foal appears to be upside down or backwards, or the fore legs are passed to the level of the knees without the nose appearing, call your veterinarian immediately.

The improper positioning of a foal at birth is known as dystocia (pronounced diss-TOE-shah) and can be a serious problem for both the mare and the foal. While you are waiting for the veterinarian, keep the mare walking, making her less likely to strain to deliver the malpositioned foal.

The thin amnionic sac has passed along with this newborn foal and is lying on the ground; the remainder of the placenta is beginning to pass and is seen hanging behind the mare.

Photo by Sarah Fryer

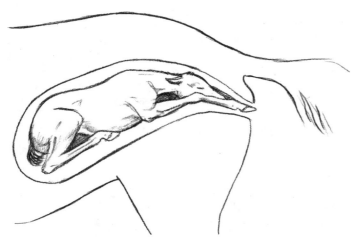

Normal position of the foal in the birth canal.

Arrival of the Foal

The foal is usually born along with the broken amnionic sac. If the foal is born inside a still-intact amnionic sac, you will need to quickly break it.

The umbilical cord will break during or soon after birth. The mare should remain lying down for a few minutes after delivery to allow the blood in the umbilical cord to be incorporated into the foal's bloodstream. If, however, she stands up quickly and breaks the umbilical cord immediately, the amount of blood lost will be minimal and will not cause a problem.

If you are present at the birth and the mare will tolerate help, clear the fetal membranes from the foal's nostrils and mouth and rub the foal vigorously with a coarse dry towel to stimulate respiration.

Foal Size

Despite their large size draft foals do not appear to be at an increased risk of fetal malpositioning or an inability to pass through the birth canal. Light horse mares are usually able to carry and deliver draft cross foals with no problems, since the size of the mare's uterus largely determines the size of the developing fetus. Foals from light horse mares bred to draft stallions can still grow to be quite a bit larger than their dams.

Most folks who crossbreed prefer to breed a draft mare to a light horse stallion to avoid any potential fetal size birth problems and to (hopefully) breed a foal with the size and bone density of a draft horse. You cannot, however, predict whether a foal will take after the draft parent or the light horse parent, and the offspring may take on some of the least desirable traits of both.

Post-Foaling Complications

Draft mares seem to be more susceptible than other breeds to post-foaling complications. Regular exercise is good for pregnant mares, as it helps them maintain strength and muscle tone and will help decrease the chance of complications. Good nutrition is also important.

Weakness and Weight Loss

A mare normally stands soon after giving birth, and certainly should be able to rise within 24 hours after foaling. A down mare needs veterinary attention. Postpartum weakness can occur in a mare with an infection, internal injury or leg nerve damage. A draft mare that stands normally after foaling may still develop a stiff hind limb gait or fail to maintain weight during nursing. In the months after foaling, severe weakness and debilitation in the mare can result in the death of or the need to put down the horse.

EPSM may be an underlying cause of many post-foaling problems in draft mares. Before blaming EPSM rule out other complications of delivery, including infection of a retained placenta, a ruptured uterus or uterine artery and a damaged intestine trapped in the birth canal during delivery. EPSM is, however, common in draft horses and ponies and the stress of delivery may be just enough to push these horses over the edge and cause obvious problems.

Providing any nursing mare the extra calories she needs by increasing the fat in her diet is always safer than feeding high levels of grain. If EPSM is a part or all of the problem, the mare needs a diet that is high in fat and low in starch and sugar.

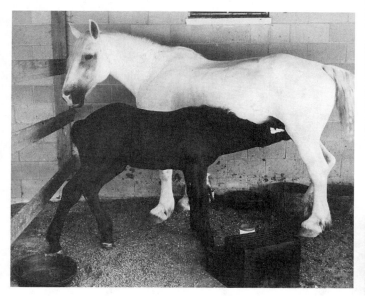

The loss of condition in a nursing draft mare indicates a need to change her diet; this mare turned around with an increased fat intake.
Photo by Alice Saczawa

Placenta Problems

The placenta should begin to pass soon after delivery. If, during this process, the membranes hang below the mare's hocks, tie them up in a knot to decrease the likelihood the mare will kick at them and possibly injure the foal. Do not cut off these membranes, as their weight helps the rest of the placenta to pass.

The entire placenta should pass within two to three hours of delivery. Carefully examine it for evidence of thickening due to infection (placentitis) or for areas of abnormal development, which may affect the foal's health. Look for missing pieces.

placentitis	
placent	= placenta (fetal membranes)
itis	= inflammation

If the entire placenta does not pass within two to three hours the mare has a retained placenta and needs prompt veterinary assistance. Retained portions of the placenta often cause laminitis and founder. Your veterinarian can administer

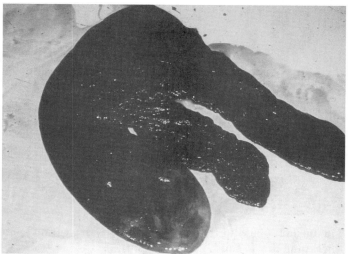

After the placenta has passed, carefully examine it and save it in the refrigerator for your veterinarian to evaluate.
Photo by Jim Brendemuehl

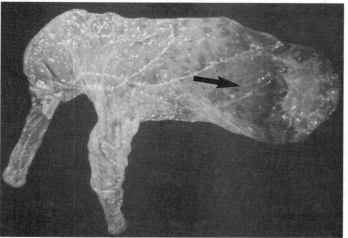

The areas of thickening and discoloration near the cervical star (right) of this placenta are indicative of placentitis.
Photo by Rob Bildfell

medications to help the remainder of the placenta to pass, and to combat infections. Retained placentas seems more common in draft mares, perhaps due to dietary deficiencies more than anything else. Be sure your pregnant mares receive adequate supplemental vitamins and minerals.

You may see some odd things in your horse's placenta that may or may not be significant. Small pouches may be dangling from the inner placental surface or a wad of brown rubbery tissue (called a hippomane) may be floating free inside the placenta. These conditions are nothing to worry about. Nonetheless, save the placenta refrigerated in a plastic bag so your veterinarian can examine it and take samples if needed.

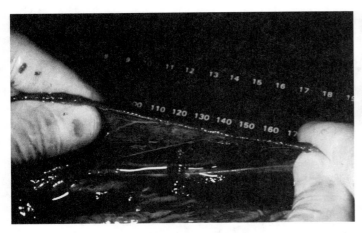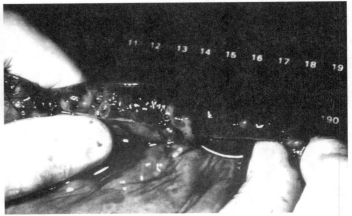

The normal placenta (left) is quite thin; mares eating endophyte-infected fescue pasture or hay develop severe placental thickening due to fluid build up (right).

Photos by Jim Brendemuehl

Lactation

A lactating mare will produce up to four percent of her body weight in milk each day. Her daily calorie needs will be almost twice the requirement during early pregnancy. Her water intake also will almost double.

Witch's milk

Occasionally a filly foal will have a watery secretion from her mammary glands known as witch's milk. Provided the glands are not swollen, hot or painful and the filly is eating and drinking normally, the condition is not considered a problem and should resolve with time.

Mastitis

Mares are much less susceptible to infection of the mammary gland (mastitis) than are cows. Although most cases of mastitis occur in lactating mares, mastitis may also occur in non-lactating mares and even in filly foals. Indications of infection include:

- increased size and temperature of the affected mammary gland
- change in milk to a watery or a thick material
- signs of illness in the nursing foal.

Mares with mastitis may not allow the foal to nurse. Effective treatment will depend on the severity and nature of the infection and on the temperament of the mare. Stripping out affected glands, hot packing, and administering antibiotic mastitis treatments into the gland through the teat are all useful. Systemic antibiotics may be necessary for a mare that would rather not have her mammary glands messed with.

A mare that was exposed to endophyte-infected fescue grass or pasture during the last months of pregnancy often fails to produce milk, a condition known as agalactia. Treatment with the drug domperidone may help, but prevention is much better than treatment.

mastitis	
mast	= breast
itis	= inflammation
agalactia	
a	= lack of
gala	= milk
ia	= condition

Colostrum

Antibodies from the mare do not pass across the placenta, meaning foals are born without antibodies to protect them from infections. Colostrum is the first milk produced by the mare. The newborn foal *must* get enough colostrum, as it contains a high level of protective antibodies the foal absorbs through its intestines.

Fat supplementation of pregnant mares increases the level of antibodies in their colostrum. Colostrum is only produced during the first 24 hours of lactation. A mare that is leaking colostrum prior to giving birth may not have enough left for the foal. In such a case, collect and store the colostrum to feed the newborn. Colostrum remains active for up to one year in the freezer.

The foal's intestines allow uptake of antibodies only during the first 24 hours of life. High quality colostrum—from the mare's first milk, and that has not been frozen for more than a year—should therefore be ingested as soon as possible after birth. If the foal does not nurse immediately, you may need to feed it colostrum by stomach tube. The tube is passed through the foal's nostril and into the stomach, a procedure best performed by a veterinarian as the inadvertent passage of the tube and colostrum into the lungs will cause serious lung damage (aspiration pneumonia).

For adequate protection, a foal should get at least 2 quarts of high quality colostrum within 6 hours of birth.

Your veterinarian can analyze the foal's blood for antibodies (immunoglobulins) at 24 to 48 hours after birth to determine if the foal has received adequate levels of antibodies. If not, equine immunoglobulins are commercially available to be given intravenously to help protect the foal. Many of these products have been produced by draft horses.

A healthy foal should stand and nurse within two hours of delivery, and continue to nurse several times per hour.

Photo by Dusty L. Perin

Photo by Sarah Fryer

The Foal

Even if your breeding program is successful, various problems may affect the health of a foal at or soon after birth. If you are breeding horses, develop a good working relationship with your veterinarian, whom you should consult often.

The Newborn

Time-honored tradition has us dipping the foal's navel (the umbilical stump) in an antibacterial solution such as Betadine (iodine) as soon as possible after the umbilical cord has separated from the foal, as well as giving the foal an enema. As it turns out, studies fail to support the value of these procedures. If the foaling area is clean, treating the navel with iodine does not reduce the incidence of infections in foals, and not treating the navel with iodine does not lead to an increased incidence of infection. If you feel strongly that dipping the navel is important, use a chlorhexidine (Nolvasan) solution rather than iodine, as it is more effective and less damaging to the tissue.

The administration of an enema to ensure passage of the meconium—the material that accumulated in the foal's gut during gestation—is also not necessary. Failure to pass the greenish-brown meconium within the first 24 hours is fairly uncommon. Furthermore, if the foal's intestines are not working normally, the amount of material in most commercial enemas is usually insufficient to have the desired effect. Watch the foal for passage of the meconium, followed by the soft tan milk stool. If the foal appears uncomfortable or is straining to defecate, call your veterinarian. If these signs are due to meconium impaction a large volume enema of warm soapy water is generally effective.

A foal should attempt to stand within minutes of birth and should be able to get around. A weak foal or one that is born with twisted legs may need to be helped up and guided to the mare's udder. If the foal cannot stand within a few hours, or if it is too weak or refuses to nurse, the foal may need veterinary assistance. Draft foals are more likely than light horse foals to need help standing.

A newborn foal should attempt to stand up within minutes of birth (left) and should be able to get around, if only on wobbly legs.

Photos by Vickie Darnell

A foal born in a clean area will likely be healthy without having its navel dipped.

Photo by Dusty L. Perin

Foal Monitoring

Examine and handle the foal daily to help ensure continued good health and smooth training in later stages. In particular, start handling the foal's feet at an early age.

Check the rectal temperature, heart and respiratory rates daily so you can discover early signs of pneumonia or other infections. Although a foal may appear healthy, it may sicken quickly and die if not treated without delay. Consult a veterinarian immediately if the foal:

- has a temperature below 99°F or above 102°F
- becomes lethargic or appears distressed
- has an increased respiratory rate (greater than 40 breaths per minute)
- has an increased heart rate (greater than 100 beats per minute)
- has a swollen umbilicus
- develops swollen joints
- has persistent diarrhea
- strains to urinate or defecate.

Neonatal Problems

Neonatal problems in draft foals are no different from those of other breeds. Proper care and nutrition of the mare will help prevent some problems. Careful observation of the foal will help you catch problems before they become life-threatening.

Patent Urachus

Occasionally a foal leaks urine from the umbilical stump. This condition, known as patent urachus (pronounced your-ACHE-us), occurs because the tube (urachus) that carried urine from the fetal bladder to the placental cavity failed to close when the foal was born. Patent urachus occurs in horses more than any other species, and is the most common birth defect involving the urinary tract of foals. The persistent moisture makes the umbilical tissue susceptible to infection.

The traditional treatment of patent urachus involves chemical cautery (sealing) of the urachus with concentrated iodine or phenol or with silver nitrate. This treatment may, however, predispose the damaged tissue to infection. Current recommendations are not to treat the area unless it is already infected, but rather to administer antibiotics to the foal.

If an infection is prevented or cured by antibiotic therapy, a patent urachus often closes on its own within a week of birth. If it doesn't, or if an ultrasound examination indicates a severe abnormality of the umbilical vessels leading to the umbilicus, your veterinarian will likely choose to do surgery to remove these structures and close the urachus.

Septicemia

Newborn foals are susceptible to systemic bacterial infections, known as septicemia. Foals that do not receive adequate colostral antibodies are particularly at risk. Bacteria may enter through the umbilicus or patent urachus, or be inhaled or swallowed.

Septicemic foals stop nursing, are depressed and generally have a fever. The mucous membranes of septicemic foals often become yellow (a condition known as jaundice or icterus). Prompt veterinary attention is essential.

> *septicemia*
> septic = infected
> emia = blood

Nutritional Myopathy

Foals born to selenium-deficient mares—even foals that are injected with vitamin E and selenium soon after birth—may develop muscle degeneration and weakness, known as nutritional myopathy. Severely affected muscles turn extremely pale to white, hence the other name for this disorder, white muscle disease. The mare should receive adequate selenium before and during pregnancy. Affected foals may recover with selenium treatment and nursing care, but prevention is much preferred to treatment.

> *nutritional myopathy*
> nutritional = related to diet
> myo = muscle
> pathy = disease

Ruptured Bladder

Rupture of the foal's urinary bladder may occur during delivery, and is most likely in colts. Affected colts are normal at birth but quickly sicken and do not urinate. Surgical repair is possible and immediate veterinary attention is vital.

Normal time for the first urination in a foal is about 8 hours after birth; a filly may take slightly longer to urinate than a colt.

Dummy Foals and Prematurity

Problems with the placenta or a reduced blood supply to the foal during birth can result in brain injury from lack of oxygen, resulting in a dummy foal. These foals have decreased brain function and are dull and often lethargic. With proper nursing care some foals recover, but those with severe brain injury do not.

Foals born prematurely have poor development of the lungs as well as of the brain. Intensive care may pull some of these foals through the critical period. Some equine hospitals have specialized neonatal intensive care units to provide around-the-clock care.

Neonatal Isoerythrolysis

A newborn foal with a blood type that is incompatible with the mare's blood type may develop a rapidly progressing weakness and jaundice caused by the destruction of its red blood cells. This condition, known as neonatal isoerythrolysis, is caused by antibodies produced by the mare and passed to the foal in her colostrum.

For this problem to occur, the mare must have had a previous foal with a similar incompatible blood type that resulted in her being sensitized and stimulated to produce the antibodies. The first such foal is typically normal, as the sensitization occurs during the birth process. The problem is somewhat similar to the human problem of women who are Rhesus blood factor (Rh) negative and give birth to Rh-positive babies. Affected foals may survive if they are treated quickly and aggressively with fluids, supportive care and, when necessary, blood transfusions.

neonatal isoerythrolysis	
neo	= new
natal	= born
iso	= equal or the same
erythro	= red blood cell
lysis	= rupture

Umbilical Hernia

An umbilical hernia occurs when the umbilical stump does not completely heal after birth, leaving a defect, or opening, in the abdominal wall. The failure of the umbilicus to properly heal can be influenced by genetics, by an infection of the umbilicus or by increased pressure in the foal's abdomen due to colic or some other abdominal problem in the first few days of life.

The hernial sac will be soft—its contents are usually just soft tissue and fat, but intestines could fall into a larger hernia. You should be able to push on the sac so its contents move back up through the opening in the abdominal wall.

Small hernias often heal by themselves. Large hernias, or those that have not healed by six to 12 months, should be repaired by a veterinarian. In some cases a clamp applied to the hernial sac results in healing, but in most cases surgery is the preferred method of treatment.

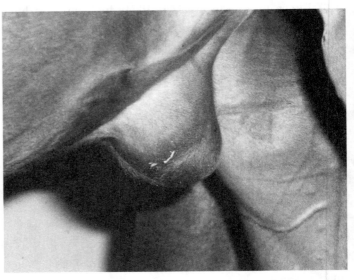

The swelling on the bottom of this foal's abdomen is an umbilical hernia.   *Photo by Mike Huber*

Leg and Joint Problems

A draft foal may be born with angular limb deformities (twisted legs) or contracted tendons. The foal may outgrow these problems on its own as it exercises and gains strength. Some foals require assistance, and your veterinarian may suggest restricting exercise or various splints, casts or special hoof trimming.

Physitis, OCD and contracted tendons may develop in young, rapidly growing horses. Such problems require the assistance of your veterinarian and possibly your farrier. Any foal with a systemic infection (septicemia) can have joint infections that may cause permanent damage if not treated early and aggressively.

Most foals benefit from plenty of exercise. *Photo by Dusty L. Perin*

Diarrhea

Diarrhea in a foal may occur due to a variety of causes. A bacterial infection of the intestines is a serious problem that requires immediate veterinary assistance. Salmonella and clostridia are two particularly dangerous bacterial infections in a foal. Diarrhea may also be due to various viruses, but these are usually fairly short-lived problems that resolve with minimal therapy. Any time a foal has diarrhea for more than a day or two, or shows signs of lethargy, poor appetite or fever associated with diarrhea, get veterinary assistance immediately.

Foal heat diarrhea

Foals often develop diarrhea during the mare's foal heat, which occurs about a week after delivery. The cause of foal heat diarrhea is not entirely clear. Some people believe it is related to intestinal parasites. Whether or not this is true remains to be proven, but it makes sense to keep the mare's worming schedule up to date, ensure that the foal is born in a clean environment, keep the foal in a clean area with the least possible exposure to parasites and worm the mare with ivermectin within a day or two after foaling.

Vaccinations and Worming

Consult your veterinarian and Chapter 4 of this book regarding the vaccination and worming of your foal. Vaccinations for foals should begin at two to three months of age. Worming should begin at two months of age. Read the package instructions carefully to ensure that the wormer you choose is safe for foals.

Orphan Foals

The ideal solution for raising an orphan foal is to find a nurse mare. Draft and draft cross mares make good nurse mares

because they are often willing to accept an orphan and may be capable of raising a second foal along with their own.

Hand Feeding

Since suitable nurse mares may be hard to find, hand raising a foal is often the only choice. Although foals have been raised on cow milk, goat milk and milk replacers designed for calves, lambs and goats, these alternatives are not nutritionally balanced for a growing foal. Use a milk replacer designed for foals. If a foal milk replacer is not immediately available, goat milk is far better for foals than is cow milk.

Bottle feeding is the way to start, and feeding every few hours will reduce the chance of the foal developing a gastric (stomach) ulcer. If at any time a newborn foal refuses to drink for more than four hours, you may need to resort to tube feeding to provide the needed fluids and energy.

A healthy foal will drink 15 to 30 percent of its body weight per day; a draft foal requires approximately 6 to 8 gallons of milk replacer per day. The foal should gain one to two pounds per day.

Switching a foal from bottle feeding to bucket feeding as soon as possible will allow the foal to have frequent feedings without completely disturbing your sleep and workday. Provide a full bucket of milk to start with and encourage the foal to nurse from your finger or a nipple while you gently guide its mouth to the bucket. Your foal may take some time to learn to drink from the bucket, but most foals learn within 12 to 24 hours.

Once the foal is drinking from the bucket, hang it so the rim is just above the point of the foal's shoulder. In hot weather keep the milk from spoiling by dropping a freezer pack or plastic bottle filled with frozen water into the bucket. Changing the milk or milk replacer often also helps avoid spoilage. Discard any remaining milk after 12 hours. Foals orphaned after a week or so of age may not take easily, or at all, to bucket feeding.

Social Skills

Hand-raised foals need to learn proper equine social skills as soon as possible. The playful antics of an orphan foal toward its owner may be cute, but they become dangerous as the foal grows bigger and stronger. Weaning the foal onto solid food as soon as possible will allow you to turn the foal out with other weanlings or with a tolerant mare or gelding to help it learn to be a horse. Allow the foal access to hay or grass and offer milk-based pellets until the foal is two to four months of age.

To learn proper equine social skills, foals need adult horse company.

Photo by Dusty L. Perin

Foal Handling

Handling a foal starting soon after it is born helps the foal get used to being with people, making its later training a lot easier. Some folks like to do more than just handle the foal by engaging in imprint training, a somewhat controversial process that establishes a life-long pattern of submission from the foal toward the person doing the imprinting.

Imprinting can be achieved only during the first 24 to 48 hours after birth. Although the process can be useful for later training and handling, if not done properly it may lead to serious training and handling problems later on.

We absolutely agree with Dr. R. D. Scoggins, equine Extension veterinarian at the University of Illinois College of Veterinary Medicine, that if you want to imprint your foal consult with someone who is experienced and knowledgeable about the process.

Weaning

We know of no adverse effects of letting a mare naturally wean her foal, other than having a larger weanling to deal with should it get emotional during weaning. Horse owners wean their foals for various reasons:

- to get the mare back into condition more quickly
- to keep the foal from gaining weight too fast on a heavy milking mare
- to put the mare back to work
- to start training the foal, which is easier when it is on its own.

Starting soon after birth, a foal should get used to being with people.

Photo by Dusty L. Perin

By four months of age the foal should be eating plenty of hay and feed, some of which it may steal from its dam. We like to have draft mares on a high fat and low soluble carbohydrate feed, and this same feed is good for foals to be weaned onto. Although time and patience may be needed to switch an adult draft horse onto one of these feeds, foals take to them more readily. We know of one foal who was stealing Mom's pellets and added oil, and then refused to eat pellets that did *not* have added oil. Supplemental vitamins and minerals will help ensure the growing foal has healthy bones, joints and tendons.

Weaning is stressful for both the foal and the mare (and sometimes for their owner). Some folks find that providing a barrier to separate the mare and foal so they can still see each other works well. Other folks prefer to move the foal to its own stall, in sight of other horses but not the mare. We have seen evidence to suggest that weanlings placed in small groups are more stressed than those placed individually in stalls, but we are reserving judgement until we see more studies on this subject. Putting weanlings either in small groups or with well-behaved and caring mares or geldings seems to us to be the more natural approach.

After weaning, the mare's udder will fill and she may become uncomfortable. Do not milk her out unless you need the milk for another foal. Milking her out only stimulates her to produce more milk and prolongs the process of drying up. Cold compresses or hosing may help, but she will begin to dry up rapidly. Some folks like to limit the mare's food supply during this time, believing fewer calories will cause decreased milk production. Others limit her water supply. We don't believe either method has an effect, but if you feel you have to do *something* we'd rather see you limit feed than water.

Castrating Colts

Draft stallions are typically more docile and easier to handle than light horse stallions, but compared to a gelding even a draft stallion may need special housing and handling. Unless you have a dynamite colt worthy of breeding, castration is in order. A horse may be castrated at any age, but most veterinarians prefer the horse to be at least six months old, since establishing immunity to diseases such as tetanus is important prior to surgery. Castrating at an early age will not alter the horse's growth or conformation. Consult your veterinarian about the best time to castrate a colt. Many veterinarians like to wait until fly season is over.

Several techniques are used for castrating horses, some with the horse standing and some involving a short period of general anesthesia. Your veterinarian will make a recommendation based on which procedure would work best for your particular horse.

Cryptorchid Testes

A colt's testes should be descended at or shortly after birth, although the small testes of a prepubescent male may be difficult to find. One or both may appear to rise and fall into the scrotum for several months. Finding both testes may be easier with the horse mildly sedated. By about nine months of age you should be able to easily feel both testes.

If one testis, or both, is not present in the scrotum, the horse is a cryptorchid. A cryptorchid horse should be castrated as soon as possible for two good reason: the condition is inherited and cryptorchid testes are susceptible to developing tumors. The surgery for castration of a cryptorchid horse is more complicated than routine castration and is usually performed at an equine hospital rather than on the farm.

Statistics tell us that the left testis is more likely to be retained than the right. Percherons have the highest reported incidence of retained testes of any horse breed. In some cases hormonal treatment causes a retained testis to drop into the scrotum. If you believe your colt is a cryptorchid, consult your veterinarian early on for advice.

> *cryptorchid*
> crypt = hidden
> orchid = testis

Stallion-Like Behavior

Geldings are generally less aggressive than stallions toward other horses and less interested in mares in heat, although some geldings do exhibit stallion-like behaviors. You may wonder if a testis or part of a testis is still in the horse, but as Cornell University animal behaviorist Dr. Katharine Houpt has said, "Most veterinarians can count to two."

Testing for blood levels of the male hormone testosterone will determine if your gelding is really a gelding. In most cases these levels will be normal. Many geldings (20 to 30 percent) engage in some stallion-like behavior regardless of their age at castration.

Foal Growth		
Age	*% of Mature Weight*	*% of Mature Height*
birth	10	60
2 months	27	71
6 months	48	81
9 months	60	90
12 months	70	92
18 months	82	95

Foal Growth

A foal at birth has already attained approximately 60 percent of its total adult height, and rapidly gains both height and weight. The accompanying growth chart is from a study of light horses. Although draft foals obviously grow to be larger and heavier than light horses, we could find no comparable study in heavy horses.

Common wisdom is that draft horses mature later than light horses, but we have not seen any studies to confirm this belief and we are betting that the rate of growth and maturity of draft foals is not much different than that of light horses. In either case, foals gain height much more rapidly than they gain weight. Small wonder that so many youngsters go through an awkward gangly stage.

At one week of age this foal is already 60 percent of its eventual adult height. *Photo by Becky Wilber*

A baby horse looks so gangly because it gains height before it gains weight. *Photo by Dusty L. Perin*

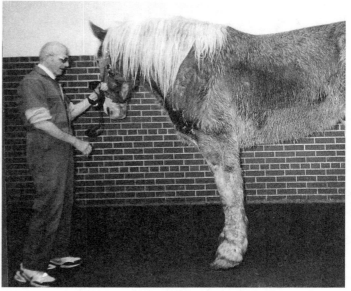

What's Ailing My Horse?

An observant horse owner will be quick to notice when something is wrong. The exact cause or causes of the problem, however, may be more difficult to determine. In most cases you will need the assistance of a veterinarian. The diagnosis of a problem may be made after considering the horse's age, breed, gender and what the horse is used for, as well as evaluating the environment and the horse's medical history, and conducting a physical examination. In some cases results of blood testing, urine analysis, cerebrospinal fluid analysis, biopsy or other procedures are needed to help make a proper diagnosis.

As a horse owner you must learn to hear what your horse is trying to tell you. *Photo by Nolan Darnell*

Making a Diagnosis

The diagnosis of disease in any animal is difficult. When the patient cannot tell us directly what doesn't feel right, where it hurts, how long a problem has been going on and how it may

have changed, we are already at a distinct disadvantage. We must learn to look for and correctly interpret clues that, in some disorders, may be subtle or easily misinterpreted. Animals also rarely respond to requests to perform certain maneuvers that would make a diagnosis easier.

When something is ailing your horse, an examination by a veterinarian may be essential in order to find out what's wrong. *Photo by Beth A. Valentine*

The diagnosis of disease in large animals such as horses is particularly difficult since we cannot pick the horse up or lay the horse down to test such things as reflexes. Palpation of abdominal organs in a horse can only be done by rectal examination, which doesn't get you far no matter how long your arm is. X-ray and ultrasound imaging of the internal organs of a large horse are extremely difficult and sometimes impossible. Instruments such as endoscopes and laparoscopes that can be used to visualize internal organs need to be extremely long and specially designed to be useful in draft horses. Exploratory surgery—often performed in humans, dogs, cats and cattle with puzzling internal disorders—is a difficult, dangerous and expensive procedure to perform in a horse.

In some cases a diagnosis can only be suspected. In such a case, a trial of a specific treatment may be instituted. If the horse responds to the treatment, then those involved assume the diagnosis was correct. Sometimes several different treatments must be tried before a successful one is found. For some disorders, tincture of time is the best therapy, as the horse's body heals itself. Fortunately for the horse and its owner, veterinarians are continuing to develop new procedures and fine-tune existing procedures in order to enhance our diagnostic abilities and capabilities.

Examining Possibilities

Most problems in draft horses can have more than one possible cause. For each condition described here we have tried to list possible causes in order from the more likely to the less likely, but of course we couldn't include *all* the various possibilities. This information is meant only to help you be informed about disorders that may occur in draft horses, and to understand how your veterinarian comes to a decision regarding a diagnosis and treatment. New tests will continue to be developed and new (or newly recognized) disorders will continue to appear. Get assistance from your veterinarian, your farrier or both when you have a problem with your horse.

Sign	Explanation
Skin Bumps	*Allergic reaction* Includes hives and eosinophilic granuloma, which may be due to insect, feed or airborne pollen allergy, and insect bite reactions; hives may also occur due to contact allergens on the skin. *Infection* Various bacteria can cause abscesses in the skin; less commonly, parasitic worms or fungi cause bumps. *Tumor* Includes sarcoids, melanoma (most often in gray horses), melanocytic nevus (any color horse), squamous cell carcinoma, lymphoma and others. *Bursal swelling* Increased fluid in bursae over bony prominences results in soft swelling. *Proud flesh* Exuberant granulation tissue, meaning excessive tissue that grows in healing wounds, most often on lower legs. *Fat bumps* The occasional horse is lumpy due to large fat deposits.
Lumps/Swelling in Throatlatch Area	*Strangles* Streptococcal infection of the lymph nodes in this area. *Thyroid enlargement* Can occur in horses on a high iodine diet or on a too-low iodine diet (goiter); usually appears on both sides of the neck. *Thyroid tumor* In an aging horse, benign thyroid tumors cause thyroid enlargement that may be visible or may be felt in this area, and may involve one or both glands on either side of the neck. *Melanoma* In gray horses, usually more than six years old. *Infected cheek tooth* Careful examination of teeth, perhaps including radiographs (X-rays), may be necessary to make this diagnosis. *Guttural pouch infection or air* Swelling caused by fluid or excess air in the guttural pouches.

Sign	Explanation
Hair Loss, Itchy	*Allergy* Often due to biting insects (the most common cause of tail and mane rubbing), but may be due to allergens in feed, contacting the skin or in the air. *Parasitic disease* Lice and leg mites are most common; other causes include parasitic worm larvae, which are less common now that ivermectin is used for worming horses. *Ringworm* Fungal infection that is sometimes itchy.
Hair Loss, Non-Itchy	*Ringworm* Fungal infection causing patchy hair loss and dry flaky skin, often not itchy, and may spread; generally does not cause severe skin irritation. *Bacterial infection* Severe skin irritation that may be painful, but usually not itchy. *Photosensitization* Loss of skin and hair in areas with white hair. *Alopecia areata* Small to large areas of hair loss with no associated skin reaction; hair sometimes eventually regrows. *Parasitic disease* Straw itch mites can cause a non-itchy skin disease of the horse's neck and withers. *Anhidrosis* Chronic non-sweating disease in horses may result in hair loss. *Immune-mediated disease* Blistering skin diseases, such as pemphigus, are uncommon but do occur in the horse. *Congenital skin disease* An inherited fatal disease in Belgian foals resulting in loss of hair and hooves; rarely a horse is born with hypotrichosis, a condition similar to baldy calves; hair loss may also occur in a foal born to a dam treated for EPM.
Poor Fertility	*Active uterine infection* Usually caused by bacteria, but may also be a yeast infection. *Uterine scarring* Damage to the uterine lining (endometrium) by previous or on-going infection. *Abnormal ovarian cycling* Abnormalities of the ovaries, or of the hormones they produce, severely affecting conception rate. *Poor nutrition* Selenium deficiency and overall poor condition may interfere with normal reproduction in both the mare and the stallion. *Stallion problems* Analysis of the stallion's breeding behavior and sperm may indicate that the fertility problem is with the stallion, not with the mare.

Sign	Explanation
Abortion	*Infections* Herpesvirus is the most common viral cause of abortion; various bacteria and fungi may also infect the placenta. *Poor placental formation* Due to previous damage to the mare's uterus or to poor nutrition. *Twins* Mares are typically unable to carry twin foals to term, and one or both may abort. *Twisted umbilical cord* The long umbilical cord may become twisted enough to compromise the blood supply to the fetus. *Illness in the dam* Various illnesses may result in subsequent abortion. *Poisonous plants* Fescue infected with endophytic fungi, as well as various other plants, cause abortion in mares.
Weak or Ill Foal	*Infection* Bacterial or viral infection can affect lungs (pneumonia), the intestine (diarrhea) or the entire system (septicemia or viremia); foals may be infected prior to, during or immediately after birth. *Selenium deficiency* An affected foal may be normal at birth, but soon becomes weak and has difficulty standing and nursing. *Neonatal maladjustment* Too little oxygen to the brain or premature birth can result in poor brain and/or lung function in a foal. *Ruptured bladder* The foal, typically a colt, is normal at birth, but then develops signs of illness and is not able to urinate. *Meconium impaction* A foal must pass the fetal intestinal content (meconium) within the first 24 hours of life or it will develop colic. *Neonatal jaundice* Caused by any bacterial septicemia or by incompatible blood types between the dam and foal leading to red blood cell damage (neonatal isoerythrolysis). *Botulism* *Clostridium botulinum* bacteria in the foal's intestine may produce toxins and result in severe weakness.
Diarrhea	*Change in feed* Especially a too-rapid change to lush pasture, rich hay or a high fat diet. *Stress* Usually fairly mild and short in duration, and the horse's appetite and attitude remain unchanged.

continued

Sign	Explanation
Diarrhea *continued*	*Antibiotics* Especially those given by mouth; can affect the bacteria normally present in the intestinal tract and allow overgrowth of potentially harmful bacteria. *Nonsteroidal anti-inflammatory drugs* Phenylbutazone (bute) and banamine may cause irritation to the large intestines. *Bacterial disease* Life-threatening disease may be caused by bacteria such as salmonella and clostridium. *Potomac horse fever* Usually the diarrhea is short lived and, if treated aggressively, rarely results in death. *Parasitic disease* Fairly uncommon due to the regular use of highly effective wormers; some smaller protozoal parasites are not killed by regular wormers and may cause diarrhea. *Malabsorption* Lymphoma and certain inflammations may affect the lining of the small intestine. *Colitis X* A serious and often life threatening diarrhea of unknown cause—seen most often in horses with a recent history of stress—likely due to overgrowth of dangerous bacteria such as clostridia.
Swollen and/or Painful Eye	*Conjunctivitis* May be an allergic reaction, a foreign body in the eye or a bacterial infection. *Injury* The lids and cornea are the most likely eye parts to be injured. *Uveitis (moon blindness)* Can cause permanent blindness if not treated quickly and aggressively. *Tumors* Tumors of the eyelids or surface of the eye are most common, but tumors may occur in or behind the eye.
Swollen Leg	*Fluid-filled joint or tendon* If non-painful, may or may not be a big problem; if the fluid is because of infection, prompt treatment is necessary to prevent permanent damage. *Bowed tendon* Appears as a firm swelling on the back of the front cannon bone. *Lymphatic obstruction/damage* Infection of the lymphatics of the leg (lymphangitis) causes poor drainage of fluids and lower leg swelling; tumors higher up in the leg that block lymphatics may also cause leg swelling. *Edema* Fluid accumulating in the legs and under the abdomen may occur with blood vessel damage (vasculitis, such as sometimes follows strangles), or may be due to Potomac horse fever, heart failure or low blood protein. *Fracture* A serious condition that must be evaluated immediately by a veterinarian. *continued*

Sign	Explanation
Swollen Leg *continued*	*Bruise* A severe bruise within muscle can cause swelling.
	Tumors Tumors within muscle can cause leg swelling but are not common.
Sudden Severe Painful Lameness	*Hoof abscess* Typically extremely painful, with heat in the hoof.
	Sole bruise May appear similar to an abscess, but with only bruising evident and no infection; may take many weeks to heal.
	Gravel Infection that works its way into the hoof wall from the white line, may break open at the coronary band.
	Laminitis and founder Horses that get into grain or are put on lush pasture, and those with pituitary tumors, are most susceptible; primarily the front feet are affected.
	Muscle injury or spasm May be due to trauma such as a fall or to underlying muscle disease such as EPSM.
	Fracture An obviously serious situation requiring immediate veterinary attention.
Stiff Hind Limb Gait	*Muscle disease (EPSM)* The first thing to look for in a draft or draft cross.
	Joint disease (arthritis) Diagnosis in a draft-related horse should be proven by either joint blocks or radiographs.
	Selenium deficiency Causes muscle stiffness and weakness in severely deficient horses, especially young ones.
	Tetanus Causes the horse to be stiff overall (sawhorse stance) and over respond to sounds and other stimuli; the horse's third eyelid commonly flashes repeatedly across the eye; prompt veterinary attention is essential.
	Lyme disease May cause stiffness that shifts from one leg to another, and lameness that may or may not affect hind limbs.
Poor Performance	*Muscle disease (EPSM)* In a draft-related horse, this disorder must be considered a likely cause of otherwise unexplained poor performance.
	Respiratory problems Airway obstruction, such as occurs with laryngeal hemiplegia (roarers), or airway disease such as bronchitis or pneumonia.
	Heart disease Less common than EPSM or respiratory causes, but possible.

continued

Sign	Explanation
Poor Performance *continued*	*Selenium deficiency* May or may not be the primary cause, as many selenium deficient horses perform just fine. *Hypothyroidism* Often cited as a cause, but uncommon in horses. *Anemia* Often diagnosed, like hypothyroidism, but must be relatively severe to affect a draft horse's performance. *Nutritional problem* Too little energy or protein, improper balances of minerals or (for an EPSM horse) insufficient fat. *Parasites* Unlikely to cause performance problems in horse that is wormed regularly. *Gastric ulcer* Much less likely in draft horses than in light horses.
Overall Weight Loss	*Muscle disease (EPSM)* The most common cause of unexplained weight loss in a draft-related horse with a good appetite. *Cancer* Causes wasting, even if the horse has a good appetite; an aging horse with pituitary tumors (Cushing's disease) may lose weight. *Other chronic diseases* Liver, kidney, heart and intestinal disease and chronic bacterial infection can result in severe weight loss that may or may not be associated with a poor appetite. *Equine motor neuron disease (EMND)* The equine equivalent of Lou Gehrig's disease (ALS) in humans, this disorder is less common in drafts as it is related to lack of pasture, the main source of vitamin E in most horses' diets. *Parasites* Often the first thing considered but not likely to be the problem with regular worming. *Bad teeth* Also often accused of causing poor condition, but less likely in most horses than other causes. *Poor nutrition* A common explanation for weight loss in a horse, but not likely unless other more common problems are eliminated.
Incoordination	*Cervical stenotic myelopathy* A form of OCD involving the vertebrae (wobbles); most common in young, rapidly growing horses, in which signs are similar on both sides of the body; may occur in aging horses due to arthritis of the vertebrae. *Equine protozoal myeloencephalitis (EPM)* Often causes incoordination that is more severe on one side than the other; generally affects only one horse in the barn, not several.

continued

Sign	Explanation
Incoordination *continued*	*Herpesvirus* Rhinopneumonitis virus may cause a sudden onset of incoordination due to spinal cord disease and may affect more than one horse in the barn. *Other viruses* Equine encephalitis viruses, West Nile virus and rabies virus may cause severe incoordination. *Trauma* Vertebral or skull fracture, or just bruising. *Equine degenerative myelopathy (EDM)* Incoordination is similar on both sides of the body; caused by low vitamin E levels in young growing horses, and relatively uncommon. *Tumors and abscesses* Any growth or swelling near the spinal cord can cause damage. *Migrating parasite* Occasionally parasites get lost and migrate into the spinal cord. *Inner ear infection* Can cause a horse to appear incoordinated because of lost balance control.
Increased Drinking and Urinating	*Pituitary tumor* In an aging horse, these tumors often cause increased drinking and urinating due to Cushing's disease. *Kidney failure* Malfunctioning kidneys cause increased thirst and passage of increased volumes of dilute urine. *Too much salt* Horses that consume salt blocks at a rapid rate may need daily salt added to feed rather than access to a block. *Too much water* Occasionally a horse drinks so much water that the kidneys are flushed out and can no longer concentrate urine to conserve water.
Dark or Discolored Urine	*Concentration* Urine will appear darker any time it becomes more concentrated due to decreased water intake. *Normal reaction to sunlight* The urine of some horses turns bright orange to red after exposure to sunlight, a phenomenon that becomes obvious in snow or bedding. *Muscle damage* The muscle pigment myoglobin, which damages the kidneys, causes red-brown urine following severe muscle damage. *Red blood cell damage* Damage to red cells for any reason causes release into the urine of the red blood cell pigment hemoglobin, which damages the kidneys. *Blood in the urine* May occur due to kidney or bladder stones, or to bleeding anywhere within the urinary tract. *continued*

Sign	Explanation
Dark or Discolored Urine *continued*	*Liver disease* Bile pigments may turn the urine a brownish green color; the horse will be jaundiced. *Melanin* A gray horse with melanomas in or near the urinary tract may pass gray to black melanin in its urine.
Hard Breathing, without Cough	*Poor conditioning* If associated with exercise. *Increased body temperature* An overheated horse or one with a fever may take rapid shallow breaths (panting). *Pneumonia/pleuritis* Some horses with pneumonia or pleuritis have rapid breathing without a cough. *Heart failure* Some horses with heart failure do not have an obvious cough.
Hard Breathing, with Cough	*Allergic bronchitis and heaves* A horse with allergic bronchitis has a periodic deep cough; a horse with heaves *always* has trouble breathing, especially exhaling. *Pneumonia* Various bacteria may infect the lungs; particularly dangerous is aspiration pneumonia, in which food material or medications have been inhaled into the lungs. *Influenza (flu)* A viral disease of the lung, generally mild in adult horses, which recover within two weeks, but can be severe and lead to death in young foals. *Rhinopneumonitis (equine herpesvirus)* A viral disease of the nasal passages and lungs, typically relatively mild and transient. *Heart failure* A failing heart may result in a fluid build up in the lungs and coughing. *Other* Fungal infection, tumors within the lungs and aspiration of irritating material such as silica from the soil are less common causes of hard breathing and coughing.
Difficulty Swallowing	*Choke* Caused by esophageal obstruction, most commonly in horses that eat concentrated feeds too rapidly. *Botulism* May occur in foals due to bacterial toxins made in the intestine, but more common in adult horses eating feed contaminated with botulinum toxin. *Equine protozoal myeloencephalitis (EPM)* This disease may affect the nerves involved in swallowing. *Selenium deficiency* Most often in foals and young adult horses that have low dietary selenium levels; may be accompanied by swelling or atrophy of jaw muscles.

continued

Sign	Explanation
Difficulty Swallowing *continued*	*Yellow star thistle and Russian knapweed poisoning* Found in the western states, this plant causes damage to the parts of the brain associated with swallowing. *Rabies* Infection with rabies virus can cause problems with swallowing that resemble choke.
Jaundice in Foals	*Systemic bacterial infection* Any generalized bacterial infection (neonatal septicemia) often causes jaundice. *Red blood cell damage* Incompatible blood type of the mare and foal results in red blood cell damage and jaundice in the foal (neonatal isoerythrolysis).
Jaundice in Adults	*Off feed* Horses that go off feed for any reason often develop mild jaundice. *Liver disease* Inflammation of the liver (hepatitis) or biliary system (cholangitis) or damage to the liver often results in mild to severe jaundice. *Red blood cell damage* A breakdown of red blood cells for whatever reason causes jaundice.
Dullness and Lethargy	*Any illness with fever or pain* Know how to take your horse's temperature. *Chronic bacterial infection* Internal infections are often hard to detect. *Liver disease* Often accompanied by yellow discoloration of the eyes (jaundice) and other tissues, and sometimes by maniacal behavior. *Kidney disease* Toxins that should, but cannot, be passed in urine cause severe illness. *Brain infection* Usually due to viruses, but may also be due to bacterial or protozoal encephalitis or migrating parasites, and may involve maniacal behavior. *Brain tumor* Fairly uncommon in horses. *Muscle disease (EPSM)* Not likely to cause severe signs of dullness, but can cause lethargy, stumbling, etc. *Anemia* A horse would have to be severely anemic to cause such obvious problems; a slight anemia in a dull and lethargic horse most likely reflects some other chronic problem. *Poor nutrition* A horse must be quite starved before severe signs of dullness and lethargy occur due solely to poor nutrition. *Hypothyroidism* Often diagnosed in lethargic horses, but rarely the cause.

Sign	Explanation
Maniacal Behavior	*Brain disease* Various bacteria, viruses and protozoa can infect the brain; less commonly, parasites migrate through and cause damage to the brain. *Liver disease* Liver failure can result in increased blood levels of the potentially toxic compounds of digestion that it normally breaks down, leading to severe brain dysfunction.
Signs of Pain	*Colic* Horse is off feed and not passing normal amounts of manure. *Muscle pain* May look like colic, and can cause secondary gas colic. *Gastric ulcer* Particularly common in foals and any horse under stress; high-grain feeds and high doses of nonsteroidal anti-inflammatory medications are predisposing factors. *Pleuritis* With or without pneumonia, this painful condition is usually accompanied by fever. *Choke* Horse is unable to completely swallow food and may be quite distressed, with saliva and feed likely to be present at the nostrils. *Ovarian pain* Associated with heat cycles in some mares. *Renal pain* Due to kidney infection or the presence of stones.
Sudden Collapse	*Anything causing weakness* Cause may be difficult to determine; in a draft-related horse consider EPSM. *Heart disease* Suspect this condition if the collapse is associated with exercise; less common in horses than in other species. *Narcolepsy* Horse suddenly falls asleep and collapses, but remains quite normal between episodes; may be inherited in Suffolks. *HYPP* In draft-related breeds, occurs only in crosses descended from the Quarter horse stallion Impressive. *Intraarterial injection* See Seizures/Convulsions
Seizures/Convulsions	*Equine protozoal myeloencephalitis (EPM)* Can cause seizures, but more typically causes incoordination. *Brain tumors* Fairly uncommon in horses. *continued*

Sign	Explanation
Seizures/Convulsions *continued*	*Brain infections* Viral or bacterial infections of the horse's brain are possible; parasites migrating through the brain are also possible, but uncommon. *Intraarterial injection* An injection placed into the artery can cause immediate seizures that may result in death; horse owners are advised not to give intravenous injections unless instructed by a veterinarian. *Epilepsy* Can occur in horses, but diagnosed only after other causes of seizures have been eliminated.
Sudden Death	*Intestinal accident* Twisting or rupture are the most common intestinal accidents to cause sudden death without previous obvious illness. *Ruptured artery* Most common are rupture of the uterine artery in pregnant mares and of the aorta in any horse. *Heart disease* Death may be due to sudden damage to the heart, or occur months to years after previous damage and scarring. *Pulmonary edema* Fluid buildup in the lungs can occur due to sudden heart failure, transient airway obstruction, anaphylaxis or bacterial toxins in the blood; in some cases an exact cause is not found. *Muscle disease (EPSM)* Underlying EPSM has been associated with sudden death in drafts. *Hyperthermia* Excessive and uncontrolled body heat, can occur in draft horses with EPSM. *Plant toxins* Ingestion of plants such as Japanese yew and oleander. *HYPP* In drafts, occurs only in crosses related to the Quarter horse stallion Impressive.

Photo by Debby Peterson

Blood Testing

To figure out what is going on inside a horse is often difficult. Drawing blood for laboratory testing gives your veterinarian a lot of valuable information. Although we sometimes hear otherwise, we are not aware of any blood values that are normally any different in draft horses compared to other horses. Included here are the normal adult ranges for the most commonly run tests on horses established in the laboratory at the College of Veterinary Medicine at Cornell University.

Normal Range

As you might imagine, establishing the normal range of blood values for horses can be difficult, and therefore normal ranges vary quite a bit between laboratories. If the laboratory your veterinarian uses has normal ranges that are different from those listed here, they are using either a different procedure for the testing or a different unit of measurement, or their normal ranges are not accurate. Some normal horses have values that are always slightly outside the established normal range. Normal values for foals are often slightly different from those for adult horses.

For values that are usually quite large—in the hundreds or thousands—a slight increase or decrease may not be significant. For values that are typically quite small, however, a slight difference may be significant. When in doubt, repeat the testing to make sure the values accurately reflect the health status of

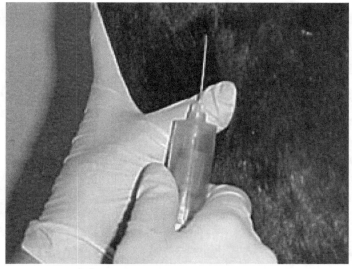

A blood sample drawn for analysis provides valuable information regarding the horse's health.

Photo by Beth A. Valentine

your horse. CBC and chemistry panel are the most commonly used tests to screen a horse's health, but your veterinarian may want to order additional tests depending on what is going on with your horse.

In any group of horses normal blood test values will vary from one individual to the next, and a value slightly outside the normal range may be normal for that particular horse.

Photo by Brian Richman

CBC (Complete Blood Count)

The complete blood count (CBC) is drawn into a blood tube (usually with a lavender top) containing an anticoagulant to keep the blood from clotting. The laboratory examines the red blood cells (RBCs or erythrocytes) and the different kinds of white blood cells (WBCs or leucocytes) that are circulating, and gets a total count of each.

erythrocytes, leucocytes
erythro   = red
leuco   = white
cytes   = cells

WBC (white blood cells)

normal range = 5.5-12.0 thousand/microliter

The white blood count increases slightly with stress and may increase markedly due to infection. A low count in a horse with suspected infection may indicate that the infection is too overwhelming for the horse's body to keep up with. An extremely high count may indicate leukemia, a form of cancer that fortunately is uncommon in horses.

HCT (hematocrit) or PCV (packed cell volume)

normal range = 31%-44%

This count tells you the volume of blood composed of red cells. It increases due to dehydration, decreases due to anemia.

leukemia
leuk   = white
emia   = blood

RBC (red blood cells)

normal range = 6.3-9.2 million/microliter

The number of red cells per unit of blood increases with dehydration, decreases due to anemia.

MCV (mean corpuscular volume)

normal range = 40-52 femtoliters

This measure of the size of the red blood cells looks mostly for decreased size due to iron deficiency anemia, although size may increase slightly in a horse trying to recover from anemia other than iron deficiency.

anemia
an   = lack of
emia   = blood

Segs or Neutrophils

normal range = 2.6-6.5 thousand/microliter

Neutrophils are the white blood cells with segmented nuclei that respond most to infection. A slight increase may be seen with stress, but a large increase suggests infection.

Bands

normal range = none

Bands are immature neutrophils that may increase due to infection, but are uncommon in horses.

Lymphocytes

normal range = 1.6-6.2 thousand/microliter

These white blood cells are involved in the immune response, for example the production of antibodies, and may increase in long term (chronic) infections. They may decrease slightly due to stress.

Monocytes

normal range = 0-0.4 thousand/microliter

Monocytes, like lymphocytes, are involved in fighting chronic infections.

Eosinophils

normal range = 0-0.8 thousand/microliter

These white blood cells increase due to allergy or parasitism.

Basophils

normal range = 0-0.1 thousand/microliter

Similar in some ways to eosinophils but present in much lower numbers, these white blood cells increase due to allergy or parasitism.

Platelets

normal range = 110-250 thousand/microliter

Platelets are involved in blood clotting. Low values often indicate bleeding tendencies. If the platelets clump together prior to testing (which they sometimes do), the count will be inaccurate but the report will indicate "platelets clumped" to explain the strange count.

Serum Chemistries

A second round of blood is often collected into a red-topped tube, or clot tube. In this tube blood is allowed to clot so the serum can be drawn off and analyzed for a variety of serum chemistries (the result of which is called a panel or profile) that indicate the health of the horse's various body systems. The tests included in these profiles may differ slightly among laboratories, and some veterinarians run some of these tests at their offices. Not all the tests included below may be on your horse's chemistry profile, and other tests may be done that are not listed.

Glucose

normal range = 75-117 micrograms/deciliter

Glucose is blood sugar. Low values may be obtained if a day or so goes by before the blood is tested. We are not aware of any common conditions in adult horses in which low glucose is important. High glucose, however, may indicate a pituitary tumor (equine Cushing's disease). Diabetes causing high blood sugar is rare in the horse. Slightly abnormal values (high or low) may be seen if blood is drawn within a few hours of a grain meal.

BUN (blood urea nitrogen)

normal range = 9-20 milligrams/deciliter

Blood urea nitrogen is a measure of kidney function. The BUN may increase if the horse is dehydrated. A persistent increase in a normally hydrated horse indicates a kidney problem. Slightly low values are generally of no importance.

Creatinine

normal range = 0.9-1.7 milligrams/deciliter

Creatinine is another measure of kidney function that is less sensitive than BUN to increases due to dehydration. Persistent high values indicate kidney disease. Low values are generally not significant.

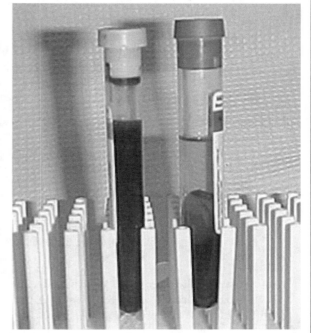

The tube on the left contains anticoagulant to allow the examination and counting of red and white blood cells; the blood on the right is in a clot tube, allowing analysis of serum for chemistries or other tests. *Photo by Beth A. Valentine*

AST or SGOT (aspartate amino transferase)

normal range = 212-426 units/liter

Aspartate amino transferase is an enzyme released into the blood from a damaged heart, muscle or liver. If this count is high, look at other values to determine where the damage is. If, for example, the increase is due to liver damage, other liver tests such as GGT, ALP, SDH and bilirubin should also be abnormally high. AST is often slightly increased due to muscle injury in drafts with EPSM. Low values are of no importance.

ALT or SGPT (alanine amino transferase)

normal range = 2-12 units/liter

Alanine amino transferase may increase due to muscle or liver damage, but this test is not often useful in the horse. Low values are of no importance.

GGT (gamma glutamyl transferase)

normal range = 8-33 units/liter

Gamma glutamyl transferase is a useful indicator of liver disease such as hepatitis and cholangitis, which will cause increased values. Horses with colic may also have slightly increased GGT levels. Low values are of no importance.

hepatitis, cholangitis	
hepa	= liver
cholang	= biliary
itis	= inflammation

ALP (alkaline phosphatase)

normal range = 75-220 units/liter

The alkaline phosphatase value increases due to active bone growth or liver damage. ALP is often slightly higher in young growing horses. Low values are of no importance.

SDH (sorbitol dehydrogenase)

normal range = 2-11 units/liter

Sorbitol dehydrogenase increases with liver damage. Low values are usually of no importance.

Bilirubin

normal range = 0.7-2.6 milligrams/deciliter

Bilirubin increases with liver damage and red blood cell damage, and in a horse that has not eaten well for two days or more. The two forms of bilirubin are direct (conjugated) and indirect (unconjugated). A horse that is not eating or a horse with red blood cell damage will have an increase primarily in the indirect (unconjugated) form. An increased percentage of direct (conjugated) bilirubin indicates liver disease. Low values are generally not significant.

Total Protein

normal range = 6.1-7.4 grams/deciliter

Total protein increases due to dehydration and may decrease due to chronic liver, kidney or intestinal disease, or following severe blood loss, vasculitis or starvation. Total protein may increase or decrease because of other diseases.

Albumin

normal range = 3.0-3.7 grams/deciliter

Albumin is a protein produced by the liver that may be preferentially lost due to liver, kidney or intestinal disease.

Globulins

normal adult range = 2.0-4.0 grams/deciliter
normal foal range = greater than 0.8 grams (800 milligrams)/deciliter

Globulins are proteins that include antibodies. This value may increase with infection or decrease due to problems with the immune system. In a foal the globulin level is measured to ensure the foal has received adequate colostrum.

CK or CPK (creatine kinase)

normal range = 93-348 units/liter

Creatine kinase is an enzyme released into the blood from a damaged heart or muscle. This value may be normal, or slightly to markedly increased, in a horse with EPSM. Increases are most likely to be seen in EPSM horses when blood is drawn four to six hours after exercise. Low values are of no importance.

LDH (lactate dehydrogenase)

normal range = 160-453 units/liter

Lactate dehydrogenase is a relatively nonspecific enzyme that may increase due to liver, heart or muscle disease. Low values are of no importance.

Cholesterol

normal range = 63-118 milligrams/deciliter

Triglycerides

normal range = 14-77 milligrams/deciliter

Measures of blood fats are typically important only when they are high in ponies or miniatures with increased blood fat levels and fat infiltration into the liver, a condition known as hyperlipemia. Horses on a high fat diet do not have abnormally high fat levels in the blood.

> *hyperlipemia*
> hyper = increased
> lip = fat
> emia = blood

Iron

normal range = 83-276 micrograms/deciliter

The iron level may decrease due to either chronic infection or iron deficiency. High blood iron indicates too much iron in the diet from feed, water or supplements. Too much iron in the body can damage the liver and other tissues.

Fibrinogen

normal range = 100-400 milligrams/deciliter

Fibrinogen is a serum protein that increases during infections or other causes of tissue damage. Low values may occur due to certain bleeding disorders.

Electrolytes

Electrolytes are important for the normal functioning of the nervous system, heart and muscles. Increases and decreases may be meaningful, and changes may occur due to excessive fluid and/or electrolyte loss, such as from sweating, kidney problems, gastrointestinal problems or poor nutrition.

Electrolyte	Normal Range (milliequivalents/liter)
Bicarbonate	22.0 - 34.0
Calcium (Ca)	11.2 - 13.0
Chloride (Cl)	95.0 - 113.0
Magnesium (Mg)	1.1 - 4.6
Phosphorus (P)	2.3 - 4.4
Potassium (K)	2.5 - 5.5
Sodium (Na)	134.0 - 143.0

Courtesy of Beaver Dam Farm

Giving Medications

We all hope our horses will remain healthy, but at one time or another every horse owner needs to medicate a horse. Some medications must be administered only by a veterinarian, while others may be safely given by the horse's owner. When you are called on to medicate a horse, a little knowledge will help you make the experience as nontraumatic as possible for both you and your horse.

Safe Procedure

Any time you give a medication or vaccine, the procedure is likely to result in some pain or discomfort to the horse, or may involve handling a painful area. No matter how mild-mannered the horse is, be ready to avoid kicking, biting, crushing or head swinging.

Stay close to the horse's side, with your feet well away from any place the horse might step. Tightly grip all medications, needles or tubes. The horse's slightest movement can cause things to be dropped and contaminated or lost.

If you plan to give vaccines or injectable medications yourself, be absolutely certain that:

● you have obtained high quality products. Watch especially the expiration date. Store medications properly in a refrigerator, when required. Giving a horse vaccinations or medications that will not be effective makes no sense.

● you know exactly how the medication should and should not be given. Injectable butazolidin (bute), for example, must be given only intravenously and *never* injected into the muscle.

If vaccines or antibiotics have been in a refrigerator or other cold environment, warming the material to body temperature before administration makes the medication more comfortable to the horse and also flow more easily on injection. Warming an eye ointment may result in less discomfort and fidgeting, and a warm ointment can be applied more rapidly, which is useful since the horse may not stand still for long. Warming may be accomplished by carrying the medication in a pocket close to your body for several minutes.

Systemic Medications

The word systemic refers to the whole body and may be used with reference to a generalized illness, such as a fever or infection, or to a medication given in a way that lets it enter the bloodstream and reach all parts of the body. Forms of systemic treatment include:

● oral medications given by mouth
● intramuscular medications given by injection in the muscle
● intravenous injections given into the jugular vein.

The newer intranasal vaccines for horses are designed to have the most effect on the immune response within the nose, but to some degree they may also get into the system.

Systemic Medications (medications that get into the entire body system)		
Type	*Abbrev.*	*Method of Administration*
Intradermal	ID	injected into the skin, not commonly used for horses
Intramuscular	IM	injected into the muscle
Intranasal	IN	squirted through the nostril into the nose
Intravenous	IV	injected into a vein, usually the jugular vein
Oral	PO	given by mouth
Subcutaneous	SQ	injected under the skin, not commonly used for horses

intramuscular	
intra	= into
muscular	= muscle
intravenous	
venous	= vein
intranasal	
nasal	= nose

Oral Medications

Oral medications may be in the form of a liquid, paste or pill. These medications include paste wormer, liquid wormer, cough mixture, and tablets crushed and mixed with water or molasses, as well as vegetable oil if you are treating EPSM. Also available in tubes are electrolytes, natural calming agents, and anti-inflammatory medications such as phenylbutazone (bute) and banamine. The abbreviation for directions to give a medication by mouth is PO, standing for *per os,* which is Latin for by mouth.

Liquids and Pastes

When done properly, the administration of liquids or pastes by mouth is a relatively safe procedure, although pastes are less likely than liquids to be accidentally inhaled into the lungs. Liquid medications are given using a dose syringe, turkey baster or tube; pastes come in a tube. Insert the end of the implement at a corner of the horse's mouth and place it on top of the tongue as far back as possible. Give small amounts at a time, rather than trying to force the entire amount at once, which may result in loss of the material onto the floor as well as onto you.

Many wormers and other paste medications in tubes have a mechanism to adjust and lock-in the proper dose for your horse's weight. Make sure you fully understand the mechanism and have it set properly so you don't overdose or underdose your horse. Take every opportunity to weigh your horse or estimate its weight using the formula in Chapter 6.

When giving oral medication, place the tube or syringe into the back of the horse's mouth from the side.

Photo by Barry Cooper

Pills

The problem with pills is how to get them into the horse. You'd be amazed at how many pills your veterinarian may prescribe to medicate a full-size draft. The pills must be ground to a powder and mixed with something tasty. You can find pill-crushing devices in catalogs and at tack shops, or you can use an old-fashioned mortar and pestle.

For the fastest and best procedure, invest in a spice or coffee grinder or a mini food processor. These devices make quick work of grinding a large number of pills, saving you time and effort. For safety's sake, relegate the grinder for use only with medications, rather than try to clean it for use with spices and coffee. Some horse medications, such as phenylbutazone (bute), are dangerous to certain people.

A powdered pill may be mixed with something your horse likes, such unsweetened applesauce or apples and/or carrots chopped in a food processor. If your horse still turns up its nose, add a little molasses. We try to avoid feeding draft horses a lot of highly concentrated sugars like molasses, but a little bit with your apple or carrot mixture, or mixed with crushed pills and water in a syringe, may be just enough to entice your horse to readily take its medicine.

Intramuscular Injections

Vaccines are most often given by intramuscular injection. Other medications, such as some antibiotics and anti-inflammatory drugs, are also given as intramuscular injections. From the injection site in the muscle the material is slowly released into the bloodstream. Compared to intravenous injections, intramuscular injections require slightly longer to take effect but release material into the system for a longer period.

Procedure

The procedure for administering an intramuscular injection is safe, provided you follow certain precautions:

● The needle must always be sterile. Never use the same needle twice, or you risk the development of clostridial or other bacterial infection, which can be life threatening. If you are careful to maintain sterility, you may be able to reuse a syringe two or three times, provided you use a new needle every time.

● If you are drawing medication from a bottle into a syringe, first wipe the top of the bottle with alcohol and let it dry. Injecting a small amount of air into the bottle at about the same amount that you are going to draw up makes drawing the medication into the syringe easier.

● Once you have drawn up the proper amount, flick the syringe with your index finger to move air bubbles to the top, and gently push the syringe plunger to expel any air before injecting.

● Brush the site of the injection clean, then wipe it with alcohol and let it dry. Cleaning reduces the chance of carrying surface bacteria into the injection site. Many veterinarians and horse owners do away with the alcohol cleaning step without any problems, and some horses seem to be more concerned about alcohol than about the injection itself.

● Always ask your veterinarian about safe procedures for the injections you are giving and follow the instructions carefully.

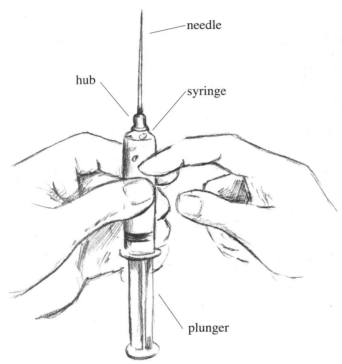

Flick the filled syringe with your index finger to move air bubbles to the top, then expel the air through the needle by gently pushing the plunger.

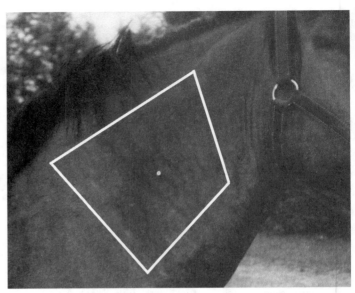

The safe zone for neck injections is the roughly rectangular space defined by the shoulder, a line several inches below the crest and the groove in the neck where the jugular vein lies; note the needle inserted to its hub and observed for blood.

Photo by Beth A. Valentine

Injection Site

Injections should be made either into the neck or into the back of the thigh muscles. Both these sites have a large muscle mass where any infection that might occur can drain by gravity. Never inject into the pectoral muscles of the brisket or the gluteal muscles of the rump.

For a medication that has to be repeated for several days, rotate sites around the horse such as right neck, left neck, left thigh and right thigh. If you return to previously injected area, place the subsequent injection in a slightly different spot.

The Injection

Separate the needle from the syringe containing the medication. Carefully handle only the outside of the end (the hub) of the needle to ensure that the inside stays sterile. Never touch the needle itself. You may place the needle into the injection site by one of two methods:

1. The most common method is to hold the needle between your thumb and forefinger while you rap the horse on the injection site two or three times with the back of your hand, then

The safe zone for an injection into the thigh is the roughly rectangular area defined by the thick muscle mass at the back of the thigh.

Photo by Beth A. Valentine

turn your hand so that on the next rap you insert the needle. The rapping desensitizes the horse to the slight pain of inserting the needle.

2. For a horse that is wise to the rapping technique, either grasp a fold of skin with your other hand or have someone grasp a fold of skin on the other side to distract the horse while you insert the needle. Although only rarely does a draft horse give us trouble with intramuscular injections, be prepared for the horse to jump or flinch when the needle goes in.

The needle will most often be either a 20 gauge (smaller bore) or 18 gauge (larger bore). It should be inserted to the hub and observed for several seconds for the appearance of blood, indicating that you have inserted the needle into a blood vessel. If this happens, withdraw the needle slightly—not all the way out—and reinsert it in a slightly different direction. Take care to touch only the outside of the needle hub.

Most medications that should go into the muscle are not designed to go directly into the bloodstream. Some intramuscular medications, such as procaine penicillin, can kill a horse if injected into the blood.

To ensure that material does not get into the blood, always draw back slightly on the syringe once it is tightly secured to the needle to make sure you don't see blood coming into the syringe. *If you see blood, do not inject into this site.* Instead redirect the needle and continue checking until you are sure you will be injecting into muscle and not into a blood vessel.

A draft horse has a lot of muscle to inject into, but may also require a lot of medication. Limit as much as possible the amount of material injected in one site, because all injected

---

If the site of an injection becomes swollen and warm or sensitive to the touch, or is accompanied by fever, depression or loss of appetite, call your veterinarian immediately.

---

materials cause a certain amount of tissue damage and irritation, which can allow bacteria to grow. Some folks maintain that no more than 25 cc of material should be injected in one site, but since a draft horse on penicillin may require 50 cc twice a day, you will fast run out of spaces to inject. In such instances, place half the material in one site, then withdraw the needle slightly (but not all the way) and redirect it into an adjacent site to help keep the horse comfortable and minimize tissue damage. After redirecting the needle, which may be done with the syringe still attached, always pull back on the syringe to look for blood before injecting.

Vigorously rub the area with the heel of your hand after giving an injection and withdrawing the needle. The idea is to help distribute the material within the tissue. We don't know if anyone has ever checked to see if that's what really helps, but it certainly makes *us* feel better.

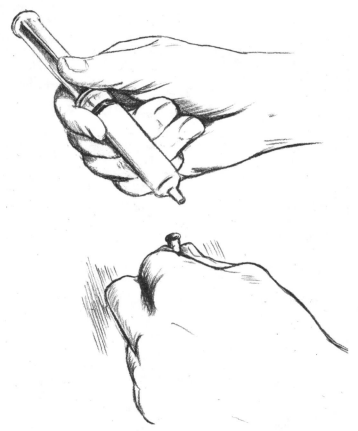

Rap the horse two or three times with the back of the hand holding the needle (left), then quickly turn your hand and insert the needle (right).

Needle Disposal

The disposal of needles and syringes is a tricky business because they are technically medical waste. Before disposal, place the needle back into the plastic casing to protect the person who picks up the garbage. Consult your veterinarian about the proper use and disposal of these implements, and remember to be careful.

Intravenous Injections

Giving an intravenous injection is a no-no for the horse owner, unless your veterinarian has put an intravenous tube (catheter) in place or you are well-trained in the procedure. The carotid artery is just below the jugular vein. Inadvertent injection into the carotid artery instead of the jugular vein may result in seizures or collapse, and can cause death. Veterinarians use a variety of procedures to avoid this tragic error, although accidents still happen to the best veterinarians. Newer materials allow the safe placement of a catheter into the jugular vein, where it can remain in place for several weeks while the horse owner or veterinarian safely and easily administers intravenous medications.

When drawing medication from a bottle for intravenous administration, wipe the top of the bottle with alcohol and inject air in the same way that you would for an intramuscular

Systemic Medications Commonly Used in Horses

Generic Name	Trade/Common Name	Category	Common Uses	How Given
penicillin	various	antibiotic	treat bacterial infections	IM, IV
procaine penicillin	Aquacillin & others	antibiotic	treat bacterial infections	IM
ceftiofur	Naxcel	antibiotic	treat bacterial infections	IM, IV
trimethoprim-sulfa	Tribrissin	antibiotic	treat bacterial infections	PO
tetracycline/oxytetracycline	various	antibiotic	treat bacterial infections	IV
doxycycline	Vibramycin	antibiotic	treat bacterial infections	PO
metronidazole	Flagyl	antibiotic	treat bacterial infections	PO
gentamycin	Gentocin	antibiotic	treat bacterial infections	IM, IV
flunixin meglumine	Banamine	NSAID*	reduce fever, pain and inflammation	IM, IV, PO
phenylbutazone	Butazolidi; bute	NSAID*	reduce fever, pain and inflammation	IV, PO
dipyrone**	Novin	NSAID*	reduce fever; treat mild colic	IM, IV
furosemide	Lasix	diuretic	reduce edema; treat exercise induced pulmonary hemorrhage	IM, IV, PO
acetazolamide	none	diuretic	reduce edema; treat HYPP	PO
acepromazine	ace	tranquilizer	sedative; treat laminitis	IM, IV
diazepam	Valium	tranquilizer	control seizures	IV
detomidine	Dormosedan	tranquilizer pain reliever	sedative pain relief	IM, IV
xylazine	Rompun	tranquilizer	sedative	IM, IV
butorphanol	Torbugesic	narcotic	pain relief, sedative	IM, IV
morphine	none	narcotic	pain relief, sedative	IV
meperidine	Demerol	narcotic	pain relief, sedative	IM, IV
oxymorphone	none	narcotic	pain relief, sedative	IV
guaifenesin	GG	anesthetic	anesthesia	IV
ketamine	Ketaset	anesthetic	anesthesia	IV
dexamethasone	Azium; dex	corticosteroid	reduce inflammation or allergic reactions; treat shock	IM, IV, PO
prednisone; prednisolone	pred	corticosteroid	reduce inflammation, especially allergic reactions; treat immune-mediated disorders	PO
methocarbamol	Robaxin	muscle relaxer	relieve muscle spasms and cramps due to nervous system problems	IV, PO
pergolide	Permax	dopamine-like***	treat Cushing's disease	PO
cyproheptadine	Periactin	anti-serotonin***	treat Cushing's disease	PO

*Nonsteroidal anti-inflammatory drug; **No longer available as of 1998; ***Brain neuro transmitter that affects the pituitary gland

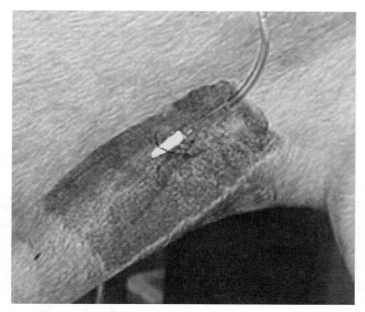

Once your veterinarian has placed a catheter in the horse's jugular vein, intravenous medicating is safe and easy.

Photo by Beth A. Valentine

injection. Be particularly careful not to have any air in the syringe when you inject.

A common practice among the owners of pulling horses is intravenously administering compounds such as vitamin E and selenium. When given intravenously, these compounds carry a risk of causing shock and collapse, known as anaphylaxis. Furthermore, the jugular vein may become damaged. The injection site at least becomes irritated, and these horses are often dangerous to work around. They will fight, often violently, to avoid a needle in their jugular vein, which becomes apparent to any veterinarian upon approaching such a horse with a needle, even if just to draw a blood sample. Subjecting any horse to this treatment is a sad state that should never be.

Intranasal Medications

Several new vaccines for respiratory infections such as strangles and influenza (flu) are designed to be squirted into the horse's nose. Such vaccines have the advantage of producing increased immunity at the site where these infectious diseases usually start, while eliminating the risk of a vaccine reaction in the muscle. To be safe and effective these vaccines must be given properly; their administration is best left to your veterinarian.

If you want to give these vaccines yourself, first consult with your veterinarian regarding proper procedure, and read the package instructions carefully. Intranasal vaccines must be placed into the true nostril, not into the overlying false nostril.

Although the effect is strongest in the nose where the material is placed, some degree of effect occurs throughout the system. The intranasal strangles vaccine contains streptococcal bacteria that have been modified so they are unable to result in a

full-blown strangles infection, but these bacteria are still alive and can get into the blood stream. Occasionally a horse will develop a mild infection for a day or two following vaccination.

> **Never give intranasal strangles vaccine and any intramuscular vaccines or injections at the same time—infection with streptococcus is possible at the injection site in the muscle.**

Topical Medications

Topical medications are powders, pastes, ointments, gels or fluids applied directly to the area requiring medication, usually the eye, skin, hooves or ears.

Skin and Hoof Medications

Skin and hoof medications include antibiotics for bacterial infection, antifungal medications, broad-spectrum antibacterial and antifungal shampoos, solutions or scrubs and DMSO. Many of these medications come as a liquid, gel or ointment.

For many uses we recommend antibiotic tubes designed for intramammary application in cows with mastitis. These formulations are inexpensive and handy to use, and the small volume and nozzle tops ensure that the medication doesn't end up badly contaminated.

Antibiotic preparations designed for treating mastitis in cows work well for treating bacterial hoof infections, as well as small areas of bacterial skin disease. *Photo by Barry Cooper*

Depending on the problem, you may have to clean or treat the area to be medicated with a weak bleach solution (diluted with water 1:10), Betadine (iodine) solution or scrub, chlorhexidine (Nolvasan) solution, lime-sulfur dip (4 of ounces lime-sulfur mixture per gallon of water) or other favorite formulation. We like Betadine scrub for its action against many bacteria and fungi. We keep a jar of medical gauze sponges soaked in Betadine scrub in the barn for cleaning hooves with thrush, mild cases of scratches and other areas of skin infection or superficial wounds. If you own gray horses you may prefer to use chlorhexidine, as it will not discolor the skin and hair.

DMSO

Dimethylsulfoxide (DMSO) is a solvent that has a strong anti-inflammatory action and the ability to penetrate intact skin. DMSO carries any compounds that are dissolved in it through the skin, therefore some precautions must be followed. The application to the skin of a toxic substance such as mercury—sometimes used in compounds called blisters, that supposedly treat tendon and ligament problems but don't work—to an area that has recently been treated with DMSO can be deadly. The DMSO carries the mercury into the bloodstream, causing severe injury to the kidney and large intestine, followed by death.

When mixed with antibiotics DMSO is useful for treating deep infections of the skin or frog. It also provides anti-inflammatory effects and is able to carry in other anti-inflammatory compounds such as corticosteroids for the treatment of tendon, joint and ligament injuries. As far as we know DMSO is not useful when applied to the skin over tense, painful muscles.

DMSO may be given into a vein to reach areas in need of anti-inflammatory treatment through the bloodstream. Intravenous DMSO has many uses for horses with colic, spinal cord or brain inflammation, tying up or muscle injury, but must always be given by a veterinarian. If your veterinarian treats your horse with intravenous DMSO, be prepared for its distinctive and pervasive odor in the air.

Always wear gloves when handling DMSO gel or liquid.

Intraocular Medications

Topical medications placed into the eye are known as intraocular medications. If your horse suffers from an eye infection or allergic conjunctivitis, develops a corneal ulcer or injury or recurrent uveitis (moon blindness), you will find yourself getting lots of practice with eye ointments.

Ointment comes in a small tube with a long nozzle for placement under (inside) the lower lid, which is easier done in an eye that is not extremely painful. Unfortunately the conditions requiring medication are usually painful, and your horse may not appreciate your efforts on its behalf. With practice and time, and as the medications cause the eye to be more comfortable, both you and your horse will find this procedure easier.

Your veterinarian may also prescribe systemic anti-inflammatory medications that may make treating the eye easier. For horses with corneal ulcers or uveitis, a small amount of phenylbutazone (bute) may help. The horse *must* be treated multiple times per day—usually at least four times daily—with intraocular ointments that control infection or medications that give added moisture to a dry eye. If the ointment has been in a cold barn, you will have a hard time squeezing out the proper amount. Carry the medication in a pocket to warm it.

With a dampened cotton ball, wipe down the outside of the eyelid to remove any discharge prior to treatment and any excess ointment after treatment. Try to keep the area around the affected eye clear of dirt and debris that could get into the eye. A well-fitted fly mask will help protect the eye against dirt, sun and flies between treatments.

Grasp all materials tightly so as not to lose a valuable medication in the bedding and manure when the horse jerks or swings its head. Keep your hands resting on the horse's head at all times. Give a light squeeze to the tube to get a small amount of ointment to the tip, to save time and ensure that the squeeze you give when the tube is in position will actually deliver medication.

While holding the tube in one hand and holding that hand steady by resting it against the horse's face, use one or two fingers to gently draw down the lower lid. Take a few practice tries. In case the tube bumps into anything, aim to place the ointment close to the inside corner, where the third eyelid helps cover and protect delicate tissues. Aim at a slight angle toward the inner corner of the eye, rather than straight into it. A quick squeeze is all that's needed.

If the horse is particularly jumpy, or continues to put its head up so high that reaching the eye is difficult, you may need to give the medication by putting a small amount (1/4 to 1/2 inch) on a *clean* finger. Even if the horse allows the ointment to be placed into the lower eyelid from the tube, if any oozes to the outer surface of the lids you may need to use a finger to gently push it back to the inside of the eyelid. Work the ointment around by gently pressing the upper and lower eyelids together to help spread the medication. If your horse does not allow you to press its eyelids don't worry, the medication will eventually spread on its own.

As you and your horse get used to the procedure, chances are good that you can go from using a finger to squeezing the tube directly into the eyelid, which decreases contamination of the medication being given.

intraocular
   intra   = into
   ocular   = eye

Ear Medications

If your horse has a bacterial infection in the ear canal, or has ear ticks, you may need to place drops or ointment into the ear canal. This eventuality is one good reason to make sure your horses are accustomed to having their ears touched and handled. Stand back after giving the medication, as the procedure will likely cause your horse to shake its head and you may find yourself being medicated, as well.

To medicate the eye, rest your hands on the horse's head, gently pull down the horse's lower eyelid, then squeeze a small amount of medication under the inside of the lid.

Photo by Barry Cooper

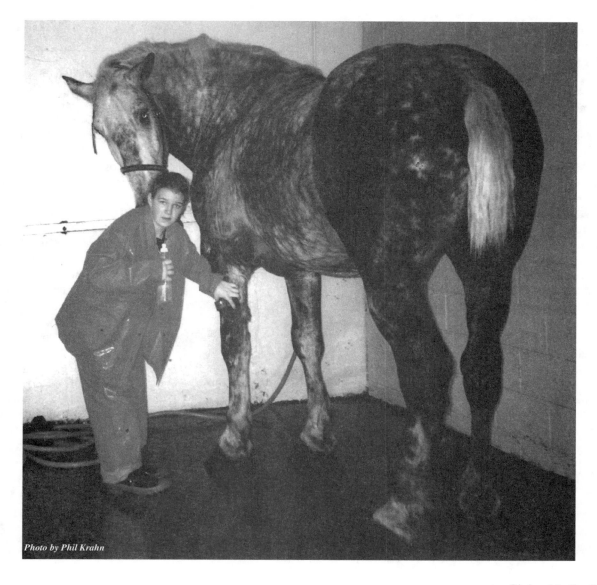

Photo by Phil Krahn

24

The End

The death or euthanasia of a beloved horse is emotionally traumatic for everyone involved. The thought of performing a postmortem examination may be difficult for the owner and even for the veterinarian to contemplate. If the cause or causes of death are well known, you may have nothing to gain from having this procedure performed, and burying the horse or calling the renderer to pick up the body may be the best way to begin the emotional healing process.

A horse that carries mortality insurance must at least have a postmortem in the field, with the submission of samples for microscopic examination, before the insurance company will be satisfied that foul play was not involved. Draft horses, however, are less commonly insured than other breeds.

If twisting of the intestine around a fatty tumor caused severe colic and death of an old horse, it may be of some relief to the horse owner to know that fatty tumors occur commonly in old horses. Nothing anyone could have done would have prevented the horse's death.

Compared to cattle, in which metabolic-related deaths may occur with few or no findings on postmortem examination, the cause of a horse's fatal illness or sudden death can usually be determined by a veterinarian or veterinary pathologist. They may be able to explain what happened, but in cases such as colitis or a ruptured stomach they may or may not be able to explain exactly why it happened.

A postmortem examination may involve simply taking a sample of the muscle at the back of

euthanasia	
eu	= good
thanasia	= death
postmortem	
post	= after
mortem	= death

the thigh to look for EPSM, or may be as involved as a complete examination of all organs, both with the naked eye and under a microscope. Additional testing may be required to identify toxins, vitamin or mineral deficiencies, bacteria or viruses. These tests are commonly available at a regional veterinary diagnostic laboratory or veterinary college. The cost of a thorough examination is usually not exorbitant and may be money well spent.

A postmortem examination may be used to gain knowledge to help prevent problems in other horses that could be exposed to the same infectious disease, poisonous plants or feed, or that are genetically related and may therefore have similar problems. Many infectious diseases and plant or feed poisonings are diagnosed following postmortem examination, and other horses that may have been exposed may be successfully treated in time to prevent their deaths.

Photo by Bonnie Nance

Resources

General

Vet Clinic:
ruralheritage.com/vet_clinic/
(The latest information on EPSM and other draft horse health care concerns, plus virtual vet Dr. Beth A. Valentine online to answer your questions related to draft animal health.)

The Evener Work Horse, Mule & Oxen Directory and Guide
Rural Heritage
281 Dean Ridge Ln
Gainesboro, TN 38562
931-268-0655
www.ruralheritage.com
(Annually updated directory.)

Chapter 2:

Vitamin and mineral supplements:
Vita-Flex Nutrition
PO Box 12308
Omaha, NE 68112
800-848-2359
www.vita-flex.com

Chapter 3:

Fat Pak 100 (powdered animal fat product):
Milk Specialty Products
PO Box 278
Dundee, IL 60118
800-323-4274
www.milkspecialties.com

Cocosoya oil:
Uckele
PO Box 160
Blissfield, MI 49228
800-248-0330,
www.uckele.com/equine.asp

Feed Companies:
Blue Seal Feeds, Inc.
PO Box 8000
Londonderry, NH 03053
800-367-2730
www.blueseal.com

Buckeye Feed Mills
PO Box 505
330 E Schultz Ave
Dalton OH 44618
800-898-9467
www.buckeyenutrition.com

Nutrena
Cargill
PO Box 5614
Minneapolis, MN 55440
612-742-7448
www.nutrenaworld.com

Purina Mills
1401 South Hanley Rd
St. Louis, MO 63144-2987
800-227-8941
www.purinamills.com

Southern States Cooperative
6606 West Broad St
Richmond, VA 23260
804-281-1180
www.southernstates-coop.com

Low soluble carbohydrate commercial feeds:
Blue Seal Demand
Blue Seal Hunter
Blue Seal Racer
Nutrena Compete
Purina Equine Senior
Purina Hi Fat Hi Fibre (Canada)
Purina Strategy
Southern States Legends 14 pellets
Triple Crown Equine Senior

High fat commerical feeds:
Buckeye Ultimate Finish

Chapter 4:

Fly masks:
Farnam Super Mask
Farnam Companies, Inc.
Horse Products Division
301 West Osborn
PO Box 34820
Phoenix, AZ 85067-4820
800-234-2269
www.farnam.com

Chapter 5:

Hoof supplements:
Farrier's Formula
Life Data Labs, Inc.
PO Box 349
Cherokee, AL 35616
256-370-7555
800-624-1873
www.lifedatalabs.com

Master's Hoof Blend
Vita-Flex Nutrition
PO Box 12308
Omaha, NE 68112
800-848-2359
www.vita-flex.com

Farrier schools:
General Farrier Short Course
& Advanced Farrier Course
Mike Wildenstein
Cornell University
College of Veterinary Medicine
Ithaca, NY 14853
607-253-3127
www.vet.cornell.edu/hospital/farrier.htm
www.horseshoes.com/schools/cornell/crunfrsr.htm

Heartland Horseshoeing School
Chris Gregory
327 SW 1st Ln
Lamar, MO 64759
417-682-6896
www.ruralheritage.com/horseshoes
www.ruralheritage.com/village_smithy

Sources of Draft Horse Shoes and Supplies:
Anvil Brand Shoe Co, Inc.
PO Box 198
500 South Spencer Street
Lexington, IL 61753
800-365-8202
www.anvilbrand.com

Will Lent Horseshoe Co.
5800 West Woodrow Road
Shelby, MI 49455
231-861-5033

Farrier Product Distribution
PO Box 1328
Shelbyville, KY 40066
800-468-2879

Remuda Tire Company (rubber shoes)
999 East 160th Avenue
Broomfield, CO 80020
303-280-0049
www.remudatire.com

Farriers Supplies and Services
American Farriers Journal
Lessiter Publications, Inc.
PO Box 624
Brookfield, WI 53008
www.lesspub.com/afj
(Annually updated directory, includes farrier schools.)

Chapter 9:

*One AC, a feed supplement being tested for horses
with anhidrosis:*
MPCO, LLC
2905 W Cholla St
Phoenix, AZ 85029
602-866-7701
r.leroy@worldnet.att.net

Chapter 15:

Orthoflex Saddle Co.
RR 2 Box 132
Nevada, MO 64772
417-667-7834
800-flex-fit
www.ortho-flex.com

Chapter 18:

Hoof cleaning solutions:
Clean Trax
Equine Technologies, Inc.
416 Boston Post Road
Sudbury, MA 01776
978-443-8078

White Lightning
Across the Anvil East, Inc.
920 Route 33, Building 7
Freehold, NJ 07728
800-872-6845

Hoof dressing:
Life Data Hoof Antiseptic
Life Data Labs, Inc.
PO Box 349
Cherokee, AL 35616
256-370-7555
800-624-1873
www.lifedatalabs.com

Some Useful Conversions

The following conversions come in handy for such things as interpreting supplement labels or calculating feed ingredients.

1 pound	= 16 ounces = 0.45 kg
1 kg	= 2.2 pounds
2 cups fluid	= 1 pint = 1 pound = 480 ml
1 liter	= 2.1 pints
1 ppm =1 mg/kg	= 0.45 mg/pound
ppm x 0.0001	= %
% x 4,536	= mg/pound

Photo by Bonnie Nance

An ounce of prevention is worth a pound of cure.

Glossary

abdominal tap. The use of a needle to obtain a small sample of abdominal fluid for analysis.

abortion. The loss of a dead fetus before it reaches full term.

acute. Having a sudden or rapid onset and following a short but severe course, as in "acute disease;" early, as in "acute stages of a disease."

adrenaline. A stress hormone produced by the adrenal glands; epinephrine.

aerobic. Energy production by cells through the breakdown of fats, protein, glycogen or sugar using processes that require oxygen.

agalactia. Lack of milk production.

allantochorionic membrane. The portion of the placenta containing the blood vessels that nourish the fetus.

allergen. A substance that elicits an allergic response in an individual that is sensitive to that substance.

allergy. An inflammatory reaction following exposure to a substance (allergen) in the air or feed, or by contact with the skin.

alopecia. Loss of hair.

alopecia areata. Localized areas of hair loss, likely caused by an immune-mediated attack on hair follicles.

amnion. The thin membranous sac portion of the placenta that is filled with fluid and surrounds the fetus.

amyotrophic lateral sclerosis (ALS). Lou Gehrig's disease.

anabolic. Building up of tissues, especially muscles.

anaerobic. Energy production by cells through the breakdown of glycogen and sugar using processes that do not require oxygen.

anaphylaxis. A severe allergic response resulting in shock.

anemia. Decreased oxygen supply to cells caused by too few red blood cells or too little hemoglobin in the red blood cells.

anesthetic. Gases or injectable agents that cause lack of sensation; may be applied to one area (local) or to the entire body (general).

angular limb deformity. Twisted leg.

anhidrosis. Lack of sweating.

anthelmintic. A compound that kills parasites, also called a wormer or dewormer.

antibacterial. A compound that reduces the growth of or kills a variety of bacteria, but not as effectively as an antibiotic.

antibiotic. A compound that kills bacteria.

antibodies. Proteins that protect against infectious disease; also called immunoglobulins.

anticoagulant. A compound that keeps blood from clotting, used in tubes in which blood is collected for analysis.

antifungal. A compound that kills fungi, such as lime-sulfur dip used to treat fungal skin disease or itraconizole, miconizole and clotrimazol used to treat white line disease.

antihistamines. Compounds that block histamine, a substance involved in causing signs of allergies.

anti-inflammatory. Compounds that decrease tissue inflammation and damage.

antioxidant. A compound that counteracts the potentially damaging effects of a cell's use of oxygen or of exposure to the sun's ultraviolet radiation.

antiseptic. A compound that can kill a variety of bacteria and fungi, but often not as effectively as antibiotics or antifungals.

antitoxin. A compound that blocks a toxin.

aorta. The large artery carrying blood from the heart to the body.

arrhythmia. Abnormal heart beat rhythm.

arthritis. Joint inflammation.

artificial insemination (AI). A procedure in which semen is collected from a stallion and manually deposited into the mare's uterus.

ascarids. Roundworms.

aspirate. To treat by aspiration; the substance or material removed by aspiration.

aspiration. The act of inhaling; to remove (liquids or gases) by means of a suction device; to inhale substances other than air into the windpipe and lungs.

ATP. Adenosine triphosphate, the molecule that provides energy to living cells.

atria. Plural of atrium, the two upper, smaller chambers of the heart.

atrial fibrillation. A kind of arrhythmia in which the atria beat too rapidly such that the ventricles do not fill adequately with blood.

atrium. A chamber of the heart.

atrophy. Lack or loss of growth; wasting.

aural. Of or pertaining to the ear.

aural plaque. A raised white hairless skin lesion in a horse's ear caused by papillomavirus infection.

autonomic nerves. Nerves that function without conscious control, such as those regulating heart rate and sweating, and are often involved in response to stress.

azoturia. Monday morning disease; also called tying up, black water, setfast or exertional rhabdomyolysis.

bacteremia. The presence of bacteria in the bloodstream.

banamine. A nonsteroidal anti-inflammatory drug (NSAID) used to control pain and fever.

base narrow. Conformation in which the legs are close together when viewed from the front or back.

bastard strangles. Abscesses inside the body caused by *Streptococcus equi.*

bean. Secretions that have hardened in the cavity at the end of a horse's penis.

benign tumor. A tumor that does not spread or invade deeply into adjacent tissue.

Betadine. A brand of tamed (non-stinging) iodine known as povidone iodine.

biopsy. A sample of body tissue removed surgically and examined microscopically.

black flies. Small biting flies.

blacksmith. A person who shapes iron with a forge, anvil and hammer and who may or may not be a farrier.

black water. Monday morning disease; also called tying up, azoturia, setfast or exertional rhabdomyolysis.

block. Injection of a short-acting local anesthetic near a nerve or into a joint.

blood count. Lab procedure in which components of blood such as red cells are counted as an indication of condition; complete blood count (CBC).

blow. To breath hard.

blue green algae. A kind of pond scum that may produce toxins that cause severe liver failure and death.

bobbed tail. A tail that has been shortened by the removal of a portion of the tail bones; a docked tail.

bog spavin. A persistent soft swelling of the hock joint capsule caused by an increase in the joint fluid; also called thoroughpin.

bone spavin. A persistent hard swelling of the hock caused by abnormal growth of bony tissue.

borborygmi. The normal digestive sounds made by a horse.

borium. A metal applied to the bottom of horseshoes to provide traction.

bot fly. A fly that lays its eggs on the hairs of horses.

bot knife. An instrument designed to remove bot eggs from a horse's haircoat.

bots. The larvae of the bot fly, which migrate and attach to the inside of the horse's stomach and the first part of its small intestine.

botulism. Paralysis caused by toxins produced by *Clostridium botulinum* bacteria.

bounding pulse. An increase of force felt in the arteries.

bowed tendon. An outward bend in the tendons at the back of the fore leg cannon bones.

breakover. The way the toe of a hoof moves during locomotion.

broken wind. An allergic lung disease; also called heaves or chronic obstructive pulmonary disease (COPD).

bulb. The soft tissue forming the heel of a horse's hoof.

bursa. A fluid-filled sac under the skin over bony prominences such as the hock and elbow, or associated with tendons or ligaments such as at the withers and poll.

bursitis. Inflammation and swelling of a bursa.

bute. Phenylbutazone, a nonsteroidal anti-inflammatory drug (NSAID).

BVSc. Bachelor of Veterinary Science, the veterinary degree conferred on graduates of European, Australian and New Zealand veterinary colleges.

cactus cloth. A woven grooming aid that may be used to rub itchy horse faces.

calcification. Deposition of calcium to form bony hard tissue.

calculi. Stones.

camped out. Standing with the forelegs placed well in front (camped out in front) or hind legs placed well behind (camped out behind).

cancer. A malignant tumor composed of cells that invade the tissue and spread through the body.

canker. Necrotic pododermatitis.

cannon bone. The bone from the knee to the fetlock in the fore leg, and from the hock to the fetlock in the hind leg.

cantharidin. Irritant contained in blister beetles; also called Spanish fly.

capillary refill time. The time it takes blood to flow back into the gingiva after finger pressure is applied.

capped elbow. The swelling and filling with fluid of the bursa over the point of the elbow; also called a shoeboil.

capped hock. A swelling of the bursa over the point of the hock.

carcinoma. Cancer of epithelial cells, such as those that form skin and the lining of the mouth, nose, and internal organs.

cardiac. Of or pertaining to the heart.

cardiac glycosides. Compounds occurring naturally in plants or manufactured as drugs that affect heart function.

carotid artery. The large artery in the neck that supplies blood to the head.

carpus. The part of the fore leg corresponding to the human wrist; in the horse also called the knee.

Caslick's operation. A surgical procedure in which part of the mare's vulva is sutured closed until she is ready to foal.

cast. Lying in such a position, usually too close to a wall or fence, that the horse cannot get its legs underneath itself to stand.

castration. The surgical removal of a stallion's testicles; also called gelding.

catabolic. Relating to the breaking down of tissues, such as muscle and fat, for use as energy.

cataract. Degeneration of the lens of the eye causing it to become cloudy white and interfering with normal vision.

catecholamines. Blood hormones, produced by the adrenal glands, that increase during stress and can stimulate or suppress various parts of the autonomic nervous system.

catheter. A tube placed into the jugular vein to administer fluids or medications, into the urethra to collect urine, or into the nasolacrimal duct to flush a blockage.

cauda equina. The last portion of a horse's spinal cord where the long nerves in the spinal canal resemble a horse's tail.

caudal. Of or pertaining to the tail or tail end of the body or of a body part.

caulks. Devices attached to the bottom of a horseshoe to provide traction.

CBC. Complete blood count.

cecum. A large, blind ended portion of large intestine attached to the end of the small intestine and the first loop of the large intestine.

cerebrospinal fluid (CSF). Fluid that bathes the brain and spinal cord.

cerebrospinal tap. The collection of a sample of cerebrospinal fluid through a needle for analysis.

cheek teeth. Molars.

chemistry profile. Serum chemistries.

chemotherapy. The chemical treatment of cancer.

chestnut. The raised pad of hairless skin on the inner surface of the leg.

chlorhexidine. An antibacterial solution (trade name Nolvasan).

choke. An obstruction of the esophagus by feed.

cholangitis. An inflammation of the biliary system of the liver.

chorioptes mites. Microscopic insects that cause a skin infection known as mange.

choroid. A part of the uveal tract in the back of the eye.

chronic. Long lasting, as in "chronic disease;" late, as in "chronic stages of a disease."

chronic obstructive pulmonary disease (COPD). An allergic reaction that causes difficulty breathing, similar to asthma in people; also known as heaves.

clinical signs. Signs of health problems that can be seen or found by physical examination, similar to symptoms except that symptoms are problems people feel and can describe to their physicians.

***Clostridium botulinum*.** A bacterium in the soil and in the intestines of many animals that can produce toxins that cause paralysis (botulism).

***Clostridium tetani*.** A bacterium in the soil that can contaminate wounds and produce toxins to cause tetanus.

clubfoot. A hoof that is abnormally upright.

coffin bone. The foot bone contained within the hoof; also called the pedal bone, third phalanx or P3.

Coggins test. A blood test that looks for indications that a horse has equine infectious anemia (EIA, or Swamp Fever).

colic. Pain caused by problems in the abdomen, such as stomach or intestinal pain.

colitis X. A severe, acute and life threatening inflammation of the colon causing colic, diarrhea and death.

collagen. Fibrous protein that helps hold cells and tissues together to form part of the skin and internal organs.

colostrum. The first milk produced by the mare that contains high levels of antibodies to protect the foal.

colt. A baby male horse.

concentrates. High energy feeds such as grains, pellets and extruded feeds.

conception. Fertilization of an ovum by sperm to result in pregnancy.

concussion. Forces on the hooves and legs that are affected by conformation, the weight of the horse on its hooves, style of hoof trimming and shoeing, and composition of the ground surface on which the horse is exercised.

conformation. The build of a horse.

congenital. Present at birth, usually referring to abnormalities that may or may not be inherited.

conjunctiva. Mucous membranes of the eye.

conjunctivitis. Inflammation of the conjunctiva.

contracted tendons. Shortening of the tendons of the legs.

COPD. Chronic obstructive pulmonary disease; also called heaves or broken wind.

cornea. The clear outer covering of the eye.

coronary band. Soft tissue around the top of the hoof from which the hoof grows.

corpora nigricans. Black bodies on the upper iris of the eye that may serve as sunshades.

corticosteroid. A compound produced by the cortex (outer portion) of the adrenal gland, or a similar manufactured drug, used to treat shock or to control allergic and other inflammatory problems.

cow hocked. A conformational defect in which the horse's legs bend inward at the hocks, resulting in hocks that are close together.

cow kick. A kick to the side, as opposed to the back.

crackles. Abnormal lung sounds caused by a lung problem and heard with a stethoscope.

cresty neck. A prominent and thick top portion of the neck from which the mane grows.

cribbing. An addictive action in which a horse grasps the edge of a board in its teeth, sharply bends its neck, sucks in air and makes a grunting noise.

crossbreed. The mating of two horses of different breeds; offspring resulting from such a mating.

cross-ties. Two ties fastened to parallel walls or posts that attach to each side of a halter to hold a horse in place.

cryotherapy. The freezing of tissue as a treatment for cancer.

cryptorchid. A male horse in which one or both testes have not descended into the scrotum.

cryotherapy. The freezing of tissue as a treatment for cancer.

cryptosporidia. Protozoal organisms of the intestine that can cause diarrhea.

culicoides. Gnats.

culicoides hypersensitivity. An itchy skin disease caused by allergy to gnat bites; also called sweet itch or Queensland itch.

Cushing's disease. A disease of horses caused by a pituitary tumor producing hormones that affect metabolism and hair growth, as well as other hormone producing organs.

cyanide. A poison that blocks the transfer of oxygen from the blood to the cells.

cyst. A thin walled, fluid filled structure.

cystic. Pertaining to the urinary bladder; any lesion consisting of a cyst or cysts.

cystoliths. Stones in the urinary bladder; also called urinary calculi.

deer flies. Flies that bite a horse's ears.

degenerative joint disease (DJD). Changes in the bones and cartilage of the joints that can cause painful lameness.

dehydration. A condition in which body tissues lack sufficient water to function normally.

denervation atrophy. A loss of muscle mass caused by a degeneration in the nerve supplying the muscle.

dermatitis. Inflammation of the skin.

dermatitis verrucosa. The irritation of the skin of the lower legs known as greasy heel or scratches.

dermatophilosis. An infection of the skin caused by dermatophilus bacteria; also called rain scald or rain rot.

dermatophytes. Fungi that cause ringworm.

desmitis. Inflammation of a ligament.

developmental orthopedic disease (DOD). A group of problems occurring in the joints, tendons and ligaments of growing foals.

deworm. To rid the body of parasitic worms.

dewormer. Anthelmintic, a compound used to rid the body of parasitic worms; also called wormer.

diarrhea. Passage of fluid feces (manure); also called scouring.

digoxin. A cardiac glycoside used as a medication to help a failing heart, also present in certain plants such as foxglove, causing heart failure if the plants are eaten.

discharge. Fluid, pus or mucus draining from any area and possibly indicating a blockage, inflammation or infection.

DJD. Degenerative joint disease.

DMSO. Dimethylsulfoxide, a colorless liquid or gel used as an anti-inflammatory medication or as a penetrant to carry other medications into the tissues.

docked tail. A tail that has been shortened by the removal of a portion of the tail bones; also called a bobbed tail.

DOD. Developmental orthopedic disease.

domperidone. A medication that may counteract some of the problems caused by fescue toxicity.

dorsal recumbency. The position of a horse lying on its back, usually occurring only during certain surgical procedures or in foals with gastric ulcers.

draft. The act of pulling a vehicle or load; an animal used for pulling.

Drill-Tek. Brand name for tungsten carbide combined with a softer carrier metal and applied to the bottoms of shoes to provide traction.

dummy foal. A foal born with brain injury caused by the lack of oxygen.

DVM. Doctor of Veterinary Medicine.

dysfunction. Abnormal functioning.

dystocia. Difficulty in delivery caused by the abnormal positioning of the foal in the birth canal.

ear flies. Deer flies.

ear tooth. Misplaced tooth tissue in the bone at the base of the ear.

Eastern equine encephalitis (EEE). A viral disease carried by mosquitoes that affects the brain.

easy keeper. A horse that easily keeps its proper weight.

edema. Fluid build up in tissues.

EDM. Equine degenerative myelopathy.

EEE. Eastern equine encephalitis.

EIA. Equine infectious anemia.

elective surgery. A surgical procedure that is not performed because of an emergency.

electrolytes. Salts that are supplied by feed and lost in sweat that are needed for the proper functioning of the nervous system, heart and muscles.

embryo. The first stages of the development of an egg, following its fertilization by a sperm, before it becomes a fetus.

EMND. Equine motor neuron disease.

encephalitis. An inflammation involving the brain.

encephalitis virus. A virus that causes inflammation of the brain.

endometrium. Uterine lining.

endophytes. Fungi, some of which produce toxins, that grow within plants.

endorphins. Substances produced by the brain that decrease pain.

endoscope. A flexible tube used to examine the inside of a horse.

endotoxemia. The presence of bacterial toxins in the bloodstream.

energy. The capacity of a physical system to do work; nutrients required by the body's cells to survive and function normally; total body energy.

enterolith. Intestinal stone.

eosinophilic granuloma. Skin lumps caused by an allergic reaction; often erroneously called protein bumps.

eosinophils. White blood cells that respond to parasitic or allergic disease.

epiphysitis. Physitis, an inflammation of the growing ends of bones.

epithelial. Of or pertaining to the epithelium, the layers of cells that form skin and that line most of the body's cavities.

EPM. Equine protozoal myeloencephalopathy.

EPSM. Equine polysaccharide storage myopathy; also known as EPSSM and PSSM.

EPSSM. Equine polysaccharide storage myopathy; also known as EPSM and PSSM.

equine degenerative myelopathy (EDM). A spinal cord degeneration resulting in incoordination due to vitamin E deficiency in young growing horses.

equine infectious anemia (EIA). A viral disease carried by biting insects that can cause anemia.

equine motor neuron disease (EMND). A disabling condition of adult horses associated with vitamin E deficiency and involving the degeneration of nerves that supply muscles, similar to amyotrophic lateral sclerosis (ALS), or Lou Gehrig's disease, in humans.

equine polysaccharide storage myopathy (EPSM, EPSSM, PSSM). A disorder affecting carbohydrate metabolism in muscle.

equine protozoal myeloencephalopathy (EPM). A protozoal disease of the brain and spinal cord.

ergot. The raised pad of hairless skin on the back of the fetlock.

esophagus. The tubular organ through which food passes from the mouth to the stomach.

estrogen. A female hormone produced by the ovaries.

estrous cycle. The three weeks of ovarian activity that culminate in a mare being in heat.

estrus. The time during which a mare is receptive to breeding; also called in heat.

euthanasia. The humane ending of a seriously sick or injured horse's life.

exertional rhabdomyolysis. Muscle injury caused by exercise; also called Monday morning disease, tying up, azoturia, setfast or black water.

expiration. The act of exhaling; the act of dying; expiration date.

expiration date. The manufacturer's estimated date at which a medication or vaccine is no longer effective.

extension. The straightening of a joint to cause its parts to move apart; a long-strided gait produced when a horse increases extension of its leg joints.

face flies. Non-biting flies that feed on eye and nasal secretions.

facial. Of or pertaining to the face.

false nostril. The blind-ended cavity above the horse's true nostril.

farrier. A blacksmith who shapes and fits horseshoes.

feathers. The long, often flowing hairs growing on the lower legs of some horses.

feces. Manure.

femur. The bone extending from the hip to the stifle.

fertility. A mare's ability to conceive and carry a foal to term; a stallion's ability to successfully inseminate a mare.

fescue foot. A foal's loss of hoof caused by grazing on endophytic-infected fescue pasture.

fetus. The developing foal within the uterus.

fever. An abnormally high body temperature caused by an infection or inflammation.

fiber. A tough elongate structure such as a muscle, a tendon or ligament fibers, or the less digestible parts of forage in the diet.

fibrotic myopathy. A mechanical lameness in which the forward swing of the affected hind leg is shortened, causing that foot to slap the ground.

filly. A baby female horse.

flare. An outward bend of the side of the hoof, usually the outer side.

flared. Having a flare on the hoof; wide open, referring to the nostrils of a horse that is breathing hard.

flat shoe. A shoe without traction devices.

flehmen response. Curling the lips, with raised head, in response to an unusual or sexually appealing taste or scent, or as a response to pain.

flexion. Bending two parts at a joint to bring them closer together.

flexion test. Bending a lame horse's joint for a period of time, then trotting the horse and looking for signs of pain in the joint.

float. The instrument used to rasp a horse's teeth.

floating. Rasping down sharp points (hooks) on the horse's molars.

flu. Influenza.

foal. A baby horse.

foal heat. A mare's first heat cycle after foaling, usually occurring at about one week post-foaling.

foal heat diarrhea. Diarrhea in a nursing foal during the mare's foal heat.

follicle. In the ovary, the fluid-filled structure containing the ovum; in the skin, the structure from which a hair grows.

forage. Hay or pasture; also called roughage.

foreign body. Any substance that is not a normal part of the horse's body, such as a plant fiber, lodged on or in the skin or eye or within body tissue or a body cavity.

founder. Sinking of the coffin bone caused by laminitis.

fracture. A broken bone.

free radicals. Potentially damaging compounds made by cells that use oxygen for energy production, or occurring in tissue exposed to certain types of damage, such as skin injury caused by exposure to sunlight.

frog. The fork-shaped soft tissue on the bottom of a horse's hoof.

fungi. More than one fungus.

fungus. Any member of a group of chlorophyll-lacking parasitic plants that includes molds, mildews and yeasts, some of which cause infection, allergic reactions or poisoning due to toxins they produce.

furosemide. A medication (trade name Lasix) that causes increased fluid loss in urine.

ganting. Limiting the water intake of a pulling horse so it will meet the weight requirements of its class.

gas colic. Intestinal pain caused by gas buildup; also called spasmodic colic.

gastric reflux. Stomach contents that come up through a nasogastric tube.

gastric ulcer. Stomach ulcer.

gastrointestinal motility. The normal movement of the esophagus, stomach and intestines to transport feed material through the digestive system.

gelding. A castrated male horse; the act of castrating.

gestation. Pregnancy.

giardia. Protozoal organisms of the intestine that can cause diarrhea.

gingiva. The gums.

gluteal. Of or pertaining to the rump muscles.

glycogen. A polysaccharide, formed of many sugars linked together, that is broken down to sugar and used for energy by muscle and other cells.

gnats. Small biting insects of the culicoides insect family that can cause allergic skin disease in horses; also called midges, no see ums, or sand flies.

goiter. An enlargement of the thyroid glands caused by iodine deficiency or excess.

grade. A mixed breed horse, often of unknown ancestry.

Gram-negative bacteria. Any bacteria that do not take on color from Gram's stain.

Gram-positive bacteria. Any bacteria that take on a blue color from Gram's stain.

granuloma. A nodular area of chronic inflammation in which macrophages are prominent.

granulosa cell tumor. The most common tumor of the ovary in a mare, often causing her to exhibit stallion-like behavior.

gravel. A bacterial infection of the hoof wall.

greasy heel. Scratches.

guttural pouch. The air-filled pouch in the horse's head that cools the blood to the brain during exercise.

habronema. A parasitic worm, the larvae of which can cause summer sores.

hackamore. A bitless bridle.

hamstrings. The muscles at the back of the thigh; also called the semimembranous and semitendinous muscles.

hard keeper. A horse that has a hard time keeping its proper weight.

head nod. The downward drop of a lame horse's head when a sound leg hits the ground, followed by an upward swing of the head when the painful leg hits the ground.

heart failure. A condition in which the heart does not function properly.

heat. Estrus.

heave line. An obvious line of increased muscle at the base of the ribs in a horse with heaves.

heaves. An allergic lung disease; also called chronic obstructive pulmonary disease (COPD) or broken wind.

hemoglobin. The oxygen-carrying protein of red blood cells.

hemoglobinuria. The presence of hemoglobin in the urine.

hemolysis. The breakdown of red blood cells.

hemorrhage. To bleed.

hepatitis. Inflammation of the liver.

hernia. A defect (opening) in the abdominal wall.

hippomane. A rubbery wad of brownish tissue floating inside the placenta.

hives. Bumps resulting from a fluid buildup in skin caused by an allergy.

hoof crack. A crack in the wall of a horse's hoof, usually in the quarters.

hoof tester. A device that puts pressure on the sole or wall of the hoof to detect and determine the location of pain.

hooks. The sharp points that grow on the inside of a horse's lower molars and the outside of the upper molars and that must be regularly floated.

horn flies. Biting flies more often seen on cattle than on horses.

Horner's syndrome. Damage to the sympathetic nerves to the head and eyes resulting in unequal pupil size and sweating on the affected side.

hospital plate. A shoe with a removable bottom plate, used to treat canker and other diseases of the sole and frog or to increase sole support.

hot. Unmanageably energetic.

house fly. A fly that feeds off skin debris through a vacuuming-type mouth.

hyperkalemia. Increased potassium in the blood.

hyperkalemic periodic paralysis (HYPP). A muscle disorder causing episodes of weakness and collapse in horses related to the Quarter horse stallion Impressive.

hyperlipemia. A condition in ponies and miniature horses in which increased fat levels are present in the blood, liver and kidneys.

hypersensitivity. An allergy.

hyperthermia. A severe and potentially dangerous increase in body heat.

hypertrophy. The increased growth of cells, organs or muscles.

hypotrichosis. A condition evident at or soon after birth that is characterized by lack of hair caused by abnormal hair follicle development.

HYPP. Hyperkalemic periodic paralysis.

icterus. Jaundice.

ileocecal impaction. A blockage caused by feed in the last portion of the small intestine.

ileum. The last part of the small intestine.

IM. Intramuscular.

immune mediated disease. A disease in which tissue damage is caused by an immune response occurring when parts of the body are not recognized and are attacked as if they were foreign invaders.

immunoglobulins. Antibodies.

impaction colic. Pain caused by an obstruction within the intestine.

imprinting. The natural bonding process by which a newborn animal learns to recognize its mother, or to accept and trust a human or other animal.

imprint training. The process of teaching a newborn foal to accept being handled by people; also called imprinting.

IN. Intranasal.

inactivated vaccine. A vaccine in which the infectious agent or toxin has been altered so it is no longer dangerous, but will cause the horse to produce antibodies.

incisors. The teeth in the front of the mouth that are used to nip off grass and other plants, leaves, twigs and bark.

incoordination. The abnormal gait of an uncoordinated horse that does not know where its feet are, the hallmark of spinal cord disease.

infection. Tissue reaction and damage caused by infectious agents such as bacteria, fungi, protozoa and viruses.

infertility. The temporary or permanent inability of a mare to conceive and carry a foal to term or of a stallion to inseminate a mare.

inflammation. Tissue reaction and damage that may or may not be caused by infectious organisms.

influenza. A viral infection of the respiratory system; also called the flu.

inguinal canal. The canal between the caudal abdomen and the scrotum, through which the testes descend.

inherited. Caused by genes and therefore capable of being passed on to offspring.

insecticide. A compound that kills insects.

insemination. The deposition of semen into the vagina by a stallion or into the uterus through artificial insemination.

insensitive test. A test that does not accurately reflect the severity of a problem, such as the skin pinch test for dehydration.

insoluble carbohydrates. Cellulose and other materials forming plant cell walls; also called structural carbohydrates.

inspiration. Inhaling.

intact. Not castrated.

interference. The action of hitting a foot with another foot during walking, trotting or cantering.

intermandibular. Between the jawbones.

intramammary. In the mammary gland, usually referring to medications placed into the mammary gland through the teat (nipple).

intramuscular (IM). In the muscle, usually referring to injections.

intranasal (IN). In the nasal cavaty, usually referring to vaccine squirted into the nasal cavity.

intraocular. In the eye, usually referring to medication placed in the eye.

intravenous (IV). In the vein, usually referring to injections into the jugular vein.

intussusception. Telescoping, as in one portion of the intestine folding into the next portion of the intestine.

iris. The portion of the eye around the pupil that gives the eye its color and is part of the uveal tract of the eye.

ischemia. Lack of blood supply to a tissue or organ.

IV. Intravenous.

ivermectin. Generic name for a highly effective anthelmintic contained in several brand name wormers.

jaundice. Yellow coloration of body tissues, most visible in the white portion of the eye (the sclera), conjunctiva, skin and gums; also called icterus.

joint capsule. The fibrous tissue surrounding the joint that contains joint fluid.

joint mice. Fragments of cartilage or bone that float freely in the joint as a result of OCD or joint trauma.

jugular vein. The large vein in the neck that carries blood from the head to the heart, used for taking blood samples and for giving intravenous fluids or medications.

keratin. The protein that makes up the surface of a horse's skin and the hoof wall, frog and sole.

kneecap. The small sliding bone in the stifle (true knee) joint; also called patella

labial. Of or pertaining to lips, referring to either the mouth or the vulva.

lacrimal duct. The tear duct extending from the eye to just inside the nostril; also called the nasolacrimal duct.

lactation. Producing milk.

lactobacillus. Bacteria that promote healthy digestion in the intestines.

lamellae. Laminae.

lameness. Abnormal gait caused by either pain or a mechanical abnormality.

lameness examination. A thorough examination by a veterinarian that may include trotting on a loose lead, flexion tests and nerve and/or joint blocks to try to localize the area causing the lameness.

laminae. Layers of tissue that attach the hoof wall to the underlying bone; also called lamellae.

laminitis. Inflammation of the laminae of the hoof that can lead to rotation and sinking of the coffin bone, a condition known as founder.

lance. To open an abscess to allow drainage; the sharp blade used to open the abscess.

laparoscope. A flexible endoscope used to examine internal organs of the abdomen.

laryngeal. Of or pertaining to the larynx.

laryngeal hemiplegia. Paralysis of the left side of the larynx; also called roaring.

lateral quarter. The side of the hoof wall on the outside of the horse's leg.

lateral recumbency. The position of a horse lying on its side.

lesion. An abnormality of body tissues that may be seen by the naked eye, through a microscope or both.

leukemia. Cancer of the white blood cells circulating in the blood.

libido. Sexual drive.

lice. Tiny insects, not always visible to the naked eye, that can affect the horse's skin and hair.

ligament. A fibrous band that connects bones to other bones.

lime sulfur. A topical antifungal medication.

lipoma. A benign tumor of fat.

locking stifle. A mechanical lameness where the stifle locks up in either a bent position (intermittent locking stifle) or in a straightened position; also called upward fixation of the patella.

locomotion. Movement, such as walking, trotting or cantering.

locomotory. Of or pertaining to the muscles involved in locomotion, as distinct from those involved in maintaining posture (postural).

Lou Gehrig's disease. Amyotrophic lateral sclerosis (ALS), a muscle wasting disease of humans that is similar to equine motor neuron disease.

lungworms. Parasites of the lungs in horses, donkeys and mules.

Lyme disease. A bacterial infection causing inflammation and pain in multiple joints.

lymphangitis. Inflammation of the lymphatics of the legs.

lymphatics. The vascular structures that carry fluid from the tissues to and from the lymph nodes.

lymph glands. Lymph nodes.

lymph nodes. The nodular organs of the lymphatic system; also called lymph glands.

macrophage. A cell that ingests bacteria, damaged tissue and matter such as plant material in the tissue.

malabsorption. A condition, caused by inflammatory or neoplastic conditions, resulting in poor nutrient absorption from the intestines.

malignant edema. The infection of muscle with toxin producing clostridial bacteria.

malignant tumor. A tumor that invades deeply into adjacent tissue and may spread to other sites.

mandible. The lower jaw.

mange. A skin infection caused by mites, in horses most often leg mange caused by chorioptes mites.

maniacal behavior. Hyperexcitability due to a brain disease that causes a horse to be out of control.

mare. An adult female horse.

mastitis. Inflammation of the mammary gland.

maxilla. The upper jaw.

mechanical lameness. A gait abnormality that is not associated with pain, seen primarily in the hind limbs and caused by the abnormal functioning of muscles, nerves, tendons, joints or ligaments.

meconium. Fetal intestinal content.

medial. Toward the midline.

medial quarter. The side of the hoof wall on the inside of the horse's leg.

medical colic. An intestinal problem that may be resolved with medical therapy.

melanin. Black pigment in the skin, hair and hooves, and sometimes in the mouth or other mucous membranes.

melanoma. A malignant tumor of melanocytes.

melanocytes. Cells that make the black pigment melanin.

melanocytic nevus. A benign tumor of melanocytes; also called a mole.

metabolic. Relating to the production of energy by cells.

metastasize. Spread, as in the spreading of a cancer.

midges. Gnats.

mites. Microscopic insects that can affect the skin of horses causing mange.

mitochondria. The structures in living cells that use oxygen to produce energy (ATP), often called the powerhouses of the cell.

modified live vaccine. A vaccine in which the infectious agent has not been killed but has been altered so it is less able to cause infection.

molars. The grinding teeth; also called cheek teeth.

mold. Fungus.

mole. A benign skin tumor of melanocytes; also called melanocytic nevus.

Monday morning disease. Massive muscle damage during or after work; also called tying up, azoturia, black water, setfast or exertional rhabdomyolysis.

moon blindness. Uveitis.

mucopurulent discharge. A discharge of pus and mucus from an infected area.

mucous membrane. Moist, hairless skin such as that lining the mouth, nose, vagina, prepuce, penis and eyelids.

multivalent vaccine. A vaccine containing several different compounds in the same dose.

myelitis. Inflammation of the spinal cord.

myoglobin. Reddish colored proteins present in muscle.

myoglobinuria. Red to red-brown discoloration of the urine caused by the presence of myoglobin from damaged muscle cells.

narcolepsy. A disorder in which the affected horse, other animal, or human suddenly falls asleep and collapses.

nasogastric tube. A flexible hose passed through the nose to the stomach to relieve an obstruction in the esophagus, to relieve pressure in the stomach, or to give medications or fluids directly into the stomach.

nasolacrimal duct. Lacrimal duct; also called the tear duct.

navel. Umbilicus.

navicular bone. The bone within the suspensory ligaments in the hoof.

navicular disease. A painful lameness caused by the degeneration of the navicular bone.

necropsy. Autopsy or postmortem examination.

necrotic pododermatitis. A severe bacterial infection of the frog, sole and sometimes bulbs of the hoof; also called canker.

neonatal. Of or pertaining to a newborn foal.

neonatal isoerythrolysis. Damage to a newborn foal's red blood cells caused by antibodies in the mare's milk when the blood types of the mare and foal are incompatible.

neonatal maladjustment. Problems caused by poor brain and/or lung development in a foal born prematurely or deprived of oxygen during late gestation or birth.

neoplasm. A tumor.

neoplastic. Pertaining to a tumor.

nephrolith. A kidney stone.

nerve block. A local anesthetic placed around nerves to temporarily block pain sensation, used to determine the site of a painful lameness.

neuritis. Inflammation of nerves.

nitroglycerine. A compound that causes dilation of arteries, used in humans with heart problems and in horses with acute laminitis caused by decreased blood flow.

Nolvasan. Brand name of the antibacterial solution chlorhexidine.

nonspecific signs. Signs of disease that may be caused by any one of a wide variety of problems.

nonsteroidal. Anti-inflammatory medications that do not contain corticosteroids.

no see ums. Gnats.

NSAID. Nonsteroidal anti-inflammatory drug.

nutritional myopathy. Muscle degeneration and weakness in a selenium deficient adult horse or a foal born to a selenium deficient mare; also called white muscle disease.

OCD. Osteochondrosis dissecans.

onchocerca. A parasitic worm that inhabits and migrates in the skin tissues of a horse's head and neck.

optic nerve. The nerve from the back of the eye to the brain.

oral. Of or pertaining to the mouth or medications given by mouth.

ossification. Hardening to a bony consistency.

osteitis. Inflammation of a bone.

osteoarthritis. Inflammation involving bone and joints.

osteochondrosis dissecans (OCD). A degeneration of cartilage and bone occurring in young growing horses.

otitis externa. An infection involving the outer portion of the ear.

otitis interna. An infection involving the inner ear.

otitis media. An infection involving the middle ear.

ovariectomy. The surgical removal of one or both of a mare's ovaries.

ovulation. Release of a mature egg (ovum) from the ovary.

ovum. An egg produced in the ovary.

oxytocin. A hormone that causes uterine contractions to aid in delivery of a foal and passage of the placenta.

P1. First phalanx, the upper pastern bone in the foot.

P2. Second phalanx, the lower pastern bone in the foot.

P3. Third phalanx, the foot bone; also coffin bone, pedal bone.

palpation. Feeling with the fingers and hands.

palsy. Paralysis.

papillomavirus. A family of viruses, many of which can cause skin growths.

parrot mouth. Having the lower jaw shorter than the upper jaw.

parturition. The act of giving birth.

pastern. The portion of a horse's leg between the hoof and the fetlock.

patella. The kneecap.

patent urachus. A urachus that fails to close at birth, resulting in urine leakage from the umbilicus.

pectoral. Of or pertaining to the muscles of the brisket or front chest area.

pedal bone. The coffin bone.

pedal osteitis. Inflammation of the coffin (pedal) bone of the foot.

pemphigus. An immune-mediated blistering disease of the skin.

perianal. The area around the anus.

peristalsis. The normal wave-like action of the gastro-intestinal system that moves food and feces through.

perivulvar. The area around the vulva.

phalanx. Any one of the three bones of the foot.

photosensitization. Sun-induced skin disease caused by damaging compounds accumulated in the skin.

physitis. An inflammation of the ends of growing bones; also called epiphysitis.

PHF. Potomac horse fever.

pigment. Anything that colors tissue cells or fluid.

pinna. The visible part of the ear.

placenta. Fetal membranes lining the uterine wall of a pregnant mare.

placental insufficiency. A condition, caused by poor placental formation, in which the fetus aborts.

plaque. A flattish raised lesion.

pleura. The thin membranes that line the chest and cover the lungs.

pleuritis. Inflammation of the pleura.

PMU farm. Pregnant mare urine farm, where mares produce female hormones used to treat post menopausal women.

pneumonia. Inflammation of the lungs.

PO. Per os, administered through the mouth; also called oral.

polyestrous. Having more than one heat cycle in one year.

polysaccharide. A carbohydrate formed by many sugars linked together.

poor doer. Unthrifty.

postmortem. After death.

postmortem examination. Autopsy performed on animals; also called necropsy.

postural. Of or pertaining to the antigravity muscles responsible for maintaining upright posture, as distinct from the muscles responsible for locomotion.

Potomac horse fever (PHF). An infection involving fever and diarrhea caused by rickettsial organisms that are carried by fresh water snails.

premature. Birth of a foal before all body systems, especially the brain and lungs, have fully developed.

premature placental separation. Separation of the placenta from the uterus before the foal is born.

prepubescent. Prior to puberty.

prepuce. The fold of skin containing the penis; also called the sheath.

pressure sores. Wounds in the skin, similar to bed sores in humans, caused by lying down excessively, especially in a wasted weak animal.

probiotic. Compounds fed by mouth to enhance digestion.

prognosis. Outlook, referring to the course of a disease.

protein bumps. Eosinophilic granuloma, incorrectly attributed to too much protein in a horse's diet.

proteoglycans. Substances important to the health of the cartilage that lines joints.

protozoa. Microscopic single-celled organisms larger than bacteria.

proud flesh. A tumor-like growth of normal tissue in a healing wound, most commonly occurring on a horse's lower legs.

PSSM. Equine polysaccharide storage myopathy; also known as EPSM and EPSSM.

puberty. Sexual maturity.

pulmonary edema. Excess fluid in the lungs.

pupil. The opening in the eye through which light passes.

purpura hemorrhagica. An uncommon consequence of exposure to *Streptococcus equi,* the cause of strangles, in which an abnormal immune response by the horse results in an attack on and damage to blood vessels.

purulent. Containing pus.

pus. Yellowish and slightly thick material discharging from an infected area.

pyrantel. Generic term for the brand name wormer Strongid.

pyrantel pamoate. Generic term for the paste or liquid wormer brand name Strongid.

pyrantel tartrate. Generic term for the daily wormer brand name Strongid C.

pyrocatechins. Compounds in the urine of some horses that cause the urine to turn red or orange red when exposed to sunlight.

pyrrolizidine alkaloids. Toxic substances present within certain plants that cause liver damage.

quarter crack. A crack occurring on the side of a hoof.

Queensland itch. An itchy skin disease caused by allergy to gnat bites; also called sweet itch or culicoides hypersensitivity.

quittor. Inflammation of the cartilage of the hoof.

rabies. A viral infection of the brain and spinal cord that is always fatal.

radiograph. The image obtained after passing X-rays through tissue to hit a certain kind of film.

rain rot. Dermatophilosis.

rain scald. Dermatophilosis.

reciprocal apparatus. The natural linking of a horse's hind leg joints by tendons, ligaments and muscles that prevents bending of the hock without also bending the stifle.

rectal. Pertaining to the rectum, usually referring to rectal body temperature or rectal palpation or ultrasound.

recumbent. Lying down.

red bag. The allantochorion of the placenta that has passed before the foal is born, indicating premature placental separation.

reflux. Fluid passing up a nasogastric tube caused by increased fluid pressure in the stomach.

regurgitate. To bring back to the mouth food within the esophagus that has not made it to the stomach.

REM. Rapid eye movement.

REM sleep. The part of the sleep cycle in which rapid eye movement occurs during dreaming.

reproductive. Of or pertaining to the production of offspring.

resection. Surgical removal.

retina. A delicate multilayered, light-sensitive membrane lining the inner eyeball and connected by the optic nerve to the brain.

retrovirus. A virus that incorporates itself into the genetic material of the cell.

rhinopneumonitis. An equine herpesvirus causing respiratory or spinal cord disease of adults and the abortion or death of foals.

rickettsia. Microscopic organisms that can cause disease.

ringbone. A bony proliferation involving the pastern joints caused by degenerative joint disease.

ringworm. Skin infection causing hair loss by fungi known as dermatophytes.

road founder. Laminitis caused by repeated concussion on hard surfaces.

roaring. The respiratory sound caused by laryngeal hemiplegia.

roughage. Hay or pasture; also called forage.

ryegrass staggers. Incoordination caused by fungi that may be present within ryegrass pasture or hay.

sand colic. Colic caused by a buildup of sand in the intestines.

sand flies. Gnats.

sarcoid. A common skin tumor in horses caused by a bovine papillomavirus.

sarcoma. A malignant tumor of connective tissues.

sawhorse stance. The stiff-legged stance and movements of a horse with tetanus.

sclera. The white portion of the eye surrounding the clear cornea.

Scotch bottom. A style of over-sized horseshoe often used for show draft horses.

scouring, scours. Diarrhea.

scratches. An irritation of the skin of the lower legs having many causes, most often bacterial; also called dermatitis verrucosa or greasy heel.

scrotum. The skin sac containing the testes.

secondary infection. Bacterial infection occurring because of decreased body immunity, often following infection with a virus or an allergic disease.

semen. The sperm-containing fluid of the stallion.

septicemia. The presence of bacteria or bacterial products in the blood throughout the body.

serous. A watery fluid.

serum. The noncellular portion of blood.

serum chemistries. A series of tests run on the noncellular portion of blood to evaluate the function and integrity of various body systems; also called a serum chemistry profile or chemistry profile.

sesamoid bones. Usually refers to the two bones in the suspensory ligament at the back of the pastern joints.

setfast. Monday morning disease; also called tying up, black water, azoturia or exertional rhabdomyolysis.

sheath. The fold of skin enclosing the penis; also called the prepuce.

shipping fever. Bacterial pneumonia associated with the stress and confinement of long-distance transport.

shivers. A mechanical lameness of the hind legs associated with abnormal hiking of an affected leg, a condition that progresses to cause overall muscle atrophy and weakness.

shoeboil. Capped elbow.

sickle hocked. A conformational defect in which the hocks are bent more than is normal, resembling a sickle when viewed from the side.

sidebone. Ossification of the cartilages of the hoof.

signs. Referring to clinical signs, or abnormalities that can be seen by watching or examining a horse.

silent heat. An estrous cycle occurring without obvious behavioral changes to indicate the mare is in heat.

silica. A kind of particle present in the soil of California's Monterey and Central Peninsulas, the inhalation of which can result in severe lung disease.

skin graft. A portion of normal skin placed into a skin wound to speed healing.

slipping the fetus. Early embryonic death.

smegma. Secretions accumulating in the areas around the vulva or penis and sheath.

sole abscess. An infection within the sole of the hoof.

sole bruise. Bruising of the sole of the hoof.

soluble carbohydrates. The part of the horse's diet that includes starches and sugars; also called nonstructural carbohydrates.

Spanish fly. Cantharidin, the toxin contained in blister beetles.

spasm. A cramp.

spasmodic colic. Intestinal pain caused by gas buildup; also called gas colic.

spavin. A swelling of the hock area, which may be bog spavin or bone spavin.

specific signs. Clinical signs that indicate a single particular problem, as opposed to nonspecific signs that could be caused by many different problems.

sperm. Cells produced by the testes.

spinal canal. The channel formed by the vertebrae through which the spinal cord passes.

spinal cord. The part of the central nervous system that connects the brain to the nerves of the body and legs and passes through the spinal canal.

splint. Swelling caused by an inflammation of the splint bones of the leg.

splint bones. The small, short bones on both sides of the cannon bones.

springhalt. Stringhalt.

squamous cell carcinoma. A cancer of the skin, conjunctiva or surface of the eye.

stable fly. A kind of biting fly.

stallion. An uncastrated adult male horse.

stall walking. Constant walking, usually circling, in a stall.

stall weaving. Action in which a standing horse sways from side to side for minutes or hours.

starch. Soluble carbohydrates in plants formed by many sugars linked together that are digested in the small intestine and stored in animal cells as glycogen, to be broken down to sugar for energy.

stay apparatus. The interconnection of bones, tendons, ligaments and muscles that allows a horse to stand for long periods of time and to sleep standing up.

stenosis. A narrowing, such as of the vertebral canal.

sterility. Permanent infertility.

sternal recumbency. The position of a horse lying down with its chest and abdomen on the ground.

steroids. Anti-inflammatory medications containing corticosteroids; a group of compounds (anabolic steroids) used to increase the bulk of muscle and other tissues.

stethoscope. A device that amplifies sounds through the body wall, used to hear sounds produced by the heart, lungs and intestines.

stifle. The true knee joint in the hind leg.

stillbirth. The birth of a full-term dead fetus.

stocking up. Soft swelling of the lower legs caused by edema.

strangles. Infection of the respiratory passages and lymph nodes of the head by *Streptococcus equi*.

stringhalt. A mechanical lameness of the hind legs in which the horse picks up an affected leg abnormally high so the hoof almost hits the bottom of the abdomen.

stringy. Showing early signs of shivers or stringhalt.

strongyles. Parasitic worms of the intestines.

structural carbohydrates. Insoluble carbohydrates.

stud. A stallion used for breeding; a metal device put into a horseshoe to improve traction.

sugar. Simple soluble carbohydrate that is metabolized by cells for energy.

summer sores. Non-healing sores on a horse's skin caused by infection by habronema worm larvae carried by biting flies.

sunblock. A lotion applied to the skin to help block the potentially dangerous ultraviolet rays from the sun.

superficial. Shallow, or on the surface.

supplements. Additions to the horse's diet of forage and concentrates.

surgical colic. An intestinal problem requiring surgery for correction.

suspensory apparatus. The tendons and ligaments that support the back of the fetlock.

sutures. Stitches used to close up a wound or surgical opening.

sweeney. Atrophy of the shoulder muscles.

symptoms. Indications of disease a human patient feels and can tell the doctor about, as opposed to signs a horse owner or veterinarian can determine only by observation or examination.

systemic. Affecting all body systems.

swamp fever. Equine infectious anemia.

sweet feed. A mix of grains and molasses; also called textured feed.

sweet itch. An itchy skin disease caused by allergy to gnat bites; also called Queensland itch or culicoides hypersensitivity.

tapetum. The reflective part of the retina in the back of the eye.

tendon. A fibrous band connecting a muscle to a bone.

tendon sheath. The fibrous tissue surrounding a tendon and normally containing only a small amount of fluid.

testes. Plural of testis.

testicular torsion. Condition of having a twisted testis.

testis. The male reproductive organ that produces sperm.

tetanus. Painful and often lethal muscle spasms caused by toxins produced by *Clostridium tetani* bacteria.

textured feed. Sweet feed.

third eyelid. The extra eyelid at the medial portion of the horse's eye that helps protect the eye.

third phalanx. The coffin bone.

thoroughpin. Bog spavin.

throatlatch. The area under the jaw at the junction of the head and neck; also the bridle strap around this area.

thrush. A bacterial infection of the frog of the hoof.

thumps. Horse hiccups, in which the diaphragm spasms at regular intervals.

thyroid. A gland composed of two lobes, one on each side of the neck.

tick. An insect related to the spider.

toe. The front portion of the hoof.

topical. Description of a medication applied directly to the area requiring treatment.

torsion. Twisting, usually referring to intestines, testes or the umbilical cord.

total body energy. A horse's overall level of energy.

toxic. Containing toxins, or being poisoned by toxins.

toxin. Any poison that causes harm, including certain drugs, plant compounds and bacterial products.

toxoid. Modified toxin used as a vaccine for protection from bacterial toxin-induced diseases such as tetanus.

trace minerals. Minerals required by the body in minute amounts.

trachea. The windpipe.

tracheostomy. An opening made into the trachea to allow easier breathing.

traction shoe. A horseshoe with traction devices such as studs, caulks, Drill-Tek or borium.

transrectal ultrasound. Soundwaves passed through the rectal wall to examine abdominal structures.

transtracheal wash. A method used to collect fluid and cells from the trachea to try to determine the cause of lung disease.

trauma. Damage to body tissues, often through violent means.

tumor. A swelling resulting from new growths of tissue, which may be benign or malignant.

tying up. Monday morning disease; also known as azoturia, black water, setfast and exertional rhabdomyolysis.

ulcer, ulceration. The breakdown of the cornea, skin or lining of an internal organ, such as the stomach or intestines.

ultrasound. A method of bouncing sound waves off of internal tissues to produce an image.

umbilical hernia. A defect in the abdominal wall where the umbilicus attached.

umbilical stump. In a newborn foal, the remains of the umbilicus that heals to form the umbilicus, or navel.

umbilical torsion. Too many twists in the umbilicus, resulting in the death of the fetus caused by a decreased blood supply.

umbilicus. The umbilical cord or the place where the umbilical cord was attached; also called the navel.

unthrifty. Having poor body condition; also called a poor doer.

upward fixation of the patella. Locking stifle.

urachus. The tube, which normally closes at birth, carrying urine from the fetal bladder to the placenta.

ureter. Tube through which urine passes from the kidney to the urinary bladder.

ureterolith. A stone in the ureter.

urethra. The tubular structure from the bladder to the outside through which urine passes during urination.

urinary calculi. Stones in the urinary bladder.

urine scald. An irritation of the skin caused by constant exposure to urine.

urolith. A stone in the urinary system.

uveal tract. The part of the eye including the iris and the choroid.

uveitis. Inflammation of the uveal tract of the eye.

vaccine. A medication that causes the immune system to be activated in order to prevent a bacterial or viral disease, or a disease caused by certain toxins.

vascular. Pertaining to the blood vessels.

vasculitis. Inflammation of the blood vessels.

VEE. Venezuelan equine encephalitis.

Venezuelan equine encephalitis (VEE). A viral disease affecting the brain and carried by mosquitoes.

ventricles. The heart's two large, powerful lower chambers that pump blood to the lungs and body.

vertebra. One of the bones that form the spine, through which the spinal cord passes.

vertebrae. More than one vertebra.

viremia. Viruses circulating in the blood.

viscera. Internal organs.

vitiligo. Lack of pigment in skin and hair, a condition that can happen for no apparent reason or that may occur in skin growing over a wound.

VMD. Veterinarian with a degree from the University of Pennsylvania Veterinary College; a graduate of any other American veterinary college is a DVM.

volvulus. A twisting of the intestine that prevents the passage of its contents and results in the strangulation of the part involved.

vomeronasal gland. An organ above the hard palate in the nasal cavity that, in horses, apparently functions as an organ of smell.

vulva. The mare's external genitals.

weaning. Separating a mare and foal until the foal becomes independent of the mare.

weanling. A foal that has been weaned but has not yet reached one year of age.

WEE. Western equine encephalitis.

Western blot. A test that looks for proteins, such as those making up antibodies, used to help diagnose certain diseases such as EPM and Lyme disease.

Western equine encephalitis (WEE). A viral disease that affects the brain and is carried by mosquitoes.

West Nile virus. A virus carried by mosquitoes and causes encephalitis in horses, people and birds.

wheezes. Abnormal sounds made by damaged lungs and usually heard with a stethoscope.

white line disease. A fungal infection of the hoof wall.

white muscle disease. Nutritional myopathy.

windpuffs. Fluid filling of the joint capsule of the fetlocks.

windsucker. A mare with a tipped and sunken vulva that draws in air, feces and urine.

witch's milk. Mammary gland secretion in a filly foal.

wobbles. A disease of the spinal cord that results in incoordination.

wormer. A medication used to rid the body of parasitic worms; more properly called a dewormer or anthelmintic.

worming. Ridding the body of parasitic worms; more properly called deworming.

X-ray. The means by which radiographs are obtained.

yearling. A horse between 1 and 2 years of age.

Photo by Ruth Freeman

Bibliography

Many of the following reference materials are available from Rural Heritage, 281 Dean Ridge Lane, Gainesboro, TN 38562, 931-268-0655, www.ruralheritage.com.

Chapter 1: Keeping Draft Horses Safe

Burch M. *How to Build Small Barns & Outbuildings*. Pownall, VT: Storey Communications; 1992.

Burger SM. *Horse Owner's Field Guide to Toxic Plants*. Millwood, NY: Breakthrough; 1996.

Cecil P. Build a Two-Stall Horse or Mule Barn. *Rural Heritage*. Holiday 1999:62-65.

Cecil P. Three-Sided Shelter. *Rural Heritage*. Spring 2000:65-67.

Clay J. *Build the Right Fencing for Horses*. Pownall, VT: Storey Communications; 1999.

Clay J. *Building or Renovating a Small Barn for Your Horse*. Pownall, VT: Storey Communications; 1999.

Ehringer G. *Roofs & Rails*. Colorado Springs, CO: Western Horseman; 1995.

Haas J. *Getting Ready to Drive a Horse and Cart*. Pownall, VT: Storey Communications; 1995.

Hill C. *Horse Keeping on a Small Acreage*. Pownall, VT: Storey Communications; 1990.

Hill C. *Trailering Your Horse*. Pownall, VT: Storey Communications; 2000.

Houpt K. Cornell University College of Veterinary Medicine, Ithaca, NY: personal communication.

Lintin M. *Harness Up*. Gainesboro, TN: Rural Heritage; 1997.

Miller LR. *Work Horse Handbook*. Sisters, OR: Small Farmer's Journal; 1981.

Walrond S. *Starting to Drive*. Great Britain: Kenilworth Press; 1999.

Webber T. *Stables and Shelters*. Great Britain: Kenilworth Press; 1999.

Chapter 2: Feeding the Draft Horse

Ewing RA. *Beyond the Hay Days*. LaSalle, CO: Pixyjack Press; 1997.

Hintz HF. Importance of Selenium. *Rural Heritage*. Holiday 1999:52-53.

Chapter 3: Fat Is Good

Briggs K. Feeding the High-Octane Horse. *The Horse*. August 1998:73-80.

Briggs K. Big Appetites. *The Horse*. March 2000:95-102.

Crandell K. Feeding Fat: Friend or Foe? *Trail Blazer*. September/October 1998:25-27.

Gill A. Advances in Equine Nutrition. *The Horse*. July 1998:55-60.

Hintz H. Animal nutrition. Cornell University, Ithaca, NY: personal communication.

Kronfeld D. Virginia-Maryland School Regional College of Veterinary Medicine, Blacksburg, VA: personal communication.

Neuman, AJ. Well, Doc, What Do You Do Now? *Draft Horse Journal*. Autumn 1990:34-35.

Ralston S. Veterinary nutrition. Rutgers University, New Brunswick, NJ: personal communication.

Thompson K. Purina Mills, St. Louis, MO: personal communication.

Valentine BA. Feeding the Pulling Horse. *Rural Heritage*. The Evener 1998:21.

Valentine BA. Shivers Is a Muscle Disease, Jerry's Story. *The Draft Horse Connection*. Fall 1998:24-27.

Chapter 4: Routine Health Care

Hill C. Waging War on Flies. *Rural Heritage*. Summer 1995:48-50.

Kirsch KL. Natural Fly Spray. www.ruralheritage.com/vet_clinic/

Chapter 5: Foot and Hoof Care

Butler D. *Horse Foot Care*. LaPorte, CO: Doug Butler Enterprises; 1995.

Butler D. *Principles of Shoeing II*. LaPorte, CO: Doug Butler Enterprises; 1995.

Duquette DA. *Hooftrimming for Horse Owners*. Lenoxdale, MA: HFH Press; 1996.

Heymering H. *On the Horse's Foot, Shoes and Shoeing: The Bibliographic Record and a Brief Timeline History of Horseshoeing*. Cascade, Md: Steloy Publishing; 1990:340.

Russell V. *Heavy Horses of the World*. Whitewater, Wis: Heart Prairie Press; 1983.

Weber T. *Feet and Shoes*. Great Britain: Kenilworth Press; 1995.

Wildenstein M. *Fundamentals of Draft Horse Shoeing*. Dryden, NY: Jokar Dane Productions; 1998.

Chapter 6: Health Clues

Kirsch KL. Gentling Horses in Montana (Pat Parelli's Training Method). *Rural Heritage*. Spring 1998:51-53.

Lintin M. Estimate Your Horse's Weight. www.ruralheritage.com/horse_paddock/

Lyons J. *Lyons on Horses: John Lyons' Proven Conditioned©Response Training Program, 1st edition*. New York, NY: Doubleday; 1991.

Meredith R. Horse Logic. *Rural Heritage*. column; Holiday 1997 to present.

Chapter 8: Analyzing Movement

Clay J. Hereditary Unsoundness in Horses. *Rural Heritage*. Winter 2000:58-60.

Houpt K. Cornell University, Ithaca, NY: personal communication.

Miller LR. *Work Horse Handbook*. Sisters, OR: Small Farmer's Journal; 1981.

Rooney JR. *The Lame Horse*. Neenah, WI: Russell Meerdink; 1998.

Rooney JR. *Video Guide to Lameness: Front Legs*. Neenah, WI: Russell Meerdink; 1994.

Rooney JR. *Video Guide to Lameness: Hind Legs and Back*. Neenah, WI: Russell Meerdink; 1994.

Chapter 10: Head

Hintz H. Animal nutrition. Cornell University, Ithaca, NY: personal communication.

Ralston S. Veterinary nutrition. Rutgers University, New Brunswick, NJ: personal communication.

Rebhun B. Large animal internal medicine and opththalmology. Cornell University, Ithaca, NY: personal communication.

Schwabe A. *Your Horse's Teeth*. Great Britain: J.A. Allen; 1999.

Webber T. *Mouths and Bits*. Great Britain: Kenilworth Press; 1999.

Chapter 12: Lumps and Bumps

Rebhun B. Large animal internal medicine and opththalmology. Cornell University, Ithaca, NY: personal communication.

Chapter 13: Breathing Hard

Kronfeld D. Equine nutrition. Virginia-Maryland Regional College of Veterinary Medicine, Blacksburg, VA: personal communication.

Chapter 14: Gastrointestinal Problems

King C. *Preventing Colic in Horses*. Cary, NC: Paper Horse; 1999.

Chapter 16: Muscles

Valentine BA. Common Horse Breeds Affected by EPSM. www.ruralheritage.com/vet_clinic/

Valentine BA. EPSM Affects Your Horse's Muscles. *Michael Plumb's Horse Journal*. July 1996:8-10.

Valentine BA. EPSM—New Muscle Disease in Draft Horses. www.ruralheritage.com/vet_clinic/

Valentine BA. Feeding EPSM Horses for Maximum Results. *Horse Journal*. October 1998:12-13.

Valentine BA. Feeding the Pulling Horse. *Rural Heritage*. The Evener 1998:21.

Valentine BA. Signs of EPSM in Draft Horses. www.ruralheritage.com/vet_clinic/

Chapter 17: Joints and Legs

Neumann AJ. Well, Doc, What Do You Do Now? *Draft Horse Journal*. Autumn 1990: 34-35.

Neumann, AJ. Doc, I'd Like to Know More About Stringhalt. *Draft Horse Journal*. Autumn 1999:71-73.

Neumann, AJ. Orange City, IA: personal communication.

Chapter 18: No Hoof, No Horse

Gregory C. Heartland Horseshoeing School and virtual farrier at www.ruralheritage.com/village_smithy/

Chapter 19: Reproduction

Damerow G. Draft Horse Twins. www.ruralheritage.com/horse_paddock/

Damerow G and Clay J. Draft Horse Gestation and Foaling. www.ruralheritage.com/vet_clinic/

Fryer S. Fertility in Suffolk Punch Draught Horses. Corvallis, OR: College of Veterinary Medicine, Oregon State University; Fall 1999

Ginther OJ. Equine reproduction specialist. University of Wisconsin, Madison, WI: personal communication.

Henton, J. Large animal clinical sciences. University of Tennessee, Knoxville, TN: personal communication.

Jones T. *The Complete Foaling Manual*. Tyler, TX: Equine Research; 1999.

Willoughby DP. *Growth and Nutrition in the Horse*. Cranbury, NJ: A.S. Barnes; 1975.

Chapter 20: The Foal

Miller RM. *Imprint Training*. Colorado Springs, CO: Western Horseman; 1991.

Probst S. Can Imprint Training Go Too Far? *Rural Heritage*. Spring 1999:62.

General

Colles C. Functional Anatomy Great Britain: Kenilworth Press; 2000.

James RB. *How to Be Your Own Veterinarian (sometimes)*. Mills, WY: Alpine Press; 1990.

Kainer RA and McCracken TO. *Horse Anatomy, a Coloring Atlas*. Loveland, CO: Alpine Publications; 1994.

Photo by Ruth Freeman

Index

(Illustrations are indicated by page numbers in *italics;* charts and tables are indicated by pages numbers in **bold.**)

antibodies, 172, 189
anticoagulant, 172, 189
antihistamines, 94, 189
antioxidant, 19, 21, 189
antiseptic, 189
antitoxin, 189
Appaloosas, 76
appetite, 51, 174
apples, 21, 51
Arabians, 97, 101, 138
Ardennes, 43, **43**
arrhythmia, 68, 189
arthritis, 113-114, 119, 124, 164, 189
artificial insemination (AI), 140, 189
ascarids, 32, *32*, 33, 189
aspartate amino transferase, 173
aspiration pneumonia, 102, 104, 151, 167
AST, 173
asthma, 100
Astragalus spp., 10, *10*, **11**
ATP, 23, 190
atrial fibrillation, 68, 190
atrophy, 116, 190
    See also muscle atrophy
atropine ointment, 75-76
aural plaque, 72, 190
autonomic nerves, 70-71, 190
Avatec, 13
azoturia. *See* Monday morning disease; tying up

B

backbone, *111*
back pain, 112
bacteremia, 190
baldness, 90, 161, 189
    See also hair loss
banamine, 190
bands, 172
barley, **25**, 29
barn design, *1, 2, 3*, 1-3
base-narrow stance, 44, *44*, 46, 190
basophils, 173
bastard strangles, 81, 190
bats, 39
bean, 42, 190
bedding, 4, 8, 91, 135, 147
bee sting, 84
beet pulp, 17-18, 29
behavior, 51, 52-53, 119, 168, 169, 199
belching, 58
Belgian blow, 67
Belgians
    and cataracts, 74

and congenital skin disease, 91, 161
and eye tumors, 77
hoof quality of, 43, **43**
and skin cancer, 98
and sunburn, 91
and twinning, 147
Berteroa incana, 9, *9*, **11**
Betadine, 190
bicarbonate, 175
big head, 19, 84
bile, 167
biliary system inflammation, 168, 174, 192
bilirubin, 173, 174
biopsy, 146, 190
biotin, 21, 43
birth, 147-148, *148*
birth defects, 116, 153, 154
birthmark, 95
bites
    insect, 36, 89, 93, 94, 160, 161
    snake, 84
bitterweed, 10
bitting, 82, *82*
black bodies, 74, *74*, 192
black flies, 35, *35*, 94, 190
black-legged tick, 38, *38*, 125
black walnut, 8, **11**, 135
black water. *See* Monday morning disease; tying up
bladder rupture, 154, 162
bladder stones, 60, 193, 206
bleeders, 81
bleeding disorders, 175
blinders, *75*
blindness, 76-77, 89, 163
blister beetle, 11-12, *12*
blisters, 91, 92, 161
blood
    from nostrils, 81
    in semen, 140
    in urine, 60, 166
blood clotting, 173
blood count, 172, **172**, 190
blood fats, 175
blood protein, 163, 174
blood sugar, 173
blood testing, 25, 126, 171
blood type, 154, 162, 168
blood urea nitrogen, 173
blood values, 171, **172-175**
blood vessel inflammation, 81, 84, 130, 163, 174, 206
blot test, 114, 206
blowing, 99, 190
blue clay, 135
blue green algae, 6, 190

CSF, 112, 191
culicoides, 35, 193
culicoides hypersensitivity 35, 193
curry comb, 89
Cushing's disease, 117, *117,* 193
   and cresty neck, 135
   and dermatitis, 86
   and glucose level, 173
   and haircoat, 89, 117, *117*
   and laminitis, 135, 164
   and muscle atrophy, 117, *117*
   and rain scald, 87
   and urine volume, 59, 89, 117, 166
   and weight loss, 51, 165
cyanide, 9, 193
cystic calculi, 60
cystoliths, 60, 193

D

dandelion, 128
death (sudden), 92, 99, 119, 130, 170, 184
decontamination, 80, 85, 105
deer flies, 35, *35,* 193
deer tick, 38, *38,* 125
degenerative joint disease (DJD), 50, 113-114, 124-125, 193
   See also osteoarthritis
dehydration, 70, 71, 174, 193
   and blood count, 172, 173
   and colic, 108
   and photosensitivity, 91
dehydration test, 71, *71*
de Lahunta, Alexander (veterinary neurologist), 27
denervation atrophy, 116, 193
dentigerous cyst, 79-80
dermatitis, 86, 89, 193
dermatitis verrucosa, 193
dermatophilosis, 86-87, *87* 193
dermatophilus bacteria, 86
dermatophytes, 193
Desitin, 60
desmitis, 127, 193
developmental bone diseases, 21
developmental orthopedic disease (DOD), 122, 193
deworming, 34, 193
diabetes, 173
diagnosis methods, 159-160
diarrhea, 57, 108, 162-163, 193
   and antibiotics, 57, 105, 163
   in foals, 108, 153, 155, 162
Dictyocaulus arnfeldi, 100
diet, 30, 113
   See also fat (dietary); feed
digestion, 56-57

digital cushion, *138*
Digitalis purpurea, 7-8, *7,* **11**
digital pulse, 69, *69,* 132
digoxin, 99, 193
dimethylsulfoxide, 86, 133, 193
dirt eating, 51
DJD, 50, 113-114, 124-125, 193
DMSO, 86, 133, 193
docked tail, 37, 193
DOD, 122, 193
domperidone, 12, 150, 193
donkeys, 100, 115, 122
down horse, 57, 64-66, *65*
   and EPSM, 65, 119, 120, 121
   post foaling, 148
dressage, *61,* 121, 126, 128
Drill-Tek, 49, *49,* 193
driving, 13, **24**
drying up, 157
dummy foal, 154, 193
dystocia, 148, 193

E

ear flies, 35, 193
ear masks, 35
ears, 72-73, 166
   drooping, 83, *83*
   pinned, 51, 52
ear ticks, 38, *38,* 72
ear tooth, 79-80, 193
Eastern equine encephalitis (EEE), 39, **40,** 194
easy keeper, 194
edema, 194
   of the cornea, 76
   of the head, 84
   of the leg, 87, 163
   malignant, 92, 130, 199
   pulmonary, 170, 202
EDM, 19, 112-113, 166, 194
EEE, 39, **40,** 194
EIA, 40-41, 194
electrolytes, 21, 66, 175, 194
embryo, 143, 194
embryonic death, 145-146
EMND, 51, 63, 117-118, 165, 194
   and vitamin E deficiency, 19, 113, 118
encephalitis, 39, 52, 53, 168, 194
encephalitis virus, 166, 194
endometritis, 135, 143, *144,* 144-145, 146, 161
endometrium, 146, 194
endophytes, 12, 194
endophytic fungus, 12, 146, 162
endorphins, 4, 194

endoscope, 102, 108, 109, 143, 159, 194
energy, 24-25, 27-28, 52-53, 165, 194
energy requirements, 15, 23
English bridle, *82*
enterolith, 19, 107-108, *108,* 194
eosinophilic granuloma, 93-94, 160, 194
eosinophils, 94, 172, 194
epidermolysis bullosa, 91
epilepsy, 170
epiphysitis, 123, 154, 194
epitheliogenesis imperfecta, 91
EPM, 40, 53, 114, 194
    and aspiration pneumonia, 102
    and congenital skin disease, 161
    and facial nerve damage, 83
    and incoordination, 165, 170
    and muscle atrophy, 116
    and seizures, 169
    and swallowing difficulties, 167
EPM vaccine, 39-40, **40,** 114
EPSM, 24, 27, 194
    and anesthesia, 25, 103, 119
    and appetite, 51
    and back pain, 112
    and behavior problems, 119
    cause of, 118, 119
    and contracted tendons, 127
    control of, 25, 28, 121
    discovery of, viii, 25-27
    and down horse, 65, 119, 120, 121
    and exercise intolerance, 53
    hereditary nature of, 118-119
    and lameness, 62, 121, 124, 164
    and lethargy, 168
    and locking stifle, 129
    and lying down, 63, 91
    and Monday morning disease, 120-121
    and muscle atrophy, 117, 118, *118*
    and muscle biopsy, 120, *120*
    and muscle enzymes, 120, 121, 173, 174
    and muscle pain, 121
    and navicular disease, 136
    onset of, 119-120
    and poor performance, 164, 165
    and post-foaling problems, 148-149
    and pressure sores, 91
    resemblance of to arthritis, 124
    resemblance of to EMND, 118
    resemblance of to EPM, 114, 118
    resemblance of to fibrotic myopathy, 129
    resemblance of to Lyme disease, 126
    and shivers, 128
    signs of, **119**
    and soluble carbohydrates, 24-25

    and stiffness, 62, 119, 126, 164
    and stringhalt, 128
    and stumbling, 63, 168
    and sudden collapse, 169
    and sudden death, 170
    and weight loss, 165
EPSSM. *See* EPSM
equine degenerative myelopathy (EDM),
    19, 112-113, 166, 194
equine herpesvirus. *See* herpesvirus
equine infectious anemia (EIA), 40-41, 194
equine motor neuron disease. *See* EMND
equine polyneuritis, 83, 115
equine polysaccharide storage myopathy. *See* EPSM
equine protozoal myeloencephalopathy. *See* EPM
equine recurrent uveitis, 74, 76, 163
equine rhinopneumonitis virus, 115
    See also herpesvirus
equine viral arteritis, 39, **40**
ergot, 122, *122,* 194
erythrocytes, 172
esophagus, 56, *56,* 194
estrogen, 145, 147, 194
estrous cycle, 142, 194
estrus, *142,* 169, 194
euthanasia, 130, 184, 194
Evener, The, 186
exercise, 6, 53, 70
    aerobic, 28, 189
    and breathing rate, 67, **67,** *99*
    and cooling down, 16, 70, 108
    and down horse, 65
    and foals, 6, 154
    and gastric ulcers, 109
    and heart rate, **67,** 67-68
    and lymphangitis, 87
    and muscle enzyme levels, 174
    and nosebleed, 81
    and sudden collapse, 169
    and suspensory desmitis, 127
    and sweating, 70
    and temperature, 69
    and tying up, 120-121
exertional rhabdomyolysis.
    See Monday morning disease;
    tying up
exuberant granulation tissue, 160
eyes, 74-75, *74*
    blindness in, 76-77, 163
    infection of, 75, 163
    injury of, 75-76, *76,* 163
    tumors of, 77-78, 163

M

macrophage, 94, 199
maggots, 34
magnesium, 19, 175
malabsorption, 163, 199
malignant edema, 92, 130, 199
malignant lymphoma, 80
mane rubbing, 89, 161
mange, 88, *88*, 133, 199
maniacal behavior, 53, 168, 169, 199
manure, 57, 195
    See also diarrhea
maple, red, 8-9, *8,* **11**
mare, 199
    estrous behavior of, 142, *142,* 143
    perivulvar area of, 42, 54
    pmu, 6, 130, 140
    stallion-like behavior in, 143
    urinary system of, *59*
    See also broodmare
massage therapy, 112
mastitis, 150, 199
MCV, 172
mean corpuscular volume, 172
mechanical bridle, *82*
mechanical lameness, 128, 199
mechanobullous disease, 91
meconium, 152, 162, 199
medical records, 41
melanin, 90, 167, 199
melanocytic nevus, 95-96, 160, 199
melanoma, 60, 77-78, 80, **95, 97,** 160, 199
    See also gray horse melanomas
Meredith, Ron (horse trainer), 52
metabolic disorder. *See* EPSM
methionine, 21, 43
miconazole, 134, 189
midges, 35, *35,* 199
milk production, 150, 157, 198
milk replacer, 155
milk stool, 152
minerals, 19, 51, 149
miniature horses (and hyperlipemia), 175, 197
mites, 38, 85, 161, 199
mitochondria, 23, 199
MMD. *See* Monday morning disease
molars, 199
moles, **95,** 95-96, **97,** 199
Monday morning disease (MMD), 25, 65, 119, 120-121, *120,* 199
    See also tying up
monensin, 13
monocytes, 172
moon blindness, 74, 76, 163, 206

Morgans, 74
mortality insurance, 184
mosquitoes, *35,* 35-36, 39
mucopurulent discharge, 81, 200
mucous membranes, 78, 200
mucus, 81
mules, 100, 115, 118-119, 122
muscle atrophy, 91, 120
    asymmetric, 114, 116-117, **117**
    and EMND, 117-118
    and EPSM, 118-120
    symmetric, 117, **117**
muscle biopsy, 120, *120*
muscle damage, 25, 62, 173, 174
    due to EPSM, 24-25, 27
    and tying up, 53, 120
    and urine color, 59-60, 120
muscle enzymes, 120, 121, 173, 174
muscle hypertrophy, 100, *100*
muscle loss, 55, 89, 114, 116, 117
muscle pain, 52, 120, 121
muscles
    locomotory, 200
    postural, 201
    trembling of, 69
    straining of, 112
    weakness in, 63-64
myelography, 113
myoglobin, 60, 120, 166, 200
myoglobinuria, 60, 59-60, 200

N

narasin, 13
narcolepsy, 64, 169, 200
nasal discharge, 81-82
nasogastric tube, 105, 200
nasolacrimal duct, *74,* 76
navel, *54,* 154, 200
navicular bone, *126, 136,* 200
navicular disease, 136-137, 200
navicular fracture, 50
necropsy. *See* postmortem examination
necrotic pododermatitis, 50, 132-133, *133,* 200
neonatal isoerythrolysis, 154, 162, 168, 200
neonatal maladjustment, 162, 200
neoplasm. *See* tumors
nephrolith, 60, 200
Nerium oleander, 7-8, *7,* **11**
Neumann, A.J. (equine veterinarian), 25, 128
neuritis, 114-115, 200
neuritis of the cauda equina, 9, 60, 114-115
neutrophils, 172
nerve block, 62, 200

nerve damage, 117
nerve disease, 62
newsprint, 4
nitroglycerine, 135, 200
nodular collagenolytic granulomas, 94
Nolvasan, 200
nonsteroidal medications, 200
    and diarrhea, 57, 163
    and gastric ulcers, 109, 169
Norwegian Fjords
    and cresty neck, 135, *135*
    and EPSM, 119
noseband, 81
nosebleed, 81
no see ums, 35, *35,* 200
nostrils, 81
NSAID. *See* nonsteroidal medications
nurse mares, 155
nutritional myopathy, 153, 200

O

oats, **25,** 29
obesity, 54, 107, 144
OCD, 113, 122-123, *123,* 200
    and arthritis, 124
    and diet, 21, 28, 123
    and incoordination, 112, 122, 165
    and spavin, 125
    in young horses, 154
oil. *See* fat (dietary); vegetable oil
oleander, 7-8, *7,* **11,** 170
onchocerca, 33, 35, 88, 200
opossums, 114
Orcutt, Bob (equine veterinarian), 25-26
orphan foals, 155
Orthoflex saddle, 112
ossification, 138, 200
osteitis, 137, 200
osteoarthritis, 124, 138, *138,* 200
osteochondrosis dissecans. *See* OCD
otitis, 72-73, 200, 201
Otobius megnini, 38, *38*
ovariectomy, 143, 201
overweight, 54, 107, 144
ovulation, 142, 146, 201
oxytocin, 147, 201
Oxytropis spp., 10, *10,* **11**

P

P1, *126*
P2, *126*
P3. *See* coffin bone

packed cell volume, 172
pain (signs of), 169
paints, 91
palpation, 143, 159, 201
palsy, 73, 75, 201
Panicum spp., 10, *10,* **11**
panting, 70, 167
papilloma, 95, **95**
papillomavirus, 72, 95, 201
paralysis, 115
    See also palsy
parasites, 57, 165, 172, 173
    and human health, 33
    and incoordination, 166
    intestinal, 32-33, 108, 155
    and maniacal behavior, 169
    and muscle atrophy, 116, 117
    non-intestinal, 33
    resistance of to wormers, 34
    skin, 87-88, 160
    and weight loss, 165
Parelli, Pat (horse trainer), 52
parrot mouth, 79, 201
parturition, 65, 107, 147-148
pastern, *138,* 201
pasture, 5-6
    and diarrhea, 108, 162
    fescue, 12, 146, 150, 162
    and toxic plants, 6-11, **11**
pasture colic, 108
patent urachus, 153, 201
PCV, 172
pecking order, 54
pedal bone. *See* coffin bone
pedal osteitis, 137, 201
peeling, 91
pelleted feed, 100, 104, 155
pemphigus, 92, 161, 201
penis
    cancer of, 98
    cleaning of, 41-42
    examination of, 54
    paralysis of, 115
    warts on, 95
Percherons
    and eye tumors, 77-78
    hoof quality of, 43, **43**
    and retained testicle, 157
    and sun-related problems, 90
    See also gray horse melanomas
peristalsis, 104, 201
peritonitis, 109
petroleum jelly, 60
phalanx, *126,* 201

Rural Heritage

a bimonthly journal published since 1976 in support of farming and logging with horses and other draft animals. Each issue is packed with how–to articles and up–to–date information related to training and working horses, mules, and oxen along with profiles of the teamsters who farm and ranch with them.

In *Rural Heritage* you will find out what's going on in today's draft animal world and discover gems of rural wisdom you won't find anywhere else. We are so sure you'll love this family magazine, we offer a money–back guarantee—if you are not completely satisfied after receiving your first issue, cancel and get a full refund. Join teamsters across North America by making *Rural Heritage* part of your life.

Call now: 319-362-3027
or visit online: www.ruralheritage.com

Just a sample of great articles from past issues:

Why Do Horses Shy?
Hitching 46 Percherons
From Hide to Harness
Gelding or Stallion?
Bits for Draft Work
Work Sleds & Mudboats
Loading the Great Circus Train
Is Your Vet a Good Horse doc?
Horses as Mind Readers
Toxic Plants in Your Pasture
Get Fieldwork Done Despite the Heat
Hitching Three Abreast
West Nile Virus—How Real Is the Danger?
Horse–Drawn Bracken Basher
Work Carts
Plowing Up an Internship
From Luxury Hotel to Horse Logging School
Canadian—The Little Iron Horse
Making and Unmaking the Balky Mule
Horse Logger's Initiative
Lighting Vehicles in Winter
Backing a Mule
Reading Horses
Resistance and Work Rates
Log Loading Aids
4–Point Trim—Help or Hoax?
Holding Back the Hurry–Up Horse

For a complete list of related books and videotapes
visit our bookstore at
www.ruralheritage.com